MIDNIGHT MARQUEE ACTORS SERIES

BELA LUGOSI

Edited By
Gary and Susan Svehla

MIDNIGHT MA
BALTIMO

ISBN 1-887664-01-7
Library of Congress Catalog Card Number: 95-080281
Manufactured in the United States of America
Printed by Kirby Lithography Company, Arlington, VA
First printing by Midnight Marquee Press, Inc., October 1995
Front Cover: David L.Daniels' rendering of Bela Lugosi from *Mark of the Vampire* (MGM 1935). Cover copyright © by David L. Daniels.

Dedication:

To our dear parents who are no longer with us, Ann Svehla and Melvin Miller. And to our wonderful parents, Richard Svehla and Aurelia Miller, for their love, support, and encouragement.

... and of course, to Bela Lugosi.

Acknowledgements:

It is so difficult to thank everyone who helped, encouraged, or generally kept our spirits up during this project. But we'll try.

Thanks to all our authors and artists, the ones who've worked so long for *Midnight Marquee* and who are now an integral part of Midnight Marquee Press: Jim Coughlin, Robert Allen Crick, David L. Daniels, John R. Duvoli, Dennis Fischer, Bruce Hallenbeck, Tom Johnson, Allen Koszowski, Don Leifert, Greg Mank, Mark A. Miller, John E. Parnum, Fred Olen Ray, Bryan Senn, James Singer, Don Smith, David H. Smith, Steve Thornton, Steve Vertlieb, and Tom Weaver.

Thanks also to our new writers and artists: Robert Clarke, Dwight David Frye, John Goodier, Richard Gordon, Jeff Hillegass, David J. Hogan, John J. J. Johnson, Bob Madison, Ted Okuda,Randy Palmer, Gary Don Rhodes, John Soister, John Stell, Bret Wood, and Nathalie Yafet.

Our appreciation to John Antosiewicz for his devotion to horror films and horror film memorabilia preservation.

Thanks to Richard Bojarski, Ronald V. Borst (Hollywood Movie Posters), Steve Hammett of Kirby Lithography, Gary Don Rhodes, and John Soister for his assistance.

Our deepest gratitude, for their help and encouragement, to: Tom Johnson, Frank Lidinsky,Tim and Donna Lucas, Greg Mank, and Tom Weaver, as well as our families (especially our little Grandma Erma Palm), friends, distributors, and to all our readers of *Midnight Marquee* who have supported us for so long.

Truly admirable is the person who gives his all to each job he tackles; today that is a quality very rare indeed. Despite obstacles in his personal life, Bela Lugosi's professional career will always represent the epitome of talent, dedication, and perseverance.

TABLE OF CONTENTS

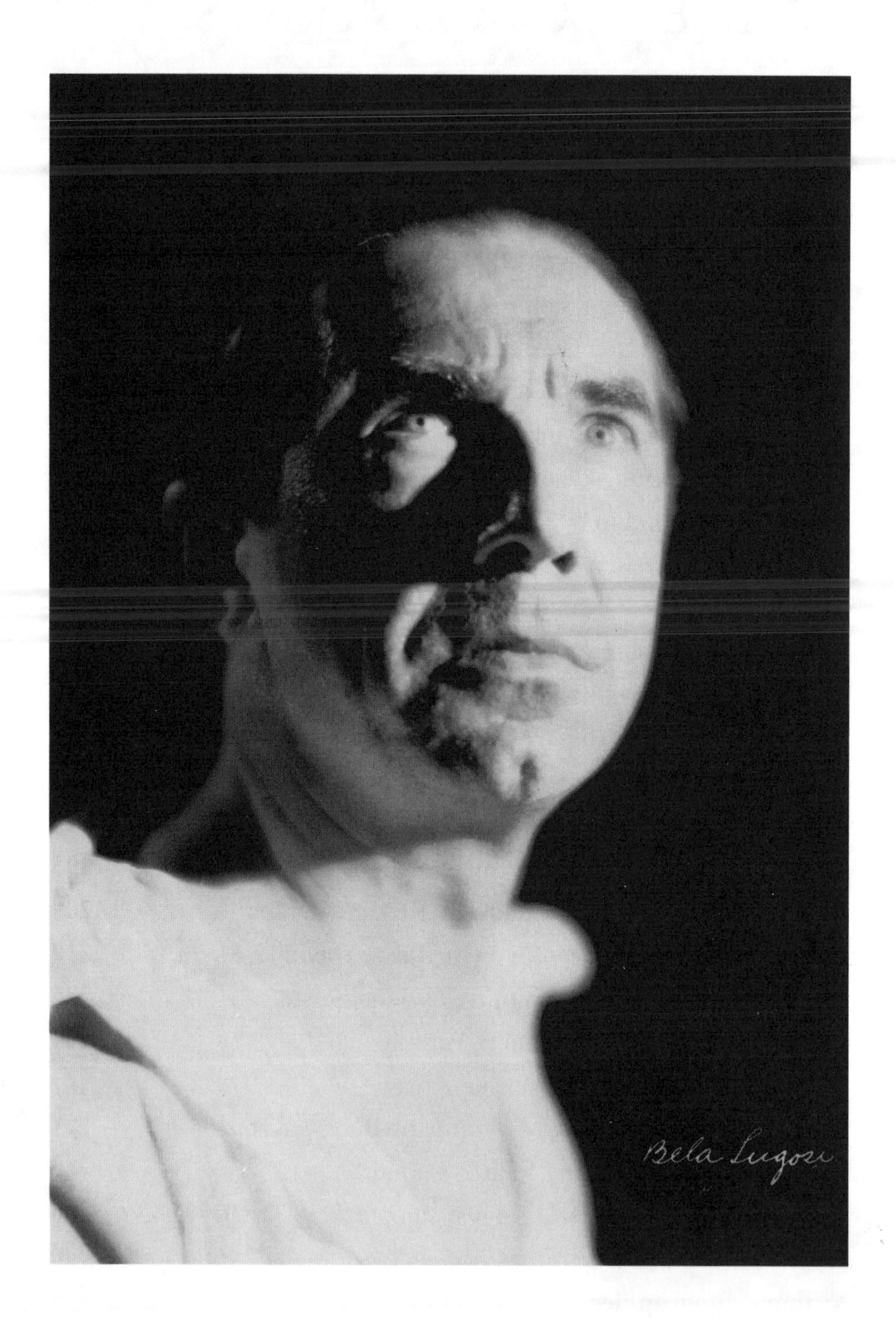
Bela Lugosi

INTRODUCTION

We decided to inaugurate the *Midnight Marquee Actors Series* with horror film icon Bela Lugosi because the nineties appear to be the decade of his rebirth and rediscovery. With the release of pristine copies of Universal horror classics in attractively packaged, low-priced videocassettes and laserdiscs, the increased interest in cult writer/director Edward D. Wood, Jr., and the artistic triumph of Tim Burton's *Ed Wood* which features Bela Lugosi (distorted history noted), a new generation of film fan is being introduced to the legendary bogeyman of decades ago. As the writers in this volume attest, Lugosi was a very gifted actor who appeared in only a handful of well-produced, quality vehicles, but whose reputation has mushroomed far beyond the movies in which he sometimes had to appear. What better controversial star with which to start our series?

First of all, a note of explanation as to what the *Midnight Marquee Actors Series* is and is not. Our intention was not to be definitive and feature *every one* of Lugosi's features. The approach to the *Actors Series* is simple. We solicited written chapters from our stable of expert film writers on the Lugosi film or films which they most desired to shed ink. Granted, these selections might not be Lugosi's best films nor his most memorable. Many writers chose to select Lugosi films on which precious little has been written. Others decided to select a favorite Lugosi film, but one that is not necessarily his best. Others opted to re-address the classics—*The Raven, Dracula, The Black Cat, Son of Frankenstein*—and try to create a new slant, a new angle on films so often critiqued. Different writers had different agendas, but the bottom line is this, most of the important Lugosi films are here included. True, only *The Ape Man* is examined as the representative Monogram Picture, but writer Mark A. Miller refers to the others in the series. I preface Miller's Monogram coverage by including Lugosi's entry into the nadir of poverty row, PRC's *The Devil Bat*. The Edward D. Wood, Jr. era is covered by a marvelous discussion of *Bride of the Monster* (which is a more effective showcase for Lugosi than *Plan 9 From Outer Space* could ever hope to be).

Films have been covered chronologically, but within each year, titles have been covered alphabetically, thus meaning that the *first* film covered during a particular year may have been released *after* other entries during that specific year.

Since writers only knew what titles were to be covered within this volume and never had the opportunity to read chapters submitted by others, some inevitable overlap of information does sometimes occur. In comprehensive anthologies such as this one, that is certainly to be expected. As co-editor of this volume, I was constantly amazed at just how effectively all the chapters seemed to merge into one book with one vision. Interestingly enough, some of our writers praise Lugosi's work to high heavens, while other writers stress the cracks and fissures within his body of work. By combining such biases and opinionated visions, the volume becomes a better balanced vehicle by which to judge the man, his work, and his contribution to film.

Gary J. Svehla
September 1995

In *Renegades* (1930), Bela Lugosi portrays the bearded Sheik Muhammed, who quite theatrically calls himself the "Marabout," making the most of his scenes with Myrna Loy. "You look very nice when you don't say nothing," he explains to her... later crudely explaining he might return her to Warner Baxter.

ENTERING THE REALM OF SOUND

LUGOSI'S FIRST SIX TALKIES (1928-1930)

by Gary Don Rhodes

Prisoners
CREDITS: Producer: Walter Morosco; Director: William A. Seiter; Screenplay: Forrest Halsey; based on Ferenc Molnar's novel *Prisoners*; Cinematographer: Lee Garmes; Editor: Leroy Stone; Copyright number: LP399; registered May 21, 1929; a First National film.

CAST: Corinne Griffith...Riza Riga, James Ford...Kessler, Bela Lugosi...Brottos, Ian Keith...Nicholas Cathy, Julanne Johnston...Lenke, Ann Schaeffer...Aunt Maria, Barton Hesse...Kore, Otto Matiesen...Sebfi, Harry Northrup...Prosecuting Attorney.

The Thirteenth Chair
CREDITS: Producer and Director: Tod Browning; Screenplay: Elliot Clawson; based on Bayard Veiller's play *The Thirteenth Chair*; Cinematographer: Merritt B. Gersted; Editor: Harry Reynolds; Copyright number: LP794; registered October 28, 1929; a Metro-Goldwyn-Mayer film.

CAST: Conrad Nagel...Richard Crosby, Leila Hyams...Helen O'Neill, Margaret Wycherly...Mme. Rosalie La Grange, Helen Millard...Mary Eastwood, Holmes Herbert...Sir Roscoe Crosby, Mary Forbes...Lady Crosby, Bela Lugosi...Inspector Delzante, John Davidson...Edward Wales, Charles Quartermaine...Dr. Philip Mason, Moon Carroll...Helen Trent, Cyril Chadwick...Brandon Trent.

Such Men Are Dangerous
CREDITS: Producer: William Fox; Director: Kenneth Hawkes; Screenplay: Ernest Vadja; based on an original story by Elinor Glyn; Cinematographer: L.W. O'Connell and George Eastman; Editor: Harold Schuster; Copyright number: LP1074; registered January 25, 1930; a Fox Film.

CAST: Warner Baxter...Ludwig Kranz, Catherine Dale Owen...Elinor Kranz, Albert Conti...Paul Strohm, Hedda Hopper...Muriel Wyndham, Claude Allister...Fred Wyndham, Bela Lugosi...Dr. Goodman.

Wild Company
CREDITS: Producer: William Fox; Director: Leo McCarey; Screenplay: Bradley King; based on an original story by Bradley King and John Stone; Cinematographer: L.W. O'Connell; Editor: Clyde Carruth; Copyright number: LP1382; registered June 16, 1930; a Fox Film.

CAST: Frank Albertson...Larry Grayson, H. B. Warner...Henry Grayson, Sharon Lynn...Sally, Joyce Compton...Anita, Claire McDowell...Mrs. Grayson, Mildred Van Dorn...Natalie, Richard Keene...Dick, Frances McCoy...Cora, Kenneth Thomson...Joe Hardy, Bela Lugosi...Felix Brown, George Fawcett...Judge, Bobby Callahan...Eddie.

Renegades
CREDITS: Producer: William Fox; Director: Victor Fleming; Screenplay, Jules Furtham; based

on Andre Armandy's novel *Le Renegat*; Cinematographer: L.W. O'Connell; Editor: Harold Schuster; Copyright number: LP1648; registered October 3, 1930; a Fox Film.

CAST: Warner Baxter...Deucalion, Myrna Loy...Eleanore, Noah Berry Sr....Machwurth, Gregory Gaye...Vologuine, George Cooper...Biloxi, C. Henry Gordon...Captain Mordiconi, Colin Chase...Sergeant Major Olson, Bela Lugosi...Sheik Muhammed, the Marabout, Victor Jory...Young Officer, Noah Berry Jr....Young Legionnaire, Fred Kohler Jr....Young Legionnaire.

Oh, For A Man
CREDITS: Producer: William Fox and Harold McFadden; Director: Harold McFadden; Screenplay: Philip Klein and Lynn Starling; based on Mary F. Watkins' short story *Stolen Thunder*; Cinematographer: Charles Clarke; Editor: Al De Gaetano; Copyright number: LP1720; registered November 5, 1930; a Fox Film.

CAST: Jeannette MacDonald...Carlotta Manson, Reginald Denny...Barney McGann, Marjorie White...Totsy Franklin, Warren Hymer...Pug Morin, the "Walloping Wop," Alison Skipworth...Laura, Albert Conti...Peck, Bela Lugosi...Frescatti, Andre Cheron...Costello, William B. Davidson...Kerry Stokes, Bodil Rosing...Masseuse.

Viennese Nights
CREDITS: Director: Alan Crosland; Screenplay: Oscar Hammerstein II and Sigmund Romberg; Cinematographer: James Van Trees and Frank Good; Editor: Harold McLernon; Copyright number: LP1463; registered August 4, 1930; a Warner Brothers film.

CAST: Alexander Gray...Otto, Vivienne Segal...Elsa, Jean Hersholt...Hofner, Walter Pidgeon...Franz, Louise Fazenda...Gretl, Alice Day...Barbara, Bert Roach...Gus, June Pursell...Mary, Milton Douglas...Bill Jones, Lothar Mayring...Baron, Bela Lugosi...an Ambassador.

As Bela Lugosi called to the "Children of the Night" in *Dracula* (1931), a screen career began... or at the least, became illuminated from mere existence into a stardom befitting the classical Hollywood paradigm. Yet, for six films prior to the Stoker adaptation, "talking" had become an adjective attached to Lugosi films, which at that time remain better described as films with Lugosi. Overshadowed by the horror films, these six become increasingly worthy of investigation. As ominous a shadow as *Dracula* and the other horror films cast, these six in some ways offer a variety lacking in the later work. In fact, they might best meet Lugosi's own hopes for his career: a little mystery mixed with comedy and drama.

Though Lugosi made numerous silent films in America, his earliest response to talkies in 1928 gave him the opportunity to laud the technical advances and exclaim, "I like your California—and who knows, I may go into pictures here." Bela actually landed in Los Angeles due to a West Coast version of the stage *Dracula,* and he enjoyed associating with the many Hungarians already involved in the Hollywood system. Trades reported him spending time with Lya de Putti, Vilma Banky, Michael Curtiz, Alexander Korda, Victor Varconi, and others. Lugosi's talk of entering sound films proved very prophetic.

Prisoners (1929) was the first of these, yet the First National film, in retrospect, seems more like a cautious swimmer wading only a short distance into unsure waters. As the "talkers" took hold, numerous films already in production became curious hybrids of sound and silence, with characters bursting into dialogue after several reels of subtitles. This particular effort consisted of only some ten percent sound, with few sound effects and a minimum of dialogue.

Corinne Griffith, whose nicknames had moved from the "Orchid Lady" to at times "the world's most beautiful woman," headed *Prisoners'* cast as Riza Riga, a nightclub showgirl who adds to her meager salary by doubling as a thief. Though she attempts to leave such shameful deeds behind her, Griffith returns to crime when she can't live without a particularly pretty dress with which to entice attorney Nicholas Cathy. Lugosi appears as Brottos, the ominous cabaret owner, a prominent role referred to in the film as "The Man" and bordering on the category of heavy. Ian Keith, later to be considered for the lead in *Dracula* (1931) and supposedly again as the Count in *Abbott and Costello Meet Frankenstein* (1948), portrays lawyer Cathy, who defends poor Corinne at trial after she is caught stealing 300 florins. Keith manages to fall in love with the girl and, despite the fact she is sentenced to several months in jail, promises to wait for her faithfully.

The Molnar novel on which the film is based, like most of his works, remains charming, if not sentimental. His tales generally featured sympathetic heroes and heroines... underdogs, starving artists, undiscovered actresses, and, in *Prisoners,* the waitress who steals. In the strictest sense, Molnar's works included no real villains, as he often stated his disbelief in their existence. The bad men in his works are just men, men who are erring but that also have some good qualities. The final paragraph of *Prisoners* finds lawyer Cathy seeing Riza to the prison cell she is to occupy: "...suddenly he felt that there dwelt between these narrow walls, all liberty, all freedom of thought, of feeling, the revolutionary liberation of human morality; while all that lay outside these four walls was but a prison, and all they who go about with head lifted high in pride, who have failed to learn the Master's lesson of forgiveness—the prison guards of convict morality—they are the prisoners."

The film's dialog itself comes in the climactic trial sequence, considered by some critics as an effective segue into sound, though others, like *Motion Picture* magazine pointed to the sometimes unusual and decidedly un-European lines spoken. "It is an interesting sidelight on the erudition of European peasantry to hear Corinne tell the judge who gives her a light sentence, 'I acquiesce in your decision.' However, Corinne's voice is as lovely as her face, so why cavil at what she says?" Despite the favorable nods to the tone of her voice, Griffith would make only three films following *Prisoners,* with one being a British production. Unlike many roaring twenties stars, she retired from the screen a very wealthy woman, having earned money not just as a top star but also as executive producer of more than twelve of her own films. Her retirement only led to further achievements as the author of a dozen novels. Griffith found much less success in her marriages, with one short-lived spouse of 1933-34 being Walter Morosco, the producer of *Prisoners.*

Lugosi himself expressed much interest in the film during production, telling Hollywood's *Citizen* on February 12, 1929, that he was, "delighted that his first talkie is written by no one else but Ferenc Molnar and the locale is in Hungary in which country Lugosi was born." Another account quoted the actor as nervously explaining, "Eighteen years ago, I buy a pair of trousers in Budapest and now I wear them in this picture when I play a Hungarian." Newspapers already identified him as the famed Count Dracula of the stage, as well as noting his popular appeal with females of the audience. His own notices from *Prisoners* were brief but favorable. *Motion Picture* told readers, "Bela Lugosi makes a very European villain," and certainly he must have enjoyed what the August 21, 1929, *Variety* called: "Some nice photographic shots and some of the scenes set a Hungarian background on a Hollywood lot."

As filmic greats like Al Jolson and Charlie Chaplin gave reporters their strong views for and against the popular advent of sound in the cinema, conflicting stories arise concerning Lugosi's personal stand on the issue. After the filming of *Prisoners* ended, the Hungarian found himself on the San Francisco stage as *Dracula,* having been replaced during his Hollywood stay in a Northern tour by Frederick Pymm. Upon Lugosi's return, Pymm moved to the role of Butterworth, the British attendant. The Hungarian not only resumed vampire status but began answering numerous newspaper requests for interviews. Fred Johnson, a writer for the *San Francisco Call* printed "Dracula Sees No Talkie Future" on July 27th, the very day Lugosi wed his third and short-lived wife, Beatrice Woodruff Weeks. Johnson quotes Lugosi as saying "The stage will not only survive, but will increase its appeal. The flesh and blood actor will become more popular—the talking pictures already have whetted the desire to see and hear him on the stage. We

Bela Lugosi appeared as Inspector Delzante in 1929's *The Thirteenth Chair.*

will continue to have pictures—silent ones, likely, and the radio will carry the dialogue of the world's best actors in broadcasting of plays."

The following day, however, Rosalind Shaffer's "Talking Language Difficulties Met" article for the *San Francisco Chronicle* carried a somewhat different cinema forecast from the resident vampire. After expressing his belief that an actor must undertake an intensive study of a role to give talking pictures the best of his/her talents and training, Lugosi confidently exclaimed, "The screen will learn to draw on the vast fund of stage technique perfected through the centuries, and when it has learned this, talking pictures will become as great a medium as the stage."

At any rate, some critics found problems with *Prisoners'* plot, not only with the lovely Griffith heading to prison at the film's conclusion, but also with a subplot that kept a cold-blooded murderer from receiving his just punishment... an early incarnation of loud moral refrains against the early thirties' gangster genre. *Variety* also claimed, "celluloid fans will be disappointed," and that the tale becomes "irksome long before its close." Director William Seiter, best remembered for comedies like *Sons of the Desert* (1934) and *Room Service* (1938), found himself overlooked in reviews that suggested exhibitors use Griffith as the film's major selling point.

Next on Lugosi's film schedule was MGM's *The Thirteenth Chair;* based on Bayard Veiller's play, this film is the one pre-*Dracula* Lugosi talkie that inevitably peaks the interest of film fans as the first collaboration of the Hungarian and director Tod Browning. Though the duo were over a year away from the filming of *Dracula,* Browning's reputation for the bizarre and unusual became insured through his several-film collaboration with Lon Chaney, Sr. The tale had not only been successful on Broadway, it had been transferred to the celluloid once before in 1919.

Though *The Thirteenth Chair* was mistakenly referred to as Lugosi's first talkie by *The Los Angeles Times,* the actor's earliest chance to do much of any speaking on film did not go unnoticed. One columnist wrote, "Talking pictures may have proved an unsurmountable obstacle to some famous foreign actors, but they have not proved so to Bela Lugosi. When Tod Browning was casting his mystery thriller *The Thirteenth Chair,* he chose the Hungarian player to enact a Scotland Yard detective who solves the mystery. For a talking picture, such a step was almost revolutionary, but Browning is elated over what he considers a discovery for the screen." *Variety* reported MGM adding Lugosi to the cast on July 10. Another article related an incident during the shooting of this "All-Dialog" mystery:

"'Interlock,' drawls director Tod Browning. 'Everybody quiet!' Lugosi begins his lines in that pronounced foreign accent of his... Bela is a detective in *The Thirteenth Chair.* He is quizzing Moon Carroll, fresh from the stage. She replies... then Browning waves his arms. For the third time the scene is spoiled. Someone has slipped on the lines. 'Tis Moon,' accuses Tod, impersonally, patiently, inoffensively. Moon acknowledges guilt, prettily, laughing. 'But it was my fault!' insists Lugosi, unperturbed, suave, gallant."

Lugosi's role as Inspector Delzante offers him a more sizeable role than any other of his first six talkies. Though at times overly theatrical, Lugosi commands attention during every scene in which appears. He towers over Wycherly and Hyams, accusing both at different times of the murder. Lugosi becomes dominant, calculating, and far more serious than the detective of Veiller's play. Lugosi appears as striking as in any of his future films, looking both dapper and a very young forty-seven.

Among the rest of the mystery's cast were Margaret Wycherly, repeating her role as the spiritualist, Mme. Rosalie La Grange. Wycherly was notably successful for her work in the Broadway version of *Tobacco Road* (1933) and her Oscar-nominated performance in 1941's *Sergeant York.* She remains a favorite character actress to film buffs through her role as Jimmy Cagney's mother in *White Heat* (1949). Though the 1916 *New York Times*' review of *The Thirteenth Chair*'s Broadway run found Wycherly only "adequate," she remains one of the highlights of the film version. Though quite comical as she introduces herself and prepares for the seance, her performance soon drifts into the eerie. "Things happen in the dark," Wycherly informs the cast members shortly before emoting anguished moans during the darkened inquiry into the murder.

Variety justly felt top-billed Conrad Nagel, in the role of Richard Crosby, was "wasted," though Leila Hyams, as heroine Helen O'Neill, "was natural and appealing throughout... [proving] that the voice can express as much through a sound box as it can over the footlights." Holmes Herbert received little mention in the reviews, though he went on to repeat the same role in a 1937 remake of the film, as well as appearing with Lugosi in *Broadminded* (1931). Many of the other cast members were criticized for their overdone English accents for a tale supposedly taking place in India.

Browning later utilized Leila Hyams in *Freaks* (1932), and the green-eyed blonde played opposite Lugosi a second time in *Island of Lost Souls* (1932). One article claimed that Hyams had a curious complex with the number thirteen, having left her home in Cincinnati on the 13th day of a month, travelling in Pullman car number thirteen, sleeping in berth thirteen, and even landing in Hollywood on a December 13th. Curiously, the *Los Angeles Times* noted that Hyams made, "valiant attempts to have the film started on Friday the 13th, without success, due to director Tod Browning, who asserted that the number held no luck for him."

Hyams herself managed to pinpoint many modern complaints about the film: "Transplanted stage plays don't seem to hit the right spot with me... action is lacking in so many of them." Yet, even in an era when sound films often seemed to borrow so heavily from the stage, some critics pointed to this problem. Philip K. Scheuer of *The Los Angeles Times* threw fault as a "far too literal

A posed MGM publicity shot casts Lugosi in a mysterious light for *The Thirteenth Chair.*

translation of a stage property which certainly attained uncommon popularity in its original form," as well as questioning the "marked tendency on the part of the director to fill his scenes with intentional disorder." To highlight the tastes of audiences who loved a good chill, Scheuer added that those "who are readily influenced by swank in production, who absorb superficialities simply because they are offered for absorption, and who ask for nothing more than dimmed lights, shrieks, and the thud of a falling body to make their evening a success... to them, the picture is highly recommended."

In some ways, the photographic composition seems stiff and stagey. Somewhat disconcerting too is the crossing of the 180 degree line (generally considered an editing *faux pas*) in the sequence in which John Davidson convinces Holmes Herbert to put off the announcement of Nagel's marriage and allow him to pursue his theory regarding the murder. Yet, other technical aspects of the film remain impressive, given the period. Multiple moving camera shots occur, one of which begins at a high angle and slowly moves, not only closer to the cast, but also down to eye level. Another effective shot utilizes a very slow track in toward Wycherly, praying alone in a room of the house.

Before its premiere, *The Los Angeles Times* reacted favorably to *The Thirteenth Chair,* noting how timely the "eerie, scary thriller" had arrived for the Halloween season. "All-Chills! All-Shudders! All Shakes! All Gasps! O-O-o-o-h!" ads read, promoting the film as hardcore horror, the "weirdest spine chiller of them all." "Shiver and shake: It's the best mystery show ever," publicity proclaimed. Screenings on October 31st at the Loew's State in Los Angeles even had an extra 11 p.m. show, complete with Halloween party.

Though Browning's name meant much on a picture of this type, the collaboration with Lugosi created only a minimal stir at the time. Some notices referred to the actor's stage portrayal of *Dracula,* with the *LA Times* dubbing him as the "frowning Lugosi." One of the more interesting pieces was a full-page portrait in a September, 1929 *Theatre Magazine.* "Bela Lugosi, famous on the stage as the sinister vampire in *Dracula,* makes his bow before the movies in the leading male role opposite Margaret Wycherly in *The Thirteenth Chair,"* the caption read. "He is also slated for the role of *Dracula* in its film version." Another portrait appeared in *Motion Picture Classic* to announce the Hungarian's appearance in the film, also mentioning the "rumor that Lugosi may repeat on the screen his stage success in *Dracula."* Several newspaper advertisements featured a menacing pen-and-ink of the actor. Many even billed him fourth in the cast, though the credits on the film itself list him seventh. As far as Browning goes, some publicity held him as the ultimate "thrill-wizard" of the cinema. Ads in New York drew the connection to Veiller's stage hit more than anything to do with either Lugosi or the director, and elsewhere exhibitors utilized their own inventions to draw in crowds.

J. Miller, manager of the Apollo in Peroria, Illinois, conducted a "superstition contest" in conjunction with the showing of the film. He arranged for *The Peoria Journal Transcript* to run the contest along the lines of the inquiring-reporter idea each day for three days prior to screening the film. Questions dealing with pet superstitions were asked in the newspaper with cash prizes going to the best replies. Naturally, the number "thirteen" superstition featured prominently among the answers. Miller also made tie-ins with area furniture stores for window displays on chairs, with photographs and placards announcing the film and theater. The number thirteen was also a strong part of lobby displays and illuminated in the marquee deck lights. Furthermore, an elaborate stage effect was put on showing two black-draped, mysterious heads and the prominent number thirteen displayed in the theater auditorium before the showing of the picture. Luminous paint, sound effects, and eerie music assisted in adding mood to these stunts.

Fox Studios next acted as Lugosi's cinematic employer, providing employment opportunities for four of his next five films. The studio had earlier produced *The Veiled Woman* (1929) with Lugosi, with initial announcements claiming the melodrama would be Lugosi's "debut in a talking picture." The released film, however, was completely silent. Another Fox project, *Luxury*, a drama to pair Lugosi with Clare Luce, was announced in mid-1930, but the drama never went before the cameras. By the end of the decade, studio assets over and above liabilities were approximately $73,000,000 and the studio itself churned out some fifty films a year. On January 3, 1930, Fox issued a statement claiming that 1930 will be "the greatest in every respect in the history of the company." Though "what ifs" are problematic to determine and

Fox proclaimed *The Veiled Woman* would be Lugosi's debut in a talking picture. However, when the film was released, it was silent.

support, Lugosi might certainly have found a home at Fox as a supporting or even lead player had Universal chosen another actor to portray *Dracula* (1931).

Speculation has led some to believe that William Fox's birth in Hungary could have been a source of kinship between Lugosi and him. This assumption is almost definitely incorrect. Fox was not only Jewish and a basically a product of America (he grew up in a New York tenement from age nine months), but he was also mired in personal problems during and after the production of the four Lugosi/Fox films. Problems ranging from the stock market collapse to a 1929 automobile injury to government anti-trust action against studios owning theaters caused Fox to sell his shares in the corporation in 1930.

The first of the Fox talkies in which Lugosi appeared was *Such Men Are Dangerous* (1930). The most notable event during production remains a two-plane collision on January 2 that killed ten men involved in the film, including director Kenneth Hawkes. The crash occurred some two miles south of Redondo Beach at an altitude of 3000 feet, with both planes plunging into the waters below and sinking almost immediately. In addition to Hawkes, an assistant director (Max Gold), two cameramen (Conrad Wells and George Eastman), two assistant cameramen (Ben Franklin and Otto Jordan), two property men, and two pilots lost their lives. The director's brother, Howard Hawkes, reportedly backed out on accompanying Kenneth at the last minute due to a change in plans. In addition to the deaths, Fox claimed $20,000 in property loss.

The scene to be filmed depicted a character's parachute drop into the sea, with a third plane in flight to allow Jacob Triebwasser (a stand-in for Warner Baxter) to make the jump. This third aircraft was not involved in the accident. Lieutenant Colonel Roscoe Turner piloted the additional aircraft and avoided the accident itself. Before being put to bed with what was described as a nervous breakdown, Turned gasped out, "I turned my ship as soon as possible, and all I could see was the flames and the smoke as the burning planes struck the water."

Other eyewitness reports commented that two men were seen attempting to parachute out of one of the planes immediately following the crash, but the mass of destruction struck the water before they could leap to safety. The chief officer of an ocean liner described the disaster as resembling a "bolt of lightning." Numerous fishermen in boats and other persons along a coastal highway also saw the explosion. The first rescue ships found only "twisted and charred portions of wings and canvas." Three bodies were also discovered, floating face down on the water's cold surface. Two were those that had almost jumped, with the third having been thrown from the aircraft due to the force of the explosion. All were badly burned and replete with broken bones. Blazing gasoline on the water marked the spot where the planes had submerged. Navy mine sweepers, aided by two speed boats, three Coast Guard cutters, eighteen Navy planes, and five commercial aircraft, found the remaining wreckage the day after the accident, though only the landing gear could be pulled to the surface.

Fox representatives quickly expressed their condolences to the bereaved. Among the family members left behind were Kenneth Hawkes' wife, actress Mary Astor. Among other notables displaying concern over the incident was aviator Charles Lindbergh, who stated "A head-on crash in the air is something so rare that it seldom enters into safety factors of airlines. The mishap was certainly unfortunate, but such a thing is practically impossible in air transportation where stunts or other than regulated flying are not involved."

Despite two attempts, teams were unsuccessful in raising the wreckage. On January 6, however, a diver searched the ocean floor sixty-five feet beneath the water's surface. The heroic diver recovered Hawkes and one other corpse from their fate, having been badly mangled and rammed against the plane's instrument board. Dangerous waters and strong winds prevented further bodies from being found, drawing the catastrophe out even longer.

A hearing held by the Coroner found little revealing information, instead making clear that each of the pilots involved had experience operating planes for cinematic use. Studio eyewitnesses offered an even stranger account of the crash than those not involved in the production. Watching carefully and waiting for the parachutist to jump, they jointly saw the two planes start to turn as their wings touched. This caused the aircraft to swing around and meet nose-to-nose. One explanation cited the "double glare of the sun and water," adding that blind spots might have allowed a pilot to turn dangerously close to another plane. Final blame was not affixed to any particular party or reason.

The essential plot of *Such Men Are Dangerous* had a wealthy Warner Baxter overhear several women discussing how unattractive he is, believing he must surely have been married for his money. Baxter's character, Ludwig Kranz, becomes so distraught that he eventually fakes his own death and goes to Dr. Goodman, a plastic surgeon, to get a more handsome face. Though Goodman at first refuses, Kranz changes his mind by offering £10,000 for the operation. He returns to his former society friends as a "new" person, Pierre Veillard, a millionaire thanks to the fortune of his previous life.

The film, originally titled *The Mask of Love,* was inspired by the real-life airplane suicide of a German financier. Fox credited Elinor Glyn, whose first name became that of the leading lady in the tale, with formulating the film's story. The screenplay itself was written by Hungarian novelist and playwright Ernest Vadja, who earlier had penned *The Love Parade* (1929), the screen's first original operetta. Along with Baxter and a sixth-billed Lugosi, *Such Men Are Dangerous* also featured Hedda Hopper, still eight years away from beginning her Hollywood newspaper column. On March 12, 1930, *Variety* claimed the finished film was "without distinction, chiefly because the theme is what flappers call dizzy... it remains mediocre fare for the better first runs." In his review (*New York Times,* subtitled "Skin Deep"), Mordaunt Hall found more kind words for the film. *Such Men Are Dangerous* for him became a "most interesting talking film" for the Roxy's third anniversary celebration, further praising Baxter's makeup as "marvellous" and his performance as "highly effective." Hall noted the dialogue as done "exceedingly well with a minimum number of words." Lugosi took the last line of Hall's notice, getting attention for a "sincere performance."

Lugosi appears quite sympathetic and kindly as the plastic surgeon, diametrically opposed to such later roles as the disturbed Dr. Vollin in *The Raven* (1935) . Though his screen time is concentrated in one section of the film, the role is more a joy than any other of his Fox "talkies." In explaining his work during World War I and thus why he cannot accept Baxter's check, Lugosi seems more human than in many of his later films. In terms of a "talkie," Lugosi curiously switches from speaking German to his secretary to a slightly broken English with Baxter. When he first takes the £10,000, Lugosi promises, "I can do *too* much good with this money," though more accurately he means "I can do *so* much good with this money." Later, removing the gauze from Baxter's bandaged head, Lugosi requests that the patient "wait a little minute," not intending to express that a minute itself can come in various lengths, but rather something like "wait a little bit" or "wait a minute." Despite such gaffes, the role of Dr. Goodman becomes one of Lugosi's most rewarding, spotlighting a range of sympathy similar to what he mustered for *The Black Cat* (1934).

Leading lady Catherine Dale Owen received less-than-encouraging comments, with *Variety* claiming that she "twitches her eyebrows during closeups until laughter is almost provoked." The actress offered her own response to talkies, mentioning how confusing it was to not work in continuity as one does in the theater. "Learning lines for the stage is much easier than for the talking pictures," she explained to the press.

Though the memory of the crash lived on in the reviews of the film and certainly the minds of theatergoers, various possibilities for exhibition publicity still remained open. The Kaufman Theater of Fox's Great Lakes in Buffalo garnered attention for planting a dialogue writing contest in *The Buffalo Times* the week previous to the showing of the film. Large layouts of stills from the picture were printed, with a coupon below each photograph. The contest had readers attempting to write appropriate dialogue for the illustrated scenes.

On May 10, 1930, *Variety* announced Lugosi would play under Leo McCarey's direction in Fox-Movietone's *Road House*. The film soon changed titles to *Wild Company,* and like so many flaming-youth films, the young have a tremendous amount of fun before learning a lesson at the end. "Thrills, parties, jazz—where does this mad speedway lead?" movie posters asked. Frank Albertson stars as Larry, the son of wealthy H.B. Warner. Constantly draining money from his father, Albertson quickly spends it in a speakeasy where singer Sharon Lynn entertains. Unfortunately for him, Lynn is the moll of gangster Kenneth Thomson, who befriends the youth only to pin a murder wrap on him. Warner turns over his son to the police, and the ensuing trial

In *Wild Company* (1930) Lugosi appeared with Frank Albertson and H. B. Warner.

means a lengthy lecture for the boy before being handed a suspended sentence.

Director McCarey's career blazed on a much more colorful path than *Wild Company* would suggest. From such comedies as *Duck Soup* (1933) and *The Awful Truth* (1937) to the sentimental *Going My Way* (1944) and *An Affair To Remember* (1957), McCarey garnered fame for successfully blending comedy with a deep understanding of human beings. Father, H.B. Warner, carried much weight as a lead in many silents, including that of Christ in *King of Kings* (1927), later moving on to such supporting roles as his Oscar-nominated performance in *Lost Horizon* (1937). Frank Albertson drifted into character and supporting roles in such films as *Room Service* (1938), *Man Made Monster* (1941), and *Psycho* (1960) . Sharon Lynn, who so strongly affects Albertson's character, was better known for her singing and dancing than any dramatic acting. Mother, Claire McDowell, makes little impact through her role, with the actress later appearing with Lugosi in *Murder By Television (* 1935).

Wild Company allows Lugosi limited screen time, but as nightclub owner Felix Brown he becomes key to the film's conclusion. Kenneth Thomson pulls a gun on Lugosi after the tuxedoed Hungarian walks in to discover him robbing the nightclub's safe. Bela immediately throws his hands up, offering a few words to save his own neck. "Don't get rough with the gunplay," he explains to the crook, promising to forget what he has seen. "I'd rather stay alive with my mouth shut," Lugosi adds just before hitting the light switch with his elbow. Thompson manages to shoot him all the same, causing the murder for which Frank Albertson becomes charged.

Billboard magazine gave exhibitors several tips for arousing added interest in *Wild Company*. "You can play up the moral of the picture particularly," H. David Strauss wrote. "If you can get the film early enough in advance for your local ministers to see it at a private presentation, it would be a good stunt and the writer candidly believes it will give the idea for a sermon to them. You might even try to stage a fathers' and sons' night, admitting the two together for the performance at a slight reduction in price, or try selling family-party tickets. To sons and daughters, mail cards or hand them out at the theater, with such a statement as 'Do your parents grant every wish? Do you think this is conducive in bringing out the best that is in you?' To parents you might mail cards asking the questions: 'Do you give your children too much liberty? Has it made them penny wise and pound foolish?' No doubt you get up some interesting arguments on these questions." Strauss correctly realized that quarrels from such an inquiry would certainly occur.

As generally dull as *Wild Company* seems now, reviews at the time were mixed. *Billboard* felt the result was a "good job," except for "a few sequences that are inclined to a lethargic pace." Warner and Albertson received nice nods, though Lynn lacked "conviction." Richard Watts, Jr. of the *New York Herald Tribune* enjoyed the film even less, summing it up as "feeble stuff." Though for him Albertson was a "rarity" and Kenneth Thompson gave a "good performance," Warner "overacts" and Lynn "isn't very good." On the whole, Watts much preferred the Roxy Orchestra's rendition of Ravel's *Bolero*. Most reviews excluded any mention of Lugosi, perhaps because of his small role and poor billing.

Lugosi's next screen appearance came in Fox's *Renegades* (1930), based on Andre Armandy's novel, *Le Renegat*. Popular Warner Baxter of *Such Men Are Dangerous* starred as one of four Foreign legion privates. Among the remaining three legionnaires was Noah Beery, Sr., famous for his appearances in such films as *The Mark of Zorro* (1920), *The Sea Wolf* (1920), and another Foreign Legion epic, *Beau Geste* (1926). Myrna Loy appeared during a period prior to her tremendous success through W.S. Van Dyke's *The Thin Man* (1934). At this point in her illustrious career, Loy was locked into the roles of exotic, often oriental vamps. Costar C. Henry Gordon would play in future Lugosi films, *The Black Camel* (1931) and *The Devil's In Love* (1933), as would Victor Jory (in 1942's *Black Dragons*) .

Behind the scenes of *Renegades,* Victor Fleming helmed the production as director. He later found his name attached to *Treasure Island* (1934), *Captains Courageous* (1937), *The Wizard of Oz* (1939), and also as the accredited director of *Gone With The Wind* (1939). Sophie Wachner provided the costumes, just as she had for *Such Men Are Dangerous* and *Wild Company*. Likewise, the cinematographer of Lugosi's first two Fox talkies, L. William O'Connell, lensed *Renegades* as well. *Renegades* also utilized Movietone, the earliest system to record sound directly onto film. The film was shot on location in the Mojave desert ,and due to the extreme heat, the studio had technicians spray water on tents and supply refrigerators to help keep everyone cool.

The New York Times called Baxter "excellent" and Loy "praiseworthy." Beery's voice was too "strident" and C. Henry Gordon talked "so loudly it seemed his voice might tear through the screen." *Billboard* also remarked about Loy, calling her the "Theda Bara" of the day, combining "stunning" looks" and the "necessary menacing portrayal that the role demands." *Variety,* however, felt Loy's performance contained "stagey" and "unconvincing qualities," giving a much more favorable nod to the "excellent" fight scenes." *Photoplay* also praised the story's action. If reviews shared any common points, the immense sets with desert fortresses and hundreds of extras aroused many kind comments, but the film as a whole was "muddled," "tedious," and "monotonous." Most reviewers cried for considerable cuts to quicken the pace and cure some of the discrepancies in the plot.

Renegades itself has a heartbroken Baxter and three companions deserting the French Foreign Legion to join a band of desert mercenaries. Baxter finds his love, Myrna Loy, as a member of a marabout's harem. Wicked and lecherous, she feels safe enough with the marabout to taunt Baxter. Soon, the Riffs side with Arab guerilla forces to destroy the French forces. As the Arabs

Jeanette MacDonald and Reginald Denny appeared with Lugosi in the romantic comedy *Oh, For a Man!*

attack Baxter's old fort, Baxter and his three companions convince the Riffs to support the French. The fort is saved, but at the cost of the Riffs' lives. With his dying strength, Baxter shoots the vile Myrna Loy.

Lugosi portrays the bearded Sheik Muhammed, who calls himself the "Marabout," quite theatrically, making the most of his scenes with Myrna Loy. "You look very nice when you don't say nothing," he explains to her ... later crudely explaining he might return her to Baxter. Lugosi views Loy as sexual property, and very disposable at that, adding that he really doesn't care one way or another. "What do you think?" becomes his recurring question. A more stern moment of domination comes as Lugosi forces her to leave the room when Warner Baxter visits. "If I say go, you go. If you don't, my little lamb, I will have you flogged." In a single scene, Lugosi's nickname for Loy changes from a "dove" to a "pig." As the uncrowned "king of the Riffs," Lugosi also finds the chance to spin a few choice sayings, such as sending word to Baxter that "Muhammed cannot go to mountain; mountain must come to Muhammed." Though most of his screen time is limited to two scenes, the role is central to the plot, adding further tension between Baxter and Loy.

Most theatergoers didn't actually see *Renegades* until 1931, with several exhibitors experiencing reactions different than would be expected, given the tone of period critics. The Hollywood Theater in Fort Worth, Texas, called the film a "box office hit," adding that their house had to hold the film over. From Keith's in Cincinnati, the management reported only "good" business for the film but still crowned it a "great action picture." The RKO in Winnipeg, Canada reported "audiences pleased" due to the "fine action." Spokane, Washington's Audian Theater admitted only fair business, but claimed "crowds like it—needs plugging."

To hopefully draw more passerbys into their theaters, exhibitors were told to "build a small fort on the marquee of your theater. Also, you can spread your lobby entrance with white sand and decorate it in the colors of the Legion. A couple of men dressed as Legionnaires, stationed in front of the house, lend color. Also, a couple of men so attired riding horseback about the streets of your city, properly placarded, should make a great ballyhoo."

Fox's *Oh For A Man* became Lugosi's next released film, and though premiering in November 1930, it didn't enter general release until early the following year. Hamilton McFadden, a graduate of the Harvard Law School and a former stage actor, directed a handful of basically undistinguished films before turning to acting on celluloid. Shortly after *Oh For A Man,* McFadden directed Lugosi again, in *The Black Camel* (1931). Cinematographer Charles Clarke went on to earn four Academy Award nominations in the forties, as well as being awarded a special Oscar in 1944 for "the development and practical application of a device for composing artificial clouds into motion picture scenes during production photography." Along with lensing films for four decades, Clarke also designed a battery-run motor camera that later became an industry standard. Prior to *Oh For A Man,* Clarke filmed Lugosi in *The Veiled Woman* (1929).

Jeannette MacDonald starred in this farce, though she was still a few years away from teaming with Nelson Eddy at MGM and becoming the target of many stand-up comics as a result of songs like *Indian Love Call.* Co-star Reginald Denny became a longtime screen actor, moving into character roles as a result of his dapper style and British accent. Along with portraying "Algy" in the Bulldog Drummond series, he appeared in everything from *Sherlock Holmes and the Voice of Terror* (1945) to *The Secret Life of Walter Mitty* (1947). Supporting player Albert Conti had previously appeared in *Such Men Are Dangerous.*

The comedy itself has Jeanette MacDonald as the talented diva with a large following of fans, even though she has her maid keep everyone at bay. After spurning one suitor by saying her career is her ultimate focus, MacDonald goes home only to be robbed by Reginald Denny. Conveniently, however, Denny is a huge fan of the singer and the two become friends. MacDonald even demands that Denny be given a job in the opera chorus. Denny later becomes disgusted at the situation and is about to leave as MacDonald proposes. The two leave for an Italian villa, but eventually Denny walks out on MacDonald and she returns to New York to sing. Later, he returns to her room and the duo are reunited with a kiss.

The tale itself originated in a story printed in the June 7, 1930 edition of *The Saturday Evening Post.* Fox soon purchased Mary F. Watkins' *Stolen Thunder,* which initially served as the film's title as well. Though much of the plot would be retained, writers Lynn Starling and Philip Klein altered MacDonald's character name from "Madame Cleo Hanni" to "Carlotta Manson." Many details were added to the short story as well, including Lugosi's character, Frescatti. Yet, perhaps the greatest problem in terms of plot became the lack of punishment Denny received for his crimes. After MacDonald's star grew brighter, the production code forbidding such unreproved crimes was firmly in place. As a result, Fox was unable to reissue this comedy and cash in.

Lugosi's role as Frescatti offers him little chance for screen time, with his first appearance at the end of a MacDonald performance. As he calls her singing "simply superb," she returns the compliment by complaining of a cast member that always eats and smells of garlic. Though not intended as anything more than an example of MacDonald's temperamental nature, in retrospect the scene becomes enjoyable given Lugosi's lifelong association with the garlic-hating vampire. A later scene finds him listening to Denny sing, with one particularly interesting closeup of his face grimacing in response to a sour moment of the performance. Well-dressed and wearing a goatee, Lugosi resembles his later role of Dr. Benet in *The Invisible Ray* (1936).

Reviews varied greatly on this film, ranging from comments like "a worthy winner" and an "excellent treatment" to "ridiculous." *Billboard* claimed on December 13, 1930 that it "is hardly to be considered as worth-while farce for the higher type of audience." The trade had no real complaints with MacDonald and Denny, save for the latter's unfitting "Irish brogue." In the end, the reviewer believed audiences would find *Oh For A Man* "trashy entertainment." *Variety* also

Vivienne Segal, Alexander Gray, and Margaret Jacobson Blanchard (second wife of Oscar Hammerstein) appeared with Bela Lugosi in *Viennese Nights.*

felt the film "is hardly of deluxe house calibre," tracing much of the trouble to the story itself. Yet, the cast, direction, and music were all applauded. *Photoplay,* however, felt it was "one of the month's brightest, without a doubt."

Management at the Alamo theater in Louisville, Kentucky brought in only "fair" business with *Oh For A Man,* mentioning it was "nothing to rave about." The Aldine in Philadelphia did "poor" business with the film, leaving a disgusted exhibitor to mention the "silly comedy never had a chance." Small, "poor" audiences also plagued *Oh For A Man* in Providence, Rhode Island, as the RKO Victory Theater suggested to Fox that the "stars deserve a better vehicle." The Golden Gate in San Francisco also cried that "business should have been better." Only a few exhibitors reported strong responses the comedy, with those that did attributing good crowds to other reasons. Chicago's Oriental drew filled seats not due the film, for example, but because the personal appearance of some radio stars proved "a big draw."

To help with business, *Billboard*'s Sidney Harris advised theater owners to "play up *Oh For A Man* by exploiting Miss MacDonald and Denny, who have been in enough films to become fairly well known. You might employ an inexpensive street ballyhoo in the form of using a girl, garbed as an old maid, to carry a sign calling attention to the picture."

Viennese Nights, a Warner Brothers' musical and Lugosi's next film, often found itself compared to such novels as Edith Wharton's *Age of Innocence.* The musical offers three young men (Alexander Gray, Bert Roach, and Walter Pidgeon) who leave their homes to join the Austrian

Army. Pidgeon becomes a lieutenant, which ends his friendship with the other two. Gray falls in love with a cobbler's daughter, the lovely Vivienne Segal, and takes her to a nightclub with Bert Roach. Unfortunately, Pidgeon meets and also takes a fancy to Segal. The officer persuades her to marry him, leaving Gray to leave heartbroken for America. Years later he struggles as a musician to support his child. When chance allows him to again cross paths with Segal, they at first decide to be together and reach happiness. After she learns of his child, however, she returns to Pidgeon. Decades later, Segal awaits the marriage of her granddaughter to a wealthy young man when she instead elopes with an American musician... Gray's grandson. Segal later dreams that Gray comes to her and sings.

Given a premiere in November of 1930, *Viennese Nights* didn't enter general release until early 1931. Along with the Vitaphone sound system, the movie utilized beautiful, two-strip Technicolor. Though many circulating dupes are a near-eyesore, the original copies themselves retain well-defined colors and real beauty. If not a revered auteur, director Alan Crosland retains a permanent place in cinema history by having helmed the first talkie, *The Jazz Singer* (1927). Sigmund Romberg and Oscar Hammerstein II wrote the story and music expressly for the screen. Hammerstein later became one half of a musical team with Richard Rodgers, writing lyrics for such popular shows as *Oklahoma!* and *South Pacific*. Though less remembered, Romberg became the subject of a film biography in *Deep In My Heart* (1954), with Jose Ferrer portraying the composer.

As per the cast, Pidgeon later achieved popularity in films like *How Green Was My Valley (1941), Mrs. Miniver* (1942), and *Madame Curie* (1943). Segal found much greater fame in operettas and Broadway musicals like *Pal Joey* than in her few cinematic ventures. Supporting players like Jean Hersholt and Louise Fazenda remain important in cinema history. The former became most famous as the character "Dr. Christian" on radio and in a number of films, as well as later appearing in *Mark of the Vampire* (1935) with Lugosi. Hersholt also founded the Motion Picture Relief Fund and is still remembered for his humanitarian efforts. Fazenda had already appeared in the first sound horror film, *The Terror* (1928), by the time of *Viennese Nights,* though she is better remembered as being an important female comic at Mack Sennett's Keystone studio, as well as performing in such features as *No No Nanette* (1930) and *Alice In Wonderland* (1933).

"If this pretty and clean musical romance, with pleasing music, does not get over, it will settle any question at present as to whether the theatre-going public wants musical talkers," *Variety* claimed on December 3, 1930. "That test comes with the general release." Reviewers had no problems bestowing laurels on the cast, with *Billboard* claiming Segal "establishes herself as an artist," and Pidgeon appearing to "excellent advantage." Yet, the question of how interested the cinemagoing public was in musicals remained a prime question in the early notices of many reviewers. *Variety* summed up its thoughts on *Viennese Nights* with, "Plenty of good production all in acceptable color, direction beyond reproach, well assembled cast and everything, but it's a musical. Let's see."

Lugosi appears all too briefly as an ambassador, making an even more disappointing experience than viewing his unbilled roles in other films like *Fifty Million Frenchmen* (1931) and *The Devil's In Love* (1933). The only saving grace might be the use of Technicolor, though *Viennese Nights* features basically no closeups of Lugosi. The result renders none of the unusual characterization in *Renegades* or the surprising versatility of *Such Men Are Dangerous,* but rather an essentially uninteresting curio.

To help with promotional materials that read, "Gay! Sparkling with the wine of life! A picture you'll remember long after others are forgotten," the "experts" told theaters to target women in their local promotions for the film, suggesting they "get some cheap lace and fade it yellow and scent it with lavender, with an appropriate card, and mail it to the ladies on your mailing list; it should arouse interest. Decorate your lobby in rosemary, lavender, and lilacs. A hope chest in your lobby of faded wedding veils, orange blossoms, and other things of a forgotten day should attract attention. Appeal to the sentiment of your female clientele. No doubt they are tired of sensationalism in films and the sympathetic touch in connection with this one should win."

Perhaps theaters that tried this idea should have purchased a better quality of lace, as many reported empty theater seats. Philadelphia's Aldine Theater received "poor" attendance, as did Baltimore's Auditorium and Jacksonville's Palace. One repeated complaint was that rental prices had driven up ticket costs to the 50¢ to $1.50 range, with managers complaining "Prices too high for this class picture" and "Baltimoreans won't pay $1 top." The Audian of Spokane noted only "fair" crowds, clamoring that the picture "needs plugging," apparently beyond any "hope chest" in the lobby. The Strand in Louisville also brought in lesser crowds, even though the management did feel it was a "fine picture" and "high class." The Music Box in Portland, New York City's Warner Theater, and the same city's Strand all did less-than-desirable business. Detroit's Fisher attempted to explain its minimal crowds by saying *Viennese Nights* was simply a "sophisticated film of limited appeal," and St. Louis' Missouri Theater complained that the "strong show at next door house hurt biz." Only a few theaters found real success with *Viennese Nights,* such as the Grand in Columbus and New Orleans' Strand. Two theatres in Washington D.C. did particularly well with the film, with the Earle delighting at the "coloring and music." Adding evidence to Detroit's belief that the film had limited allure was D.C.'s Ambassador, asserting there was "real appeal" but "for a *first-class* residence section."

In the final analysis, these six films themselves have limited allure today. On the whole, Lugosi has small parts... offering mere glimpses of the very reason most of these films are remembered at all. Furthermore, just as one might read these varied films as a signal of lost opportunity for the Hungarian—a path not traveled due to *Dracula*—they just as easily could be an indication of an actor wallowing forever in supporting roles. They could be indicative of obscurity, a fate not too distant from the ever-diminishing light of actors Warner Baxter, Conrad Nagel, Reginald Denny, Frank Albertson, and others that today are essentially forgotten. More than mere curiosities but far less than anything "classic," these six films maintain a unique place in the Lugosi canon. Varied and worthy of investigation, they become evidence in exploring one phase of the screen icon's evolution.

Dracula has the impact of a nightmare, not a nightmare of blood and thunder and chaos, but of deathly quietude, with Lugosi the silent, slowly stalking figure who evades capture as easily as he escapes logical analysis. The steady, creeping pace at which he encroaches upon his victims is far more dreamlike and terrifying than leaping and clawing would ever have been.

Dracula

(1931)

by Bret Wood

CREDITS: Associate Producer: E.M. Asher; Producer: Carl Laemmle, Jr.; Director: Tod Browning; Screenplay: Garrett Fort; Continuity: Dudley Murphy; Based upon the Bram Stoker novel and the 1927 stageplay by Hamilton Deane and John L. Balderston; Scenario Supervisor: Charles A. Logue; Cinematographer: Karl Freund; Art Director: Charles D. Hall; Film Editor: Milton Carruth; Supervising Film Editor: Maurice Pivar; Recording Supervisor: C. Roy Hunter; Set Designers: Herman Rosse and John Hoffman; Photographic Effects: Frank J. Booth; Musical Conductor: Heinz Roemheld; Makeup: Jack P. Pierce; Set Decorations: Russell A. Gausman; Costumes: Ed Ware and Vera West; Casting: Phil M. Friedman; Research: Nan Grant; Art Titles: Max Cohen; Released February 14, 1931 by Universal Pictures, 75 minutes

CAST: Bela Lugosi...Count Dracula, Helen Chandler...Mina Seward, David Manners...John Harker, Dwight Frye...Renfield, Edward Van Sloan...Professor Van Helsing, Herbert Bunston...Dr. Seward, Frances Dade...Lucy Weston, Charles Gerrald...Martin, Joan Standing...Maid, and Moon Carroll, Josephine Velez, Michael Visaroff, Daisy Belmore, Nicholas Bela, Donald Murphy, Carla Laemmle, John George, Tod Browning

While critical opinion on Bela Lugosi's appearance in *Dracula* (1931) varies from unqualified adulation to revisionist views that strongly disparage his efforts, his portrait is an incontestable cornerstone of the horror cinema, bearing profound influence not only on the actor's subsequent work but on the performances of other horror stars throughout the generations that followed. The same might be said of the film itself, whose reputation has suffered beneath the pens of some contemporary aficionados but which—in spite of the poison ink that mocks it—eloquently asserts its undeniable puissance with every fresh screening.

The source of the backlash against the film, the star, and for that matter the director, seems to reside in the context in which *Dracula* is being considered. It is tempting to judge it according to the standards set by the influential motion pictures that arose in its wake. Films such as the *Frankenstein* series, *Dr. Jekyll and Mr. Hyde, Island of Lost Souls,* and the Val Lewton films may offer convenient reference points but are virtually immaterial to an assessment of their predecessor, yielding little substantial insight into the aesthetic and historic importance of such a vanguard film. The more challenging task is to examine *Dracula,* and Lugosi's titular performance in particular, in the proper context—the circumstances under which the film was produced by Universal and the climate of the movie marketplace, which was encased within a barrier of narrative plausibility, a barrier *Dracula* defiantly punched through, thereby allowing for the appearance of other horror films both original and derivative. A brief history of the project's evolution is therefore in order.

Since the supernatural was systematically denied in the pre-1930 American cinema (otherworldly creatures routinely unmasked as elaborate, human-made hoaxes, as in *London After Midnight, The Cat and the Canary,* and *The Bat*), it was a daunting challenge for director Tod Browning to make the unreal plausible without alienating his audience. For Browning, at the peak of his career following a prosperous five-year stint at MGM, *Dracula* was to be his crowning achievement, transcending the intense (yet always rooted in the realm of the possible) thrillers he made there with Lon Chaney. After signing on with Universal, which had purchased the rights to Bram Stoker's novel, he departed on a European vacation to celebrate his new contract and revitalize his creative spirit.

But when he set foot back on American soil, he found his visionary plans beginning to crumble. The stock market had crashed in his absence, which caused Universal production chief Carl Laemmle, Jr. to radically amend his campaign for lavishly produced pictures that refused to bow to the Hollywood code of the happy ending (e.g. *All Quiet on the Western Front*). *Dracula* was an early victim of Universal's belt-tightening. The budget was promptly slashed, meaning Browning could no longer afford the services of Lon Chaney—not that it mattered, since Chaney had signed a new contract with MGM in Browning's absence and would be dead of bronchial cancer long before cameras ever started turning on *Dracula.* Just as damaging to Browning's dream was Laemmle's conservative-minded dictum that the film should closely adhere to the text of the popular stage play, the rights of which Universal had simultaneously acquired with the novel. This explains why the latter half of the film is so awkward and setbound in comparison to the extended prologue (where Browning's devious imagination was allowed momentarily to roam), which is atmospheric, relatively dynamic, and genuinely haunting.

Laemmle's edict of adherence to the play was a sort of insurance policy for the studio's investment in the film, following the flimsy belief that a stage play literally adapted to film was a guaranteed success—a misconception widely subscribed to during the dawn of sound. Since Deane and Balderston's *Dracula* had been criss-crossing the nation since its 1927 premiere, the more faithfully Browning could transcribe the play onto celluloid, the better.

Enter Bela Lugosi.

Although a perfunctory search among different actors was conducted by Universal once they acquired screen rights to the property, from its first American performance on October 5, 1927, *Dracula*'s titular role belonged to the veteran of the Hungarian stage. The filmic vampire, Laemmle et al. ultimately decided, was to be his as well... again adhering to the elements of the successful stage production.

How this decision of casting affected Browning is impossible to discern today, but since the director had seen Lugosi in the play and had directed the actor in his 1929 film, *The Thirteenth Chair,* it is safe to assume that Browning was satisfied with, if not enthusiastic about, the choice of leading man.

As Tod Browning once told an aspiring actor, "There is only *one* Lon Chaney and he has gone, *forever.* No one can take his place." When the director stepped onto the set of *Dracula* on Monday, September 9, 1930, it was not his intention to mould Lugosi into a facsimile of his late collaborator. Such an effort would have been foolhardy to say the least. It was Chaney himself who truly defined his roles, not any director or screenwriter. Browning's acknowledgment of this fact was what made their partnership so fruitful. And ultimately, *Dracula* called for a departure from the seething, ferocious characterizations Chaney had pioneered. In compliance with Laemmle's wishes, Browning deferred to the persona Lugosi had carved for himself on stage and built the film around that, rather than forcing Lugosi to calibrate his performance to comply with a pace, tone, and style preconceived by the director. Browning's crucial role was in helping Lugosi tone down his outward, presentational stage acting style for the more subdued, representational mode of performance suitable to the screen. Lugosi later recalled, "for the screen, in which the actor's distance from every member of the audience is equal only to his distance from the lens of the camera, I have found that a great deal of the repression was an absolute necessity. Tod Browning has continually had to 'hold me down.'"

Because Lugosi's characterization was initially designed for the stage, it emphasized the "normalcy" of this hideous monster, on-stage physical transformations and elaborate makeup effects being extremely difficult to accomplish on a nightly basis without shattering the audience's suspension of disbelief. Though it may be considered heretical to some, it may have been fortuitous that Lugosi rather than Chaney portrayed the stage-derivative Dracula. Chaney's gift was for larger-than-life personages who often overwhelmed the thin narratives of his films, employing a presentational acting style that, when not captured on film in a proper manner by someone acquainted with his forceful performance method, often vaulted over the boundary of plausibility into pure excess. Such an approach was not appropriate to a film like *Dracula,* which was considered volatile not only by Laemmle but his advisors ("Were this story put on the screen, it would be an insult to every one of its audience," one script-reader wrote in 1927). Even the press acknowledged the kid gloves with which the property needed to be handled. Upon the film's release, *Variety* wrote:

> "Such a treatment called for the utmost delicacy of handling, because the thing is so completely ultra-sensational on its serious side that the faintest excess of telling would make it grotesque. Nice judgment here gets the maximum of shivers without ever destroying the screen illusion, the element that makes it possible is the pictorial plausibility of the scenes of horror in which impossible creatures move."

Lugosi functions so beautifully in the role because he is not monstrous but suitably mysterious. This would, of course, all change in time as subsequent films encouraged him to abandon the enigmatic detachment and play monsters and mad scientists more flamboyantly, reducing his subtle and complex presence to stereotypical hamming. In *Dracula,* however, he is remote in behavior and alien in appearance, just enough to unsettle an audience, while maintaining the necessary ordinariness to keep the drama rooted in the realm of the real. The subtlety of Lugosi's performance is remarkable, for the film exerts its chilling influence without many of the now-tired trappings of the vampire subgenre it established. Lugosi has no fangs. No puncture marks appear on the necks of his victims. But for a droplet on the tip of Renfield's finger, there is no blood. The devices of the repugnant crucifix and mirror pass through the film quickly, without histrionic emphasis. In *Dracula,* the mechanics of how a vampire operates are secondary to the drama and dread of finding one's self in such a ghoul's presence.

Much of this subtlety was censor-inspired but it works to the film's advantage. One might even argue that *Dracula* functions better without the groans and noises deleted by the Production Code Administration after the film's initial release, later restored in the currently circulated prints.

While this was his third sound film, Browning was reluctant to rely too heavily on the newly developed cinematic element. Like Chaney, he was leery of the still-imperfect technology, preferring to understand its limitations and potential before gambling his career on it. Resisting the temptation to fill the soundtrack with forceful music, excited dialogue, and startling bursts of noise—and from this hollow thunder derive chills—Browning took a more insinuating approach, calling upon the suspense-generating power of the silent cinema, which was well within his control. Under his direction, emotional tension was created through the manipulation of stark imagery, concisely-composed *mise-en-scéne,* inconspicuous editing and the all-permeating darkness characteristic of his work.

Dracula has the impact of a nightmare, not a nightmare of blood and thunder and chaos, but of deathly quietude, with Lugosi the silent, slowly stalking figure who evades capture as easily as he escapes logical analysis. The steady, creeping pace at which he encroaches upon his victims is far more dreamlike and terrifying than leaping and clawing would ever have been.

Lugosi didn't have to rant and growl and hiss to cast his spell. His power over the viewer (like Dracula's power over the characters who surround him) is akin to that of the snake over its prey, moving silently, gradually, hypnotically, tapping into some primordial sense of danger every animal shares, and which involuntarily wells up in one's soul in the presence of such an imposing and alien figure.

The first image of Dracula, freshly risen from his casket in the catacombs of his Transylvanian castle, is one of the most unsettling in the film, yet Lugosi does nothing but wear the appropriate, stony expression. The shot begins after he has just taken a step, so his black robe sways gently, inexplicably. Otherwise, he doesn't seem to move. Rather, Browning deviously

Lugosi functions so beautifully in the role of Dracula because he is not monstrous but suitably mysterious.

nudges the cautious audience closer to this silent, motionless, Sphinx-like creature by dollying the camera into a medium closeup, forcing the reluctant viewer within reach of the dreaded Count.

And it isn't solely Lugosi's silence and stillness that make him such a frightful being, but rather these qualities in contrast to the behavior of other characters. This suspense-generating difference is especially evident in the Castle Dracula scenes, where there is a detachment, a clear schism between Lugosi's slow-motion mannerisms and Dwight Frye's nervous speech and movement—like two pieces of a jigsaw puzzle that do not fit together.

While Renfield the clerk struggles to conceal his fear and attempts to conduct real estate business, Dracula confidently floats about, occasionally stopping in dramatic poses (with a shuttered baby spotlight accentuating his eyes vs. Renfield's conventionally-lit visage). While Renfield speaks cordially and directly, Dracula waxes poetic about the music of the wolves and survival of the spider: "The spider, spinning his web for the unwary fly... The blood is the life, Mr. Renfield." To which a perplexed Renfield responds, "Uh... yes," little realizing the clue to his own horrible fate offered by the Count's nonsensical mumblings.

The effect is a disconcerting one. One feels frustration in sympathy with Renfield at his inability to converse with the Count. This a heightened reflection of an earlier, equally confounding scene, in which Renfield is unable to express to the superstitious villagers the necessity of his nocturnal visit to Castle Dracula.

Dracula responds to Renfield's questions and comments but one could hardly call what they share a conversation. What results is a nightmarish sequence in which the viewer shares Renfield's alienation and insecurity (especially since the spectator in the theater is held immobile in a chair just as Renfield sits helplessly at the table Dracula has prepared for him). Words hold little meaning, and are little else than a means of passing time while Lugosi performs a waltz of death around him (us), an expressionistic ballet of predator and prey in which the reality of the film —the narrative concern with Renfield's arriving and carrying out his task —is put on hold. The plot intentionally stalls while we watch the ceremonious process by which the snake charms the mouse, nervously waiting for it to strike, a gruesome *pas de deux* that would be devoid of power were it not for Lugosi's exquisite performance as the mystifying Count Dracula. The film is a sort of low-key precursor to *Psycho,* in which the ostensible leading character (Renfield/Marion Crane) and plot (real estate deal/impulsive embezzlement) are introduced solely as means of leading the viewer into the lair of a deceptively polite, oddly charming, murderous fiend.

Every line of dialogue Lugosi delivers in *Dracula*'s *danse macabre*, no matter how insignificant, is given the same dreamlike delivery that frustrates the viewer trying to find meaning in his words, and by deciphering them, discover his intentions. Offering Renfield drink, Dracula croaks forth, "This... is... very old.... wine." Does this refer to his age and immortality? Or is it merely a suggestion of his wealth and sophisticated taste? The sequence is so stupefying that, under its spell, one is inclined to excuse the occasional moment of dark comedy that occasionally slips in, such as Dracula's comment, "I never drink... wine." When considered rationally, this line is merely cheap and campy, but situated within the other cloudy ingredients of the scene, it is appropriately disconcerting, another clue to Renfield's fate of which he is oblivious.

The slow, cadenced precision with which Lugosi pronounces his lines was not due to any lingual barrier. He had spoken many of the same phrases almost every evening for the previous three years as he performed Dracula on stage.

The lingering, formal approach to dialogue—savoring the exotic inflections that creep into his carefully enunciated speech—was a calculated ingredient in the character's cryptically mesmerizing charm. To understand how much Lugosi's manner of speech enhances his performance as Dracula, one need only compare it to that of Inspector Delzante in *The Thirteenth Chair*, made a year and a half earlier by Browning at MGM. In ordinary street clothes, speaking ordinary lines at ordinary rhythms, moving in an ordinary manner, Lugosi is thoroughly demystified. In this character role of the detective trying to solve a pair of supernatural murders, he is no more impressive than any other supporting actor on the studio roster.

The Hungarian accent works to his detriment—hardly enhancing his character, if anything convoluting it. Lugosi's Eastern European intonation is distracting and incongruous with the film's milieu of upper class Britishers in the heart of India (where the leading character speaks with a thick Irish brogue).

Further hindering the performances in *The Thirteenth Chair* is the rather crude 1929 sound technology with which the dialogue was recorded. Often Lugosi is, like most of the cast, poorly coached, (this being Browning's first film with synchronized sound), so that lines are often spoken so quickly that, when not entirely unintelligible, they fail to carry any of the sinister impact they were composed to deliver.

Lugosi, more than anyone else in the cast, seemed aware of this flaw in *The Thirteenth Chair*'s pacing and occasionally slipped into his *Dracula* mode and stylized the filmic role with some of the dramatic pauses and menacing stares that he employed during his stage performances. In one scene, Delzante allows a key suspect to spend a few minutes alone in the room in which a murder was committed. As he slowly backs out the doorway, he issues a stern warning, allowing the words to uncurl menacingly from his mouth, "The constable outside has orders... to arrest anyone... leaving..." (closing the door behind him), "... this house."

Impressive as Lugosi's delivery may be, these ominous enunciations are merely hamfisted theatrics when coming from a character who hasn't been given the proper dramatic treatment by the filmmakers. He is somewhat exotic but so is every other character in the film. It is the exceptional strangeness of Dracula—contrasting so harshly with the polished, uptight Britishers—that gives these same performatory ingredients profound meaning in the 1931 film. When Lugosi delivers dialogue in a similar manner as the Count, the words and gestures cease to be thespian efforts to dress up a shallow character. The gradually paced alien intonations rise from the belly of the beast, ooze through lips moistened with saliva and spread through the room like some gaseous, lethal spirits, snaking into the ears of Renfield and the theater audience held similarly within the vampire's grasp.

On board the ill-fated Vesta, after the businessman's blood has been spilled, the chemistry between Dracula and Renfield changes. Lugosi is still enigmatically silent and still, while Frye's Renfield is manic, unkempt, and grovelling at the feet of his master. We fear Dracula not so much because he is a monster (which Lugosi certainly is not) but because he is capable of turning *us* into monsters—from officious real estate agent to sniveling, bug-eating wretch. Lugosi's Dracula is fearsome, because he brings about this change without violence or even threats of violence. He politely seduces rather than brutally attacks.

Lugosi maintains Dracula's icy detachment in every scene, moving through the London fog in formal attire like the angel of death after wordlessly murdering the impoverished flower girl on a dingy streetcorner. One unsettling factor is that he commits these heinous crimes seemingly without emotion or guilt (prefiguring a modern obsession with the seductive, guilt-less serial killer). He shows no pity and offers no dramatic flourishes—not even the hackneyed swoop of a cape—things all sympathetic victims are supposed to be entitled to in the laws of melodramatic cinema.

This explains why the scene in which Dracula slaps the mirrored cigarette box from Van Helsing's hand is such a potent moment. It is the first time he has actively expressed any emotion and made any sudden physical movement in the entire film. (The scene in which he recoils from Renfield's crucifix was the closest he had yet come to an emotional outburst, but that moment was softened by Browning's framing and editing, showing only the end of Lugosi's movement and hiding his face behind his arm.) Lugosi's slapping of the cigarette box indicates that a turning point has been reached. Dracula's secret has been discovered and he must now defend himself against the blood-thirsty do-gooders. Immediately after the incident, he regains his composure and once again any readable thoughts or emotions are hidden away. For a moment, though, a significant crack in his sophisticated veneer has been exposed, hinting at the degree of cold brutality that lurks within.

In the remaining minutes of the film, Dracula's stonelike reserve wavers a few times and Lugosi resorts to more theatrical gestures and poses that lack the icy subtlety of the preceding scenes and thus tend to conventionalize his character. When he attempts to hypnotize Van Helsing, he performs the unnecessary gesture of extending a claw-like hand and furrowing his brow—surely a pose left over from the stage play, a medium which cannot suggest such malevolence as subtly as the cinema.

When he is pursued into Carfax Abbey, Dracula's composure further disintegrates, as he is reduced to a running, panicked beast, probably Browning's attempt to bring the film to a climax through standardized techniques of rousing action. As a result, the character becomes more human—therefore less mystifying—and Dracula's ability to evoke fear in the viewer quickly evaporates. The thrill of *Dracula* is over. The process of finding his body and penetrating its heart with a stake are but necessary technicalities in concluding the narrative which the audience politely tolerates. Dracula's censored groans, as the stake is pounded in, are the final, most blunt expression of his tumble from detached immortality into the domain of human emotion. The only suspense-generating element is the question of Mina's well-being, but even that is mild since her character is so two-dimensional and dull in comparison to the more richly-detailed but just as subdued performance Lugosi delivered.

As Lugosi portrays him, Dracula is a stranger whose words and gestures offer no indication of his personality or intentions. The villains of ordinary Hollywood thrillers clearly communicate their intentions through standardized words and gestures which—through repetition and traditions in melodramatic acting—have come to carry encoded meaning. Their very appearance consists of symbolic details the audience is schooled in interpreting. For example, when a swarthy antagonist strokes his long moustache and smiles his gold-toothed smile at an innocent woman, the viewer is telegraphed his very thoughts and intentions: his low social station, his villainy, his sexual desire, his ruthless greed. Words usually do little more than redundantly reinforce these nonverbal impressions.

Lugosi's Dracula, on the other hand, is a cipher who defies simple interpretation. He doesn't look like the typical villain. He doesn't behave like the typical villain (He doesn't even behave like a typical *human*). He doesn't say villainous things. He is a bewitching anomaly to be watched carefully, approached cautiously... studied... suspected... feared. He is not the hissable villain of the simple monster movie. He is not the complex, heart-broken beast of the Lon Chaney films such as *West of Zanzibar* and *The Unknown.* Lugosi baffles the viewer, refusing to let us understand anything about this uncanny figure.

This alien-ness is probably the ingredient most responsible for *Dracula*'s eerie impact upon the viewer. The role is carefully designed and flawlessly portrayed so that the audience is systematically unsettled by this creature who seems human but bears little resemblance to anything we have yet encountered (at least not until the characterization, through overuse, became a not only familiar but tiresome cliche). Perhaps better than any other cinematic creation, Lugosi's Dracula is the ultimate representation of the Other.

Defined by Jacques Lacan, the Other stems from repressive society's conflict with that which is not accepted or understood. In his essay "The American Nightmare: Horror in the '70s" (*Hollywood from Vietnam to Reagan.* New York: Columbia University Press, 1986), Robin Wood explains:

> "The concept of 'the Other'... represents that which bourgeois ideology cannot recognize or accept but must deal with... by rejecting and if possible annihilating it... It functions not simply as something external to the culture or to the self, but also as what is repressed (though never destroyed) in the self and projected outward in order to be hated or disowned...the projection on to the Other of what is repressed within the Self (is done) in order that it can be discredited, disowned, and if possible annihilated."

Wood breaks the Other down into eight components of society's disinherited: other people, woman, the proletariat, other cultures, ethnic groups within the culture, alternate ideologies or political systems, deviations from ideological sexual norms, and children (several of which directly apply to *Dracula*). Dracula's wives (including Mina) threaten the patriarchal system by their independence, their sexual appetites, and their refusal to remain ornamental love objects to masculine law. Dracula is an intruder in that he comes from outside the Sewards' close circle of friends and, more disturbing still, from outside their nation's borders. Coming from an alien culture, he is instantly viewed with suspicion by the others, a disruptive intrusion into the family that Browning made every effort to play up in casting the role. Once Chaney was ruled out of the cast, Browning wanted someone foreign and little known to the moviegoing public in the role; he told the *Los Angeles Examiner*, "I favor getting a stranger from Europe, and not giving his name. (Casting a well-known star) takes away from the thrilling effects of the story." The Count's ideological system, his perversion of *their* religious practices and rules of behavior, directly conflicts with the Sewards' as will later be discussed. And, most calamitously, there is the sexual deviance.

These elements of the Other—not in themselves very terrifying—become a source of horror once they are carefully meshed with the truly horrific crimes of the vampire, who drinks the blood of the living, murders children, and drives the most refined and self-controlled person to a frothing insanity. This figure of unadulterated profanity is bestowed with all the insecurities, prejudices, and secret sins of his creators: he practices polygamy, he is a foreigner, and he does not subscribe to Anglo-Saxon religious mores. The writers who have embellished and originated the lore of the vampire, from Stoker through the playwrights and screenwriters, have added their own feelings of bigotry, religious intolerance, and sexual insecurity to the story, unconsciously ridding themselves of these everyday haunts and reassuring themselves that they and the world can rest easy with a clean conscience once this evil is annihilated. These concerns make *Dracula* frightening and make his threat not merely fantastical but one enshrouded in society's shared, real anxieties.

Dracula is particularly unsettling and engaging because of the conflict it presents with religion. The Count not only operates outside the boundaries of the bourgeois Christian family, he inverts its most sacred laws—a terrifyingly real Dark Prince whose communion is the blood of virgins and whose aristocratic immortality is a mockery of Christ's resurrection. The Count and his three lamia defile numerous sacred codes, including the innocence of children (in Dracula's killing of the flower girl and Lucy's infanticide), marriage and monogamy (Dracula's multiple wives and pursuit of another's fiancée). By their eternal life on earth they defy the liturgy of burial. Dracula's aversion to the crucifix is sacrilege at its most literal. Other, less overt images add to this catalogue of Dracula's blasphemy. When Renfield is in the castle, he sees three bats flapping outside a gothic, stained glass window, much like a cathedral's, which has significantly been smashed, so that its frame is now empty and is used as an entrance by the winged predators. The appearance of the three wives, with their white gowns and hands reverentially folded at their breasts supplies another evocative image of religious ceremony or formality, a wedding or communion, somehow corrupted.

Much has rightly been made of the sexual overtones of the vampire's attack, which seems much more telling (especially in Browning's version) than the need for life-sustaining human blood. From the project's inception, Dracula's bite was conceived as a sexual act as much as a homicidal one. Upon reading the screenplay, Carl Laemmle, Jr. dictated firmly that "Dracula should go only for women and not men," (a command Browning complied with on paper but defied on celluloid by having Dracula and not his ghastly wives descend upon the unconscious body of Renfield).

Lugosi's suave, slightly smarmy good looks do much to establish a romantic link between vampire and victim; but the sexuality is far from healthy and "normal." A dark taint to sexual desire is expressed in the morbid flirtation between Dracula and Lucy in the opera box ("Quaff a cup to the dead already. Hurrah for the next who dies!" she coos dreamily) and Dracula's murderous embrace (molestation) of the juvenile flower girl. The sexual nature of the vampire's attack makes the undead Lucy's off-screen murder of an infant all the more disturbing.

In one particularly profound scene, Lugosi, through facial expression, conveys the gruesomeness of *his* variation on the sexual act. When he approaches the neck of Mina (moving up to and below the lens of the camera, as if encroaching upon the neck of the viewer), he wears not an expression of carnal desire but a rather disturbing, sickly grimace, suggesting his repugnance at the act of violating this woman, while suggestively hinting at the bloody mess the encounter will result in.

In spite of the power it exerted in 1931, Lugosi's performance as Dracula has, in the years since, lost some of its insidious power. This comes as no fault of the original performance but as the result of actors and directors of a lesser calibre who rose in Lugosi's shadow. No sooner had *Dracula* shaded the movie screens of America than the singularly uncanny film was set upon

Mark of the Vampire **is a fascinating little film that manages to engage and surprise even though it is laden with vampire-movie formula.**

and commodified into a formulaic genre. Other filmmakers imitated it. Other filmmakers appropriated from it. Other filmmakers pillaged *Dracula* of the components they considered most effective—the components most easily plagiarized and repackaged and sensationally marketed. As a result, cinematic horror changed forms, having less to do with the dynamics of the vampire's intrusion upon the rigid moral fiber of the pampered Brits (and all the sexual tension that accompanied it) and became instead a series of mechanized shadows and scares, like a haunted house in an amusement park—brash and startling, with its ghouls of painted plaster, but less deeply menacing to be sure.

Within a few years of *Dracula*'s release, the horror film was already becoming mired in cliche, as studios of all sizes sought prosperity through mimicry rather than innovation. The Depression inspired conservative attitudes in studio chiefs, who preferred a reliable remake or sequel such as *Dracula's Daughter* to a financially unpredictable genre-bending film like *Freaks.* By the mid 1930s, the horror movie was entering into a phase of unconscious self-parody, with Lugosi offered few options but that of replaying his legendary role with slight modification and decreasing subtlety.

When Lugosi and Browning were reteamed for the last time to make *Mark of the Vampire,* MGM's requisition was not for an original thriller but a remake of the Chaney/ Browning silent *London After Midnight,* which would capitalize on the popularity of the 1931 film version of *Dracula* the same way *London After Midnight* had plagiarized the 1927 stage play.

In spite of these studio-imposed restrictions (such obstacles plagued Browning's career), *Mark of the Vampire* is a fascinating little film that manages to engage and surprise even though it is laden with vampire-movie formula. But it is the very familiarity and predictability of *Mark of the Vampire* that constitute its charm and allow for the startling gut-punch that it delivers the horror movie audience in the end. The plot replicates the *Dracula* scenario of a mansion of wealthy Brits whose grounds are haunted by vampires (primarily Count Mora, portrayed by Lugosi) who wander in from a nearby decaying estate. A scientist well versed in the supernatural arrives to help the family, whose daughter has fallen under the spell of the undead neighbor.

By this time, Lugosi's face was so instantly recognizable and inextricably associated with vampires, demented scientists, and the like that he needed to do nothing else but stand and grimace to deliver the charge the audience awaited. He was such an icon of movie monstrosity that, tragically for him, such details as speech and character were superfluous. Filmmakers felt it a waste of time to give his roles any depth.

Browning, who always privileged character over plot (nowhere better evidenced than in the Chaney films) recognized this flawed trend but was trapped within it, since *London After Midnight*'s plot dictated that the character of Count Mora should not really be a vampire but a fake—hired by the scientist in an effort to solve a crime. At the same time, Count Mora functioned as a cheap tool to attract ticket-buyers and satisfy their shallow expectations of frightening sights, devoid of significance beyond Lugosi's standardized appearance.

Dissatisfied with the situation, Browning tried to develop the character somewhat, returning to the pre-Stoker folklore of the vampire, which asserts that before a vampire can roam the countryside in search of blood, he must first attack members of his own family. Even if Lugosi was forbidden to interact with the other characters (and reveal himself to be merely a hoax), he might be endowed with some deeper meaning by the legends of the townspeople that fear him. Browning and screenwriter Guy Endore introduced the character of Luna, Count Mora's daughter (Carroll Borland), and developed a semi-incestuous link between her and her father. Not daring to violate the provisions of the censorial Production Code under which Hollywood filmmakers were subdued, MGM executives quickly ripped these pages from the screenplay. Any depth Browning and Lugosi may have hoped for was lost.

Rather than give up and allow Lugosi to be wasted as such an empty, meaningless figure, Browning and Endore devised a brilliant coda to *Mark of the Vampire* that apologizes for its own limitations and offers wry criticism of the two-dimensionality of the unambitious horror film. In this scene, which has no correlative in *London After Midnight* (where the vampire was the detective/hypnotist in disguise), the vampires are revealed to have been little more than theatrical illusionists hired to haunt the Balfour estate.

Here, as Lugosi packs away his black cape, the filmmakers acknowledge that the film was little more than a cheap but effective gag: makeup, costume, and special effects that are easily unfurled before a gullible audience and conveniently packed away at the conclusion of each performance. That's how self-consciously formulaic the horror film had become. *Mark of the Vampire*'s surprise ending is a pointed bit of cynicism that has never really been acknowledged, especially by those critics to whom makeup, costume, and special effects constitute the basis of suspense and dread.

Having accomplished their tasks with a smirk and having fulfilled all obligations to MGM regarding *Mark of the Vampire,* both star and director hoped to retire their well-worn horror props and move on to new terrain—more challenging roles, less conventional narratives—but the move never came. No one realized that *Mark of the Vampire* was a half-parody, half-indictment of the conventional horror film. Instead, audiences gasped and critics proclaimed it, "the horror film to end all horror films." Lugosi and Browning suddenly realized that there was no defying this genre they had been instrumental in creating. The horror film had become so formula-bound and rigid, parody didn't register, lost in the repetitious conventions audiences mindlessly craved.

There was only compliance or obsolescence. Actor and director separated there and followed their own separate courses.

Browning found obsolescence. After his audacious screenplay of *The Witch of Timbuctoo* was hacked apart and rewritten by the studio, he directed a mundane whodunit (*Miracles for Sale,* which also suffered studio tampering) and never made another picture.

Lugosi, on the other hand, attempted to survive within the industry. He fought for roles which might allow him to demonstrate a greater range as an actor, but unfortunately the die had been cast and the remainder of his career would be fraught with professional frustration. Though he might find roles that allowed him to display his expressiveness at greater volumes, never again would there be a film such as *Dracula,* carefully tailored to showcase his remarkable abilities, furtively channeling his quiet, mysterious, unsettling charms into the lens of the camera and releasing them magnificently upon a tension-filled audience.

Bela Lugosi, in costume from *Mark of the Vampire,* appeared at a social function for the Los Angeles Junior Soccer League.

Lugosi, fresh from his turn as Murder Legendre in White Zombie, is in fine form as the wild-eyed madman Roxor in *Chandu the Magician*.

CHANDU THE MAGICIAN (1932)

by Dennis Fischer

CREDITS: Directed by Marcel Varnel and William Cameron Menzies; Based on radio broadcast series by Harry A. Earnshaw, Vera M. Oldham, and R.R. Morgan; Adaptation and Dialog: Philip Klein and Barry Conners; Film Editor: Harold Schuster; Assistant Director: Walter Maryo; Art Director: Max Parker; Photography: James Wong Howe; Sound: Joseph E. Aiken; A Fox Production release, 72 minutes.

CAST: Edmund Lowe...Chandu, Irene Ware...Princess Nadji, Bela Lugosi...Roxor, Herbert Mundin...Albert Miggles, Henry B. Walthall...Robert Regent, Weldon Heyburn...Abdulah, Virginia Hammond...Dorothy, June Viasek...Betty Lou, Nestor Aber...Bobby

The "Chandu the Magician" series began life as a West Coast radio program starring Gayne Whitman in 1931. William Fox's Fox studio, which later merged with 20th Century to form 20th Century-Fox, bought the rights and selected Edmund Lowe, who had played a magician in the Fox film *The Spider*, to essay the role of Chandu. The co-director of *The Spider* and co-director of *Chandu the Magician* was the legendary William Cameron Menzies, noted for such SF film classics as *Things to Come, The Whip Hand,* and, of course, *Invaders From Mars*.

Menzies was a genius in film design, and his selection seems obvious because of the many ingenious special effects that the film incorporates. For an early sound film, it has very fluid camera movement and the marvelous effects work stands up well in comparison to today's cinematic magicians.

Later Lugosi himself would perform the role of Chandu the Magician in Principal's 1934 serial, *The Return of Chandu,* which was shot on sets leftover from *King Kong*. However, Lugosi's charismatic and commanding presence is the only thing to recommend this pedantic serial, and although he makes a fine Chandu (with his long expressive fingers, few actors could match Lugosi in hand gestures suggestive of putting the whammy on somebody), he's even better in the villainous role of the ruthless Roxor.

Chandu's humor is probably attributable to French-born co-director Marcel Varnel, a former actor turned director, who was later noted for handling the comedy stylings of bumbling British comic Will Hay and the Crazy Gang. Varnel's best films are reputed to be *Oh Mr. Porter, Alf's Button Afloat, Old Bones of the River, Ask a Policeman, The Frozen Limits*, and *The Ghost of St. Michael's*, the latter a borderline genre entry starring Will Hay (and not Peter Ustinov who doesn't even appear in this Ealing comedy despite often being attributed as such) with a ghost supposedly piping before deaths occur. (Ustinov actually appeared in the Will Hay comedy *The Goose Steps Out*).

However, the most notable man connected with the production apart from Lugosi was the other director, William Cameron Menzies, a man of myriad talents, most notably in design. A Yale graduate, Menzies joined the Famous Players as an art director after serving in World War I. He began working in Hollywood as an assistant to famed art director Anton Grot (né Antocz Franziszek Groszewski), who later invented and patented a "ripple machine" to create weather and light effects on water scenes for his long-time collaborator, director Michael Curtiz, on *The Sea Hawk*. Grot and Menzies began to work together on *The Naulahka* (1918), which was set in India

***Chandu the Magician* is almost an encyclopedia of early special effects techniques, featuring one inventive effect after another throughout its fast-paced running time.**

and which established them as experts in creating exotic settings.

Menzies came to prominence for his fabulous work with Grot on the Douglas Fairbanks/ Raoul Walsh silent version of *The Thief of Bagdad*, still considered by many to be one of the most consummately designed Hollywood films ever, though the look of the film was clearly influenced by the Fritz Lang silent *Destiny* (aka *Der Müde Tod*), designed by Walther Röhrig, Robert Herlth, and Hermann Salfrank.

Menzies worked with the idiosyncratic director Roland West for whom he designed three films, *The Bat* (1926), later remade by West in 70mm in 1930 as *The Bat Whispers* in which form it inspired Bob Kane to create the comic book character The Batman; *The Dove* (1927) for which Menzies won the first assistant director Academy Award ever, and *Alibi* (1929) which features Menzies' fascinating art deco-cum-Expressionistic set designs obviously inspired by *The Cabinet of Dr. Caligari*.

Menzies helped create the wonderful costumes and worked on the script for the elegantly elaborate 1933 version of *Alice in Wonderland*, was assistant director and created the special effects for the war scenes for *Cavalcade*, and designed the cave sequence climax for Selznick's colorful *The Adventures of Tom Sawyer* (1938).

Selznick was so pleased with Menzies' work that he created a new post for him, that of production designer, for Selznick's masterpiece, *Gone With the Wind*, for which Menzies won a well-deserved Academy Award. In essence, Menzies ghost-directed the entire film by re-creating the entire script in sketch form, showing the actual camera set-ups, lighting, and all other pictorial elements which were used. Selznick also placed on his production designer the task of all montage sequences, which Menzies not only designed and laid out but also directed, including the famous burning of Atlanta sequence, which for the record marked the last appearance of the huge gate from *King Kong*'s Skull Island, redecorated as a row of households before being burned.

Menzies also designed with Vincent Korda the magnificent spectacle of Korda's *Thief of Bagdad* (1940), one of the most opulent and beloved fantasies of all time. He worked with Hitchcock, creating the memorable windmills in *Foreign Correspondent* (1940). He began a collaboration with director Sam Wood and together they did *Our Town* (1940), *The Devil and Miss Jones* (1941), *King's Row* (1942), *The Pride of the Yankees* (1942), *For Whom the Bell Tolls* (1943), and *Ivy* (1947).

Menzies' design work was marked by a "predilection for broken diagonal barriers which cross the frame like jagged slashes and usually turn up during scenes of tension, grief, and separation in the form of fences, walls, palisades, railings" according to Léon Barsacq in *Caligari's Cabinet and Other Grand Illusions: A History of Film Design.* Gillett's *International Encyclopedia of Film* acclaimed him "the most influential designer in Anglo-American cinema..."

Menzies' first two films as a director were both co-directed by Kenneth McKenna and were both concerned with magicians doing tricks which showcased Menzies' knowledge of special effects techniques. The first, *The Spider*, features Edmund Lowe performing a series of tricks to unveil a murderer in the audience, and the second, *Always Goodbye* (not to be confused with the Barbara Stanwyck film with the same title made seven years later), was much the same.

Both films, as well as *Chandu,* were made for Fox films, the outfit started by Hungarian immigrant William Fox in 1915 out of his Box Office Attraction Company. Fox developed such stars as Theda Bara and Tom Mix, financed the Murnau classic *Sunrise*, provided a home for such directors as John Ford, Raoul Walsh, and Frank Borzage, and after the sound challenge of Warner Bros., his company countered with Movietone, the first sound-on-film process, which was developed in association with General Electric.

At the end of the '20s, Fox made a bid to dominate Hollywood by trying to buy a controlling interest in Loew's Inc., the parent company of MGM, as well as a 45 percent interest in British Gaumont. Unfortunately for Fox, his timing proved disastrous as he had to deal with an automobile crash which immobilized him for two months while the famous stock market crash of 1929 and a government antitrust action took place.

Fox was saved by the success of Shirley Temple's films; however, continuing litigation forced Fox to sell his shares in 1930 to a group of bankers for $18 million for a studio that had been valued at $200 million mere months before. In 1935, Fox merged with Joseph M. Schenk and Darryl Zanuck's two year-old Twentieth Century, forming the now familiar 20th Century-Fox.

Chandu's cinematographer was the great James Wong Howe (*Mark of the Vampire; Seconds*) who later worked with Menzies again on *King's Row*. In *The Art of Hollywood*, Howe is quoted as saying, "William Cameron Menzies designed the sets and sketches for the shots; he'd tell you how high the camera should be, he'd even specify the kind of lens he wanted for a particular shot. The set was designed for one specific shot only; if you varied your angle by an inch you'd shoot over the top... Menzies created the whole look of the film."

Chandu begins inventively with a waving hand seemingly conjuring up the titles, with the name Chandu looking as if it were fashioned out of sparkling sequins. Unlike many early sound films, *Chandu* has a very fluid look thanks to the many dollies through miniatures that break up the more static shots typical of productions of the period. Miniatures are also used to extend sets and at times were shot and backprojected behind actors to create the impression of immense antiquities on the film's frugal budget.

Indeed, the film is almost an encyclopedia of early special effects techniques, featuring one inventive effect after another throughout its fast paced running time. The opening sets up that Frank Chandler (Lowe) has learned all the secrets of the Yogi and is now christened Chandu. To demonstrate his powers, Chandu does the famous Indian rope trick, disappearing a boy at its apex, performs an example of astral projection, and walks across hot coals, all tricks he will need to use later in the film.

Edmund Lowe was considered a dependable leading man who could play both two-fisted heroes and drawing room Romeos in the '20s and '30s, and while his Chandu lacks the mystery and other-worldly quality that marked Lugosi's interpretation, his down-to-earth style makes for a clean-cut hero with a wry sense of humor. Lowe's most notable work was as Sergeant Quirk in 1926's *What Price Glory*, as Sgt. Mickey Dunn in 1929's *In Old Arizona*, and as Dr. Wayne Talbot in 1933's classic *Dinner at Eight*. He carried the plot with cameos from Karloff and Lugosi in Karl Freund's otherwise unnoteworthy *The Gift of Gab* (1934). Lowe eventually descended uninterestingly into character parts, popping up in such films as *Dillinger*, *Around the World in Eighty Days,* and *The Last Hurrah*.

Chandu's teacher shows the magician a crystal ball with the image of Roxor (Lugosi), warning of "death and destruction rising from the brain of a madman." He is told that Roxor lives in the cliffs above the third cataract of the Nile and that this great danger will threaten him personally through his family.

Chandu's sister is Dorothy (Virginia Hammond), who has married scientist Robert Regent (Henry B. Walthall). Ralph Morgan (*The Power and the Glory, The Life of Emil Zola, The Monster Maker*) was originally cast as Regent, the inventor of a death ray, but was replaced by Henry B. Walthall, who is best remembered as the Little Colonel in D. W. Griffith's *Birth of a Nation*, as Dr. Manette in the 1935 *A Tale of Two Cities* , and as Edgar Allan Poe in the 1915 film *The Raven*.

Regent has invented a secret death ray capable of destroying whole cities, though his motivation for doing so is never explained. He demonstrates the ray's destructive power by blasting a large block of stone into non-existence. Such rays were commonplace staples in the mainstream pulp magazines of the '20s and '30s, inspired by the discovery of X-rays by Wilhelm Konrad Roentgen in 1895 and perhaps the heat ray of H.G. Wells' *The War of the Worlds* (1898).

The machinery in Regent's laboratory is clearly manufactured by famed electrical wizard Kenneth Strickfaden, who provided similar services for *Frankenstein, The Mask of Fu Manchu, Bride of Frankenstein,* and *Young Frankenstein* for that matter.

Roxor arrives at Regent's laboratory and arranges his kidnapping on the spot with the help of some stealthy henchmen who abduct the scientist and lower him into a boat waiting below. Nor does Roxor forget to take Regent's equipment with him as well. We divine his purpose when he promises, "An end to all that is noble, all that is sane."

Lugosi, fresh from his turn as Murder Legendre in *White Zombie*, is in fine form as the wild-eyed madman Roxor, though for the most part his performance harkens back to his turn as Dr. Mirakle in *Murders in the Rue Morgue*. He gives his lines a very similar, exhuberant reading with his larger than life delivery and expressive voice making for a commanding presence.

Unlike Mirakle, Roxor has no "advancement of science" justification for his actions. Here he is simply a vindictive, albeit clever, fiend with an unslaked thirst for destruction. He is a meglomaniac who wants to bring down civilization in order that it regard him in awe and acclaim him as ruler. Like the later Dr. No, he has no real understanding of the technology he wishes to control, it is simply enough that he can ruthlessly extort others into doing his will.

A sandstorm rages outside the building where Regent's family, Dorothy and her daughter Betty Lou (June Viasek) and son Bobby (Nestor Aber), await word from Robert. Sinister figures peer through the windows and the family grows anxious. To the accompaniment of *mysterioso* music, they see the shadow of Chandu at the end of the hallway. (We later learn that this music is an "astral bell" which alerts Chandu to the presence of great danger, though, of course, it sounds nothing like a bell).

Clearly, the family is in danger, but Chandu makes for a reassuring protector. He uncovers a letter that Regent wrote to Roxor in response to Roxor's demands for the death ray warning him that Regent will expose Roxor's nefarious plans to the government if he persists. Chandu has thus far been unable to contact Regent with his mental powers, suggesting that Regent is drugged or otherwise been rendered mentally insensible.

In a clever ploy, Roxor's henchman leaves a kitten at the doorway, causing Betty Lou to open it to rescue the mewling furball; however, the astral bell warns Chandu to check his crystal ball where he espies the henchman grabbing the young teen. Dashing to the door, Chandu stops the henchman with a gesture, putting him under an instant hypnotic spell which causes the henchman to reveal Roxor's whereabouts.

Princess Nadji (Irene Ware, who also appeared with Lugosi in *The Raven*) arrives at a wine seller's seeking Roxor. There Roxor is conferring with Adbulah (Weldon Herburn) who becomes excited at news of the princess' arrival. "I don't know if she is to be a friend or an enemy," Roxor admits, but if she opposes him and Abdulah serves him, she will join Abdulah's harem, promises Roxor.

Nor is Roxor himself immune from Nadji's charms when the princess arrives at his office. He tries to take her cloak so he can feast his eyes on her figure, but she demurs. Frustrated, he simply offers her a chair to sit upon. Lugosi performs these actions with gentlemanly flourish.

Meanwhile, Chandu infiltrates the wine seller's by hypnotizing the doorman and seeks Roxor disguised as an Arab. Roxor reveals his intentions to destroy the great dams that have brought prosperity to Princess Nadji's people unless they make him a modern pharaoh.

"I shall be greater than any pharaoh," Lugosi exults. "Civilization and all its works shall be destroyed. Man shall return to savagery, leaving only one supreme intelligence—me!"

This, in a nutshell, is Roxor's mad plan, achieving greatness by undermining the advances of the present. It is true that many people today are skeptical about the advantages of modern civilization, but just try to imagine a time when there were no supermarkets and most of a man's day was spent eking out a bare existence by working all day to gather some food and where the average life expectancy was about 40 years of age. That time was as little as a hundred years ago, even in Industrial Age England.

Roxor gloats, and finding that she won't cooperate, takes Nadji prisoner and informs her that she is to be sent to a friend of his as a present. However, he finds that the servant he has handed her to turns out to be Chandu who has taken the servant's place. Chandu escapes from Roxor's lair by overturning a flaming brazier and carrying Nadji through the flames.

We discover that Chandu and Nadji are old flames who are still in love with each other. We are also introduced to Albert Miggles (Herbert Mundin), a former soldier who used to be an orderly in Captain Chandler's outfit, who is now reduced to wearing a fez and holding camels. He begs Chandu to hire him, which Chandler does after first applying a hypnotic spell which causes Miggles to see and hear a miniature version of himself every time he tries to take a drink—in order to cure Miggles of his alcoholism. Miggles, of course, supplies the comic relief in the film, and does so far more effectively than most others of his ilk.

This is largely because the part is played by Herbert Mundin. Mundin's most famous role was as Barkis in George Cukor's adaptation of Dickens' *David Copperfield*, but he proved a delightful diversion in many Hollywood films of the '30s, especially *Adventures of Robin Hood* as Much the Miller, as well as in *Tarzan Escapes, Mutiny on the Bounty, Cavalcade*, and *Love Me Tonight*. His career was cut short by his death in a fatal car crash in 1939.

Roxor's spies learn that the expedition plans to seek Roxor at the ruins of Madune above the third cataract. Meanwhile, Abdulah makes an appearance, but when Nadji orders wine for them, the astral bell sounds. Sure enough, one of Nadji's servants who is actually in Roxor's employ poisons one of the drinks hoping to kill Chandu. Just as he is about to take the glass, the astral bell sounds again, so Chandu tries to force the hapless spy to drink while Miggles drops the glass he swiped upon hearing that the wine has been poisoned. The spy leaps into the Nile to escape

Bela Lugosi, the villain in *Chandu the Magician*, threatens Irene Ware and Edmund Lowe in a serial-style adventure thriller, directed by William Cameron Menzies and Marcel Varnel.

with his life. Roxor is indeed a treacherous foe.

Menzies establishes the ruins with a long pan through the corridors of a miniature and then a tilt down to a large set where Roxor has assembled Regent's death ray which he is still unable to work. Roxor's ruthlessness is further established by his arranging to blind the servant who failed in the poisoning attempt with a red-hot two-pronged poker. He threatens to do the same to Regent if he will not reveal the secret of the death ray, but Regent steadfastly refuses.

Nadji guides the heroes to the base of the tremendous ruins. Miggles pulls on a large ring which causes the wall to pivot open, allowing Chandu, Nadji, and Miggles to enter. Miggles is left behind to keep watch while Chandu and Nadji explore. Behind him, one of the statues of pharaohs proves to be a sentinel, and the frightened Miggles seeks out Chandu. The sentinel shuts the trio in a room. Sarcophagi tip forward to reveal armed Arabs behind them, but Chandu is able to hypnotize the men into believing that their rifles have turned into snakes and they flee, but he manages to keep one of them under his control and from him discovers the whereabouts of Regent.

Meanwhile, Abdulah has sent two men aboard Nadji's boat who kidnap the unprotected Betty Lou. Roxor summons Regent and reveals that he will sell Robert's daughter on the slave auction block if he does not cooperate. Regent begs Roxor to kill him instead and let her go, an offer which Roxor refuses.

Outside the slave market, Chandu disguised as an old bearded Arab beggar makes a duplicate of his image to distract the guard away from the door. Once inside, he turns invisible (via mass hypnosis), reappearing to bid on Betty Lou and buy her. He hands the auctioneer what appears to be a bag of coins and whispers in her ear, "Courage, Betty Lou."

Still viewing the proceedings from up above, Roxor tells Regent, "It's not too late to save her." But Regent still refuses. The auctioneer rushes up to split the proceeds, but dumping the contents of the bag reveals a collection of crawling bugs rather than coins. Roxor spots Chandu drawing Betty to the door and alerts the crowd.

Chandu pulls a pistol to keep the crowd at bay and gets Betty astride a horse. Then using his hypnotic powers, his hand and then his body disappears, leaving his empty clothes hanging in the air until they fall to the ground and disappear before the amazed crowd. Roxor realizes that Chandu's powers are a form of extraordinary hypnosis emanating from his eyes and formulates new plans against him.

After more fun with the desperate-for-a-drink Miggles, involving scoldings from a miniature version of himself and his seeing a goldfish in his drink, Chandu and Nadji ride off into an ambush led by Abdulah, who, taking his cue from Roxor, arranges to have henchmen throw teargas, blinding Chandu and incapacitating the source of his power. While Nadji escapes, Chandu is quickly bound and blindfolded.

Roxor reveals that he will threaten Regent's entire family which encourages Robert to send a message to them. Regent bribes a guard to send the message: "There is no chance of saving my life. Give the man who brings this a reward. My prayers be with you tonight. Father." The guard brings this message to Roxor who quickly eliminates four words and alters the message to read: "There is a chance of saving my life. Go with the man who brings this and reward my prayers. Be with you tonight. Father." Roxor then sends the altered message to Dorothy.

Roxor then gloats over the helpless Chandu, who tries to taunt him into removing the blindfold. "Your eyes would have no affect on me. If I were alone I would. These silly natives, they believe your tricks," thereby assuming his superiority to his underlings in all matters. However, the more cautious Abdulah prevents Roxor from removing the bandage to prove that his is the superior will.

Instead, a sarcophagus is brought in and the bound Chandu is deposited therein. "A favorite punishment of the priests of Isis who built this temple," Roxor explains. Roxor is aware that yogi can remain buried underground for a long period of time, but he hasn't heard of them surviving underwater, so he arranges for Chandu to be deposited in the nearby Nile.

With Regent's family now in Roxor's jail, Regent promises Roxor to show him how to use his machine in exchange for Roxor letting his family go. "There is a way out of that cell and I'll show it to them, but not with you in there," offers the double-crossing Roxor. Once Regent is removed from the cell, Roxor has a trap door tripped showing a pit that descends to the Nile beneath. The floors start tilting downward as Regent's family cling to handholds and the furniture slides into the pit and splashes into the river.

"Will you serve me now?" demands Roxor. Regent, faced with the destruction of his family before his very eyes, acquiesces.

Underwater in his casket, Chandu breaks his bonds and escapes the watery prison prepared for him.

Regent's beam can go halfway around the world, and Roxor now fires up its dreadful power. "At last, I am king of all," he intones in a series of closeups. "That lever is my scepter. London, New York, Imperial Rome! I can blast them all into a heap of smoking ruins. Cities of the world shall perish." The directors then show us Roxor's dreams of destruction while he continues his soliloquy:

"All that lives shall know me as master. They'll tremble at my words. Paris. City of fools. Proud of their Napoleon. What will they think when they feel the power of Roxor?!

"Even England. The sacred tradition. Its king, its triumph, its navy will be helpless. They shall bow before me in worship. Me, Roxor!

"I will destroy the dams of the Nile and its roaring floods shall speed down upon hundreds of thousands, drowning them like rats. Roxor the God whose hand deals death."

The miraculously dry Chandu appears and stops Roxor with a hypnotic command. Roxor resists and re-aims the ray at Chandu, but Chandu's will proves stronger than Roxor's, whose hand releases the ray's control lever.

Chandu frees Regent's family while Robert reveals that he set the machine to explode. Roxor is left frozen in place in front of the now-glowing death ray machine. Chandu searches for Nadji, as Abdulah tries to ambush him and gouge his eyes out, but Chandu flips him and the pair fight while Nadji hits Abdulah with a chain and Chandu knocks the wily Arab out with a right cross.

The heroes escape the ruins in the nick of time when the raygun explodes, killing Roxor and bringing the ruins down around everyone's ears. Chandu pulls the unharmed Nadji from the wreckage and they embrace beneath a romantic moon. Miggles is followed by his miniature conscience, who asks where they can get a drink. "You ought to be ashamed," the now reformed Miggles tells him. The film ends with the same gong logo that opened it.

Chandu the Magician has no great themes or thoughts buried in it, but was simply cannily crafted as entertainment. While it does present stereotyped Arabs as villains, it doesn't come across as racist, with Roxor's ethnicity left open to question. In fact, one of the most admirable characters is the Arab Princess Nadji, who loves Chandu but who has chosen to devote her life to the well-being of her people. Unlike many movie heroines who stand by the sidelines and scream, she takes an active part when the hero is threatened. In all, she is presented as an admirable woman of true heroic stature, someone who is brave and dedicated, but is also human and feeling.

The film presents a simplistic moral universe conceived entirely in blacks and whites with no grays. That Chandu is a superhero who traffics in deception presents no moral dilemmas because he is on the side of the good and the righteous. Roxor's insane plan and utter ruthlessness come from the fact that he wears the black hat of the piece. He has suffered no wrongs which serve as a whetstone to his appetite for destruction, he simply craves power and feels that the most effective way of achieving it is to wipe out everybody else until there are no challenges to his ultimate authority.

Of course, Lugosi excels at this kind of portrait. Both as an actor and as a person, he had a ravenous appetite for life, sinking his teeth into it and savoring its juices. No other actor could deliver ripe dialogue with the same memorable relish that Lugosi would bring to it. Much has been made in recent years of the tragic aspects of his life, of the fact that he ended up with smaller salaries, worse parts, and more terrible pictures that his chief rival Karloff, so that he has frequently been referred to as "poor Bela," with the epithet almost inseparable from his first name. However, according to those who knew him, he was far from pathetic.

Instead, here was a man who worked regularly as an actor into his 50s, 60s and even 70s, who had made an indelible impression on mass culture, and who liked to live extravagantly and in style. People who knew him well describe him as "warm and gracious" or "genial and easy-going." According to one-time manager Don Marlowe in *Classic Film Collector* (Winter 1970), "[Lugosi] never worried about money. He spent it faster than anyone I have ever known. He lived luxuriously in a stately mansion with lavish furnishings—wore elegant clothes and entertained in superlative taste." Here was an actor who far from being miserable and pitiable, truly enjoyed life and was at his best in bigger than life characterizations such as Ygor or Roxor.

As a film, *Chandu the Magician* is neither Lugosi's worst nor his best. Instead, it is a fast moving kid's film with a story typical of the later movie serials but with better design and special effects courtesy of some of the most talented men in Hollywood. It is designed to present wonder after wonder with the result that no particular effect stands out above the rest (although the combining of Miggles with his miniature counterpart seems particularly seamless to these eyes). The film itself therefore becomes a tribute to movies' ability to become a magic carpet that can take the viewer to new and wondrous realms where evil villains disintegrate whole cities with destructive death rays and courageous conjurers pass through foes and flames, making marvels and rescuing pretty princesses. Of such delicate delights are childhood memories made, and such is the enchanting entertainment that *Chandu the Magician* provides.

Poster courtesy of Ronald V. Borst/Hollywood Movie Posters

Bela Lugosi and ape friend Erik from Universal's *Murders in the Rue Morgue.*

Murders in the Rue Morgue (1932)

by Gregory William Mank

CREDITS: Producer: Carl Laemmle, Jr.; Director: Robert Florey; Associate Producer: E. M. Asher; Adaptation: Robert Florey, based on Edgar Allan Poe's 1841 tale, *The Murders in the Rue Morgue;* Screenplay: Tom Reed and Dale Van Every (additional dialogue by John Huston); Cinematographer: Karl Freund; Art Director: Charles D. Hall; Set Designer: Herman Rosse; Recording Supervisor: C. Roy Hunter; Film Editor: Milton Carruth; Supervising Film Editor: Maurice Pivar; Musical Director: Heinz Roemheld; Special Effects: John P. Fulton; Makeup: Jack P. Pierce; Scenario Editor: Richard Schayer; Special Process Work: Frank Williams; Technical Advisor: Howard Salemson; Assistant Directors: Scott Beal, Joseph McDonough, Charles S. Gould; Running time: 61 minutes; Original Budget: $164,220; Budget for retakes and added scenes: $21,870; Final cost: $190,099.45; Filmed at Universal City, California, October 19-November 13, 1931; retakes and added scenes filmed at Universal, December 10-December 16 and December 19, 1931; monkey closeups shot at the Selig Zoo, December 22, 1931; New York City premiere: RKO-Mayfair Theatre, February 10, 1932; A Universal Picture

CAST: Sidney Fox...Mlle. Camille L'Espanaye, Bela Lugosi...Dr. Mirakle, Leon Waycoff (aka Leon Ames)...Pierre Dupin, Bert Roach...Paul, Betsy Ross Clarke...Mme. L'Espanaye, Brandon Hurst...Prefect of Police, D'Arcy Corrigan...Morgue Keeper, Noble Johnson...Janos, the Black One, Arlene Francis...Woman of the Streets, Charles Gemora...Erik the Ape, Edna Marion...Mignette, Charlotte Henry and Polly Ann Young...Girls, Herman Bing...Franz Odenheimer, Agostino Borgato...Alberto Montani, Torben Meyer...The Dane, Harry Holman...Landlord, John T. Murray and Christian Frank...Gendarmes, D. Vernon...Tenant, Michael Visaroff and Ted Billings...Men, Charles T. Millsfield...Bearded Man at Sideshow, Monte Montague...Workman/Gendarme, Hamilton Green...Barker, Tempe Pigott...Crone, Joe Bonomo...Double for Charles Gemora, John Carradine...Audience Member

What were Bela Lugosi's greatest performances?

Dracula, of course. Sadly vengeful Dr.Vitus Werdegast in *The Black Cat*; gloriously mad Dr. Richard Vollin in *The Raven*. And Bela's Old Ygor of *Son of Frankenstein* and *The Ghost of Frankenstein* was just as deserving of an Oscar as was Martin Landau's portrayal of Lugosi in *Ed Wood*.

However, as far as Lugosi performances go, I have a personal "pet" favorite: Dr. Mirakle of Universal's *Murders in the Rue Morgue* (1932). Indeed, for me, no performance quite captures the theatricality, the passion, and the flamboyance of Bela Lugosi as does Dr. Mirakle.

This is Satan playing Shakespeare, a mad, 19th century-style performance that Edgar Allan Poe would have enjoyed and applauded. Bela, in cloak and high black hat, creeping through the night in Universal's back lot "Paris"... chattering soulfully and riding in a carriage with Erik the Ape... shrieking "Rotten Blood!" at Arlene Francis's trussed-to-a-cross prostitute... in all these baroque episodes, he is unforgettable.

Once again, it's a sterling example of Lugosi's bombast saving a movie.

Murders in the Rue Morgue always has been a controversial film in Universal's canon; perhaps the worst fate that hit it was Brian Taves' book *Robert Florey: The French Expressionist—*

a very well-researched book which insisted that... *Rue Morgue* was superior to James Whale's *Frankenstein*. The brickbats have been flying at *Murders in the Rue Morgue* ever since, smacking everything from the cupie doll heroine of top-billed Sidney Fox, to Florey's bizarre intercutting of Charlie Gemora in an ape suit to chimpanzee closeups.

Yet Bela triumphs over it all. This is Bela Lugosi, flushed with stardom after the hit of *Dracula*, happily freed from playing the Monster in *Frankenstein*, still unaware of the gravity of that disastrous career blunder and still clearly believing in his own sex appeal, dramatic powers, and Hollywood future.

And, as such, it's not only a richly entertaining performance—but a quite touching one.

"HIS CRAZED MIND PLANNED the MOST AMAZING WEDDING THE WORLD HAD EVER KNOWN... She—an innocent girl—fascinated by his evil power... What dire fate awaited? THE ANSWER IS TOLD IN BOLD, VIVID, UNFORGETTABLE DRAMA!"

—Universal Publicity, *Murders in the Rue Morgue*

Paris, 1845... 4 years before Edgar Allan Poe died ignominiously in Baltimore.

Murders in the Rue Morgue opens on Carnival Night in Paris. Ladies and gentlemen ride swings, weird music intermingles, sideshows flourish. My favorite: Lady Fatima and her "Arab Angles," all adorned in harem girl costumes, Lady Fatima herself bumping and grinding with a look of wonderfully ditzy boredom. Two old lechers watch in glee.

"Do they bite?" asks one codger, hopefully.

"Oh yes!" assures the other. "But you have to pay extra for that!"

Indeed, the opening episode of *Murders in the Rue Morgue* is so colorful, the wonders of Carnival Night in Paris so delightfully cartooned, that one instantly sympathizes with Robert Florey (1900-1979), for all the indignities he suffered at the hands of Universal. Feature writer for France's *Cinemagazine*; crony of Douglas Fairbanks, Mary Pickford, Fatty Arbuckle, Valentino, Von Sternberg, et al; director of the acclaimed 1928 experimental short *The Life and Death of 9413—A Hollywood Extra* (which Florey made for a total cost of $99): director of *The Cocoanuts* (1929), starring the Marx Brothers—Florey loved the movies and deserved Hollywood success. That James Whale directed *Frankenstein* as a classic does not excuse the cavalier way in which Whale usurped the film from Florey after the Frenchman had adapted it and directed the Lugosi-as-Monster test reels. Even with *Murders in the Rue Morgue* as his consolation prize, Florey had seen the budget slashed; he even had walked out on the project after economy-minded Universal demanded he make the film in a modern day setting (which would have smashed the "startling" nature of Mirakle's evolution theory).

Now, however,the 6'4", 31-year-old Florey had his 1845 period, and his adaptation scripted by Tom Reed and Dale Van Every (with "additional dialogue" credited to John Huston)—and Bela Lugosi. Florey even had the bonus of cinematography by 350-pound master Karl "Papa" Freund, who had photographed *Dracula*. To be fair, the original budget of $164,220 should be placed in perspective; this was almost $100,000 less than Whale had been given on *Frankenstein*, and over $190,000 less than Tod Browning had been provided for *Dracula*. (It was also about $70,000 more than Edgar Ulmer would be given for 1934's Karloff and Lugosi *The Black Cat*).

On Monday, October 19, 1931, Florey had begun shooting *Murders in the Rue Morgue*; on the Saturday night of the first week, he was shooting the carnival street scene.

Freund's camera picks up our ingenues: Pierre Dupin (Leon Waycoff, later Leon Ames), medical student and amateur detective, and his lady friend, Camille L'Espanaye (Sidney Fox). For many horror fans the 4'11" brunette Miss Fox already had one strike against her as soon as *Murders in the Rue Morgue* began: the opening credits (accompanied by *Swan Lake*, of course) award her top-billing before Lugosi! Poor Miss Fox never overcame the gossip in Hollywood that she was the lover of Universal "baby mogul" Carl Laemmle, Jr., even after she ran away to Europe to act with Feodor Chaliapin and Emil Jannings. In 1932 she left Universal, and the tiny starlet wed Universal's 250-pound New York story editor Charles Beahan, embarking on a series of

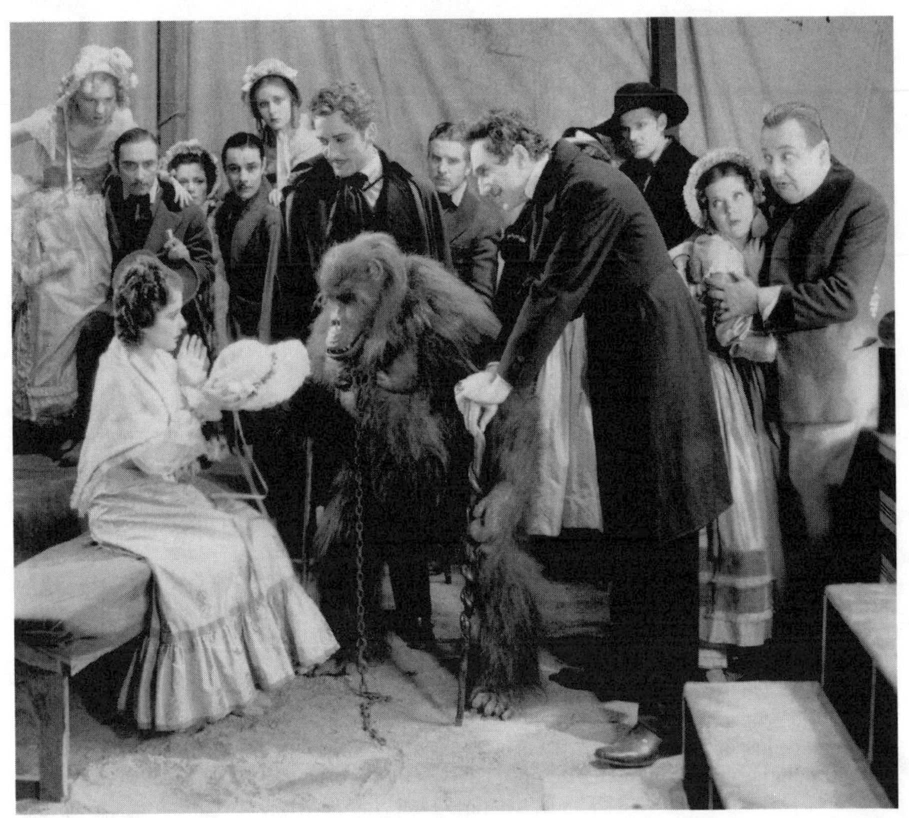

The innocent Camille (Sidney Fox) ventures forth to make the acquaintance of Erik. "Erik is only human, Mademoiselle, " leers Lugosi. "He has an eye for beauty!"

spectacular marital battles which upstaged what was left of her career.

In truth, the real-life Sidney Fox was a feisty New Yorker who once walked away from an accident that sent her somersaulting in her car 40 feet over a Hollywood hill. But you'd never know it in *Murders in the Rue Morgue*; her fluttery, baby-talking performance proves to be one of the movie's top liabilities. Sidney Fox would die in her Beverly Hills home in 1942, following an overdose of pills.

Leon Ames/Waycoff is not much better; he has an advantage, in that we know he matured into Leon Ames and shed the klunky mannerisms that nearly sink him here. Pierre, Camille, Pierre's comic pal Paul (tubby Bert Roach), and Paul's girlfriend Mignette (Edna Marion) all observe the dancing girls; as they depart, Miss Fox sticks her tongue out at Lady Fatima.

They move to a new sideshow—the tent of Dr. Mirakle. A large, 20 foot high cutout of Erik the Ape serves as an entrance to the tent (could that prop still be stashed away somewhere on the Universal lot?), and a barker in top hat and walrus mustache orates:

"...Behind this curtain is the strangest creature your eyes will ever behold: Erik, the ape man, the monster who walks upright and speaks a language—even as you and I. The ruler of the jungle, whose giant hands can tear a man in half. Erik, the ape man, the beast with a human soul! More cunning than a man, and stronger than a lion!"

The crowd moves into the large tent. The four young lovers select a seat, but a tall man, on profile, suggests otherwise:

"No, Mademoiselle, not there. Take a seat in front, where you can see everything!"

"What a funny looking man," marvels Sidney Fox, confidentially to Ames. "He's a show in himself."

Despite the curly hair and that infamous, one-long-eyebrow, Bela is strikingly handsome as Mirakle; he's also almost startlingly skinny—pounds less than the well-fed (but still sleek) Dr. Vollin of *The Raven* three years later. The actor seems to radiate madness—and launches into a soliloquy to the crowd, waving a crooked cane, his giant shadow cast against the evolution chart backdrop:

"I am Dr. Mirakle, Messieurs and Madames, and I am not a sideshow charlatan—so if you expect to witness the usual carnival hocus-pocus, just go to the box office and get your money back! I'm not exhibiting a freak—a monstrosity of nature—but a milestone in the development of life!"

Lugosi motions to his warped assistant, "Janos, the Black One," played by black actor Noble Johnson (in white face!) Johnson pulls the curtain—and there sits Erik, the Ape, played by Charles Gemora, the Filipino actor who would sport the same ape suit in Laurel and Hardy's 2-reeler *The Chimp* (1932) and many Hollywood films. Florey would intercut closeups of a real chimp, filmed on the last day of retakes at the Selig Zoo, with long and medium shots of Gemora—a bizarre and silly effect.

The crowd gasps. And among the gaspers, in the crowd, just behind Leon Ames, is an extra, with a moustache and a broadbrimmed hat, who just might be 25-year-old John Carradine. (Fred Olen Ray, Tom Weaver, and David Carradine himself believe the extra to be Carradine, who never listed *Murders in the Rue Morgue* in his credits).

"Listen to him, Brothers and Sisters!" cries Bela as Erik chatters away. "He is speaking to you! Can you understand what he said—or have you forgotten?" beams Bela, in a wonderful Karl Freund closeup. "I have relearned his language. Listen..."

With a smile both evil and tender, Bela moves to the cage. Freund's camera angle is intriguing: peeking over Erik's shoulder, capturing Bela through the cage bars. The actor speaks "ape talk" to Erik—then, turning one ear to the ape, Bela translates the ape's soliloquy:

"My home is in the African jungle, where I lived with my father and my mother. And my brothers and sisters. But I was captured by a band of hairless white apes, and carried away to a strange land. I am in the prime of my strength! And I'm lonely."

This little scene is wonderfully illustrative of the Lugosi magic—what other actor could so sincerely play a role in which he translates the chatterings of an ape? The affection as he recites Erik's early beginnings... the savage contempt with which Bela says "hairless white apes"... both are striking. But my favorite is Lugosi's tag of this speech. The way Bela almost sings the line, "And I'm lonely," giving Erik a pat, is so over-the-top cornball, yet so soulful, so full of poetry, so incredibly sincere, that it rates as my all-time favorite Lugosi line of dialogue.

"Behold—the first man!" climaxes Bela.

The crowd hisses, Florey intercutting fast closeups of the various extras. "Heresy!" cries one old man—thereby cueing one of Bela's best speeches:

"Heresy? Heresy? Do they still burn men for heresy? Then—burn me, Monsieur! Light the fire! Do you think your little candle will outshine the flame of truth? Do you think these bars and curtains are my whole life? They are only a trap, to catch the pennies of fools.

"My life is concentrated to great experiment. I tell you I will prove your kinship with the ape. Erik's blood shall be mixed—with the blood of man!"

Off goes the crowd. Bela might be discussing "mixing blood," but his leers and ogles leave no doubt what he really wants to do: mate "lonely" Erik with a lady. Despite the innuendo, innocent Camille ventures forth at Mirakle's invitation to "make the acquaintance of Erik." The ape coos in delight.

"Erik is only human, Mademoiselle," leers Lugosi in closeup, his face shining like an evil man-in-the moon. "He has an eye for beauty!"

Camille, realizing that Erik wants her bonnet, hands it to him. The ape (who spends much of the rest of the film in a state of noisy gorilla ardor) destroys the bonnet, and almost destroys Pierre as he grabs him through the bars of the cage. Bela is sorry about the bonnet—"I will send you a new one, with Erik's compliments!" he promises. But Ames' Dupin is not about to divulge Camille's address, and they depart—the ape chattering a farewell. Mirakle dispatches Janos to follow Camille and find her house.

"You liked her—didn't you, Erik?" leers Lugosi.

This carnival opening is perhaps the most enjoyable part of *Murders in the Rue Morgue*—featuring Florey's atmospherics of carnival night, Freund's terrific cinematography and—best of all—Lugosi's showboat diabolics. As many film buffs know, the carnival originally was in the middle of the film, and most believe that Florey's original opening (the street fight and Lugosi's "pick-up" of the prostitute, moved to mid-film) would have served the movie far better. It's debatable. The carnival episode is splashy, colorful, and gives Lugosi his best chance to strut his stuff. One can certainly understand why Universal's front office decided to move this to the beginning of the film to bolster the movie's first impression.

To be honest, however, part of the reason this episode is so strong is because Florey got to do it twice. Florey originally shot the "Int. Mirakle's Tent" scenes on the 3rd and 4th days of production, October 21 and 22. On Tuesday, October 27, Florey spent the entire day on retakes of this scene. One wonders why. (Is it possible Bela had played it even more wildly than he does in the final film—and had to be toned down?)

Murders in the Rue Morgue takes time to try to justify Sidney Fox's top billing. On a balcony, with Caligari-like rooftops in the night, Pierre woos Camille, profile-to-profile, comparing her to the wonders of Mayday. Later, Sidney's Camille, in her new bonnet (indeed sent with Erik's compliments), stands on a balcony, high on the back lot European villages of Universal City, serenaded by her horse-riding friends in operetta fashion, and serenading them in return. There's a picnic episode, where Sidney takes a ride on a swing, modeling her bonnet and giggling coquettishly as Freund manages to have his camera "swing" with her. Bert Roach takes a few stabs at comedy relief, although whatever (intentional) humor is in *Murders in the Rue Morgue* comes via D'Arcy Corrigan's wonderfully grim, nose-blowing morgue keeper. With his funereal expression and manner, and high top hat, Corrigan acts and looks like a character out of Dickens; he also has one of *Murders in the Rue Morgue*'s best lines: "Since that whole body disappeared last week, the Inspector is very strict about medical students!"

But it's Bela's show all the way.

In the original opening, two men fight a duel on the bridge above the Seine; the reason for their fight—a "Woman of the Streets" (Arlene Francis, long before TV's *What's My Line?*), who stands by, watching and screaming. The doxy's two prospective customers kill each other with knives. While many historians praise this episode, it's actually almost lost in the back lot mist and plays like stiff and awkward silent film footage. And it, too, was a scene which Florey did twice, retaking the sequence after Universal put the film into emergency post-shooting work.

Meanwhile, as the men kill each other and, the Woman of the Streets screams, a carriage has arrived, driven by Janos the Black One. Bela, in a black cloak, his high, black, pilgrim-style hat, and twisted cane, emerges, moving wickedly through the fog, shrouded in the mist, his face finally moving into the street lantern light and asking:

"A lady—in distress?"

It's a wonderfully dramatic, spine-tingling entrance, made magic by Lugosi, and superbly staged by Florey and Freund. Indeed, it's one of the assorted very fine moments in R*ue Morgue*.

"My carriage" invites Bela.

"No... Your hand is cold," shivers the prostitute. "It chills me."

"Come!" orders Bela, clutching her, grinning satanically and "doing a Dracula" as he

No performance quite captures the theatricality, the passion, and the flamboyance of Bela Lugosi as does Dr. Mirakle.

ensnares the woman in his cloak. "I will help you."

The Woman of the Streets gets into the carriage—and we hear her laughing hysterically. Little wonder... Apparently along for the ride that night is Erik.

What follows is *Murder in the Rue Morgue*'s most notorious scene, and one that still packs a wallop today. Bela has strapped poor Arlene Francis to a tilted cross, where she stands bound in her full-length-but-torn underwear, and her lace-up 1845 high heels; she cries and screams piteously as Lugosi's Mirakle, in apron and shirtsleeves, prepares for his great experiment. He none-too-gently takes a blood sample.

"...we shall see," he exults, "we shall know, if you are to be the Bride of Science!"

Mirakle certainly seems to be a man of the world; yet he's shocked to see that this girl he picked up on the banks of the Seine, near the bodies of two men fighting for her, is a whore. "Rotten blood!" he screams, smashing laboratory instruments. "Your blood is rotten, black as your sins. You cheated me! Your beauty was a lie!" The Woman of the Streets dies—presumably a victim of torture, fright, and shame. "Dead... you're dead," says Bela, suddenly chagrined. And Lugosi's Mirakle falls to his knees before this prostitute on a cross and clasps his hands as if in prayer—surely forming one of the most bizarre and perverse religious images of the movies.

"Get rid of it," Bela tells Janos. "The Black One" cuts her ropes with an axe, and the body falls through a trapdoor and into the Seine. We later learn she's Mirakle's third victim. "Will my search never end?" sings Bela as the incredibly morbid scene concludes.

Once again, while many historians feel this original opening would have made *Murders in the Rue Morgue* a more effective film, it's also possible that this truly horrible sequence might have been so off-putting to 1932 audiences that they would never have recovered. While the episode is powerful, it's totally without any of the charm that graced *Dracula* and *Frankenstein* (but more on that "charm" aspect later).

Eventually, Bela pays a midnight call to Camille at her room and tries to win admittance; "...I have a message for you, from Erik!," says Bela, through the crack Sidney allows in the door. "He speaks only of you. He can't forget you! There is something you must know!"

"Are you insane, Monsieur?" asks the ingenue, closing the door in his face. Bela's Mirakle, almost in tears, retreats to the streets, where Erik awaits his bride.

"There, Erik! She's up there!"

Erik climbs up the several story house, sneaks into the L'Espanaye apartment—and goes for the girl. Camille's attractive mother (Betsy Ross Clarke) hears her scream and runs to the rescue; in a touch actually concocted by Poe, Erik stuffs the mother feet first up the chimney. Florey's direction is at its strangest here; he intercuts those real monkey closeups, the genuine chimp madly bobbing its head. While the ape is supposed to be shoving Madame L'Espanaye up the chimney (not filmable, as it was sure to be cut by the censors), the existing scene (and the woman's screams) make it appear that Erik is violently raping the Mother.

Erik makes off with Camille... We have another dash of Poe (and "comedy relief") as the German, Italian, and Dane all argue about the murderer's "voice" they heard during the attack... Dupin, who's been investigating, finally persuades the police that Mirakle and Erik are the culprits... and Mirakle prepares for his great experiment between Erik and Camille.

"Her blood is perfect!" rejoices the mad Mirakle. But the police arrive, and Erik—his jumpy hormones in a complete uproar—turns on Mirakle.

"Erik... get back into your cage...!" roars Bela, but it's too late: the ape strangles the doctor, the death captured in shadows on the wall. The police shoot Janos the Black One, and after a few nice shots of the old *Frankenstein* watchtower set (here doubling as Mirakle's quarters), Erik takes off over the rooftops with Camille.

The ape, carrying the leading lady, cavorts about the roofs of Universal's back lot Paris, the crowd oohing-and-ahhing in the streets below. At length, Pierre himself gets up on the rooftops, shoots poor lonely Erik—who rolls off the roof and splashes into the Seine. To the cheers of the crowd, Camille and Pierre embrace.

Back in the morgue, a gendarme irreverently files a report to D'Arcy Corrigan's Morgue Keeper about the dead Mirakle.

"Death caused by?" asks the Morgue Keeper.

"Ha! Ha! Ha! An ape!" laughs the gendarme.

The End. It's a Universal Picture

"...Edgar Allan Poe wouldn't recognize his story. They dropped everything but the gorilla killer and the title, completely changed the characters, motives, and developments and sexed up the whole affair to the limit..." *Variety* review of *Murders in the Rue Morgue,* February, 1932.

Robert Florey had completed *Murders in the Rue Morgue* November 13 (a Friday), 1931, finishing up on the "Ext. Roof Tops" and the arch-under-bridge set. Although Florey went five days over the 18-day schedule, he had closed the film at a cost of $156,782.83—over $7400 under budget.

Trouble lurked ahead. On December 4, James Whale's *Frankenstein* premiered at New York's RKO-Mayfair Theatre; Boris Karloff was an overnight sensation, and the film was making show business history. Meanwhile, Junior Laemmle and Universal's front office were so underwhelmed by Florey's film—so fearful it would kill the sensational horror cycle after *Dracula* and *Frankenstein*—that the economy-minded studio did the almost unthinkable: they blueprinted a "Retakes and Added Scenes" schedule, alloted $21,870 for a budget, and put *Murders in the Rue Morgue* back into production on Thursday, December 10, 1931.

Florey did new work in the interior of Mirakle's lab; he redid the Duel Sequence; he filmed new scenes in Dupin's room and Camille's room. On Saturday night, December 12, Florey began 5 days of reshooting the rooftop climax; on Monday, December 14, the ...*Rue Morgue* company worked from 12:30 p.m. until 3:10 a.m. The last day was December 22—spent by Florey shooting closeups of a monkey at the Selig Zoo, later spliced in with footage of Charlie Gemora in his ape suit. When all was finally said and done, *Murders in the Rue Morgue* still came in at a bargain price, with a final tab of $190,099.45.

At 9:00 p.m. on the evening of Wednesday, February 10, 1932, *Murders in the Rue Morgue* premiered at New York City's RKO-Mayfair Theatre, where *Frankenstein* had opened two months earlier. The *NY Times* reported:

"*Murders in the Rue Morgue*, which was offered at the Mayfair Theatre last night, represents a collaboration between Edgar Allan Poe, Tom Reed, and Dale Van Every. Poe, it would seem, contributed the title and the Messrs Reed and Van Every thought up a story to go with it... The crowning spectacle of the ape clambering over the Paris roofs with the unconscious Camille on its arm brought some irreverent squeals from last night's audience... The entire production suffers from an over-zealous effort at terrorization, and the cast, inspired by the general hysteria, succumbs to the temptation to overact..."

Variety, meanwhile, saluted Bela's "customary fantastic manner," panned Sidney Fox, noted that a high-wheeled bike used in the street scene was anachronistic, and also reported that the "cynical" Broadway crowd "hooted the finale hokum," which must have annoyed Universal, after the studio had spent all those extra dollars to beef up the climax. Neither reviewer mentioned Robert Florey at all. Despite the reviews, business was good, and *Murders in the Rue Morgue*—released in the depth of the Depression—was one of the few Broadway attractions to make money during that bitter February of 1932.

Over the years, *Murders in the Rue Morgue* has always inspired controversy. Why hasn't it won the affection that greets such Universal classics as *Dracula, Frankenstein, The Mummy, The Invisible Man, The Black Cat*, and even *The Raven*?

There are several reasons:

The first is Robert Florey. True, his atmospherics are often wonderful, and all Lugosi fans should be indebted to him for staging that wonderful entrance for Bela through the Paris mist. One is also tempted to salute the director for unleashing a Lugosi so savagely entertaining. Yet, in later interviews, Florey sniped about Bela's tendency to "chew the scenery" (one of the few things that makes the film watchable today!), and even opined that the film would have been better if Lugosi's character had not been in it at all. This supports the contention that Florey was far more interested in painting shadows on walls and achieving a European "look" for his film than he was in the dynamics of the plot and performance.

The cast (aside from Lugosi) is largely without merit. One wonders why Florey allowed (and probably encouraged) such a vapid performance from Sidney Fox; Leon Waycoff could only

"His crazed mind planned the most amazing wedding the world had ever known... She—an innocent girl—fascinated by his evil power... What dire fate awaited? The answer is told in bold, vivid, unforgettable drama!"

play Poe's Dupin as he was written—a lovesick dolt.

The story has little charm. Ironically charm was one of the key ingredients of Universal's horror shows; the beautiful, epic opening of *Dracula*; the Monster's discovery of light in *Frankenstein*, and his flower game by the lake with little Maria; the romanticism of *The Mummy*—all make these stories beloved classics. But *Murders in the Rue Morgue* has no real charm; as Danny Peary writes in his book *Guide for the Film Fanatic*, "The 'best' sequences—i.e., Lugosi draining the blood from the streetwalker... are the most tasteless." There's no sweep of legend as in *Dracula*, no moving Man-Playing-God theme as in *Frankenstein*. True, Poe, in writing the original story, wasn't as ambitious as *Dracula*'s Bram Stoker or *Frankenstein*'s Mary Shelley; his goal was simply to pen a clever, shocking detective saga. Yet Florey and his band of writers should have found a way of investing more depth in *Murders in the Rue Morgue* if he wanted to be in the league of Universal's two horror predecessors.

One additional note: for me (and, I suspect, many members of the film's audience today), *Murders in the Rue Morgue* is decidedly anti-climactic after the death of Lugosi's Mirakle. The true menace is dead, and the Ape's final chase over the Caligari rooftops with Camille lacks excitement without the film's prime mover.

Had I been in the writers quarters at Universal in 1931 (a presumptuous thought!), with Florey, Tom Reed, Dale Van Every, and John Huston, I'd have made this suggestion: Don't have Erik kill Mirakle. Instead, have Mirakle (back in that wonderful cloak and pilgrim hat) lead Erik (who is carrying Camille) to the rooftops as both mad doctor and ape try to kidnap Camille and escape. As the mob watches below, Dupin reaches the roof, and shoots Erik. The ape falls into the Seine—and Bela's Mirakle is so enraged by the loss of his crony that he madly grabs Camille for himself, clutching her insanely, his cloak blowing about behind him. Dupin finally overpowers the villain, and as Camille is saved, Mirakle falls into the Seine, which had swallowed up his prostitute victims—and Erik.

However, considering that Florey thought the film would have been better without Lugosi's Mirakle, I doubt if he would have listened to me.

One can't shed too many tears over *Murders in the Rue Morgue*. Robert Florey's priorities were askew, but his great atmospherics in *Murders in the Rue Morgue* give testimony of his talent; he would direct 50 more films (including 1946's *The Beast with Five Fingers*) and over 250 TV episodes, receive the French Legion of Honor and outlive James Whale by over 20 years. As bad as Sidney Fox and Leon Ames are, they play like Vivien Leigh and Laurence Olivier compared to Madge Bellamy and John Harron in *White Zombie*. And Charlie Gemora, the ever-lonely Erik, would enjoy a long and legendary career in his gorilla suit—and go on to play the ape again in Warner Bros.' 1954 color and 3D remake, *Phantom of the Rue Morgue*.

Best of all, *Murders in the Rue Morgue* bequeaths us an unbridled Bela as Dr. Mirakle. There's a great line in Hamlet, in which Shakespeare's sad prince warns the players at Elsinore against over-acting: "It out-Herods Herod," says Hamlet. In *Murders in the Rue Morgue*, Bela Lugosi, fresh from *Dracula*, many years away from drugs and Ed Wood, truly "out-Herods Herod." Yet he does so gleefully, charmingly, and—in the heroic energy and sincerity of his dramatics—quite movingly. Here, Bela Lugosi triumphs over all—bastardized Poe, a leading lady named Sidney, a misguided director, and an actor in an ape suit—to be, as Sidney Fox expresses it in the movie, "a show in himself."

It remains my favorite Bela Lugosi performance.

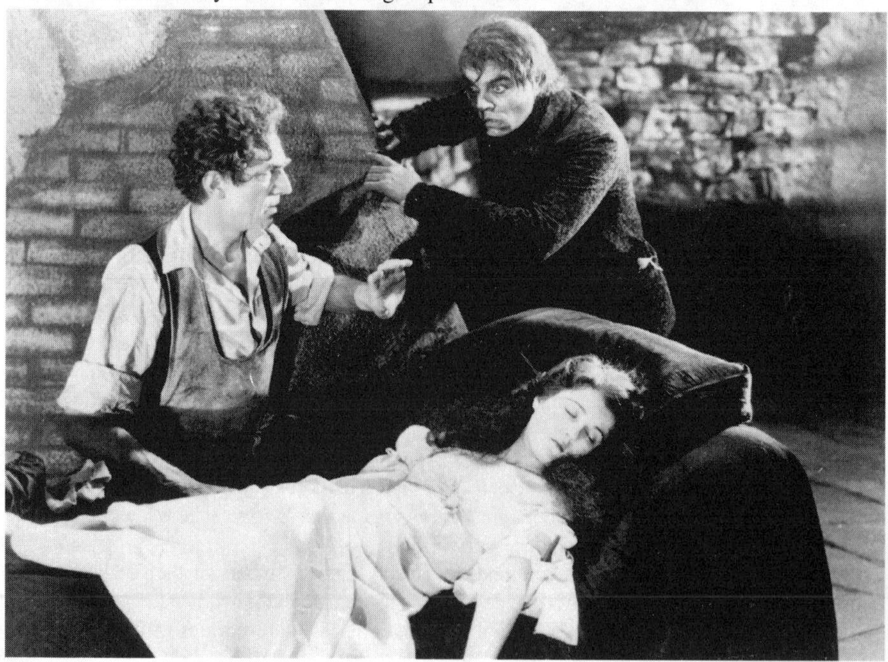

White Zombie

(1932)

by John Stell

CREDITS: Producer: Edward Halperin; Director: Victor Halperin; Screenplay: Garnett Weston; Director of Photography: Arthur Martinelli; Art Direction: Conrad Tritschler and Ralph Berger; Editor: Harold MacLernon; Special Effects: Howard Anderson; Musical Arrangement: Abe Meyer and Guy Bevier Williams; Makeup: Jack Pierce and Carl Axcelle; Assistant Directors: William Cody and Herbert Glazer; Sound Engineer: L.E. Clark; Camera Operator: J. Arthur Feindel; Assistant Camera Operators: Charles Bohny and Enzo Martinelli; Dialogue Director: Herbert Farjeon; Production Assistant: Sidney Marcus; Released July 28, 1932 by United Artists, 68 minutes.

CAST: Bela Lugosi...Murder Legendre, Madge Bellamy...Madeline, Joseph Cawthorn...Dr. Bruner, Robert Frazer...Beaumont, John Harron...Neil, Brandon Hurst...Silver, George Burr MacAnnan...Von Gelder, Frederick Peters...Chauvin, Annette Stone...Maid, John Printz...Latour, Dan Crimmins...Pierre, Claude Morgan...Zombie, John Fergusson...Zombie, Velma Gresham...Maid, Clarence Muse...Driver.

"Here's a burning glamorous love-tale told on the borderland of life and death... the story of a fiend who placed the woman he desired under the strange spell of "White Zombie," rendering her soul-less, lifeless yet permitting her to walk and breathe and do his every bidding!"

From publicity materials

In 1932 horror was at its most creative stages. Universal had released *Dracula* and *Frankenstein* just ten months apart in 1931. Paramount had released the first sound version of *Dr. Jekyll and Mr. Hyde,* a film that would earn actor Fredric March an Academy Award. First National experimented with the two-color Technicolor process in *Doctor X.* And MGM released the Boris Karloff vehicle, *The Mask of Fu Manchu.*

But *White Zombie* is something of a "bastard son" of horror's first golden age. That is, while the film is of historical importance in that it plays a key role in defining the "horror genre" as we know it today, the quality of *White Zombie* has been ferociously debated amongst the most diehard of horror fans. Certainly it can stake a claim as the first "zombie" film, but whether the film's actually any good is another issue altogether. Yes, *White Zombie* may be a bit crude if compared to the more polished films that dominated the 1930s, but the film weaves a fairy tale-like spell due to its simple good versus evil story line, boasts wonderful use of cinematography and sound, and, most importantly, features a haunting, malevolent performance by Bela Lugosi.

White Zombie opens with the arrival of Madeline (Madge Bellamy) and Neil (John Harron) who have come to Haiti to be married. Their excitement is replaced with uneasiness as they happen upon a funeral taking place in the middle of the road. Their carriage driver (Clarence Muse) informs them that such an event is a typical practice, since a body buried beneath a well travelled road is not as likely to be stolen.

Further down the road the driver stops to ask a stranger, Murder Legendre (Bela Lugosi), directions to the home of a Mr. Beaumont. Without answering the driver, Murder looks inside the carriage and places his hand on an exposed part of Madeline's scarf, which is draped over the coach's door. When a group of poorly clad villagers begin to move toward the carriage, the driver yells, "Zombie!," and hurries the coach away, leaving Murder holding the scarf of the lovely but terrified passenger.

Upon finally reaching the home of Mr. Beaumont (Robert Frazer), Neil scolds the driver and asks why he hurried away so quickly from those "men." "They are not men," is the reply, "they are zombies, the living dead, corpses taken from their graves who are made to work at the sugar mills and fields at night."

As the driver leaves, the young lovers are greeted by Dr. Bruner (Joseph Cawthorn) who asks Neil if he has a match. Bruner tells the momentarily spooked couple that he has been summoned to perform the wedding ceremony. The trio enter the impressive looking mansion and, while waiting for their host, Madeline informs Bruner that she met the "very kind" Mr. Beaumont on her trip from New York. After knowing Beaumont for only a few days, the couple have agreed to be married at the home of their new friend! "Very strange," is Bruner's reply.

The butler Silver (Brandon Hurst) advises his master that the couple has arrived. Beaumont asks if "the other person" has arrived. (Silver expresses his displeasure over Beaumont spending time with "that man.") But this other guest has not, so Beaumont greets his friends and, after the usual small talk ("You must be tired after your drive"), instructs Silver to show the visitors to their rooms. Beaumont then sneaks away to the sugar mill for an unholy rendezvous with Murder Legendre, a plantation owner whose sole (pun intended) source of labor is a horde of zombies.

It is at the mill where Beaumont's diabolical plan is explained. Madly in love with Madeline himself, Beaumont thinks he can win her love and wishes Murder, who has mastered the voodoo arts, to make the bride-to-be disappear for a month. "A month is all I need," the sadistic suitor reasons. But Murder has his own idea: by faking Madeline's death via a small amount of zombie poison, Beaumont can have all the time he needs. Reluctantly Beaumont takes the powder, swearing to use it only as a last resort.

Beaumont returns to his home and, during the wedding, makes one last plea for Madeline to give him a chance. When she refuses, he gives her a flower laced with a poisonous scent. Madeline politely sniffs the offensive offering, unaware she has just sealed her fate.

At the wedding night dinner, Beaumont proposes a toast to the happy newlyweds, while right outside the estate, Murder arrives and places a voodoo doll of Madeline, made of candle wax and wrapped in the stolen scarf, into a candle flame. Looking into her wine glass, the bride sees the face of Legendre and collapses. She is believed dead, and a funeral is held that very same night. (Apparently such an immediate burial would really take place due to the humid conditions in the West Indies.)

While the bridegroom/widower drinks himself into oblivion, the conspirators remove the "corpse" from her resting place. Paying a drunken visit to his late wife's crypt, Neil discovers the body missing and turns for help to Doc Bruner, who theorizes that either the body was stolen by a death cult for use in an evil ceremony, or that Madeline is still alive.

Meanwhile at Legendre's castle, Beaumont, regretting what he has done, begs Murder to return the soul to Madeline's body. Pretending to acquiesce to Beaumont's wishes, Legendre poisons him with a glass of wine under the pretext of proposing a toast to the "future." Too late, Beaumont realizes the zombie master has plans of his own for the soulless beauty (it is never explicitly revealed what Lugosi plans to do with Bellamy, but considering she's the only female around other than the maids, his intentions are fairly obvious). The poisoned Beaumont, now under Murder's control, is reduced to an incoherent idiot. Attempting to help his master, Silver (who apparently accompanied Beaumont to the castle) is attacked and killed by the horde of the undead.

Consulting a native witch doctor, Dr. Bruner has learned of Murder's zombie practices. He and Neil travel to Murder's castle but become separated. Neil stumbles into the castle, but passes out(!) before he can be a hero. Discovering the uninvited guest, Murder "wills" Madeline to stab her husband. But at the last minute, an arm reaches out from behind a column and shakes the knife from her hand. Momentarily free of Legendre's influence, Madeline flees the castle.

As the personification of pure evil Bela Lugosi is without peer. Never hiding behind a pretense of "meaning well," Lugosi is able to invest his character with a plethora of ghoulish touches.

At the same time Neil, awaking from his nap, catches sight of Madeline and follows her, grabbing her just as she is about to throw herself into the ocean below. Murder summons his "angels of death" to dispatch Neil, who fires a couple shots at the zombies, but to no avail. Suddenly the same arm that saved Neil from the knife gives Murder a crack on the noggin. Dr. Bruner emerges and tells Neil to get out of the way as the zombies then march one by one off the cliff into

***White Zombie* marks Bela's first appearance in a low budget horror film. Despite its low budget, however, the film stands favorably alongside many of the early horror classics.**

the same ocean that almost claimed Madeline.

Rushing over to Madeline, Neil and the heroic doctor attempt to break her out of Murder's spell. Legendre takes this opportunity to escape up the stairs but is attacked by Beaumont, who hurls Murder off the cliff to join his zombies. Beaumont then jumps himself. The reunited couple are about to share their first kiss in a long time when Dr. Bruner, pipe in hand, politely interrupts and asks if Neil has a match.

After completing *Murders in the Rue Morgue* in November 1931 (with some re-shooting in December), Bela Lugosi had completed his contract with Universal studios. In February, 1932 Lugosi signed on the dotted line to star in *White Zombie.* Filming was done in March on the leased back lots of Universal. The film was shot at night over a period of eleven days (of which Bela worked three days) and utilized sets from both *Dracula* and *Frankenstein.* Lugosi received somewhere around $800 for a film that was budgeted around $50,000, and whose financial success (it made about $8 million) was attributable to Lugosi's star power (he was still a big name in 1932.) Thus *White Zombie* marks Bela's first appearance in a low budget horror film. Despite its low budget, however, the film stands favorably alongside many of the early horror classics

But unlike its peers such as 1931's *Dracula, Frankenstein,* or *Dr. Jekyll and Mr. Hyde, White Zombie* has no classic literary source. The film is based upon an original story by Garnett Weston, which was, in turn, inspired by a travelogue written by William Seabrook in 1929 called *The Magic Island.* This work first utilized the term "zombie" and described the habits of "the living dead." (*The Magic Island* also inspired a 1932 play called *Zombie* which closed after twenty-one days.) Thus *White Zombie* is one of the first "original" horror tales, which must have added to an audience's excitement when seeing the film for the first time.

As a result of the film's modern sources, *White Zombie* is one of the few early horrors set in contemporary times. Instead of taking place in a gothic locale or a foggy, 18th-century London setting, the film is set in the present. (This is evidenced by the early discussion of the importance of being a New York banker.) Even though the story takes place in a far away land, the implication that zombies were "just a boat ride away" probably had viewers wondering what would happen if zombies ever made travel plans.

Thus with its recent discovery, the zombie must have seemed like the perfect monster to join Universal's Dracula and Frankenstein's Monster on the horror hit parade. The job of creating the makeup for the as yet unseen-by-Americans zombie was given to Jack P. Pierce, who was, of course, responsible for the Universal monsters. Pierce gave Lugosi a Satan-like face, with adjoined eyebrows, split moustache, and goatee. All Lugosi needed was a pitchfork. The zombies themselves are frightening creations, looking disheveled and staring unblinkingly into space.

The film's director, Victor Halperin, was born in August 1895 in Chicago, and attended the University of Wisconsin and the University of Chicago. He worked as a stage actor and directed several silent films before venturing into horror terror-tory with *White Zombie.* The producer, brother Edward, attended Northwestern University, and with Victor, would make several horror films including *Supernatural* (1933) with Carole Lombard, and *Revolt of the Zombies* (1936), a sort of follow-up to *White Zombie.* (But more on those later.)

With respect to the film itself, *White Zombie* is structured as pure fairy tale. (In fact Dr. Bruner cynically refers to Beaumont as playing an unlikely "fairy godfather" in an early scene.) All the characters (except Lugosi's) are given just a first or last name keeping their identities simple. Madge Bellamy is the "damsel in distress" (and the "white zombie" of the title), desired by the three male leads: Lugosi, Frazer, and Harron. Lugosi is the quintessential villain, dressed in a dinner suit, seldom without a smile on his satanic puss, and as polite as all get out. Frazer is Lugosi's uncertain henchman whose ultimate change of heart can be seen coming almost immediately. Rounding out the story are the doctor-cum-detective Joseph Cawthorn, the slippery butler, a couple of gossipy maids, and the zombies themselves, who are nothing more than Bela's well trained pets with no will of their own (quite unlike the zombies in George Romero's *Night of the Living Dead* (1968) where the zombies are clearly aggressive, albeit slow moving, eating machines.) Add to this a poisoned flower, instead of an apple, and you have *Bela Lugosi and the Nine Zombies.*

As the personification of pure evil Bela Lugosi is without peer. Never hiding behind a pretense of "meaning well," Lugosi is able to invest his character with a plethora of ghoulish touches. His first scene (aside from his eyes being superimposed over Bellamy and Harron's arrival) has him approach the carriage and lustfully study, while saying nothing to, the new female arrival. Later at his castle he delights in toying with Frazer as Frazer decides what to do to win Madeline's love. Bela's "there, there now" movement of his hands as he is about to turn over the zombie poison indicates his contempt for Frazer as well as his feeling of superiority. These feelings are reinforced when, later, a poisoned Frazer attempts to get the attention of Bela, who continues to nonchalantly whittle a voodoo doll out of candle wax. "We understand each other better now," Bela tells him.

But Frazer's Beaumont is not the first character with whom Murder has had problems. The fact is most of his key zombie henchman are those who were enemies of Murder's in their former life. When the "servants" are introduced, we learn that the zombies include Murder's former teacher, a witch doctor whose secrets were "tortured out of him," and Chauvin, an executioner who once tried to execute Legendre. Lugosi's character is clearly one who enjoys having the last laugh.

Furthermore Lugosi's line readings are some of his best, and some of the best heard in horror films. Of course there is Bela's famous response when Harron asks about the zombies, "For you, my friend, they are the angels of death." But there is also the delight Bela takes in explaining how to administer the zombie poison, "Only a pinpoint, Monsieur, in a glass of wine, or, perhaps, a flower." And then there's Lugosi's "toast to the future" in which he is clearly talking about his and Madeline's future while leading Beaumont to believe otherwise. Lugosi makes the most of what little dialogue he is given.

Many of Lugosi's scenes, however, seem to consist of him staring into the camera, eyes wide, his face in a hideous grin. Whether he is practicing a satanic rite, such as burning a Madeline voodoo doll, or "willing" Madeline to kill her husband, Murder is a guy who obviously delights in his work.

As for most of the other cast members, however, their roles are not nearly as interesting. In reality one of the criticisms by *White Zombie*'s detractors is in its one dimensional, one note characters, some of whom are not even particularly likable.

For starters there is the lovely Madge Bellamy as the beautiful Madeline. Bellamy was born Margaret Phillpot in June 1900. She started acting at age 15 and became a silent screen star appearing in such films as *Soul of the Beast* (1923) and *The White Sin* (1924). She had been in retirement for two years when she agreed to appear in *White Zombie,* hoping to stage a comeback. The big comeback never happened, although she did continue to work in films, such as *Northwest Trail* (1945).

In fact Bellamy's off-screen life is more interesting than her zombified character. In 1943 she shot her boyfriend when she discovered he married another woman, and received a six-month suspended sentence for her crime. She died in 1990 after completing her autobiography *Darling of the Twenties.*

But as the darling of *White Zombie* Bellamy isn't given much to do. Her character's sole purpose in the film is to look beautiful and virginal, and little else. All we know about Madeline is that she's from New York. And any woman who would agree to postpone her own wedding at the request of someone she has known only three days cannot be playing with a full deck to begin with.

As Madeline's hubby Neil, John Harron fares little better. Born March 31, 1903, "Johnnie" Harron, like Bellamy, had been active in silent films, having appeared in *West-Bound Limited* (1923) and *The Night Cry* (1926). He was the younger brother of Robert Harron, also a silent screen star, who frequently worked with the great D. W. Griffith and appeared in Griffith's *The Avenging Conscience* (1914), an early horror masterpiece based upon Edgar Allan Poe's *The Tell-Tale Heart.* Robert's career ended tragically when he was accidently shot in 1920, which makes for an eerie connection between the two "lovers" considering what happened in Bellamy's future. Brother John died in 1939.

Harron's performance in *White Zombie* makes it tough to care about Neil. Not unlike

David Manners' irritating "romantic leading man" role as the bossy and whiny Jonathan Harker in 1931's *Dracula,* Neil comes across as a guy only a zombie could love. The first thing Neil does in the film is to holler at the carriage driver for hurrying away from Legendre. (Neil must not have noticed Murder leering at his fiance and promptly stealing her scarf.) When Mr. Beaumont hugs and greets Madeline, Neil folds his arms and goes into a jealousy routine. (Of course Neil is perfectly correct in his feelings, but at this point in time he has no knowledge of Beaumont's intentions. Besides, Neil *did* agree to be wed at Beaumont's estate.)

After Madeline "dies," he gets even worse, becoming a drunken, whiny wimp. What few lucid moments he does have he spends yelling at the only person (Dr. Bruner) who is trying to help. When he does arrive at the castle he faints. When he gets the girl at the end, we hardly care.

But Neil's competition may be the oddest one of them all. Beaumont falls in love with Madeline after only three days, yet somehow comes up with the idea he needs a month to "convert" her. What he expected Murder to do to help him in his plan is never really clear. (Murder wasn't sure either.) Granted Beaumont turns to the zombie poison only as a last resort. But he has seen what the poison can do (the "taxi" Beaumont takes to Legendre's castle was driven by a zombie), so we are left wondering how Beaumont expected to woo Madeline were she in such a state. Beaumont's conversion at the film's climax is less a heroic act than that of a guy who has just said, "to hell with it all."

Before playing Mr. Beaumont, Robert Frazer had a lengthy film career that included 1912's *Robin Hood* and a 1929 courtroom drama called *The Drake Case.* Born in June 1891, Frazer continued to work in B-pictures and serials such as *Monte Carlo Nights* (1934) and *Dick Tracy Vs. Crime Inc.* (1941) until his death in 1944. Frazer's over the top line deliveries such as, "No...no...not...that!" inspire giggles rather than fright, and his Beaumont character comes across as one big loser.

Thus the only interesting main character besides Lugosi's Murder is Joseph Cawthorn's Dr. Bruner. (Cawthorn's other credits include *The Taming of the Shrew* (1929) and 1935's *Sweet Adeline.*) The good doctor is not so subtly identified as the film's true hero in that he smokes a Sherlock Holmesian pipe in his first scene.

But in reality the character serves many functions. He's both the disbeliever and believer: he claims not to believe in zombies, yet admits he's seen strange things in his thirty years in the West Indies. Later of course he does the research that sheds light on what has happened to Madeline, and traces her to Legendre's castle.

He also serves as the film's "prophet" in that he warns the young couple to stay away from Beaumont. And he is the story's true hero since he saves both newlyweds from certain death. Lastly he provides the film's only (intentional) laughs when he asks for a match at some of the most inopportune moments: when he and Neil are in the midst of their investigation of voodoo practices, and right after Murder has fallen to his death. However Bruner is not merely the "comedy relief," since he emerges as the most intelligent and heroic of the cast.

A curious oversight in the opening credits is the omission of Clarence Muse. Perhaps the most impressive of *White Zombie*'s cast, Muse was born in Baltimore in 1889 and went on to earn a law degree from Dickerson University. He was active in radio and vaudeville, as well as film, and helped found the Lafayette Players of Harlem. In 1973, he was inducted into the Black Filmmakers Hall of Fame.

Muse contributes the most memorable supporting performance: the carriage driver. He informs the couple of the Haitian burial practices, as well as providing the audience with the definition of "zombie." Muse rises above the typical horror roles given to black performers of the time, and delivers his lines in a low-key, straight-forward, and thus chilling, manner. His character comes across as intelligent, not a stupid "scaredy-cat." In addition to his performance, Muse also composed several of *White Zombie*'s spiritual dirges.

Muse had a lengthy film career spanning from 1929 until his death in 1979, with films like *Way Down South* (1939) and *The Black Stallion* (1979). He even appears in another Lugosi

"American movie fans will... learn... of the occult practices in Haiti in which... dead bodies are dug from their graves and put to work as slaves."

film, 1941's *The Invisible Ghost,* where he plays Bela's faithful servant, again rising above the typical servant shenanigans. Muse contributes an important role to *White Zombie,* and performs it well.

But with such a mixed bag of performances, it is quite possible that director Victor Halperin was not attempting a character driven horror film (outside of Lugosi's personification of evil, of course). Instead *White Zombie* could very easily have been a silent film. Dialogue, which is very limited to begin with, is usually delivered in short, not very colorful sentences, except of course for Lugosi's. Most of the performances (Bellamy, Frazer, Harron) are the sort of exaggerated histrionics found in silent movies. (The entire cast had their beginnings in silent films.) The lack of any attempt of character development outside of what we "need to know" is further evidence that Halperin wanted us to "witness" a series of chilling events rather than to be told a conventional horror tale.

Furthermore, Halperin frequently requires Lugosi to use his hands, instead of words, to convey his feelings, such as when he pats Beaumont on the arm as Beaumont pleads for some attention. Bela folds and twists his hands whenever he is up to no good. Those involved with the film seem intent on creating a mood, rather than memorable banter.

Halperin worked very closely with his cinematographer, Arthur Martinelli, to create a fluid, haunting film filled with disturbing images. The burial in the road at the beginning of the film disrupts the couple's happiness. The parade of emotionless zombies scares the carriage driver. The superimposed eyes of Bela Lugosi reveal his character sees all. Madeline is dressed in a beautiful wedding gown which quickly becomes her burial shroud. When Beaumont boards the carriage that will take him to Murder's castle, the camera slowly pans to reveal the zombie driver, then slowly pans back to reveal the occupant's horrified expression.

But one of the film's most unsettling moments comes when Harron is shown at a tavern, drowning his sorrows in the grape after Madeline's death. There are no other patrons actually seen, only their shadows on a back curtain. When Harron starts hallucinating, he grabs at superimposed images of Madeline, only to be grasping at nothingness, and gives the impression of dancing amongst the shadows of the patrons, their unintelligible chatter serving as a haunting background chorus.

Several scenes evidence Halperin's presence as director. For instance, consider the scene where Neil has travelled to Dr. Bruner's home after discovering the theft of Madeline's body. The scene begins with the camera focused on Neil's jacketed back, giving the impression of a fade-in. But then the camera moves to the right and stops, giving a view of Dr. Bruner (who is sitting at his desk) through the gap between Neil's (who is standing) side and his outstretched hand, which is resting on Bruner's desk. During the scene the two characters move about the room discussing the fate of Madeline. As the scene is about to end, Bruner sits back down at his desk, and Neil, still standing, once again rests his hand on the desk. The camera then moves to give the same point of view of Bruner as that which opened the scene. The camera then pans left to Neil's back, and the scene ends having come full circle.

Other interesting moments include Madeline coming down a staircase, which is shot through a flower shaped opening on the stairway bannister (she is referred to as "flower" by Murder); the zombies turning a large wheel and knocking one of their counterparts over the side, only to continue with their work unfazed (the absence of music when this happens gives the scene some extra zing); a split screen showing Madeline, who is in a castle bedroom, "summoning" her husband, who is below on the rocky cliffs; and the audience being warned of Murder's demise by showing Beaumont's shadow closing in on Murder just before he is thrown to his death.

Also key to *White Zombie*'s success are the striking sets utilized throughout the film. Beaumont's mansion is large, ornate, and well lighted enough to suggest an absence of danger. Murder's castle, on the other hand, is dark and foreboding, stands on the edge of a perilous cliff, and comes complete with large staircases, a piano, and a curious lack of furniture. The large wheel at the sugar mill, continuously turned by the zombies, is also a memorable creation. The film also includes a well utilized cemetery, and an easily accessible crypt.

Rounding out *White Zombie*'s impressive technical feats is the film's use of sound and music. A vulture gives out a horrible screech when someone is about to die. The sugar mill's wheel creaks and groans as Beaumont is led to Legendre, while the zombies turning the wheel themselves remain silent. The film opens to the sounds of voodoo drums which are used to keep away the dead. These same sounds are heard shortly before the wedding. The music which cues Lugosi's "appearance" in Bellamy's wine glass is turned up just a bit which causes a nice "jump" reaction. Later Madeline plays *Liebstraum* on Legendre's piano as Beaumont pleads with her to smile. The film makers show an uncanny knowledge of when, and when not, to use music and sound effects.

Thus with its underdeveloped characters, impressive technical tricks, and stylish touches *White Zombie* premiered at the Rivoli theater in New York City on July 28, 1932. The film was a hit with audiences, but a miss with most critics (although, truth be told, few horror films were hits with critics when first released.) The papers panned the film calling it "heavily acted" (*New York Daily News*), "clumsily wrought" (*New York Herald Tribune*), and "forgettable" (*New York Times*) On the plus side, *Variety* opined the "fine work of Lugosi is backed by a good cast and bizarre staging." In any event, the film was a financial success, and the Halperins landed a contract with Paramount, while Lugosi went on to make *Island of Lost Souls* for Paramount that very same year.

The publicity for *White Zombie* focused on both its mysterious lead performer, Lugosi, and the fact that the film was based on truth. A quote from Lugosi contained in *White Zombie*'s press book did much to give Bela an air of mystery:

"People—thousands of them—chained by monotony, afraid to think, slinging always to certainties and terrified by the unknown. They live like ants. I want to get away from people. I must get away somewhere where I can be free. And I can do it soon, too. Not many more years and I will have enough of this world's goods to pursue my own course and to pay for whatever research I desire to make. I'm going into the mountains, completely away from people, to study."

As far as any one could tell, however, Lugosi never made it to those mountains. But whatever his feelings really were for his fellow man, *White Zombie* was well received by horror fans. Perhaps Lugosi's bizarre off-camera persona contributed to his on-screen appeal.

Another selling point of the film seemed to be its promise (contained in the pressbook) that, "American movie fans will... learn... of the occult practices in Haiti in which... dead bodies are dug from their graves and put to work as slaves." The press book further alleged that the film was based on, "personal observation in Haiti by American writers and research workers, and... its entire substance is based upon fact." As icing on the cake it was reported that, because of her experience on *White Zombie,* Madge Bellamy was a "convert to cremation."

There is, in fact, probably more truth in *White Zombie* than other horror classics of the same period since zombies, as opposed to vampires and man-made monsters, actually did (and still do?) exist. The voodoo religion was brought over from Africa during the slave trade, and with it, the zombie. Although the real center of the voodoo religion is the worship of the snake god Dambala, other elements do include "devil dolls" and zombies.

While the devil doll was constructed as a means to take revenge on any enemy, the zombie was created by witch doctors to work as slave labor. Like in the film, the zombie candidate is poisoned, and is believed dead. After the burial the body is removed and given another poison which yields a practically brain dead, and thus easily controlled, individual who is put to work by the plantation owner who hired the voodoo priest. Although *White Zombie* combines the concepts of devil dolls and zombies for its own purposes, the film does have some validity in its explanation of West Indian superstition.

But whatever the real story is behind the role of a zombie, the fact is that *White Zombie* is one of the few zombie films made that is considered any good at all. With the exception of Val Lewton's *I Walked With A Zombie* (1943), no other zombie film made prior to 1966 is worth talking about: *Revolt of the Zombies,* made by the Halperins in 1936; *King of the Zombies* (1941); *Revenge of the Zombies* (1943); *Zombies on Broadway* (1945), which also featured Lugosi; *Valley of the Zombies* (1946), which featured no zombies and no valley; *Zombies of Mora Tau* (1957); *Invasion of the Zombies* and *Teenage Zombies* (Both 1960); and *The Incredibly Strange Creatures Who Stopped Living and Became Mixed-Up Zombies;* and *I Eat Your Skin* (Both 1964) .

In 1966 Hammer studios made the intelligent *Plague of the Zombies* which again showed zombies utilized as slave labor. The film's characters were better developed than *White Zombie*'s and thus more sympathetic. The film also features a terrific scene where a zombie rises from the grave. But the film isn't up to *White Zombie*'s aesthetic values and does not feature a lead villain as vicious or engaging as Murder Legendre.

Then, in 1968, George Romero redefined the notion of zombies with *Night of the Living Dead,* a film whose dead are revived via space waves, or some such method. This film linked zombies to flesh eating beasts and created a whole new version of a zombie that is a far cry from the creature found in *White Zombie.* When most people think of zombies today, they think of Romero's cult classic.

While the producing/directing team of the Halperins created one of the most important and long-lasting staples of the horror genre's gamut of no-goods, they also zombified their own film career. Reportedly they made over two dozen films by the 1940's (including *Torture Ship* in 1939 and *Girl's Town* in 1942), but only *White Zombie* is ever paid any attention. (In fact Victor Halperin died in such obscurity that the date of his death is uncertain.) Two of their other films, however, do bear some discussion here.

As a result of the financial success of *White Zombie*, the Halperins were offered a contract with Paramount to make *Supernatural* in 1933. The film features *White Zombie*'s cinematographer Arthur Martinelli, who no doubt contributed to the film's knockout opening montage sequence which relates that a psychopath (Vivienne Osborne) is about to be put to death for the murders of several men.

Meanwhile the man who turned her in, a phony spiritualist played by Alan Dinehart, is attempting to bamboozle a wealthy socialite (Carole Lombard) who has just lost her brother. By an amazing coincidence Lombard's doctor friend (H. B. Warner) is performing experiments on the recently electrocuted murderess. Her spirit is transferred to Carole, who then plays up to the fake psychic with the ultimate goal being murder. All works out fine in the end as Carole is saved by her boyfriend (Randolph Scott) and Dinehart pays for his betrayal.

Aside from the film's opening moments, *Supernatural* is missing most of the cleverness and creativity the Halperins brought to *White Zombie* just a year earlier. Perhaps it was due to the contemporary, big-city setting of *Supernatural* that limited their imaginations. Or perhaps they did not care for the Harvey Thew and Brian Marlowe script, which is hopelessly contrived even for a horror film. Aside from a few superimposed images of Osborne, it almost impossible to tell that *White Zombie* and *Supernatural* were made by the same people.

Even worse than *Supernatural* is *Revolt of the Zombies,* a pseudo sequel to *White Zombie.* In reality this 1936 travesty is a remake of the earlier film and combines the Bela Lugosi and Robert Frazer characters into one, namely Dean Jagger's. Jagger loves Dorothy Stone, but Dot loves Robert Noland. So Dean uses the zombie formula to control Stone, but then has a change of heart and is killed. (Sound familiar?) To add insult to injury, the film even contains the Lugosi "eye shots," which are supposed to be Jagger's peepers, from *White Zombie. Revolt of the Zombies* is certainly revolting, not to mention unimaginative and incredibly boring, and makes one wish for more than just Lugosi's eyes to appear in the film.

The Halperins certainly did have something going for them when they made *White Zombie,* namely Bela Lugosi. Whatever talents the Halperins did possess seemed to have been exhausted in this, their first horror film. For Lugosi this film served as a worthy addition to his gallery of grotesques. Despite his dissatisfaction with his salary, Lugosi gave his all in this film and considered Murder Legendre to be one of his best roles. Thanks to Lugosi, Legendre emerges as one of horror's most memorably evil and sadistic villains.

Despite what the initial reviews may have been, time has been kind to *White Zombie.* Most modern reference books have nice words for the film. *Halliwell's Film Guide* calls it a "genuinely eerie horror film" with "an interesting sense of composition." William K. Everson included it in his historic *Classics of the Horror Film* stating it is "one of the most satisfying films of its period." Phil Hardy's *The Encyclopedia of Horror Movies* considers it "impressive" and says the film's images "weave a potent spell." Leonard Maltin's *Movie and Video Guide* rates it three (out of four) stars, as does James O'Neill's *Terror on Tape,* which calls *White Zombie* "the best independently made horror film of the 1930's."

With its classic fairy tale roots, poetic visual style, and commanding central performance by Bela Lugosi, *White Zombie*'s status as a horror classic is secure. Although the film is certainly important as the first zombie movie made, it is also worthy of the "classic" status frequently ascribed to it. The filmmakers wisely let Bela take center stage, and Lugosi's screen charisma is at its peak in *White Zombie.* Next to his classic portrayal of Ygor in *Son of Frankenstein,* Murder Legendre is perhaps Bela's most fondly remembered performance.

A distraught and wounded Bela Lugosi, from the climax of *The Black Cat*, prepares to blow up the vile home of of Hjalmar Poelzig. In his first pairing with Boris Karloff, Lugosi portrays Vitus Werdegast, a man who has lost both his wife and daughter to the evil character played by Karloff.

THE BLACK CAT

(1934)

by Don G. Smith

CREDITS: Director: Edgar G Ulmer; Production Supervisor: E. M. Asher; Screenplay: Peter Ruric (based on a story by Edgar G. Ulmer and Peter Ruric, suggested by *The Black Cat* by Edgar Allan Poe); Continuity: Tom Kilpatrick; Assistant Directors: W. J. Reiter, Sam Weisenthal; Director of Photography: John J. Mescall; Film Editor: Ray Curtiss; Camera Operator: King Gray; Special Photographic Effects: John P. Fulton; Musical Director: Heinz Roemheld; Art Director: Charles D. Hall; Makeup: Jack P. Pierce; Released May 7, 1934 by Universal Pictures, Running time: 65 minutes

CAST: Boris Karloff...Hjalmar Poelzig, Bela Lugosi...Dr. Vitus Werdegast, David Manners...Peter Alison, Jacqueline Wells [aka Julie Bishop]...Joan Alison, Lucille Lund...Karen Werdegast Poelzig, Egon Brecher...the Majordomo, Harry Cording...Thamal, Albert Conti...the Lieutenant, and John Peter Richmond [aka John Carradine]

Story:

Newlyweds Peter and Joan Alison are traveling by train on their honeymoon to a European resort. As a result of a seating mistake, a pleasant yet somber stranger enters their car, excuses himself, and prepares to leave. The couple, however, insists that he stay since there is not far to go. The stranger, who introduces himself as Dr. Vitus Werdegast, says that he is going to visit an old friend. Later, when Peter awakens to find Werdegast lovingly stroking Joan's hair, the doctor explains that Joan resembles the wife he left behind years ago to go to war, and that he spent years in a prison camp as part of that experience.

Since they are all going near the same destination, they board a bus together and set out into the stormy night. Amidst thunder and lightning the bus driver provides "tourist" information:

"All of this country was one of the greatest battlefields of the war. Tens of thousands of men died here. The ravine down there was piled twelve deep with dead and wounded men. The little river below was swollen—red—a raging torrent of blood. That high hill, yonder, where engineer Poelzig now lives, was the site of Fort Marmaros. He built his home on its very foundation. Marmaros! The greatest graveyard in the world!"

Due to weather conditions, the bus crashes, killing the driver and leaving Joan injured and unconscious. Peter and Werdegast, aided by Thamal, Poelzig's servant, carry the girl to Poelzig's nearby house.

Upon entering, Werdegast sends someone for Poelzig and attends to Joan's injuries. When Poelzig rises from his bed and goes downstairs, it is obvious that he and Werdegast share a mutual animosity.

When Werdegast and Poelzig are alone, the psychiatrist accuses Poelzig of war crimes. Werdegast recounts the tortures he endured as a prisoner and tells Poelzig that he has returned for his wife Karen. Poelzig attempts to evade the subject as Werdegast becomes increasingly hostile.

When Peter walks innocently into the room, Poelzig suggests that they all have a drink. As Werdegast proposes a toast, a black cat runs into the room. Seeing the cat, the psychiatrist succumbs to a fit of anger and hysteria, and hurls a knife into the animal. Joan enters in a trance-like state, and Poelzig explains Werdegast's problem: "You must be indulgent of Dr. Werdegast's weakness. He is the unfortunate victim of one of the commoner phobias, but in the extreme form. He has an intense and all-consuming horror—of cats." A worried Peter persuades Joan to return to her room. Werdegast composes himself and explains that he does indeed fear cats. Furthermore, he says that, according to superstition, the black cat is a symbol of evil, and at death the evil enters into the nearest living thing. With a smile, Poelzig adds that the black cat never dies. Then the High Priest of Satanism shows his "guests" to their bedrooms.

Later, in the dead of night, Poelzig strokes a black cat while prowling the Marmaros cellars. There he has preserved his many female sacrifices to Satan. His prize, displayed upright behind glass, is Karen, Werdegast's former wife. Suddenly Werdegast enters and discovers the perverse exhibit. Poelzig tells the grieving psychiatrist that his wife died of pneumonia two years after the war, and that his daughter later died also. Werdegast calls Poelzig a liar, vows that he will help Joan leave the house alive, and pulls a pistol. Before he can fire, however, the black cat appears, completely immobilizing Werdegast with fear. When Werdegast recovers (sans weapon), he and Poelzig play a game of chess to decide whether Joan leaves or stays.

The next day, Joan has recovered, and Peter tries to make plans to leave. Poelzig conveniently arranges excuses that keep the newlyweds in the house, one ruse being that of a dead phone. As Poelzig and Werdegast play chess, Poelzig smiles and says, "You hear that Vitus? The phone is dead. Even the phone is dead."

When Poelzig wins the game of chess and the Alisons try to leave. Thamal knocks out Peter and takes Joan back to her room. Shortly afterward, Joan meets a young woman she presumed dead: Karen, the daughter of Vitus Werdegast. She reveals that she is the wife of Poelzig and warns Joan to get out of the house before it is too late. Poelzig appears and attacks the screaming Karen. When Werdegast later comes to rescue Joan, she tells him of having met his daughter, Karen. An enraged Werdegast disrupts Poelzig's Black Mass and forces Poelzig down into the cellar where he skins his nemesis alive. When Werdegast later tries to help Joan escape, Peter misunderstands his actions and shoots him. Joan and Peter flee the house, and the dying Werdegast sets off the dynamite in the cellar, destroying the house and everything in it.

Production and Marketing:

After Boris Karloff's success in *Frankenstein* (1931), *The Old Dark House* (1932), and *The Mummy* (1932), Universal was eager to return his name to lights in *The Return of Frankenstein, A Trip to Mars*, or *The Golem*. When for various reasons these plans were scotched, Edgar G. Ulmer approached Carl Laemmle, Jr. with an idea to film Poe's *The Black Cat*. Universal already had a 1932 Richard Schayer script of that title in which Karloff was to play the drunkard of Poe's tale in a scenario at least roughly following the original story. It also had a 1932 script titled *The Brain Never Dies*, based on Poe's *The Fall of the House of Usher* and *The Black Cat*, as well as yet a third script, penned in 1933, titled *The Black Cat*, which was to feature the wicked torture-laden plans of a mad count in a Carpathian castle.

Of course, Universal was also eager to combine the talents of Karloff and Bela Lugosi in a single film. Though the studio considered Karloff their premiere horror star, Lugosi had proven his mettle in such productions as *Dracula* (1931), *Murders in the Rue Morgue* (1932), and *White Zombie* (1932). The box office potential of such a teaming was attractive.

Upon receiving permission to make *The Black Cat*, Ulmer left the other scripts in the vault and ignored the original Poe tale as well, although he was under orders to feature Poe prominently in the advertising. While the resulting screenplay is one of the most intriguing of horror's golden age, it owes little to Edgar Allan Poe.

About the only plot connection between Poe's *The Black Cat* and Ulmer's film is just that—a black cat. In Poe's story the narrator's wife refers to the superstitious belief that black cats were "witches in disguise." In the film, Werdegast refers to the black cat as "the living embodiment of evil," and Poelzig adds that the black cat is deathless. This last concept may have been gleaned from Poe, since in the original story the narrator is convinced that the black cat he killed has returned to life, and in the film, after Werdegast has killed a black cat, another (or the same one!) soon appears.

If *The Black Cat* borrows little from Poe's plot, most contemporary reviewers acknowledge that Ulmer does expertly convey the Poe atmosphere. In his book *Classics of the Horror Film* (The Citadel Press, 1974), William K. Everson grants that "in its mood and in its oppressive, claustrophobic, and generally unhealthy atmosphere, (the film) does evoke a very definite feeling of Poe." In *Cinema of Mystery* (Bounty Books, 1975), Rose London agrees that "Ulmer's direction of the film and his inventive and brooding atmospherics and contrasted black-and-white effects are possibly more faithful to the world of Poe than those of any other filmmaker; he is, indeed the Aubrey Beardsley of the cinema as an illustrator of Poe." In his book *Karloff and Lugosi* (McFarland and Company, 1990), Gregory William Mank also notes the film's Poesque spirit:

"True, Poe's talk of revenge is suggested only by the black cat pet of Poelzig. Nevertheless, Poe probably would have found much to admire in this moody, sinister movie; indeed few films have ever evoked the twisted nightmarish Evil that haunted Poe's stories as did *The Black Cat*. The motifs of revenge, souls that have been 'killed,' and the demonic flamboyance would have fascinated Edgar Allan—as would have the marriage of Poelzig and step-daughter Karen. Poe, after all, had married his beloved Virginia (who was truly the 'core and meaning' of his life, and whose death destroyed him) when she was only 13 years old; and as Philip Van Doren Stern noted in his introduction to *The Portable Poe*, Poe's personality indicated 'he was sexually abnormal, but there is no way of proving it.'"

Beyond the connections cited above, Ulmer left Poe unconsulted. Instead, the main source of inspiration seems to be the reputation of Aleister Crowley, an infamous self-proclaimed Satanist who also inspired Somerset Maugham's 1908 story *The Magician.*

Initially Universal estimated a meagre $91,125 production cost, much lower than that spent on *Dracula* and *Frankenstein*. Apparently the studio believed that the dual billing of Karloff and Lugosi could carry the film to financial success regardless of other circumstances. Therefore, Universal scheduled a very brief 15-day production schedule. Ulmer began shooting on February 28, 1934, and "wrapped" on March 17, 1934, after which Laemmle, Jr. ordered the film's extreme sadism and suggested necrophilia toned down. And finally, Lugosi, who wanted to play a sympathetic role this time around, became particularly unhappy when finding his character attempting to rape poor Joan. That, among other unsavory footage, was cut and re-shot.

Of course, the ads for *The Black Cat* heralded the first time teaming of Karloff and Lugosi, and for once, when the ads promised "Stranger things than you have ever seen or even dreamed of," they were probably right! Most of the pressbook ballyhoo recommended that theaters exploit the black cat angle. Typical of the feline-infested showmanship were recommendations that two men in a giant black cat outfit roam the streets, that a sidewalk projector beam the image of a black cat, that the theater sponsor a black cat contest, and that an art contest be held for the best black cat drawing, and that an illuminated cat's head be employed. There was, however, one appeal based on Edgar Allan Poe:

"Because of the tremendous reputation which Edgar Allan Poe enjoys, his words are used in many literature classes throughout American schools. Under the circumstances, tie-ins with the showing of your picture should be easily arranged.

"Contact principals or teachers in your locality and arrange for visits of pupils to see the picture in groups, or to stimulate extra interest, sponsor an essay contest on the subject of Edgar Allan Poe's life or why *Black Cat* can be considered one of his most outstanding masterpieces. Be sure that bulletins or cards announcing your showing appear in every school and at spots patronized by school children."

One can only imagine the real horrors that would have been created had well-meaning teachers carted busloads of impressionable pupils to see this dark tale of necrophilia, sadism, and torture, only to discover that the goings-on had little to do with the story in their literature books. In 1960, when Roger Corman approached American-International with an idea of filming Poe's

Most critics consider *The Black Cat* "Karloff's film." And while Boris does give the most malevolent performance of his career, Lugosi's character is arguably the most multi-faceted and consequently, the most interesting.

The Fall of the House of Usher, the executives initially balked partly because they felt that youngsters subjected to Poe in school textbooks would hardly rush out to repeat the unwelcome experience at a movie theatre, all of which reminds of W. H. Auden's sad observation that Poe was "doomed to be used in school textbooks as a bait to interest the young in literature, to be a respectable rival to the pulps."

When the screen season ended, *The Black Cat* turned an impressive $140,000 profit for Universal. Realart Pictures re-released it in 1953 as *The Vanishing Body.*

One original pressbook merchandising angle recommended that theaters pass out black cat good-luck charms. Perhaps many individuals associated with the film acquired such charms, for the future was bright for most. Boris Karloff, of course, would give two of his finest performances in *The Black Room* (1935) and *The Bride of Frankenstein* (1935), David Manners would play in several more good films before retiring as Universal's most recognizable horror leading man, and Edgar G. Ulmer would enhance his reputation in the horror genre by directing such films as *Bluebeard* (1944), *The Man from Planet X* (1951), *The Daughter of Dr. Jekyll* (1957), *The Amazing Transparent Man* (1960), and *Beyond The Time Barrier* (1961). As for Bela Lugosi, though a sad career decline was about to commence, he would soon star in *The Raven* (1935) and *The Son of Frankenstein* (1939), the only two films in which he undeniably outshines his career rival, Boris Karloff.

For those interested in knowing virtually all there is to know about the production of *The Black Cat*, I heartily recommend Gregory William Mank's *Karloff and Lugosi*, which is the last word on the subject.

Critique:

When *The Black Cat* opened at New York's Roxy Theater on May 18, 1934, *The New York Times*, almost always deprecatory toward horror films, first informed readers that the film "is not remotely to be identified with Poe's short story." While the review grudgingly commends the camera work and the screams of Jacqueline Wells, it concludes that: "*The Black Cat* is more foolish than horrible. The story and dialogue pile the agony on too thick to give the audience a reasonable scare."

Variety was also unkind: "Because of the presence in one film of Boris Karloff, that jovial madman, and Bela Lugosi, that suave fiend, this picture probably has box office attraction. But otherwise and on the counts of story, novelty, thrills, and distinction, it is subnormal... skinning alive is not new. It was done in a Gouverneur Morris story, *The Man Behind the Door*, filmed during the war. A truly horrible and nauseating bit of extreme sadism, its inclusion in a motion picture is dubious showmanship. That devil worshiping cult is also close to the border."

In his book *Horror in the Cinema* (Paperback Library, second revised edition, 1971), Ivan Butler pronounced the film a failure: "There is not much of Poe in this, and in spite of a splendidly sinister performance by Karloff and a surprisingly moving one from Lugosi, the final result is a rather scrappy and ineffectual film. Karloff's Latin incantations are impressively delivered, but otherwise the Satanic rites, admittedly interrupted before they can get under way, look like being even less diabolical than English Druid junketings, and the guests are clearly not going to allow any orgiastic carryings-on to disarrange their elegant evening dresses and coiffeurs. The black cat of the title (and Lugosi's abhorrence of it) is completely expendable. Even the final revenge fizzles out in shadows and switch-triggered castle-dynamiting."

More recent perspectives on *The Black Cat*, however, have been more positive, many lauding it as a classic horror film:

"...*The Black Cat*, with its weird and terrifying clashes between good and evil, is one of the most genuinely horrific films of the genre... Few films have managed to generate such dread, and in such a stylish and shadowy way. That *The Black Cat* succeeds so singularly well makes it a memorable addition to the cinema of fantastic horror." (Chris Steinbrunner and Burt Goldblatt, *Cinema of the Fantastic*, Galahad Books, 1972)

"...the striking pictorial quality of the film creates a decidedly non-Hollywood and non-stereotyped horror film... The cold modernistic sets, the rich quality of eroticism (often involving the change of focus within a shot to give added sexual emphasis), and the slow gliding camerawork of John Mescall are all helped in their creation of mood by a brilliant musical score which draws heavily on the classics." (William K. Everson, *Classics of the Horror Film*, The Citadel Press, 1974)

"...*The Black Cat* is quintessential Poe in that it weaves an almost abstract web of anguish out of its all-pervasive sense of evil... Strange, hypnotic, tormented, and eliciting the best performances of their careers from Karloff and Lugosi, *The Black Cat* is one of the masterpieces of the genre." (Phil Hardy, editor, *The Encyclopedia of Horror Movies,* Harper and Row, 1986)

"A work of great artistry and sinister beauty, *The Black Cat* occupies a very special niche in the history of macabre cinema... The picture is rife with excellent lines and Karloff, getting the lion's share, serves them up with chilling understatement." (Michael Brunas, John Brunas, and Tom Weaver, *Universal Horrors*, McFarland and Company, 1990)

"...all the morbid quirks of *The Black Cat* serve as the ideal backdrop for the first teaming of Karloff and Lugosi, a wonderful showcase for the macabre chemistry which would make the unions of these men vital movie history... Karloff's Lascivious Lucifer versus Lugosi's Avenging Angel makes *The Black Cat* transcend the horror movie genre, and become a grand lunatic fairy tale, sparked by a wickedly imaginative director, a bewitched camera, and a properly romantic score." (Gregory William Mank, *Karloff and Lugosi*, McFarland and Company, 1990)

The superior assessments of the modern critics again prove that the passage of time is necessary for maximum critical insight. The greatness of the film lies in five areas. First, Edgar G. Ulmer's direction is creative, eliciting the best from the actors involved. Second, the expressionistic sets create a mood of pervasive evil. Third, John Mescall's camera is sometimes itself cat-like as it creeps about the chilling sets. Fourth, the musical score, which includes Tchaikovsky's *Romeo and Juliet* and Bach's *Toccata and Fugue in D Minor*, perfectly evokes Ulmer's intended moods. And fifth, Boris Karloff and Bela Lugosi both give one of the best performances of their careers. Reports from the set indicate that Lugosi was jealous of the time Ulmer and Karloff spent together, but if that was so, it never hindered the director from getting Lugosi's very best work. I will devote the remainder of this chapter to an analysis of Lugosi's performance.

Most critics consider *The Black Cat* "Karloff's film." While Boris does give the most malevolent performance of his career (several choice lines drip from his lips like arsenic-spiked honey!), Lugosi's character is arguably the most multi-faceted and, consequently, the most interesting.

The opening train scenes brilliantly showcase the complexities of Lugosi's character. Entering the compartment, he politely apologizes, "Do please forgive this intrusion. (Then to the train employee) It is not necessary to make it so important. You need not disturb these people. I can make myself quite comfortable in the passageway." Lugosi tips the employee and soon catches a piece of falling luggage before it hits a frightened Wells. "Better to be frightened than to be crushed," Lugosi quips with a smile.

These scenes establish Lugosi as cordial, generous, and compassionate—quite a switch for the man so identified in the public with Dracula! But there is another side to Lugosi's Werdegast as well.

When Lugosi tells Manners and Wells that he is going to visit "an old friend," his sideward, darkly reflective glance betrays the sarcasm of his statement. Werdegast is obviously a troubled man. Later, when Manners awakens to find Lugosi lovingly stroking Joan's hair, the latter explains:

"I beg your indulgence, my friend. Eighteen years ago I left a girl—so like your lovely wife—to go to war. (Pause). For Kaiser and country, you know. (Pause). She was my wife. Have you ever heard of—Kurgaal? It is a prison below Omsk on Lake Bakail. Many men have gone there. Few have returned. I have returned. After fifteen years—I have returned."

Though due to typecasting Lugosi's stroking the hair of a young married woman would usually signal some nefarious purpose, the gesture here is tender—solidifying Lugosi's presence as both a beneficent man of sorrow and as a spirit of indomitable determination and character. These are elements of Lugosi's thespian talent rarely evinced in the American cinema.

Lugosi then pulls up the blind on the window, and the steam obscures his reflection in the glass. This nice touch by photographer Mescall reinforces the hint that Lugosi is troubled and that the core of the man is unclear, possibly even to himself.

As the bus transports its passengers, and as the driver delivers his "tour guide" explanations of the area's horrors, Lugosi simply closes his eyes. He is a man repelled by violence, death, and torture. Yet, the opening scenes suggest ambiguity—that perhaps his unfortunate experiences have created psychic conflicts regarding the very type of acts that repel him.

At Poelzig's home, Lugosi tenderly ministers to Well's injuries. Then Karloff enters the room to ominous music. There is no doubt as to who the villain is here. When Lugosi and Karloff stand face-to-face, the discomfort is palpable. Karloff is clearly the "old friend" Lugosi has come to see, but it is also clear that Karloff is no friend. Karloff is clearly uncomfortable meeting Lugosi after all those years.

Shortly afterward, Lugosi confronts Karloff: "You sold Marmaros to the Russians—

A posed publicity shot from *The Black Cat*. The ads promised "stranger things than you have ever seen or even dreamed of."

scuttled away in the night and left us to die. Is it to be wondered that you should choose this place to build your house? The masterpiece of construction—built upon the ruins of the masterpiece of destruction—the masterpiece of murder. The murder of 10,000 men returns to the place of his crime!" Werdegast recounts the tortures he endured and tells Karloff that he has returned for his wife, Karen. Poelzig attempts to evade the subject as Werdegast becomes more hostile. Though delivering emotionally charged lines, Lugosi's acting is remarkably restrained. Juxtaposed against a purposeful, accusatory stare is an almost nonchalant raised eyebrow. He gives the impression of a man struggling to control seething anger, deep sorrow, and an almost overpowering lust for vengeance.

When Manners enters the room and the black cat first appears, Lugosi makes his character's phobia believable. That an eminent psychiatrist is played upon by a phobia suggests contradictions in Werdegast's personality and underscores his other major contradiction of pre-war gentility and post-war vengefulness.

As talk continues, Lugosi makes detached and light-hearted comments about Marmaros, Poelzig, and death. Though he addresses Manners—Lugosi's intended audience is really Karloff—who is quite aware by this time that his wife is acting strangely because of a strong narcotic Lugosi administered, Lugosi reveals that the taker of that particular drug sometimes becomes mediumistic, absorbing the atmosphere of her environment and those around her. Manners laughs off Lugosi's explanation as supernatural baloney. "Supernatural, perhaps," Lugosi replies, "Baloney, perhaps not. There are more things under the sun..." Lugosi here obviously refers to Karloff's Satanic evil which is supernatural, yes, but certainly not baloney. Lugosi's faint allusion to Shakespeare re-establishes his character as a man of culture, while his reference to mediumistic responses points out the seriousness with which he takes Karloff as a truly evil man involved with a very real and dangerous supernaturalism. Within the context of the film, it is through Lugosi's responses to Karloff that the audience truly begins to grasp Poelzig's potential for horror and death.

When Lugosi explains to Manners that the black cat is a symbol of evil, and that at the time of the cat's death, the evil enters into the nearest living thing, the audience is introduced to a new twist. If Lugosi's Werdegast was a genuinely beneficent person, is he still so? Has the evil of the cat entered him? If so, the change is not readily apparent, for what soon follows is one of the most sympathetic scenes in which the actor ever appeared.

As Lugosi looks up at the preserved corpse of his wife, which he treats almost as a religious icon, tears well in his uncomprehending eyes. He asks Poelzig, "And why, why is she like this?" In a few golden moments, his eyes reflect both sorrow and reverence, and his face takes on an almost angelic aura. Again, we should be struck by Lugosi's ability to evoke empathy and sympathy. He does so rather perversely in *Island of Lost Souls* (1932), very convincingly in *The Mystery of Mary Celeste* (1935), and briefly but effectively in *The Wolf Man* (1941), but really nowhere else, unless one counts a few of his more pathetic moments as Ygor in *Son of Frankenstein* (1939) or *The Ghost of Frankenstein* (1942). Regardless, none of these examples approach what Lugosi gives us in those brief, precious moments in *The Black Cat*.

When Karloff lies about the real cause of Karen's death and about the true fate of Lugosi's daughter, the Hungarian pulls a pistol, threatens to kill his nemesis, and vows that he will help Wells leave the house alive. While this is Lugosi's first attempt at revenge, it is coupled with his desire to help Wells survive. Lugosi's yin-yang continues. Of course, the second appearance of the black cat renders him helpless. Karloff then confiscates the pistol and asks Lugosi if they, as a result of the war, are not both of "the living dead?" This could well be an inside joke since Lugosi was famous for playing Dracula, the king of the living dead, and Karloff had gained fame as the Frankenstein Monster, a living creature constructed from corpses.

Lugosi, disturbed when Karloff steals a lustful glance at Wells, suggests a game of chess to decide the fate of the young woman. Having failed with a pistol, he now turns to chess as a way of resolving the conflict—certainly a gentleman's approach. The contrast again suggests the nature of Lugosi's dual personality.

During the chess game, Lugosi watches as Karloff carries on another chess game of sorts to keep the newlyweds at Marmaros, during which time Lugosi's expression is one of keen observation, with a slight tinge of disgust. Karloff wins the chess game and proceeds to put his plans into action.

With the newlyweds behind locked doors, Karloff plays the organ and Lugosi sneaks off with a key to Wells' room. After assuring her that he is her friend, his countenance darkens. "We're all in danger," he tells her. "Poelzig is a beast. I know. I have seen the proof... I wait my time. It shall be soon, very soon. Until then, I must do his bidding." If Lugosi was almost angelic facing his wife's corpse, we now get hints that the angel is truly an avenging one. During this scene, Lugosi is filmed from below, emphasizing his power and presence. Then, when he takes Wells in his arms, he assumes an almost fatherly concern and sense of responsibility, saying, "Dear child, be brave. No matter how hopeless it all seems." We can see Lugosi wrestling with inner demons, and we wonder, when the time comes, if the driven psychiatrist can indeed rescue the girl if doing so might postpone his vengeance.

When Lugosi discovers that his daughter is still alive and later breaks up the Black Mass, he flies into a controlled rage. Upon finding his daughter's corpse, however, he emits an animal-like cry of pain and disbelief. Shortly afterward, when Lugosi has Karloff at his mercy, his face is wild with rage and expectation. "Do you know what I'm going to do to you now?" he gleefully asks. "No? Did you ever see an animal skinned, Hjalmar? That's what I'm going to do to you now. Tear the skin from your body slowly, bit by bit." Lugosi reportedly so enjoyed saying those lines that several retakes were necessary. Indeed, Lugosi is positively demonic in his glee, and it is the pitifully vulnerable Karloff who for the first time elicits audience sympathy. This finale suggests a later one in Michael Reeves' highly regarded British production *Witchfinder General* (1968), in which atrocities committed by Witchfinder Matthew Hopkins (Vincent Price) drive a young soldier (Ian Ogilvy) vengefully insane. When the soldier maniacally chops Hopkins to pieces with a hatchet, the audience realizes that the previously innocent young man has been driven to a level of sadism almost exceeding that of Hopkins himself. Coincidentally, the title of *Witchfinder General* was changed for U.S. release to Edgar Allan Poe's *The Conqueror Worm*. *The Black Cat* and *The Conqueror Worm*, both fine films with similar endings, also share the distinction of taking almost nothing from Edgar Allan Poe, their alleged source.

So, was Werdegast really mad? Did the black cat's spirit of evil enter him as he himself suggested? As the wounded Lugosi, his face sagging like melting wax, leans heavily next to the red lever of destruction, we realize we will never know. He delivers his final words to Karloff with weakness and resignation. The hatred is gone. His quest is over. The dynamite explodes, and so ends one of Lugosi's finest screen performances. When *The Black Cat* crossed Bela Lugosi's path, a number of positive elements united to create one of the greatest horror films of all time. The fact that "horror man" Lugosi gave his best horror film performance as a largely heroic, though problematic, protagonist is testimony to his versatility as an actor—a versatility that Hollywood unfortunately rarely exploited.

Universal's dynamic duo, Karloff and Lugosi, along with Harry Cording. The bizarre film, directed by Edgar Ulmer, still shocks today.

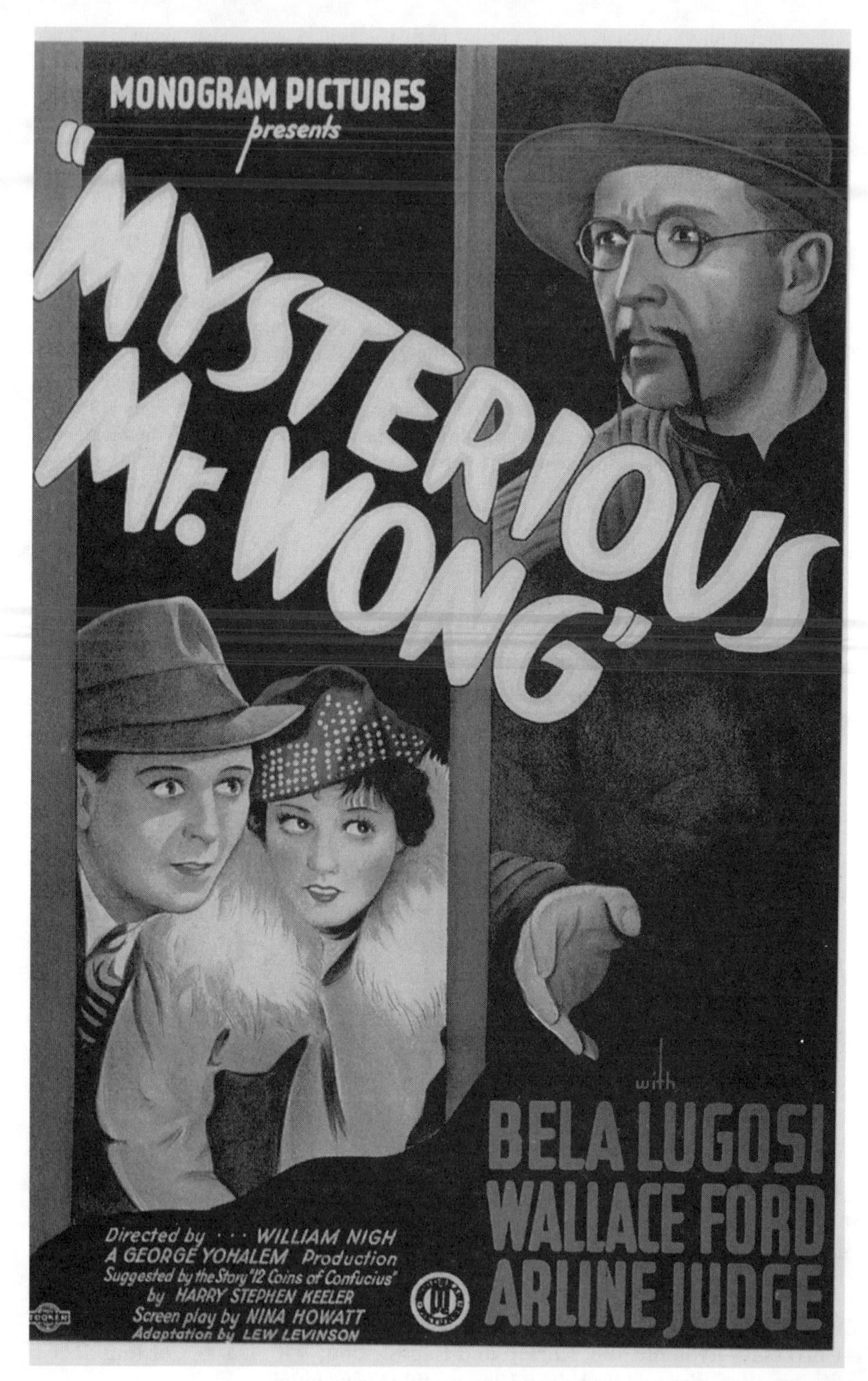

Poster courtesy Ronald V. Borst/Hollywood Movie Posters

Mysterious Mr. Wong

(1935)

by John Soister

CREDITS: Vice-President in charge of production: Trem Carr; Director: William Nigh; Supervised by George Yohalem; From *The Twelve Coins of Confucius* by Harry Stephen Keeler; Adapted by Nina Howatt; Continuity: Lew Levensen; Additional dialogue: James Harbuveaux; Photography: Harry Neuman, ASC; Film editor: Jack Ogilvie; Settings: E.R. Hickson; Recorded by John A. Stransky; Musical Director: Abe Meyer; Sound System: Western Electric; Monogram Pictures Corporation, Released 1/25/35; Running time: 68 minutes

CAST: Bela Lugosi...Mr. Wong/Li See, Wallace Ford...Jason H. Barton, Arline Judge...Peg, Fred Warren...Tsi Tung, Lotus Long...Moonflower, Robert Emmett O' Connor...McGillicuddy, Edward Piel...Jen Yu, Luke Chan...Chan Fu, Lee Shumway...Brandon, Etta Lee...Maidservant, and Ernest F. Young, Theodore Lorch, James B. Leong, and Chester Gan

With a bankruptcy behind him, and his two years of forced unemployment still a couple of years down the pike, Bela Lugosi was in the midst of his first "fat cat" period in 1935.

Universal's big hit of the previous year, *The Black Cat,* had made a profit of well over $100,000 for that studio, and certainly helped to restore Lugosi to the Laemmles' good graces. Having tipped his hand once too often over the title role in *Dracula,* and having gotten his Hungarian up during preproduction on *Frankenstein,* the middle-aged star had earlier found himself nearly *persona non grata* at Uncle Carl's. In addition, the woeful receipts of *Murders in the Rue Morgue*—Bela's alternate assignment and Robert Florey's consolation prize—had done little to convince management of his professional judgment, acting ability, or box office draw. The windfall of the "second Edgar Allan Poe" piece, however, had gone a long way toward erasing those earlier ill feelings.

True, *The Black Cat* had required Bela to appear opposite the contemptible Boris Karloff, but the billing (KARLOFF and Bela LUGOSI) had been acceptable, and the money hadn't been *too* bad, especially with the added bonus of the extra scenes, shot after production had wrapped in order to soften the deviant overtones painted by Edgar Ulmer and to placate the horrified Laemmle *pere et fils.* Other projects for 1934 were falling into place as well, assuring him of a respite from financial worry or insolvency.

There were, for example, the prospects of *Dracula's Daughter* and an adaptation of Robert Louis Stevenson's *The Suicide Club,* the two films remaining in his three-picture deal with Universal. (Both films would ultimately be made without him: a wax dummy taking his place in the former, and MGM taking Universal's place in the latter.) A few (and only a few) dollars were to be had appearing (again opposite Karloff) in *Gift of Gab,* and a few more for a novelty cameo (*again* opposite Karloff!) in Columbia's *Screen Snapshots* #11.

More satisfying to the ego and the wallet than either of these were Bela's efforts away from the Universal lot. *The Return of Chandu* may not have had the production values of the 1932 Fox feature Bela had stolen from hero Edmund Lowe, but the Principal Films serial allowed him a sympathetic part, title-card billing, and the opportunity to keep the Lugosi name (and the Lugosi "charisma") in front of audiences everywhere for three months running. (Viewers who didn't have the cash or the time to spend twelve weeks in a row watching Bela mutter incantations or trade punches with turbanned extras could catch the gist of it all in *The Return of Chandu* or *Chandu on the Magic Isle.* Released in 1935, both features were edited from the chapterplay by enterprising producer Sol Lesser, whose plans for additional filmed exploits of the mysterious magician were shelved in favor of the adventures of Edgar Rice Burroughs' cash-cow, Tarzan.)

Columbia's *Best Man Wins* started 1935 off rather profitably for Bela, who didn't mind playing opposite Edmund Lowe yet again. (The two had first appeared together in Fox's *The Silent Command,* released in 1923.) Unable to steal this one from Lowe—Columbia not only buoyed up the original movie Chandu's screen time, but provided him with a partner, Jack Holt—Bela did enjoy playing a more conventional role in a non-horror assignment. Moreover, at this point in his career, the Hungarian still hoped to be given more opportunities to "act against type" in broader, more mainstream productions.

In fact, he managed to veer away from horror parts twice more that year. In *Murder by Television,* the viewers got two Lugosis for the price of one; the actor played twin brothers, only one of whom was a blackguard. The limited release the tedious picture received had little effect on Bela's image or his professional future, however, while his barnstorming portrayal of one-armed seaman Anton Lorenzen in Hammer's *Mystery of the Mary Celeste* proved to be (in the words of Lugosi scholar Richard Bojarski), "More tragic than gruesome, disappointing Lugosi fans who expected more of the latter."

The year would end, however, with Lugosi's vampire image not only reinforced, but his further association with the much-despised Karloff more firmly entrenched in the minds of ticket buyers everywhere.

MGM's *Mark of the Vampire* gave Tod Browning yet another opportunity to prove that the popularity and resilience of his features with Lon Chaney were in no way due to his (Browning's) genius. Nevertheless, Lugosi's Count Mora was a far more frightening presence than was his Dracula. Inasmuch as both films were helmed by Browning, the more impressive performance in the latter film can only be attributed either to Bela's growing identification with and mastery of the role (which, for all intents and purposes, was that of Dracula, sans the vocal bravado), or the dynamics of the screenplay. As the latter offered a fantastically expensive, unwieldy, long-term police "sting" operation as the *raison d'etre* for the plot, and a modus operandi which, in the words of William K. Everson (in *Classics of the Horror Film*), "must have been long, laborious, tedious, utterly impractical, and finally, rather messy," the nod must go to Bela's portrayal.

Back at Universal for *The Raven,* Bela had not only to contend with Karloff's presence, but his superior billing, his higher salary, and—to Lugosi's mind, at any rate—his condescending attitude. On the plus side, Bela had more screen time, a good deal of articulate dialogue, and a second opportunity to maim and/or disfigure his hated rival and get away with it. (He got to flay Karloff's Hjalmar Poelzig alive at the climax of *The Black Cat,* and the operation on Boris' facial nerves in *The Raven* provided the proud Hungarian with, at the very least, vicarious revenge.)

Way before all of this (late 1934, as a matter of fact), Bela was sporting shaved eyebrows over at Monogram Studios. The promise of a leading role and above-the-title billing (as well as the means to meet mortgage payments and host some of the parties for which he'd become noted) had lured him back to the independents.

Monogram had been cranking out features (mostly westerns) since 1931, and was on the verge of a merger that would shake the very foundations of the also-rans in Hollywood. Late in 1935, Monogram, Mascot Studios (for which Bela had starred in the serial *Whispering Shadows* back in '33), Herbert Yates' Consolidated Film Laboratories, and several *really* minor film concerns would unite to form Republic Pictures. The end result, alas, would be dissatisfaction for W. Ray Johnstone and Trem Carr, Monogram's front-office big-wigs; before 1937 had shuffled off, their corporate identity and logo, as well as their old studios, would be reopened for business as usual. Monogram would look forward to Sam Katzman, Crash Corrigan, Tom Keene—and Bela Lugosi—for years to come.

January 25, 1935, then, saw the release of the very first Bela Lugosi starring-feature for

Monogram Pictures—*Mysterious Mr. Wong*. Viewed some 60 years after the fact, the film is unremarkable and disjointed. Cheaply budgeted, poorly written (*The Twelve Coins of Confucius,* Harry Stephen Keeler's pulpish work, "suggested" the framework of Nina Howatt's woefully dysfunctional screenplay), and shoddily directed, *Wong* nevertheless is the result of a trend—not only in film-making, but in popular taste—which had extended through the thirties and forties from the previous century.

The earliest, most dramatic indication of the fascination which things oriental have held for modern westerners can be found in the popular reaction to Gilbert and Sullivan's *The Mikado.* At the time of its debut, trade routes to Japan had already provided English sophisticates with any number of exotic Japanese imports, so those famed purveyors of operetta had merely capitalized on an extant attraction. The result, therefore, was box-office gold for the team and for impresario Richard D'Oyly Carte. Incremental income was nothing to joke about, either; royalties came rolling in on such items as music boxes, sheet music, pianoforte rolls, posters, derivative artwork "Mikado" paraphernalia (including dolls, parasols, and fans), amateur performance rights, and candies.

(A similar interest—albeit with a more-than-slight geographical shift—would occur in the early decades of the twentieth century, when the world would acknowledge a platonic love affair with the Egyptian teenage pharaoh, Tutankhamen. That attraction had already been exploited by Uncle Carl's underlings in 1932's *The Mummy.*)

Oriental fashion, oriental deportment, oriental *anything* guaranteed a fabulous return on money invested in early 20th-century USA. America's fascination with life "on the other side of the world" lead artists, interior decorators, magicians, photographers, lecturers, and myriad others to seek a buck by revealing the exotic side of life on the flip side of the globe. Hack writers, who otherwise would have occupied their time (and increased their yield) with tales of sex, betrayal, or baseball, turned their attention to things Chinese or, to a lesser extent, Japanese. (In the mindset of most Americans during this century's first three decades, there *was* no Korea, no Mongolia, no Singapore.)

In the late 1920s, Earl Derr Biggers concocted Charlie Chan, whose attraction to the *literati* is hard to understand (at least from the earliest of the novels; Charlie is therein the most artificial of *dei ex machina*). Although only five of his novel-length investigations saw print, the Honolulu-based Chinese sleuth found immortality in the course of dozens of screen adventures, ranging from early sound, semi-prestige productions to low-budget (but always top-of-the-bill) B's in the late 1940's.

John Marchand's Mr. Moto, and Hugh Wiley's Mr. Wong (no relation to the subject at hand) filled in the available slots in "B" literature, and assured respectable numbers at the "B" movie adaptations. (Marchand was always discomfited by the attention his Mr. Moto series received; Wiley, presumably, took the money and ran.)

Arthur Sarsfield Ward donned chung-sams and split infinitives to create Fu Manchu, surely the most notorious (and popular) of the breed which came to be known as the "Yellow Peril." Ward, writing under the *nom de plume* of Sax Rohmer, demonstrated not only a flair for pulp composition (his works, of which the Fu Manchu series is but a part, seem always to be in print), but offered an apt, if slightly ungrammatical guideline for its style. (Just what is a "decapitated head?")

It's possible to trace the oriental presence on the silver screen back to the mid-teens, with such novelty featurettes as Edison's *The Mission of Mr. Foo.* Described as the "rarest type of cinema play" (due to the fact that the Chinese actors wouldn't face the camera!), this early effort stressed exotica, "Chinese cunning, and political intriguing." (sic) This perception of the oriental mindset being steeped in deceit and lust for power (and for white women!) lead to the elevating of all Chinese males to the status of evil geniuses, or to the relegating of them to the (non-threatening) level of coolies, laundrymen, and railroad workers.

The unique talents of Lon Chaney, Sr. were used in no less than four "oriental" features,

Jason and Peg seem annoyed, but Mr. Wong couldn't be happier that things are finally hopping in the Dungeon of the Faithless.

ranging from Tod Browning's *Outside the Law* (for Universal/Jewel in 1921), to MGM's slick *Mr. Wu* in 1927. Only in 1922's *Shadows* (and, to a lesser degree, in the no-longer-extant *Bits of Life* from 1921), however, were Chaney's characters permitted to exhibit qualities other than bloodthirstiness, avarice, or lust. As William K. Everson wrote, in his compulsory *The Detective in Film:* "...the Oriental was a standard villain in such films as *Old San Francisco*...; or, if he was depicted sympathetically (as in Griffith's *Broken Blossoms* or the Lon Chaney vehicle *Shadows*), he compensated for that sympathy by dying very conveniently at the end."

Cinematically, the Yellow Peril *always* assured good returns. The Brits had a field day with their silent serials, the *Mystery of Fu Manchu* (1923), and *The Further Mysteries of Fu Manchu* (1924; both with Harry Agar Lyons as the eponymous villain). Rohmer's anglicized mandarin packed the houses and separated both the working class and the "swanning" upper crust from their coin-of-the-realm. (In all fairness, however, the British cinema of the twenties was so stolid—apart from an emerging Alfred Hitchcock—and nationalistic, that almost anything smacking of "exotica" would have guaranteed both audience interest and revenue.)

With the coming of sound, Paramount Studios went on to construct not one, but three profitable features from that same body of work, all starring Swedish/Russian actor Warner Oland. Oland, soon to be the first actor to repeat the role of Charlie Chan in the Fox series' run, brought with him not only box-office popularity—he had been projected on sheets and screens since the teens—but an Oriental cast to his features. (He would be the first—and, to date, the only—Fu Manchu to eschew eye make-up, but had been preceded in the role of Charlie Chan by a couple of genuine orientals (neither Chinese, both Japanese): noted actor, magician (and eccentric) Sojin and George Kuwa. As reported in Ken Hanke's excellent *Charlie Chan at the Movies,* Oland explained his countenance to Keye Luke as a byproduct of the Mongol invasion. "That's true," Luke agreed, "because the Mongols did get up there around Sweden and Finland and naturally they sired some children."

In the Oland canon, however, Fu Manchu's character was changed from that of a megalomaniacal super-genius to the head of a small, influential mandarin family. Rather than seeking to subjugate all white devils, Oland's doctor is content to vent his spleen at Nayland Smith and his circle of family members and friends. (Seeking to avoid offending either potential far-Eastern markets or oriental ticket-buyers in the States, Paramount sought to justify Fu's actions by depicting his family's accidental annihilation at the hands of the British during the Boxer Rebellion.)

Oland railed and plotted against the British in general and against the Smiths in particular for two fairly lucrative features (*The Mysterious Dr. Fu Manchu,* 1929, and *The Return of Dr. Fu Manchu,* 1930), and then, in a virtual cameo performance, entrusted his daughter to pick up where he left off at the outset of a third (*Daughter of the Dragon,* 1931). For all this, however, Oland's mandarin failed to capture either the spirit of the Rohmer novels or the hearts of their followers.

Come 1932, MGM's money and production capabilities lured freshman celebrity Boris Karloff from Universal; *The Mask of Fu Manchu* promised to restore to the evil doctor his bent on world conquest. Accompanied by his "ugly and unworthy daughter," Fah Lo See (*nee* Suee, portrayed by the highly lovely and sporting Myrna Loy), Fu indulged in the most *polite* nefarious campaign to have "the world grovel at my feet" that the screen had seen to that point. Parrying hot-tempered slurs from Lewis Stone, Jean Hersholt, Karen Morley, and Charles Starrett, Karloff responded with his lisping English cadences and the ingratiating oiliness of a veteran headwaiter.

The Mask of Fu Manchu turned a healthy profit for MGM, but whether the notoriety it inspired (Was Fu indeed an incestuous homosexual? Fah Lo See a nymph? Was reverse racism—putting ethnic slurs into the mouths of the heathen Chinese—too uncomfortable?) whetted the appetites of viewers, or, ultimately, turned them off, is still a matter for discussion.

Apropos of all of this, late 1934 found Monogram Studios eyeing properties for "that Dracula man," Bela Lugosi; the Hungarian had been signed for a one picture deal earlier that year. While something with a oriental flavor seemed the ticket (one had only to look at the Fox lot, with Warner Oland's Charlie Chan helping to lug bags of money off to the bank), a one-shot detective film didn't seem the way to go. Lugosi had played a detective—and rather well, too—in 1929's *The Thirteenth Chair,* and he had stolen every scene he'd shared with Oland in *The Black Camel* a couple of years after that, but still... Nope; with audiences virtually conditioned to hiss a villainous Bela (many viewers were uncomfortable with his operating on the side of the angels in *The Return of Chandu*), there was little point (or profit) in messing with a winning formula.

(Actually, *most* of the studios for which he worked during the early thirties screwed around with the Lugosi name and presence. Apart from Universal, only the Halperin Brothers allowed the star full rein as villain extraordinaire in their atmospheric *White Zombie.* Paramount's *Island of Lost Souls* had offered the proud actor little more than a cameo (lost in a mound of the make-up he so depised), while MGM's *Mark of the Vampire* maliciously guyed the audiences with the ultimate revelation that the "vampyre ferocious" was fraudulent.

This propensity to "waste" Bela while he was at the height of his powers caused many of the star's fans down through the years to shake their heads in wonder and disbelief. In most of the genre films in which he appeared for several years subsequent to *Dracula,* Bela was either a red herring (as in Columbia's *Night of Terror,* or Mascot's serial, *The Whispering Shadow,*) or a piece of human furniture, designed to lend some ominous dressing to an otherwise dreary mystery (cf. World-Wide's *The Death Kiss,* or *Murder by Television,* Imperial-Cameo's definitive snoozer.)

At any rate, the major problem was in finding a property which was available, cheap, and which featured an oriental fiend, a small cast, and limited, contemporary sets. Fu Manchu was out of the question; MGM had not only the rights, but also a film which still had box-office potential upon reissue, and—in the eyes of most aficionados of Rohmer's novels—the definitive portrayal of the mad mandarin by Karloff. Besides, walking in the footsteps of the rival he had helped to create would not have spurred the edgy Lugosi on to his finest performance. (This is an irony which no concerned party could forget during the filming of *Frankenstein Meets the Wolf Man.*)

The solution, happily, was the purchase of *Twelve Coins of Confucius*, penned by Harry Stephen Keeler in *his* attempt to cash in on the mania for orientalia. Lew Levenson worked at adapting the story to existing sets and contract players, while Nina Howatt got the actual screenplay credit. Studio writer James Herbuveaux, whose dialogue additions ranged from the mildly fruity to the overripe, aided and abetted in the attempt to bring Keeler's "Yellow Peril" to the big screen.

Mysterious Mr. Wong begins with an insert from the *International Encyclopedia*: "There is a tradition that 12 coins given by Confucius on his deathbed to 12 trusted friends, will some day come to the possession of one man and give him extraordinary powers in the province of Keelat."

While focusing the plot goal rather succinctly, the insert doesn't get into what those "extraordinary" powers might be, or just what the importance of the "province of Keelat" is in the cosmic scheme of things. (Nor are the next few visible words of the insert—"The principles of morality"—of much help; either we're in for some heavy philosophical sailing with Monogram, or we've intruded into the next entry.)

The succession of killings represented in the opening montage, however, makes it abundantly clear that *Mysterious Mr. Wong* is not concerned with ethical niceties. As a wounded man collapses in the street, someone rifles his pockets and retrieves a coin, leaving a note emblazoned with a Chinese character on his chest. The small notice the slaying receives in the newspaper ("Mysterious Killing in Chinatown: Police Investigate New Oriental Murder") indicates not only its relative unimportance, but also the racist overtones which will pervade the film.

A second incident, with another corpse and another coin/note exchange, garners more coverage from the paper, and talk of "Tong Wars" begins to circulate.

With the third depicted murder—a coin of Confucius is found within the shoe of a (sockless) cadaver—a bonafide headline, "Tong War Claims New Victim," explodes onto the screen.

Not only are the papers concerned; a group of sober-looking Chinese men are holding a meeting. Their leader, identified as such both by the pipe he smokes sagaciously and by some impressive tailoring, keeps the audience current while chastising his men that "We have been sent here to put an end to Wong's plot. And so far, we have failed. This mad Manchurian must be found, and the coins of Confucius restored to Keelat. In the hands of Wong, they mean its destruction."

While the crowd from Keelat is puffing smoke and wringing its collective hands, the "mad Manchurian" is sitting at a desk, presumably deep within the bowels of his secret headquarters. Looking neither quite mad nor (despite the most ornate Chinese chung-sam the Monogram wardrobe department could stitch together) terribly Manchurian, Lugosi is playing with his coins of Confucius with the amiable intensity of a pre-teen numismatist. A gong—the first of many, many—sounds, and Bela's Wong, who surely must have become used to such things at this point in his career, visibly starts.

Through a sliding door enter three hatchetmen, each of whom presents a coin to the glowering aristocrat. Waving the three away, Wong quickly gets back down to business. Having satisfactorily accounted for all the booty, he stares at a point off-camera and, in the finest tradition of screen villains everywhere, declaims to no one in particular, "One more, and the province of

Keelat shall know its rightful ruler!"

Elsewhere in the labyrinthine reaches of his lair, Wong's niece, Moonflower (Lotus Long), huddles for comfort along with her maidservant. Unbeknownst to them, Wong has entered their apartment and stands imperiously at the door. Another gong sounds (albeit *after* the mandarin has entered), prompting Moonflower to explain that "Every time it sounds, Wong gives dreadful orders and terrible things begin to happen." (This may be *her* impression of what goes on at the sound of the gong, but subsequent tollings reveal the gong to be trivial, capricious, and—to Wong, at any rate, unfailingly irritating.

The authenticity of the dialogue drops a notch lower as Wong and his only surviving family member engage in a battle of *bons mots:*

He: Did the ancient and honorable name of Wong fall from the lips of his gracious and honorable niece?

She: If doors must have keyholes, there will always be those who listen at them.

He: It would be unfortunate to have to shut so beautiful a personage in the dungeon of the faithless.

She: You wouldn't dare!

He: Wong has dared many things. He will continue to dare, and one day, when he is acclaimed by all Keelat...

She: You are wrong! You were never intended by fate to rule Keelat!

He: Time will teach you to guard indifferent speech!

The dialogue, as plummy as it is, is one of the joys of the film. Not that it's very good; apart from Wong's (and Harbuveaux's) strange idea of what "indifferent" means, the exchange just quoted is as close to classic bad writing as one can safely get. It's the *delivery* that one enjoys so much. Listening to Bela trade quips with his niece (he so gets into it at one point that he mispronounces his character's name as "Vong"), or hearing the vocal distinctions he attempts to draw between Li See's "very old" oriental speech patterns, and Mr. Wong's full-throated, undisguised Hungarian-English, offers a most enjoyable reward for staying attuned.

As Wong turns on his slippered heel and storms out, his gracious and loyal niece reveals her true feelings in one of the great dadaesque lines found in thirties' potboilers: "He frightens me; this madness of his is driving all reason from his mind."

A quick cut to a current newspaper column ("Have Tong Wars Gone Out of Style?") serves to introduce the hero of the piece, Jason H. Barton (Wallace Ford), via byline and photograph. The newspaperman's theory, that the authorities must look elsewhere to explain the recent rash of murders in Chinatown, is read by Wong, who feels that the reporter is getting too close to the truth. As a henchman silently draws a knife from his sleeve, Wong demurs: "No. He cannot be dealt with as one of our own race. This Mr. Jason H. Barton; I trust, for his own good, his interests will not bring him too close to the House of Wong."

Mr. Wong is unaware, though, that Barton places little credence in his own published views: "I ran out of gas. I slipped on a little banana oil," he tells his city editor (Lee Shumway). There's been another killing of a Chinese, however, and the editor wants Barton to follow up a lead that's just come in. "Did you ever run into a Chinaman named Wong?" he asks. Setting the tone to come, Barton parries that "you never run into one that ain't named Wong." Still, off he goes, in search of the mysterious Mr. Wong.

Pausing for a moment on his way out, Barton flirts with Peg, the receptionist at the newspaper. (The character of Peg is etched in the "quick-witted ingenue" style popularized by actresses such as Glenda Farrell and perfected by Myrna Loy in her various associations with William Powell. As Barton's girlfriend, Arline Judge is more than adequate, hitting the mark more often than not.) Peg and her beau "chat cute," and are clearly meant for each other, thus fitting to a "T" the quasi-cowardly hero/smart-alecky heroine mold that would endure at least until the end of Bob Hope's film career.

Mere moments later, in Chinatown, Barton zeroes in on the laundry where the dirty deed had been done. True to the spirit of ethnic stereotyping, the cop on the beat is Officer McGillicuddy (Robert Emmett O'Connor), a most profoundly Irish harness bull who isn't adverse to offering some pithy observations of his own. ("I was sent over from the Globe to do the murder." "You're too late. It's already been done." Rim-shot.)

Exhibiting the lackadaisical attitude typical of most cops in early sound whodunits, McGillicuddy allows Barton to nose around both the scene of the crime and the *corpus delecti*, which is still lying on the floor. Both men notice a pencil in the dead man's hand, but, says the cop, "we couldn't find nothin' the poor devil could have been writin' at the time." When asked whether *he's* ever heard of a Chinaman named Wong, McGillicuddy tosses any remaining doubt as to his powers of deduction or observation down the bunghole when he admits that, "They all sound alike to me, and these Chinamen ain't much for talkin'... Except for old Li See, the herb dealer down the street. He knows everybody and he's a regular old gossip."

Back at the House of Wong, its master is busy kowtowing before a lacquered plaque and a statue of Buddha, when another stroke of the gong jars him from reverence to petulance. Enter the three henchmen, failure written on their otherwise inscrutable faces: "Sam Toy no have coin." Angered by the prospect of still being one coin away from a full load (and suspecting employee pilfering), Wong has two of the hatchetmen seize the third, and they toss him through a trapdoor into a pit below. The mandarin glowers magnificently: "A few hours with the rats will make him speak the truth."

At Sam Toy's, McGillicuddy opens the door to shoo away a handful of locals, and the ensuing draft allows Barton to discover the paper containing the dying laundryman's last words on a high shelf. Acting in the manner of all cinematic reporters and amateur sleuths, he withholds the evidence from the police, and heads down the street to visit "old Li See, the herb dealer."

In the twinkling of an eye, Barton is at the herbalist's shop. As he enters, Li See glances suspiciously over his shoulder before plopping something (An herb? 5 cents worth of licorice?) into the open mouth of a waiting child. The disguised Wong and Barton engage in some banter—probably meant to be clever, but mostly just annoying—before another stroke of the gong causes both men to react: Barton quizzically, and Li See, as if royally pissed off. (Just what *does* the gong signify, and who's sounding it?)

Barton produces the laundryman's note; catching a quick glimpse, Li See's eyes light up. Via the miracle of superimposition, the lefthand column of Chinese characters is revealed to mean "The Golden Coin of Confucius." Snatching the paper away before the herbalist can get a good gander, Barton announces that he's off to have the paper translated by Chan Fu, a noted linguist at the university.

Scarcely has the reporter left when Li See punches a concealed button, opening the swivel door which connects the modest little shop with Wong International. Li See exits as Barton reenters the store through the inadvertently-left-unlocked front door. (At one point or another during the film, either the front door, the swivel door, or both, are left ajar, affording tremendous inconvenience to the otherwise meticulous plans of the criminal mastermind.) Scratching his head at the absence of the "very, very old Li See," Barton hightails it to the university, not noticing that he's being tailed.

Inside his chambers, Wong pulls himself erect and summons Jen Yu (Edward Piel), his chief hatchetman. Torn between elation at his discovery of the existence of the clue and grave displeasure, Wong snarls, "Your men have eyes that see not. Sam Toy left a message; the white newspaper devil has it. He takes it to Chan Fu at the university. You will see that the ticket does not arrive at Fu's."

Once again, the sleeved knife makes its appearance and, once again, Wong reminds the assassin that "This white devil cannot be dealt with as one of our own race." If it looks like an accident, however... Off trots the hatchetman.

In the university elevator Barton catches (the remarkably speedy) Jen Yu with his hand in the reporter's jacket pocket. Excusing his action with a pricelessly lame piece of Harbuveaux dialogue, "A very evil-looking spider was about to visit your pocket," the villain waits until Barton has exited the lift, and then follows him to Chan Fu's Department of Orientology.

Things take an interesting turn as, after a few moments of putting up with the reporter's patronizing questions, Chan Fu (Luke Chan) becomes engaged in a telephone conversation (in Chinese) with Wong!

(The logic of Wong's plans—sending a killer to make sure that the laundry paper never reaches Chan Fu, then advising Chan Fu to expect just such a paper—can only be explained (other than by the usual recourse to finding fault with hack writing) by Wong's profound lack of confidence in his henchman's abilities. For a parallel, but even more disheartening experience, catch Bela's Dr. Zorka (in Universal's *The Phantom Creeps*) trying desperately to take over the world despite the "help" of Jack C. Smith, surely the most inept, disloyal assistant in cinematic history.)

Barton, understandably put off by Chan Fu's sudden, surprising knowledge of the paper, plays it close to the vest and gives the linguist only half the laundry slip for translation. Unfortunately, the half presented to the professor is the same half Wong had espied, so no new information is forthcoming. Before leaving the university, Barton stops to check the entry on Confucius in the very popular *International Encyclopedia*, while Chan Fu meets with the pipe-smoking leader of the Keelat delegation, who advises the linguist that the Province of Keelat would be *very grateful* for any assistance he could render in their efforts in recovering the coins.

The reporter spends the next half-hour "re-uniting cute" with his girlfriend at a lunch counter, while Li See is lurking inobtrusively (to the extent to which it was within Bela Lugosi's power to do *anything* inobtrusively) around the doorway of Sam Toy's laundry. Slipping into the shop, Li See/Wong senses the presence of another, but a casual glance reveals no one. (Actually, there are *two* "others" hiding behind counters: Chan Fu, and an unknown Chinese man. During the remainder of the scene, the three dance about the confines of the little laundry with the precision choreography of the Bolshoi Ballet.)

While Wong pokes about, Barton meets up on the exterior set with McGillicuddy, whose absence from the laundry is explained by yet another local murder: "Seems like they just can't help from killing each other off." (This latest in the series of murders is puzzling. If all Wong has to do to find the last coin is get his hands on Barton's paper, why does he have this last victim killed? And if Wong *didn't* kill him, is the viewer to chalk up the latest murder to coincidence, or is this another facile indictment of the Chinese race (and its bloodthirstiness) by the screenwriters?)

Meanwhile, back at the laundry: Wong, in the course of one of the most cursory searches ever filmed, hears a noise behind a curtain. He finds no one. Moments later, while he's splintering some furniture, *another* noise prompts him to squeeze off a couple of shots through that same curtain; still nothing back there, save for a mortally-wounded ceramic bowl. While Wong is making enough noise to wake the dead, Chan Fu decides that he's had about enough and exits, slamming the front door for all it's worth.

Somehow, the mad Manchurian manages to hear the door above all the racket he's making, and heads out that same door. (Cut to the back room, where the unknown man is seen creeping out from behind that damned curtain. It is hoped that one of the "powers" the 12 coins offer to Fu Wong is that of 20-20 vision.) Outside, the mandarin summons one of his hatchetmen, conveniently skulking at the corner. A shot rings out, and Chan Fu falls, to translate no more. Barton and McGillicuddy abandon the previous corpse to the onlookers and walk the few steps needed to come upon the fresh one. As the Irish cop takes charge, the reporter heads back to the laundry.

Drawn as if by some unseen force, Barton moves to the curtain in the back room. In two shakes, he finds the 12th coin, sitting atop the broken shards of bullet-riddled pottery like a cherry on a sundae. At this very moment, though, he's attacked from behind by the unknown man, who bundles the reporter up in the curtain, seizes the coin, and beats it out the front door. As Barton

Squinting inscrutably through lenseless glasses is Mr. Wong's alter-ego; "very old" Li See, the Chinese coughdropsman.

struggles to free himself, someone else slinks into the laundry; it is the leader of the Keelat delegation (Fred Warren).

The Keelater (Keelatian?) takes his turn plowing through the shirts, while Barton does a bit of his own slinking as far as the front door, where he does an about-face and jauntily "enters" the shop. After a bit of questioning, Barton obtains several useless items of information: the translation ("The Golden Coin of Confucius is Concealed in the Yellow Bowl") he could have used several moments earlier; the identity of the mysterious mandarin—he's Tsi Tung, the head of the Keelat Secret Service(!)—a fact which ultimately will prove to be of no value to him; the theory that the 12th coin, seized by "another Chinese gentleman wearing a dragon ring," is now in the possession of an unfriendly Tong, the existence and efficacy of which he has questioned from the get-go.

Uneasy allies, the two men part company, with Barton headed for "old Li See's," and the mandarin off to God-knows-where. During another tiresome battle of wits between the reporter and the herbalist, a hand (Li See's?) presses a hidden button, and that blasted gong (an *electric* gong?) sounds again, summoning a trio of idle hatchetmen to the swivel door.

Moments before the slaughter can commence, however, in strolls McGillicuddy, who has presumably left the several cadavers spreadeagle in the streets in order to get "some of those

Chinese coughdrops." The ubiquitous Tsi Tung paddles in just behind the conscientious patrolman, thus making it a full house.

After several brain-numbing statements, wherein Tsi Tung avers that "my eyes see something in Li See that is very familiar, but my mind does not recall it" (Does *anyone* really speak this way?), and the herbalist cannily lets it slip that he may or may not know where Keelat is, and may or may not have been there, the secret serviceman moves in for the kill. "You know anything about a man named... Wong?"

Startled at the mention of his own name, Li See spills the coughdrops (but not the beans), but recovers sufficiently to admit that "Wong, uh, no come shop" (as if the name "Wong" were no more common in Chinatown than "Rumplestiltskin" would be in the heart of San Francisco).

This is apparently good enough for Barton and McGillicuddy, who exit, leaving a smirking Tsi Tung with his back to Li See and the emerging hatchetmen. The wily secret-serviceman whips a revolver from the sleeve of his robe, however, and is within a noodle's width of taking them all in when he's jumped from behind by a henchman who has hidden (not surprisingly, considering the French farce earlier in the laundry) behind a counter.

The next scene finds a gloating Wong sucking on his pipe, as Tsi Tung is chained to a wall in (can it be?) the dungeon of the faithless. Things are less what they seem than ever before: the mad Manchurian, it turns out, is neither Li See *nor* Wong, but "Li Chee, the traitor!" Wong does not react well to this revelation and (in what could only have been an unrehearsed bit of business—there is no camera movement to cover the shot), gives the helpless secret agent a good swift kick in the shins!

While this fiendish torture is taking place, Barton and Peg are dining at a chop-suey joint only a short distance away. As they "eat cute," Peg reacts to a pair of hands reaching menacingly over Barton's head from the adjoining booth. One of the hands painfully drops the 12th coin of Confucius onto the reporter's hat before it, its partner, and the rest of the attached human apparatus sink down to the floor in death. The coin, stolen from Barton by the Tong, has come back to him, full circle.

Taking the coin (and the corpse) as their cues to leave, Peg and her fella start a desperate (and perversely comic) exodus from Chinatown. They narrowly avoid being garotted, being on the receiving end of falling masonry and being skewered by a second-story knife-hurler. (This last is prevented only by the unexpected appearance of McGillicuddy, who works one hell of a long day!)

Boarding a cab, they are menaced by a chloroform-soaked-handkerchief-tosser, clinging precariously to the runningboard. Pausing only to shake Peg awake (that tossed hankie managed to put her out momentarily), the two reverse direction and head back *into* Chinatown, after the oriental equivalent of Skelton Knaggs informs them that "Golden coin and man called Wong, you find in back of old Li See shop."

In one of the strangest tableaux of the film, Barton and Peg arrive at Li See's shop, whereupon the newspaperman begins to pound on the front door like a man possessed. A few feet above his head, on the second-floor veranda, stands Wong, who has snuck out for a smoke or something. Wong reacts (as only Bela Lugosi *can* react), and runs into headquarters. Within a heartbeat, Jen Yu enters the herb shop through the swivel door (carelessly leaving it ajar) and creeps to the front door, turning the lock.

Barton and Peg virtually fall through the now unlocked door, only to be attacked by Wong's lackey. The plucky reporter and the villain wrestle together until Peg whacks the bad guy over the head with a nasty-looking pestle. (Peg's successful beaning of the heavy is a refreshing departure from the B-movie convention which demanded that the heroine, in seeking to help the hero out of some tussle, would accidentally brain him at least once in the course of the film. In not adhering to this most sacred of traditions, Nina Howatt probably felt that she was striking a blow for creativity.)

Noticing the open swivel door, the plucky couple muster their reserve and enter. After meandering up a staircase and down a brick corridor, the two are (momentarily) separated from each other per standard formula, only to "meet up again cute" for the (thankfully) last time. A pushed button causes a sliding door to do so, and they confront Wong's niece, Moonflower, and her maid (whose indulgence in a little reverse racism—"Do not talk to the white devil!"—echoes Wong's earlier slurs).

Having demonstrated her unease with her uncle's methods throughout the picture, Moonflower agrees, despite her servant's warning, to lead the crusaders to Wong's *sanctum sanctorum.* As he follows the troubled girl, Barton pauses to secret the 12th coin of Confucius among the coils of a handy ceramic dragon.

Even as the foolhardy three are wending their way toward him, the redoubtable mandarin is seen heating an impressive branding-iron in a flaming cauldron. Despite his having seen Barton at the entrance to his shop moments earlier, Wong is floored when the sliding door opens at Moonflower's touch and the reporter enters the dungeon of the faithless.

With the arrival of a group of hatchetmen (including a revived and cheesed-off Jen Yu), however, all hope of rescue or escape is lost. Both the pestle and the niece are removed. Somewhat emboldened by these developments, Wong cracks cryptic: "Sometimes politeness is a virtue; again it is but a better part of judgment." (Whatever the hell that means!)

Fastening the newspaperpersons to nearby available surfaces, Wong gets down to business and begins laying on the giddy aphorisms mercilessly: "Time came before man; there is plenty of it. Haste is such a futile gesture..." Before the mandarin can do his worst and bore the fettered good guys to death, the gong sounds again. As expected, Wong jumps a foot and a half, and then leads his minions out of the dungeon, to investigate.

In another classic blunder, though, the would-be ruler of Keelat has failed to notice that he has imprisoned his enemies within wriggling distance (cf. Woody Allen's *Broadway Danny Rose*) of a telephone. Maneuvering to within arms-reach of the instrument, Barton phones for help, *not* from the police (all those expensive uniforms and cars), but from the newspaper office.

In the mastermind's absence, Barton gives the skinny to Brandon, his boss. Another bizarre touch has Brandon, heart-in-mouth, anxiously asking the operator if the call (from Barton) has been cut off. When informed that his party is "still on the line," the editor abruptly slams down *his* receiver, and storms out the door.

Wong re-enters the dungeon, intending to search the reporter for the coin. (Peg: "Come in and cut yourself a piece of throat.") Barton is untied, patted down fruitlessly (why are *his* shoes not removed?), then affixed to a wall. Upstairs, in the herb shop, McGillicuddy (yes, he's *still* on duty) noses around, looking for more Chinese coughdrops. The policeman inadvertently strikes the button controlling the swivel door, but fails to take note of the now-gaping entrance. A moment later, the stalwart cop is elbowed aside as the city editor and a group of plainclothesmen hie it through the door, which *they* had noticed in a flash.

Yet another gong alerts Wong, who is poised to do vile things to Peg's nails. Dispatching his flunkies to deal with the intruders, he chooses an even more wicked-looking probe with which to work on the heroine. The suits overpower the henchmen, however, and force open the sliding door. The mad Manchurian is caught once again with an expression of profound surprise on his map and is plugged at least twice during the brief flurry of gunfire that follows. Fu Wong sinks to the floor, his hand clutching desperately at the doorknob.

Barton, Peg, and Tsi Tung are released, banal chatter and painfully ungrammatical statements are made, and the camera cuts to Wong's hand which, through it all, is *still* grasping that handle. The hand finally falls, lifeless; the danger to Keelat is at an end.

Fans familiar with both films regard *Mysterious Mr. Wong* as nothing more than a vest-pocket version of *The Mask of Fu Manchu.* Whereas the two pictures trace both the movements of a Chinese criminal genius towards his goal of domination and/or destruction, and the efforts of the forces of Caucasian law and order to thwart that goal, their respective treatments are as vastly different as a top-notch Broadway musical is from your average high-school production. No savvy contemporary movie-goer, however, would have dreamt of finding an iota of MGM-type gloss under the Monogram logo. As Keeler's story was intended as a cheap vehicle for Lugosi (the operative word being "cheap"), it was inherently unfair to Monogram for the audience to expect a silk purse from a sow's ear. Then again, as the film had been shot to lure as many takers as possible to the box office, it was equally unfair to the audience for Monogram to cadge pennies on cut-rate imitation than to spend the same pittance on low-budget originality.

The poverty-row studio did what it could with the monies on hand; budget apart, it would have taken a more creative designer than E.R. Hickson to make the public forget Cedric Gibbons' sets. More pertinent to villainy than mere flats, however, were devices of pain and torment. Fu Manchu's incredibly varied instruments of torture—the maddening peal of the giant bell, the inexorable progress of the "silver fingers," the horrifying descent into the alligator pit—are scaled down to Fu Wong's terrifying flaming cauldron in the dungeon of the faithless, the craftily concealed chamber of the rats, and the extremely painful kick in the shins.

Saving additional dollars was most likely part of the enforced duty of the screenwriters, as well. By having most of the 12 coins within Wong's grasp at the outset (and the others readily available from the local citizenry), expensive establishing scenes at museums or in exotic, ominously lit tombs could be avoided

There is a downside to all this cost conservation, however, apart from the obvious results visible on the screen. If Wong's mad plans to control the destiny of Keelat seem a bit cheesey in comparison with Fu Manchu's desire to annihilate the cursed white race, dogged adaptation of the original story must be blamed; after all, it costs no more to talk about taking over the world than it does to talk about ruling Keelat. (Still, if you pay all that money for screen rights to a novel, you may as well adhere to as much of its plot as you can.)

The Keeler work fails to provide sufficient dramatic weight to its cinematic child; coins aren't as inherently romantic or exciting as are other archaeological artifacts. At the end of the MGM opus, Karloff's evil genius, masked with the legacy of Genghis Khan and waving that impressive golden scimitar, creates an unforgettable picture of frenzy and megalomania. One can only envision Lugosi's mandarin—successful in attaining all the objects he covets—parading in front of a Monogram-sized group of oriental cutthroats and declaiming madly, all the while jingling his bag of coins(!)

The original novel can't take all the heat, though. A good chunk of the confusion must be chalked up to Messrs. Levensen and Harbuveaux, as well as to Ms. Howatt. One of the most priceless moments of illogic serves to emphasize the significance of the title of the film itself. While trussed up like a Peking duck, Tsi Tung (as stated earlier) lets it fly that Lugosi's character is *not* Wong, is *not* Li See, but is "Li Chee, the traitor!"

This admittedly jaw-dropping revelation opens the (swivel) door to some undeniably perturbing questions. If Lugosi's character is *not* Wong, why does he strut around blathering about the "ancient and honorable house" to his niece? Doesn't *she* know that this guy is not Wong? If "Wong" is the criminal mastermind the screenplay would have us believe, why does he spend most of his time in disguise, selling herbs? Is the persona of Li See the villain's best means of obtaining information from the locals, or does the "rightful ruler of Keelat" actually need the money he makes through the sale of candy and Chinese coughdrops?

The racist statements uttered by both sides in the course of the film are typical of thirties' sentiments: ethnic humor had been popular in vaudeville, and the propensity to view blacks as lazy and shiftless, Irish as drunkards, etc., survived this form of entertainment to take solid root in film for several decades to come. Over at Fox, William Demarest would later refer to Warner Oland's Charlie Chan as "Chop Suey," and no one (who wasn't Chinese, at any rate) would think a thing of it.

Mask of Fu Manchu went back into production after a wrap in order to deal with myriad complaints about ethnic slurs and sexual suggestiveness; there is no evidence that *The Mysterious Mr. Wong* received any such notoriety, or underwent any such postproduction adjustments. (Trem

Carr and the rest of the gang over at Monogram would have undoubtedly been tickled pink at any media mention of their oriental epic.) The picture was made (to use a popular phrase) "in simpler times," and to attempt to ascribe '90's sensitivities to films, plays, or literature produced over a half-century ago is inane. In the larger framework of the screenplay, however, any such verbal peccadillos exist amidst a more disturbing factor; no one—from the hero and heroine to the cop on the beat to Mr. Wong, himself—has any regard at all for the value of oriental life.

Mysterious Mr. Wong could have benefited from some tighter editing; the innumerable treks between the laundry and the herb shop do little other than than to pad the running time. At the same time, Harry Neuman's camera demonstrates more mobility than a picture shot for this kind of money deserves. Given the shoestring budget and the galloping shooting schedule (eight days), Neuman manages to imbue the film's "spookier" moments (few as there are) with decent lighting and even pulls off a tracking shot around an existing wall (even if it is in the damn laundry).

Surprisingly (or maybe *not* so surprisingly), there is virtually no music in the film. Apart from a few snatches under the titles, and some perfunctory stock insertions at odd moments, there is so little music in the film that one cannot help but to think that Abe Meyer's credit as musical director must have been a cushy union deal.

While William Nigh didn't specialize in films with a oriental basis, he did direct more than his fair share of them. After helming MGM's glossy "A", *Mr. Wu,* Nigh's "oriental magic" was divided between Bela (*Mysterious Mr. Wong* and *Black Dragons*) and Boris (all of his Hugh Wiley/ Mr. Wong features), but always at Monogram.

The director, who had entered films in 1911—first as an actor, then as a writer/ director—died in 1955.

In a cast populated by poverty-row regulars, only the three leads (and, given the narrow parameters the role offers, Robert Emmett O'Connor, whose Officer McGillicuddy has nearly as much screen-time as Peg) deliver the goods with any nuance or impact.

O'Connor entered the movies in late 1909, after a long stint with the circus, and a subsequent career in vaudeville. Initially an extra, later almost exclusively a cop, the actor made his most indelible impression late in 1935, as the brogueless Henderson, the policeman bedeviled by the Marx Brothers in their classic *A Night at the Opera.* (O'Connor: "I'm Henderson, plainclothesman." Groucho: "You look more like an old-clothes man to me.") The husky Irish actor made a good living refining a stereotype, and the vast majority of his more than 50 films saw him wearing not only an official scowl, but a badge as well. Working mainly for the majors, O'Connor played across the field, appearing in such disparate films as 1931's *Public Enemy* (opposite Jimmy Cagney), and 1944's *Whistling in Brooklyn* (opposite Red Skelton's continuing character of "The Fox"). The quintessential Irish cop checked into the Big Station House in 1962.

Not quite pretty enough to land a lead in the big studios, Arline Judge (1912-1974) usually headed the supporting cast roster. Her specialties—the other woman, the ingenue's confidante, a gal "just like one of the guys"—enabled her to run the gamut from raucous comedy (*Girl Crazy,* 1932) to "women's" pictures (the epitome of which being the near-mythic tearjerker, *Valiant Is the Word for Carrie*). With her character "types" firmly embedded in thirties styles and mores, Judge saw her film work decrease as the decades passed; her last appearance of note was in Preston Sturges' *Mad Wednesday,* starring veteran silent comic, Harold Lloyd.

The role of Peg was Judge's only real genre contribution, obtained at the last minute as Judge stepped in to replace Wheeler and Woolsey perennial foil/love interest, Dorothy Lee. The actress gives Peg's derivative and sketchy dialogue the drive it needs, and the fact that the humor of the bickering newspersons' many "cute" encounters still holds up today, is a tip of the hat to both Judge's and Wallace Ford's talent and appeal.

Mysterious Mr. Wong was not Wallace Ford's first genre film effort, nor was it his first (nor last) picture with "Mr. Dracula," Bela Lugosi. Born Sam Grundy in England, in 1897, and moving to the United States during the twenties, Ford quickly became known around Hollywood

Among the most unusual (and least expensive) of Mr. Wong's torture devices is the dreaded Giant Chinese Nail File; Peg the Stalwart keeps up a brave front.

as a warm and dependable character artist. With a career spanning four decades (he died in 1966), the diminutive actor (like Arline Judge) brought an innately likable quality to his many roles.

Appearing in such mainstream hits as *The Informer*, *The Last Hurrah*, and *Harvey* (among dozens of others), Ford was equally at home in the mystery/horror field, working with such dark giants as Tod Browning (in *Freaks*), Lon Chaney, Jr. (in *The Mummy's Tomb*), and George Zucco (in *The Mummy's Hand*). In addition to appearing with Claude Rains (in the decidedly non-horrific *The Man Who Reclaimed His Head*), and with Boris Karloff (in the equally monster-less *The Lost Patrol*), he made three low-budget shockers with Mr. Lugosi: Columbia's *Night of Terror* (1933), *Mysterious Mr. Wong,* and *The Ape Man* (1943).

Unlike the numerous other films which exploit his name but stint on his characterization, *Mysterious Mr. Wong* is pure, vintage Lugosi. Despite the low budget and the illogic, Mr. Wong allows Bela free rein to snarl venomously, to mug outrageously, and to chew scenery with the throttle wide open. In the light of subsequent modest parts, humbling experiences, and wasted, red herring assignments, it is a pleasure to witness the proud actor clearly enjoying one of his few genuine starring roles in the burgeoning horror field he had once had all to himself.

It's fun, but ultimately futile, to debate Bela's portrayal of the Chinese mandarin. His trademark accent is admittedly no more at home with a character named Wong than with an Arthur Perry or a James Brewster. (On the up-side, the mad Manchurian's improbably florid speeches *do* receive more attention than they deserve, tripping—forgive the pun—as they do across the Hungarian's tongue.) To quibble, however, is to miss the point; Lugosi was Wong because **he was Bela Lugosi**—a name, a unique personality, a box office draw—not because Monogram needed an actor to emulate an oriental.

Criticism that Bela's mandarin is drawn in strokes too broad to be realistic is likewise bizarre. As the most reprehensible modern real-life villains (bent, for real, on worldwide domination and ethnic subjugation) have displayed (to say the least) type "A" personalities, the proposed portrait of an *understated* megalomaniac is too ludicrous for words. The role of Wong demanded to be played operatically, and Bela barnstormed with all his heart.

With very few exceptions (Joseph, in Val Lewton's *The Body Snatcher,* perhaps), most of the roles that came Lugosi's way were etched in only black and white. Neither the genre with which he was normally associated, nor the various studios with which he became affiliated attached much importance to nuance. Monsters and bogeymen were considered the provinces of children and the young-at-heart, and so, the powers-that-were felt (with some justification) that the simpler the former were kept, the happier the latter would remain.

Lugosi would play an oriental (a Eurasian, actually), only once more, in the 1936 Victory serial, *Shadow of Chinatown.* Victor Poten is, in the opinion of most Lugosiphiles, a more complex role for Bela than Wong. With more rudimentary (and clearly delineated) motivation, Victor Poten's hatred of the white race (*and* the yellow race as well, doing Fu Manchu one better) allows Bela not only the opportunity to plot and scheme as a sinister mastermind, but also the chance to trade quips and punches as a no-nonsense action villain. Ironically, the Eurasian madman is foiled time and again, not only by the occidental good guys, but also by *Mysterious Mr. Wong* alumnus, James B. Leong, playing a detective named Wong(!)

Mysterious Mr. Wong was the first of several times that Bela would be called upon to play a "double role" in a film. Here, as in *Dark Eyes of London,* Lugosi's true character has a disguised alter-ego, who acts as a legitimate "front" to the police and the law-abiding gentry. Whereas the benevolent Dr. Dearborn serves a true dramatic purpose—it is his Institute for the Blind that keeps the doomed marks coming for Dr. Orlof's insurance scheme—the use of English actor O.B. Clarence's voice for the disguised Lugosi denies the latter complete authorship of the portrayal.

On the other hand, in *Wong,* despite no clear cut dramatic reason for the herbalist's existence, Lugosi gives it his (own) all in an attempt to provide "old Li See" with a different cadence than that of the Mad Manchurian. (When all is said and done, the most impressive display of Bela's vocal technique must remain his gruff rumblings as Ygor in *Son of* and *Ghost of Frankenstein.*) In neither film, however, is the role a true "double," as clever as is the subterfuge; Bela is playing one man playing another. This is not a dismissal; in *Dark Eyes of London,* the (in effect) *mimed* delineation of the saintly Dearborn allows Bela the chance to prove that, apart from his "imperfect" English, his capacity for creating a character from mannerisms alone was masterful.

Murder By Television is the only opportunity to study Lugosi putting in a double shift as two separate individuals. Starring as twin brothers, the actor never quite brings it off, due to no fault of his own. The script keeps the existence of the benevolent brother a secret until the evil one is done in, thus depriving the critical viewer of a fair chance at comparison. To compound the felony, the evil brother poses as the good one for the lion's share of the film; for all intents and purposes, the screenwriters have Lugosi playing the same role twice.

Wong did nothing to upset the oriental apple cart, and made enough of a profit to insure that more of the same would be forthcoming at reasonable intervals. Before the decade would end, fans of the Yellow Peril would be treated to *Chinatown After Dark, Law of the Tongs, Secrets of Wu Sin, Secrets of Chinatown, Captured in Chinatown, Hong Kong Nights, I Cover Chinatown,* Lugosi's Victory serial, and, of course, *The Mysterious Mr. Wong.*

Bela's mad mandarin is definitely worth a look. His first effort at Monogram uncannily (and depressingly) foreshadows his extended series of programmers at that studio a decade later. The lethargic direction, illogical story elements, penny-pinching production values: all the "qualities" so typically Monogram are present here, already full blown and ready to go.

Whether eagerly viewed by fans of the Lugosi/Monogram "canon" (and thus savored), or grumpily endured by aficionados of Bela's (limited) major studio output (and thus deplored), *Mysterious Mr. Wong* remains an interesting, if decidedly minor, foray into a still popular genre by an ever popular star.

The Raven

(1935)

by Gary J. Svehla

CREDITS: Director: Louis Friedlander (Lew Landers); Associate Producer: David Diamond; Screenplay: David Boehm; Suggested by the poem *The Raven* and the short story *The Pit and The Pendulum* by Edgar Allan Poe; Director of Photography: Charles Stumar; Film Editor: Albert Akst; Editorial Supervision: Maurice Pivar; Dialogue Director: Florence Enright; Art Director: Albert S. D'Agostino; Assistant Directors: Scott Beal & Victor Noerdlinger; Sound Supervisor: Gilbert Kurland; Musical Score: Clifford Vaughan, Heinz Roemheld & Y. Franke Harling; Dance Staged by Theodore Kosloff; Makeup: Jack P. Pierce; Released July 22, 1935 by Universal Pictures, 61 minutes

CAST: Karloff...Edmond Bateman, Bela Lugosi...Dr. Richard Vollin, Lester Matthews...Dr. Jerry Halden, Irene Ware...Jean Thatcher, Samuel S. Hinds...Judge Thatcher, Spencer Charters...Colonel Grant, Inez Courtney...Mary Burns, Ian Wolfe...Pinky Burns, Maidel Turner...Harriet Grant, and Arthur Hoyt, Jonathan Hale, Walter Miller, Cyril Thornton, Nina Golden, Raine Bennett, Bud Osborne, Al Ferguson, Madeline Talcott

"You will live in this place *forever*! It will be the perfect marriage, the perfect love. You will *never* be separated, *never*! Forever and ever (tortured laughter emanates from the demonic Bela Lugosi, his arms flapping to and fro)... What a torture, what a *delicious* torture... Greater than Poe! Poe can say that I have done it! Poe—you *are* avenged!"

Bela Lugosi as Dr. Richard Vollin at the climax of Universal's 1935 classic *The Raven*, one of the few movies in this volume where the talents of Lugosi and the craftsmanship of the production merge to create a truly satisfying viewing experience in a classic horror film production.

Even though billed second to KARLOFF, LUGOSI (paid half the salary that Karloff earned) is truly the dominant star of *The Raven* and his performance literally towers over Karloff's.

After the success of *Frankenstein* and *Dracula* in the early thirties, Universal decided to humanize their monsters by creating flesh-and-blood characters for the king of vampires and the man-made monster to portray. Using icon horror writer Edgar Allan Poe as the catalyst, Universal first unleashed *The Black Cat* in 1934, the heavily censored and recut Edgar Ulmer vehicle. Long considered dense, dark, and perverse, *The Black Cat* allowed Karloff and Lugosi the opportunity to terrify the audience by creating living, breathing, *human* fiends. While Satanist Karloff (Poelzig) played the obvious villain, psychologist Dr. Werdegast (Lugosi) does sadistically skin alive his arch-rival in the bowels of his home in the film's climax. However, in *The Black Cat* both actors shine and neither performance dominates over the other.

However, one year later, in 1935's *The Raven*, Bela Lugosi has the opportunity to outshine his rival-in-horror Boris Karloff by submitting one of his most peculiar and yet tailor-made signature horror performances, some might say his finest screen performance, period.

A decade later fans might complain of Lugosi's consistent *supporting* performances and reduced screen time, or his major starring vehicles in *substandard* poverty row productions; *The Raven* is truly the vehicle by which to assess the talents and contributions that Bela Lugosi made to the horror film genre, for here all the component elements congeal to produce a bonafide classic movie: good production values and a hefty budget, a worthy supporting cast with the marvelous

Boris Karloff as costar, well-paced (if not visually inspiring) direction by Louis Friedlander (soon to be known as Lew Landers), and a fine, literate script which allows Lugosi to have some of the greatest lines of dialog in his entire career.

THE STORY:

Dr. Richard Vollin (Lugosi), a surgeon retired from practice who does research by day and erects a monument to Edgar Allan Poe (a dungeon of torture in his home's basement) by night, agrees to operate on a young dancer who is seriously injured in a car accident. After the accident Vollin is physically attracted to this sensuous young woman, Jean Thatcher (Irene Ware), who honors the doctor by choreographing a tribute to Poe's *The Raven.* After the performance, the girl's father, the respected Judge Thatcher (Samuel S. Hinds), observes first-hand the infatuation that Vollin feels toward his daughter. Visiting Vollin and voicing his disapproval, reminding Vollin that Jean is engaged to Vollin's assistant Dr. Jerry Halden (Lester Matthews), Thatcher warns Vollin to *not* see his daughter anymore. Vollin reacts violently.

Escaped murderer Edmond Bateman (Karloff) goes to Vollin's home to have his face altered, pathetically stating that ugly people do ugly deeds (besides, the criminal needs a disguise). Quickly improvising a scenario whereby the surgeon will use Bateman to enact revenge upon the Thatcher family and fiance Jerry, Vollin attempts to enlist Bateman's help to do deeds of torture and murder. Bateman refuses. Vollin agrees to alter his face, disfiguring Bateman horribly, promising to restore his former looks after first performing these horrendous deeds.

Staging an elaborate party at his home, inviting Judge Thatcher, Jean and Jerry, and several other couples, Vollin entertains the guests and then at night uses Bateman to carry out his grand scheme: torture and murder Judge Thatcher using his pit and the pendulum knife, and kill lovers Jean and Jerry in the torture room where the walls come together to crush victims to death. Vollin feels that by destroying the objects that are torturing him, by ripping this torture out of his life forever, that he will once again be free from his obsessions. In a serial-style ending, Bateman sacrifices his own life to free the innocent victims and forces Vollin into the torture room whereby Vollin dies an agonizing death.

The success of Bela Lugosi's performance in *The Raven* can be boiled down to three major components, each to be fully discussed here—Vollin's obsession, Vollin's vision of himself as god, and Vollin's split personality: aristocratic and dominating doctor vs. ranting/raving lunatic. Whether one points an accusing finger and declares this performance over-the-top, stilted and theatrical, or whether one steps up and declares passionately how this performance is focused, mesmerizing, and top-of-his-craft, Bela Lugosi's major filmic contributions are all seen here in the best light: his dominating and romantic presence, his uncanny ability to weave a web of intrigue using only his gesturings and his eyes, and his unique European method of delivering a line of dialogue, sometimes spitting out the syllables in rapid-fire sputterings, other times emphasizing and drawing out syllables for the most sinister effect. The artistry of Lugosi, for both the critic and the fan, appears in its most fully realized context here.

First, let us examine the split personality of Dr. Vollin in *The Raven* to isolate one reason for Lugosi's brilliance here. Often times Vollin projects a specific personality for manipulative purposes, but as the story unravels, it becomes more and more apparent that Vollin is a "stark, staring lunatic," as Judge Thatcher calls him, and that he erupts into egotistic, vile outrages which are beyond his control.

For instance, the beginning of the movie projects Vollin as aristocratic doctor, a man of obvious skill and importance, a man who calls his own shots in life and kowtows to no man. "The Raven is my talisman," Vollin says.

"Curious talisman, bird of ill omen, symbol of death!" Mr. Chapman responds.

"Death is my talisman, Mr. Chapman. The one indestructible force, the one certain thing in an uncertain universe... death," Vollin declares staring off into space.

A posed publicity shot featuring Karloff and Lugosi falling asleep on the set as they read the script for The Raven.

"Dr. Vollin, the museum that I represent will pay you a very handsome price for your Poe collection."

Vollin, though interested, is tired and next time promises to show Chapman the models he built, down in his cellar. "Yes, I've actually built, you know, several of those torture and horror devices that Poe described in his tales..."

"Imagine building those things—a very curious hobby."

Vollin's eyes are intense but a million miles away. "It's more—than a hobby." A dashing host, an entertaining eccentric, but also a man who abruptly informs his guest that it is time for him to leave.

On the lam, escaped criminal and murderer Edmond Bateman (Karloff) visits the home of Vollin in order that "I want that you should—change my face!"

Vollin agrees to do the deed if Bateman first does a favor for him. Bateman asks, "Like what?"

"Torture and murder," Vollin nonchalantly answers.

"That's not my line. My line is—," Bateman is interrupted.

Vollin, now growing more emotional, reveals he knows the entire criminal history of Bateman. "You shot your way out of San Quentin—two guards are dead. And in a bank in Arizona a man's face was mutilated, burned, a cashier of the bank."

Bateman, raising his voice for the first time, "Well, he tried to get me into trouble. I told him to keep his mouth shut. He gets the gag out of his mouth and starts yelling for the police. I had the acetylene torch in my hand."

Vollin, excited, rising from his chair, gleeful, states, "And so you put the *burning* torch into his *face*, into his *eyes*!"

"Sometimes you can't help things like that!" Bateman responds.

"This job I want done is in your line, Bateman. Accept my word for it!" Vollin orders.

This sequence reveals the dual nature of Vollin: a skillful, intelligent doctor, but also a man who delights in tales (and is knowledgeable) of torture and mayhem and plans to use Bateman to execute those deeds Vollin can only concoct in his mind.

The pensive, manipulative, and evil genius of Vollin comes through as Bateman continues. "I'll tell you something, Doc! Ever since I was born, everybody looks at me and says—you're ugly. Makes me feel mean."

Disinterested at first, Vollin mutters, "Why are you telling me this? I'm not interested in your life story."

Bateman continues: "I'm saying Doc, maybe because I look ugly, maybe if a man looks ugly, he does ugly things!"

Vollin solemnly digests the importance of these words and says, "*You* are saying something *profound*. A man with a face so *hideously ugly*—"

Bateman states, "Don't ask me to do this job for you, Doc! I don't wanna do them things no more. Fix me so I'll look good, then maybe—"

"All right, Bateman!" Vollin agrees.

Even though the good-hearted Bateman still refuses to commit torture and murder for Vollin, Vollin understands only too well that if he makes Bateman monstrous and ugly, that Bateman will be more easily motivated to do horrendous deeds, or will do whatever is necessary to be changed back to his natural appearance. Vollin understands that by controlling Bateman's appearance he can also control Bateman's actions and deeds.

Thus, this sequence again reveals the dual nature of Vollin, an evil genius yet a man who delights in torture and violence, a man who becomes visibly excited by the sight and thought of pain.

Not a plastic surgeon, Vollin instead intends to perform a ten-minute operation by operating on the nerve ends of the seventh cranial nerve, the nerve that lies in the back of the head, and the one that controls the muscles of the face. "If something happens to these nerve ends, it alters your expression. In other words, *I*, who knows what to do with these nerve ends, can make you look anyway *I* choose. Now loosen your collar, lie down."

After the operation, Vollin removes the bandages from Bateman's head and the audience sees that half of his face has been hideously paralyzed. Bateman, who cannot see himself, states, "It's hard... to talk!... I can feel something's the matter!... My mouth, I want to see myself."

In a ridiculously cruel gesture, Vollin dismisses himself from the operating room and leaves Bateman alone sitting before six full-length curtains. From outside, Vollin opens each of the six curtains, one at a time, revealing a full length mirror underneath. Vollin suddenly sees the result of Vollin's knife work, all in multiple, mirror reflected images of his disfigured self. "No!" Bateman screams, pulling out his pistol, and shooting out the mirror panels.

Suddenly a hideous cackling of insane laughter echoes throughout the room. From above, behind a protective metal grid, the face of Vollin appears laughing wildly out of control, cruelly flaunting his poor victim's misfortune and signaling to the audience the dual Jekyll-Hyde nature of his also fragmented personality.

Later, after Bateman calms down, the face of Lugosi again appears at the metal grid. "I can't use my hand to do it. *Your* hand is used to torture. *Your* hand must do it. *My* brain... *your* hand. Speak up, Bateman! Do you wish to remain the ugly monster that you are? Then you will do this job for me."

The blending of Lugosi's cruel yet aristocratic personality juxtaposed to these sequences of utter insanity only compound the dual personality of Richard Vollin and his lapses between cool control and ragdoll maniac.

Even at the climax of a conversation with Judge Thatcher, the father of the young woman he saved from death, he explodes, "You driveling fool! Stop talking!" And later, after inviting Judge Thatcher, his beautiful daughter Jean, and her fiance to his house for the weekend, he takes Judge Thatcher aside and states, "I am sorry for all the stupid things I said to you the other day. I want you please to forget."

Judge Thatcher, realizing the manipulative nature of Vollin, states, "One can't forget a man saying—"

"But I was under a terrible strain," Vollin, smiling, calmly apologizing.

"Well, I suppose a man...," the Judge momentarily softens.

"Oh, you *do* forgive me," Vollin now delighted, rushes the Judge away.

In another mood swing, at the film's conclusion, as Vollin has Judge Thatcher manacled to his slab with his pendulum knife quickly and fatally descending, the Judge inquires, "What are you trying to do to me?"

Smiling, Vollin answers, "Torture you!"

"*Try* to be sane, Vollin," the judge implores.

And Vollin erupts into his violent histrionics, "I'm the sanest man that ever lived. But I will not be tortured. I tear torture out of myself by torturing you! (laughs) Fifteen minutes... Torture waiting, waiting! Death will be sweet, Judge Thatcher!"

Moments later, setting up a forced marriage ceremony so he can marry Jean Thatcher, Vollin's mind is too far gone with which to be reasoned. Even Jean warns, "It's no use... look at his eyes," realizing that this poor devil has gone over the brink one time too many.

Vollin continues to rant and rave: "I'll soon be rid of my torture, rid of it, and I'll be the sanest man who ever lived!"

Granted, when Lugosi plays insanity, he literally howls. His eyes bulge outward, his smile turns diabolical, and his words sputter and spurt in violent outrage. But Lugosi is not chewing up the scenery. His performance goes over the top as a direct contrast to his "sanity-rigidly-held-tight" performance whereby the good Dr. Vollin acts callously and coolly, logic and reason overcoming his hot-driven emotions underneath. The outward Dr. Vollin is a rubber band wound so tight that the viewer understands that when the band snaps it will spin out of control dramatically and painfully. Just as the Vollin who quotes Poe's *The Raven* is so stiff, unemotional, and under control, the Vollin who cackles, bugs out his eyes, and threatens with dynamic verbal outbursts is the mirror image opposite. Lugosi may not perform a true textbook psychotic here in *The Raven*, but his performance of passion always boiling just under the surface and which ultimately spill over displays Bela Lugosi at his finest. Lugosi can be subtle when the performance requires subtlety, but here, Lugosi fires off a fantastic performance of ballistic intensity and carries it off well.

Next let us examine Vollin's vision of himself as a god. Not a god in the sense that he can create life or have a supernatural influence over his surroundings, but a god in the sense of being center of his universe, a man who feels himself superior to all those around him, a man who depends on no one and yet manipulates people to do his bidding for self-serving purposes.

In the beginning of the movie, while speaking to museum curator Mr. Chapman, Vollin

The Raven is truly the vehicle by which to assess the talents and contributions that Bela Lugosi made to the horror film genre.

is interrupted by the telephone at home by colleague Dr. Halden, then by father Judge Thatcher, involving a serious car accident in which Thatcher's daughter Jean was involved. The three doctor team is stymied and only the reclusive Vollin may be able to help—if he chooses to help. "Yes, Dr. Halden—you know I've retired from actual practice and am only doing research. Who's on the case? Well, I'm satisfied... they can handle it as well as I can." When Judge Thatcher replaces Halden on the phone to make his personal plea for his daughter's life, Vollin is adamant: "...that's very flattering, but no! *No!*...I'm sorry" and he abruptly hangs up the phone.

Judge Thatcher, refusing to accept no for an answer, drives out to Vollin's home to personally make a plea. "You can't say no!"

"I have said it," Vollin icily responds.

"I'll pay you any amount of money," Thatcher implores the surgeon.

"Money means nothing to me!" Vollin continues.

"But someone is dying... your obligation as a member of the medical profession—" Thatcher further adds.

But Vollin is cold as ice and seemingly unmoved by Thatcher's pleas. "I respect no such obligation. I am alone and to myself!" Vollin states.

"My daughter is dying," the Judge begs.

"Death—hasn't the same significance for me as it has for you," Vollin adds eccentrically.

But Thatcher hits a nerve when he mentions the team of doctors specifically stated "you're the only one" who can save Jean.

Dramatically rising from his seat and smiling, Vollin beams, "So *they* say I am the *only* one... Very well, I will go!!" Very obviously a plea for decency and the saving of a human life means far less than having the respect of his colleagues.

Immediately after the operation, Jean is sprawled out seductively on the couch which sits below the elevated tier where proud surgeon Vollin dramatically plays at his organ. Almost cooing, Jean mutters, "You're not only a great surgeon but a great musician too... You're almost not a man but—"

"A god—with a taint of human emotions," Vollin finishes her thought.

Notice the manner in which Lugosi and Karloff perform their scenes together; the cinematographer makes Vollin the magnificent god compared to the lowly, street punk Bateman. Working against the stereotype that Karloff is the horror king, Bateman nervously seems to be hiding inside his own skin when he knocks on Vollin's door. When the servant answers the door, Vollin is standing in the background on the second step of his home's staircase, visually erect, towering above the criminal Bateman who enters nervously. In those sequences whereby Bateman implores Vollin to change his face, as quick sequences cross-cut from Lugosi to Karloff, notice what the cinematographer has purposely done. Whenever filming Lugosi, the scene is a low-angle shot looking up at Vollin who appears master of his domain. In those shots of Karloff, a high angle stance is taken looking down at the sniveling, petty murderer. Lugosi stands fully elongated, his good posture and long, lanky figure demonstrate that inner confidence dominates his personality. Karloff, at times almost mimicking his character of the Monster from *Bride of Frankenstein*, ambles about very animal-like, almost simian in certain sequences. Karloff's Bateman is hunched over, seemingly succumbing to the weight of the world. He always appears afraid as though he fears the police are ready to barge in from the next room. Lugosi, who seemingly seizes upon a plan by which to manipulate Bateman and force the sadist to do his bidding, always appears calm and under control compared to the antsy Karloff. Lugosi tells Bateman to lie down on the operating table, and after the operation, Bateman is seated in a chair as the towering Lugosi loosens his bandages. And when revealing Bateman's disfigured body to him via the six mirrors, he appears above Bateman appearing omniscient from the round metal grid area near the room's ceiling from which Vollin pontificates godlike decrees to captive and crippled Bateman. "Bateman, are you ready to do it for me!" Vollin orders.

Edgar Allan Poe is the god figure in Vollin's existence and Vollin sees Poe as his symbol of what a man must strive for in life. Toward the end of the film, at his private party in his home, Vollin is asked about his interpretation of Poe's *The Raven*. Vollin, enjoying the opportunity to lecture about Poe, answers, "I will tell you. Poe was a great genius. And like all great geniuses there was in him the will to do something big, constructive in the world—he had the brain to do it. *But* he fell in love. The name was Lenore—'Longing for the lost Lenore.' Someone took her away from him. When a man of genius is denied his great love, he goes mad. His brain has been cleared to do his work, has been tortured, so he begins to think of torture, torture for those who have tortured him!" Clearly, Vollin is not describing Poe but himself, and like Poe he considers himself a genius and a great man. As he stated earlier, a god with the taint of human emotions.

Vollin's divine confidence is finally illustrated in the sequence where he first takes his servant Bateman down to the cellar to show off his torture devices. Especially proud of his set based upon *Pit and the Pendulum*, Vollin points out the slab on which a man is manacled as the knife/pendulum mechanism lowers itself within 15 minutes to penetrate the heart of the victim.

Using himself as demonstration model, Vollin lies on the slab and tells Bateman about the manacle switch which he immediately activates, thus literally holding Vollin captive. "Got ya!!" Bateman gleefully smiles, thinking the hunter has finally been captured by the hunted, that the tables have been turned.

Yet surprisingly, Vollin is still confident and calm, unperturbed by the changing course of events. Calm and smiling, "Come on, Bateman." Growing more forceful and demanding, "Release me. Release me, Bateman!" Quickly regaining his composure, Vollin devilishly smiles and utters, "And please to remember, should anything happen to me, you will remain the *hideous* monster you *are*. Come on, Bateman." With that final leverage which Vollin holds over Bateman, Bateman releases the captive madman. "It's all quite simple, huh, Bateman!" Vollin beams triumphantly. A god has no reason to fear, not even a murderer.

Interestingly enough, Vollin's position of wealth and power (not just as surgeon but as an independent, wealthy, and aristocratic one) allows him to think he has ultimate power over all individuals, that he is superior, and that he has to answer to no one. This megalomaniacal stance allows Lugosi to literally go over the top in his performance because the character as written is definitely a man who sees himself in godlike terms, a man who sees himself towering over pathetic humanity. Even the meaning of life and most notably death has taken on new significance to Vollin, another way in which he differentiates himself from the rest of humanity. As Vollin states and restates, he is a genius, a great man, and a god.

Finally, time to investigate obsession as the third significant characteristic of Vollin's character in *The Raven*. Besides the already documented obsession with power and his own stance as isolated genius with godlike abilities, as he notes about Poe, falling in love becomes his Achilles' Heel, his tragic flaw. His obsession with Jean Thatcher and falling in love with her, acting upon that taint of human emotion, is almost Vollin's way of accepting defeat for succumbing to love, giving in to his baser human instincts, something certainly not worthy of a god. Thus, the emotion of love, being solely a human trait, must by definition be the downfall of any genius, great man, and god.

Romancing Jean after her operation, it is apparent that the great Vollin is smitten with this sweet young thing. Her own gratitude allows her to create a godlike aura around the gifted surgeon: "A month ago I did not know you, now I owe my life to you. I wish there were something I could do."

Vollin, grimacing, intense, says, "There is!... the restraint which we impose upon ourselves can drive us mad!!!" He clutches her close in a warm embrace, but this overt display of physical emotion upsets the young lady and she immediately reminds Vollin of her engagement to colleague Dr. Halden. Referring to how Vollin made Halden his new assistant after the operation, Jean says, "I owe you another debt."

But Vollin is disturbed realizing that the love he feels for her is a one way street. "You owe me nothing! I did it to give *him* something... to take the place of what *he's* losing." Vollin is once again smiling, romantic, drawing closer to Jean, his eyes dancing downward toward her sensuous form.

Still, owing a debt to the doctor, she announces that tomorrow night at her dance recital she has a special surprise for Vollin. And when Vollin looks upon her dance interpretation of Poe's *The Raven*, as the figure of Poe reads the poem aloud seated at his desk, the erotic Jean, wearing a flowing bird-like dress and a dark face mask, whips her body to and fro using her motions to express Poe's imagery and ideals. Vollin is visibly overcome by this dedication to his master. After the recital, backstage, in front of her father, Vollin smiles and bows down to her and simply states, "Whom the angels call Lenore," gently kissing her hand, enthralled.

Judge Thatcher of course does not like what he sees and visits Vollin to voice his disapproval, in no uncertain terms. "You see, last night while Jean was dancing I've observed something that worried me. Later on in Jean's dressing room I felt the same thing. Then I questioned Jean and she made a confession. She is in danger of becoming infatuated with you..."

"Whom the angels call Lenore." Lugosi greets Jean Thatcher backstage after she performs a dance recital of Poe's *The Raven* as her special surprise to him.

"You're saying, Judge Thatcher, that Jean has fallen in love with me?" Vollin smiles.

"No, I'm not quite saying that," Thatcher answers.

"You do not approve," as though Vollin would be surprised by the Judge's answer.

"Well, you disapprove yourself. You don't want a young girl like Jean falling in love with you..." Thatcher states, obviously fearing the answer to the question he asks. "Dr. Vollin, I came to you once and asked you when death was near to save Jean. I come to you again—"

"But this time—is it from death you want to save her from—or from me!" Vollin says cutting to the quick. Holding a test tube in his hand, his passions boil over causing his fist to tighten, shattering the glass and cutting his hand.

The Judge immediately understands the passions that Vollin feels. "I never realized, Vollin. I'm sorry you feel like this." The Judge's face registers great concern and worry.

"Now that you know, you still say your greatest wish for her is to marry Jerry?" Vollin asks.

Thatcher is immediate in his answer. "More than ever! There's no point in saving Jean's life if we're going to sacrifice her happiness. You *mustn't* see her again!!!"

Vollin is a man who gets everything that he wishes when he wishes. The fact that this petty human emotion, love, has him under its grip, that Jean is promised to another man, and that her father favors this other man over himself, is more than Vollin can tolerate.

Near the end of the movie, at his private house party, glancing over to the lovely Jean who is having the back of her hair twirled by finance Jerry Halden, Lugosi flashes a quick, dynamic glance of hatred in seeing his love being fingered by his younger assistant. Quickly, he regains his composure and assumes a pleasing hostlike smile. But that poison-dagger glance lingers long in the viewer's mind.

Vollin's obsession with Jean even affects his relationship with poor, pathetic Bateman. During the middle of the night, during a thunderstorm, the lumbering Bateman attempts to enter Jean's bedroom via a hidden trapdoor in the floor. A falling tree that breaks her bedroom window awakens her, but she screams when she sees the shadowy figure begin to appear from the trapdoor, than disappear below.

Moments later Vollin holds Bateman at bay with a pistol in hand. "What do you mean sneaking up from the trap door! Don't compel me to treat you as an animal. You were looking for the girl, weren't you! Answer me!

"Yes," Bateman willingly confesses.

"The girl does not concern you! Why did you try to go to her? Answer me, *why*!!!" Vollin demands. All the mad, obsessive love permeating Vollin's body comes to a head when he flings a riding whip painfully across Bateman's face and shoulders.

Even Vollin admits that his obsessive love for Jean is like a cancer that must be cut out immediately. It is that unfortunate human taint that shatters his godlike intensity of focus and direction in his life. As he screams to Judge Thatcher, "I am mad and I tell you the only way you can cure—"

The Judge interrupts, "I can't talk to you Vollin... I find you stark, staring mad..."

Hatred welling up in Vollin's eyes, Vollin mutters aloud even after Thatcher leaves — "Send her, Judge Thatcher! I warn you!!!"

Even at his own party, after delivering the speech about inflicting torture to those who have tortured him as a release from one's own pain, Vollin begins obsessing about the medical profession: "...a doctor is fascinated by pain, death and pain. And how much pain a man can endure."

Of all people present only Dr. Halden interrupts. "I disagree with you Dr. Vollin. That's not why I'm a doctor."

Then in a clever retort, Vollin solemnly declares, "You are a doctor because you want to do good." The statement infers that Vollin is a doctor for some other agenda, the agenda of obsessing about death and pain endurance. Once again, doctors are doctors because they wish to do good, but Vollin, as he started earlier, is alone and to himself and his reasons for doing anything are his own.

Thus, at the film's climax, Vollin forces young lovers Jerry and Jean into another one of his torture devices, Poe's room "where the walls come together, until they're crushed dead." Vollin believes by destroying these two lovers and their love for one another, that this act will set him free of his obsessions. "I'll soon be rid of my torture, rid of it, and I'll be the sanest man who ever lived!"

When Bateman becomes upset over "that girl, dead???" and refuses to act as slave to Bateman if it means Jean's death, Vollin coldly answers him, "Why not!...I like to torture!"

When refusing to flip the switch crushing Jean and Jerry to death, Vollin shoots Bateman who literally crawls across the floor and forces Vollin into the room of death. Vollin, panicking, pulls his hands upward to cover his face, and he drops to his knees, collapsing as the walls rush together to finally crush the fiend.

Bela Lugosi, in 1935's *The Raven*, is at the top of his form. He looks healthy, elegant and tall, a romantic, charismatic madman, a tortured individual who believes that only in torturing can he be set free. He sees himself as a genius, as an all-powerful doctor, a doctor who has retired from helping lowly humans so he can devote his full efforts to research (that and erecting monuments of torture to honor his role model, Edgar Allan Poe). He sees himself as a god with the taint of human emotions, and he sees love as the obsession that ultimately defines his humanity and thus defines his weakness as a man superior to all other men. Thus in his misguided superiority, Richard Vollin becomes pathetically sympathetic. As he declares, he is alone and to himself, but when he states it, Vollin makes it seem as though being alone and to himself puts him above everyone else. But as he demonstrates by his victimization and control of Bateman, in his sad little society party, and by his obsession to love Jean Thatcher and for her to return her love to him, Dr. Vollin is desperately alone and lonely, a man who must employ a murderer to do his bidding because his hands are not capable of murder (or so he claims to Bateman), yet a man who loves to torture and to maim (by his own hand, or so he demonstrates throughout the movie). In other words, Vollin is a walking contradiction of a madman, a man who possesses so much (property, status, and intelligence) yet desires what he cannot or should not have, a man who is god of his own twisted, demented, and perverse universe. Ultimately a god of nothingness and of triviality.

Lugosi's performance is not subtle for he milks every drop of every line of dialogue to the final degree, his eyes convulse, his smile turns too demonic, and when he raves, he literally contorts his body as well as his sputtering language delivery. But in this performance of utter, vile insanity, Lugosi does exude subtlety. He can transform himself, often within seconds, from intelligent conniver, evil manipulator, superior aristocrat, to cackling madman, scorned lover, perverse sadist, and megalomaniacal Napoleon. What a performance and what a vehicle *The Raven* became for Lugosi.

It's a small miracle that sixty years after headlining this film that Bela Lugosi's star has risen to the heights it has obtained, for such well produced movies and well written characterizations were rare in Lugosi's career. It's a shame that Lugosi was not given more opportunities to mesmerize audiences with his talents to the extent that *The Raven*, being a complete package, allowed.

In fact, it's a damn shame!

"I want that you should—change my face!" Bateman demands. And Vollin complies with devilish glee and enthusiasm.

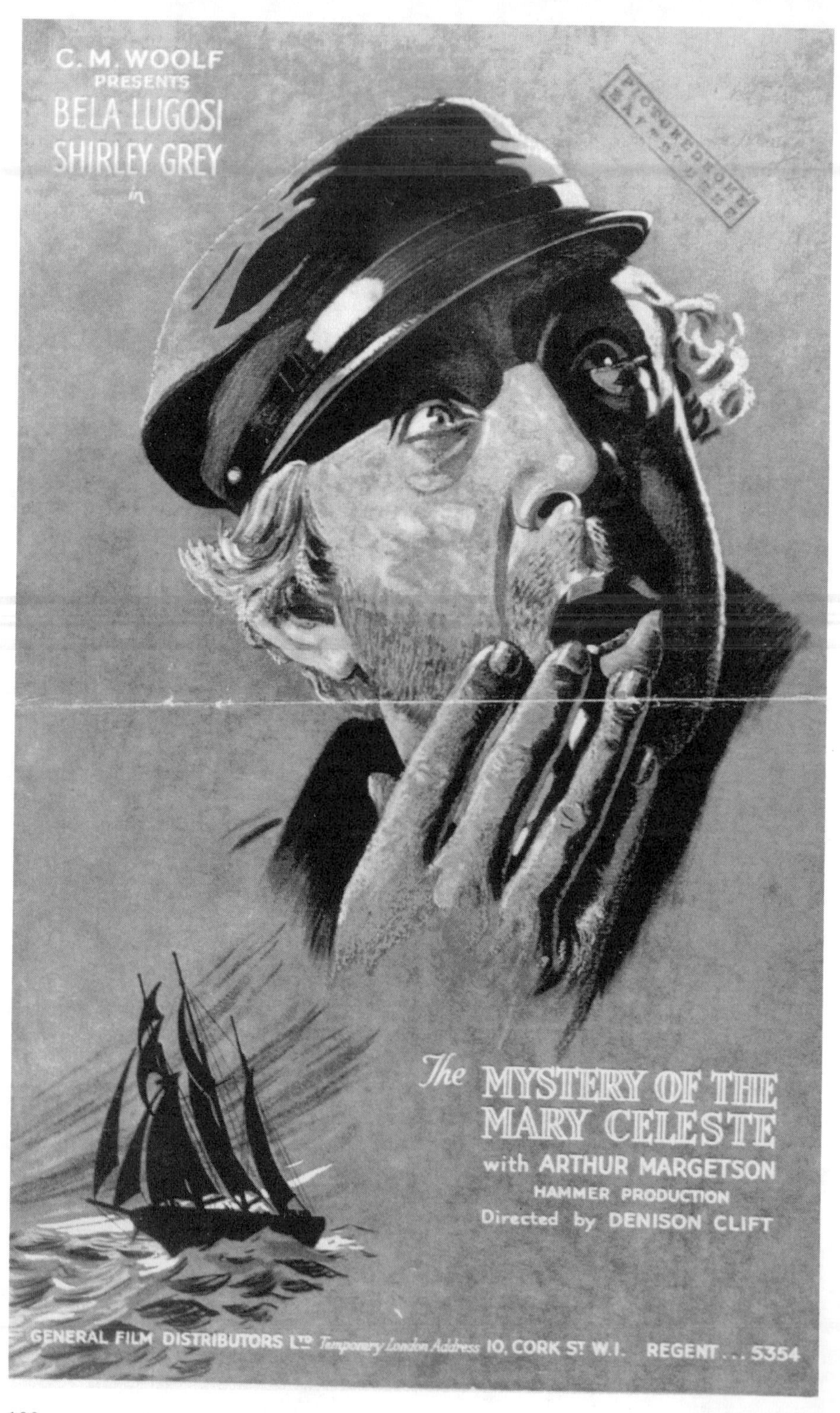
C. M. WOOLF
PRESENTS
BELA LUGOSI
SHIRLEY GREY
in
The MYSTERY OF THE MARY CELESTE
with ARTHUR MARGETSON
HAMMER PRODUCTION
Directed by DENISON CLIFT
GENERAL FILM DISTRIBUTORS LTD Temporary London Address 10, CORK ST W.1. REGENT ... 5354

The Mystery of the Mary Celeste (1936)

by Bryan Senn

CREDITS: Director: Denison Clift; Producer: H. Fraser Passmore; Screenplay: Denison Clift; Scenario: Charles Larkworthy; Photography: Geoffrey Faithful, Eric Cross; Art Direction: J. Elder Wills; Musical Direction: Eric Ansell; Continuity: Tilly Day; A Hammer Production and General Film Distributors release, 1935; Alternate Title: *Phantom Ship* (American retitling); Running Time: 80 minutes

CAST: Bela Lugosi...Anton Lorenzen, Shirley Grey...Sarah Briggs, Arthur Margetson...Captain Benjamin Briggs, Edmund Willard...Toby Bilson, Dennis Hoey...Tom Goodschard, George Mozart...Tommy Duggan, Johnnie Schofield...Peter Tooley, Gunner Moir...Ponta Katz, Ben Welden...Boas Hoffman, Clifford McLaglen...Captain Morehead, Bruce Gordon...Olly Deveau, Gibson Gowland...Andy Gilling, Terrence DeMarney...Clarlie Kaye, Ben Soutton...Jack Sampson, J. Edward Pierce... Arian Harbens, Herbert Cameron...Volkerk Grot, Wilfred Essex...Horatio Sprague, James Carew...James Winchester, Monti DeLyle...Portunato, Alec Fraser...Commander Mahon, J . B. Williams...The Judge, Charles Mortimer...U. S. Consul, and The Famous 'Q' Ship 'Mary B. Mitchell' as...Mary Celeste

"When this ship sailed, death sailed upon her."—Bela Lugosi as Anton Lorenzen.

The immortal Count *Dracula* (1931) inspiring both passion and terror in his victims; the insanely zealous evolutionist Doctor Mirakle committing *Murders in the Rue Morgue* (1932); the benign yet twisted Vitus Werdegast, deathly afraid of *The Black Cat* (1934); the Poe-obsessed Dr. Vollin (a "god with the taint of human emotions") holding forth *The Raven* (1935) as his talisman—these are Bela Lugosi's best remembered moments of triumph. Later, toppled from his Hollywood aerie through the shortsightedness of producers and his own lack of business acumen, the fallen star brought us (courtesy of Sam Katzman) the kindly Charles Kessler, tormented by an *Invisible Ghost* (1941); the insanely devoted Dr. Lorenz, driven to see that *The Corpse Vanishes* (1942); the split-personality Professor Brenner/Mr. Wagner presiding over the *Bowery at Midnight* (1942); and the hypnotic Dr. Marlowe, the *Voodoo Man* (1944) himself. In the early 1930s, Universal was Lugosi's meat and potatoes studio, offering the actor consistently choice cuts upon which to chew. For the following decade, Monogram became his bread and butter provider, though more often than not the threadbare productions seemed more akin to bread and water. Seen in stark contrast, these two well-known and oft-discussed cinematic subsets represent the apex and the nadir of Lugosi's Hollywood career (excepting, of course, his final, sad Ed Wood phase). Though the films from these studios varied wildly in quality, each and every entry offered the actor a legitimate starring role and allowed Lugosi full reign to stretch his histrionic abilities. As such they remain dear to Lugosiphiles, the gold and the iron pyrite alike. But what of the many pictures that fall between the diamonds of Universal and the zirconium of Monogram? Outside of these two studios, Lugosi often fared poorly, with starring roles coming surprisingly few and far between. For every substantial characterization allowed by a *White Zombie* (1932) or *Chandu the Magician* (1932), a plethora of short-changed parts fell to the slighted actor in the likes of *Night of Terror* (1933) or *The Gorilla* (1939). One of the most shamefully overlooked Lugosi films of that actor's 'golden era' (the 1930s) sailed forth from across the Atlantic—*The Mystery of the*

Mary Celeste. Though the picture features a full-blooded Lugosi standing proud and erect at the helm, it remains largely ignored—a small, unpretentious foreign sloop overshadowed by Universal's gigantic flagships.

"I'll be truthful and admit that the weekly pay check is the most important thing to me.... It's a good business; so I can buy steamship tickets, give tips, and invite the boys for a drink. If I wouldn't make such pictures—maybe trash—I couldn't do it."—Bela Lugosi in 1935.

The year 1935 saw Lugosi in six features: *Best Man Wins* (a deep-sea melodrama), *The Mysterious Mr. Wong* (a cheesy 'Monogrammer'), *Mark of the Vampire* (Tod Browning's atmospheric remake of *London After Midnight*), *The Raven* (a Karloff/Lugosi pairing), *Murder by Television* (a dismal technological mystery), and the British-made *Mystery of the Mary Celeste*. Of the first five, the only ones worthy of mention are *Mark of the Vampire* and *The Raven*, and of those only *The Raven* really allowed Lugosi any range as an actor. Fortunately, Lugosi's final film of the year was quite another story.

While in New York awaiting the departure of the oceanliner Berengaria for England to begin work on his last production of 1935, Lugosi admitted that he was unacquainted with the script of his upcoming project (the actor rarely read even so much as a scenario before signing on the dotted line). Thankfully, *The Mystery of the Mary Celeste* proved one of the more (sea)worthy vehicles of this busy period.

Released in the U.K. in November 1935, *The Mystery of the Mary Celeste* (retitled *Phantom Ship* when the picture finally docked at American shores) was a very early production by Hammer Films (in fact only their second), the British production company that single-handedly revived gothic horror in the 1950s with T*he Curse of Frankenstein* (1957), *Horror of Dracula* (1958), and their numerous sequels and successors. This generally forgotten thriller provided Lugosi with one of his most sympathetic roles, allowing the actor a rare opportunity to stretch his all-but-atrophied thespian compassion without ignoring altogether his trademark brand of menace.

"LUGOSI CHANGES IMAGE ABROAD" read the Los Angeles *Examiner* headline on September 20, 1935. "Bela Lugosi... is definite proof that a change of scene is often of great value.... In his English picture, *The Mystery of the Marie Celeste* [sic], Lugosi abandons bizarre makeup and terrifying roles. Instead, he appears as an old sea captain, a sympathetic, crusty old salt, and his performance, playing straight, is reported to surpass any of his efforts in the improbable horror films of recent release."

Originally announced as *The Secret of the Mary Celeste* (ultimately changed to *Mystery* before its release), the film takes its inspiration from a true incident in 1872 in which an American clipper ship, the Mary Celeste, carrying Captain Benjamin Briggs, his wife, his baby daughter, and a crew of seven, was found adrift on the Atlantic ocean with no one aboard, remaining a real-life enigma to this day. Up until the Jack the Ripper murders over two decades later, no single occurrence fired the imaginations of the London populace like the mystery of the Mary Celeste. (The ship was found and salvaged by an English vessel.) Many explanations (some of them quite fanciful) have been offered over the years, ranging from pirates to giant squids to finding the lost continent of Atlantis! In one article published in the British *Strand Magazine* in 1913, an Oxford M.A., Howard Luforth, offered a less fantastic (though no more likely) solution. He suggested that the crew built a platform from which they could observe a swimming race between the captain and his mate. The two swimmers, conjectured Luforth, were eaten by a shark and the platform collapsed, dumping the crew into the sea.

Fortunately, screenwriters Denison Clift and Charles Larkworthy chose a somewhat more believable explanation upon which to build their script for *The Mystery of the Mary Celeste*.

"This story was inspired by the findings of the Attorney-General at Gibraltar," begins the film's opening written narration, "and portrays the grim sea tragedy of the American brig 'Mary Celeste,' found drifting and derelict in the Mid-Atlantic on December 5th, 1872—one of the strangest and most dramatic chapters in maritime history." The suppositional story then begins

"Anton Lorenzen (Bela Lugosi)... Holy cats! I thought you were dead. Six years! I wouldn't have known you."

in "New York harbor, 1872." At the dock rests the Mary Celeste, set to sail to Genoa soon with a cargo of alcohol. Captain Benjamin Briggs orders his first mate, Toby Bilson, to "get a crew," and then goes to see his beloved Sarah and ask her to marry him. "You'll love the sea," enthuses Briggs, "There's something about it—the hot red dawn, the towering sails, the wake on a tropical night." His enthusiasm wins her over and she accepts. She's troubled though, because Briggs' good friend and fellow captain, Jim Morehead (a naming nod to the real-life captain 'Morehouse' who found the Mary Celeste), had also asked for her hand in marriage. When Morehead finds out that Sarah has chosen Briggs over him, the two men almost come to blows.

Meanwhile, a one-armed, derelict sailor (Bela Lugosi) staggers wearily into Jack Sampson's dockside bar. His name is Anton Lorenzen, a friend of Sampson's, but the bar owner barely recognizes his old crony. "Anton Lorenzen," marvels Sampson, "Holy cats! I thought you were dead. Six years! I wouldn't have known you." When the two are alone in the back room, Sampson demands, "What happened?" "Shanghaied," answers Lorenzen bitterly. Sampson can't get over the change in his friend. "Why, you were a fine, high-kicking buck," he remembers, "a great fella, 'handsome Anton.' We'd have owned this place together. You'd have had a packet of money in the bank by now." But Lorenzen, his spirit broken, only responds with, "Please Jack, let me sleep here. That's all I want—sleep."

Back on the Mary Celeste, Mr. Bilson has had no luck raising a crew, so the Captain himself goes to Sampson's bar to see what he can do. After breaking down Sampson's resistance with a fat five-dollar-a-head bribe (apparently Captain Briggs had previously gotten "too particular" for Sampson's liking), Sampson puts the squeeze on a handful of his bar's denizens. He also offers the job of bosun to Lorenzen. When Sampson names the Mary Celeste and mentions Bilson as the mate, however, Lorenzen becomes almost violent. Jack is taken aback and thinks his friend doesn't want the job. But Anton angrily insists, "I want it, I want it!" At the ship Anton gives an alias to Mr. Bilson—A. Gottlieb. Bilson closely scrutinizes the new man, as though he's seen him before but can't place him, then allows him onboard.

When it's time to cast off, Captain Briggs finds he's still one crewman short, so he goes to see Captain Morehead and "borrow a man." Though Morehead initially seems angry ("You stole my girl!" he accuses), he readily agrees to Briggs' request and appears to reconcile with his old friend. But when Briggs leaves, Morehead calls Grot, the man he's sending to the Mary Celeste, to his cabin and bribes him to see that "something might happen to Briggs. He might never reach Genoa alive."

With the Mary Celeste under sail, Bilson wakes up two men asleep on deck. When one of them, Katz, shakes off his hangover enough to realize that he's been shanghaied, he attacks Bilson, who beats him into submission. The violence horrifies Sarah. When she asks her husband, "Why do you have to shanghai men?," Briggs answers matter-of-factly, "Well, I couldn't get a crew. I had to pick the best men I could and no questions asked—the scum of the dock."

Soon, things begin to go wrong. Grot complains about the food. Briggs responds by ordering Mr. Bilson to "take this man out and teach him respect... flog some decency into him." That night, Grot, club in hand, creeps towards the Captain as he stands at the wheel. Fortunately, Duggan the cook spots Grot and kills the assassin with a knife.

Later, during a violent storm, a sailor named Goodschard, who'd ogled Sarah when she first came on board, sneaks into the Captain's cabin and attacks her. Anton, who'd seen the man lurking outside the cabin, breaks in, grabs a sword hanging on the wall, and strikes him down, killing the would-be rapist. Though Briggs thanks his wife's savior, Anton is inconsolable, wailing, "I've killed my fellow man."

After this second killing, the death toll mounts at a rapid pace. First Briggs loses a man in the storm when some rigging comes crashing down on the deck (which also smashes the solitary lifeboat). Then another sailor (Hoffman) turns up dead at the wheel from a knife wound. Soon afterwards, an unknown hand aims a pistol through the portal in Briggs' cabin and takes a shot at the Captain. Then, in quick succession, two more men are found dead and a third becomes so terrified that he races up the rigging in a panic and half-falls, half-leaps into the sea.

With only a skeleton crew left and the body count mounting, Briggs orders Anton to take his wife to the safety of his cabin. There the old sailor begins an impassioned reverie about his past. "I was shanghaied," he tells her bitterly, "flogged by the mate... When I was too weak to work, the mate tied a rope around me and dragged me in the sea." As Anton stares off into the haze of his own memory, his single hand inadvertently clutches at his armless sleeve and he exclaims, "a shark!" Briggs enters the cabin, dismisses Anton and then orders his wife to lock the door and not

Bela Lugosi has his makeup touched up on the set of the British film *The Mystery of the Mary Celeste* (aka *Phantom Ship*).

admit anyone until he returns.

This is the last we see of Briggs and his wife, for Bilson next tells Anton and Katz that not only is another sailor missing, but the captain and his wife have disappeared as well. "Only three of us left on the ship," announces Bilson, adding "when the next man goes, I'll know who it is." In a three-way standoff, each man accuses the others.

After Bilson goes up on deck, Katz remembers that when Anton killed Goodschard earlier to save Mrs. Briggs, the old sailor "felt terrible" and "cried like a child." Suddenly, Katz concludes, "Bilson did it!" Grasping a knife, Katz leaves Anton below and goes up on deck to confront the murderous mate. As Anton waits below, we hear sounds of a struggle, then a shot, followed by a splash. Bilson comes racing down the ladder shouting, "Gottlieb, Gottlieb, it was Katz! I shot him, flung his carcass overboard. He hates us all because we shanghaied him."

That night Bilson and Anton celebrate. "We own this ship now!" exclaims the drunken mate as he plans to loot the cashbox. But Anton remains strangely silent. Finally, Anton rises and announces, "I am Anton Lorenzen," and pulls a pistol from his coat. "Six years ago on this ship," he continues to the astonished Bilson, "Anton Lorenzen was shanghaied on the Mary Celeste. Now again the Mary Celeste, and again Mr. Bilson the mate. It wasn't Katz killed them," raves Anton, "*I* put them overboard—for the sharks. Briggs tried to get away on a raft with his pretty bride, but I got him. I got her too and now—you!" Bilson makes a break for the door but Lorenzen shoots him, then dumps his body over the side. Laughing hysterically, he fails to see the unattended boom come swinging toward his head, knocking him to the deck. Dazed, Lorenzen struggles to his feet.

Now confused, he frantically searches the empty ship, calling plaintively, "Where are you all?" With a final despairing cry, he plunges overboard.

Later, Captain Morehead's sloop runs across the Mary Celeste and boards the ghost ship. When Morehead's mate gloats over the "1700 pounds salvage money," Morehead only stares inwardly and grates, "I'm not thinking of the salvage, I'm thinking of Briggs and—and her—dead!"

The original British version differed slightly from the film seen by American audiences. It begins with Captain Morehead filing a salvage suit before the Admiralty court at Gibraltar after having found and towed the derelict Mary Celeste into port. The film then picks up with the events described above before returning back to the maritime court for its conclusion. The American distributors removed these courtroom scenes so that the story played in a straight linear fashion rather than in a flashback format, perhaps feeling that the American viewers would not be so familiar with the Mary Celeste mystery as the British public and so would be better served with a straightforward presentation. As a result of these excises, several actors listed in the credits (such as J. B. Williams, who plays the Judge, and Charles Mortimer, playing the U.S. Consul) failed to make the Atlantic crossing along with the Americanized *Phantom Ship*.

Director Denison Clift began shooting *The Mystery of the Mary Celeste* in mid-July at Nettlefold Studios, while the exteriors were filmed in the English Channel onboard the Mary B. Mitchell, a rented schooner. Clift, working with cinematographers Geoffrey Faithful and Eric Cross, makes effective use of the camera to convey the story. At Lorenzen's initial meeting with Jack Sampson, for instance, Clift stations his actors so that Lorenzen and Sampson appear in profile with a dumbfounded barkeep framed between them in the background. The bartender stares incredulously at the man he once knew (Lorenzen) but now barely recognizes. This careful positioning adds a visual depth while at the same time creating a powerful intimacy that draws the viewer into this pivotal introductory scene. We, like the barkeep, become privy to the startling revelation of a man transformed.

In the next scene the conversation continues in Jack's private office. Here the camera peers over Sampson's shoulder as he demands to know what happened to his friend. The camera positioning places all the viewer's focus on Lorenzen as the broken man sorrowfully pleads, "Let me sleep here. That's all I want—sleep."

Clift shoots much of his picture at night, adding to the doom-laden atmosphere, and takes full advantage of the claustrophobic possibilities of his small ship setting. (Though the rearranged American version loses a few moments of courtroom drama, it greatly benefits by both beginning and ending in the dark of night.) Clift uses a preponderance of tight shots and closeups rather than the more mundane medium or long shots to enhance the claustrophobic feel. Even for group scenes, he often begins the sequence in tight closeup on one man before drawing the camera back to reveal the entire crowd.

The nearly continual sounds of howling wind, lapping waves, creaking timbers, and the men singing sea shanties combine with the surrounding darkness and shadowy lighting in the cramped cabins to produce a mood ominous enough for any shudder story.

Denison Clift's screenplay contains some evocative dialogue which effectively foreshadows the dire events to come. After Jack Sampson informs Harbens that he'll be shipping onboard the Mary Celeste, he adds, "Take your music box along with you. If anybody should die on this trip," he says and looks pointedly at the Captain, "Mr. Briggs might like a little sweet music."

American-born Denison Clift, a graduate from Stanford University, began his career as a publicist before hiring on as a writer during WWI for Cecil B. DeMille and Famous Players. He started directing in 1917 and went to England in 1920 where he directed a number of British silents during a three year stint. Back in the U.S., Clift helmed pictures for Metro and 20th Century-Fox before once again going to England in the late '20s where he continued his prolific career (directing a total of 20 films in 10 years on the British Isles). Besides frequently penning his own scripts, Clift also authored a number of Broadway plays, including "A Woman Disputed" and "Scotland Yard," and published seven novels. *The Mystery of the Mary Celeste* proved to be his last film as director, for after a few more years of screenwriting Clift retired from the industry in the late 1930s. He died in 1961.

Anton Lorenzen (aka A. Gottlieb) is one of the more infrequently seen Lugosi characterizations and that is a pity because it's also one of his best. For the most part his is a sympathetic role, and Lugosi deftly handles the pathos while occasionally balancing it with his more expected chilling delivery. In fact, apart from the naive Sarah, Anton is the most sympathetic character in this maritime melodrama. Lorenzen is an almost pitiable man who appears soft spoken and kind (lovingly tending a cat, for instance) but who will react to the brutality around him with a ferocity that betrays his circumstance-induced violent nature. When the superstitious Bilson cruelly tries to fling the feline (a black cat) overboard, for instance, Anton stops him by nearly choking the life out of the man.

Lugosi makes the most of his role in several standout scenes, foremost among them the one in which he kills a man while defending the Captain's wife. Lugosi reacts to this heroic deed with horrified remorse. "I —I killed a man," he says, his voice trembling with emotion. Lugosi turns his sorrowful eyes heavenward and clutches his hand to his chest while sinking slowly to his knees, using his face and body to paint a portrait of abject contrition. "Oh God," he continues, almost sobbing in anguish, "I've killed my fellow man. I've murdered my brother." His eyes glisten and his lips purse tightly together as his face trembles in torment. Lugosi's sincerity is utterly convincing and he creates a truly heartrending moment.

In another sequence, Lorenzen explains that once he was "full of the hope of living" but, because of the brutal treatment he received, is now only a shell of his former self. "Now look at me," Lugosi invites, "My hair white, my arm—gone. Look at me now, derelict—like that ship" [pointing to a painting]. (For the Lugosiphile, this telling self-revelation possesses a chilling and prophetic sadness in view of the drug-dependent actor's final desperate years.) Lugosi's delivery is perfectly timed, with pregnant pauses and pointed emphasis, and his demeanor effectively evinces anger coupled with self-pity to inspire compassion in the viewer.

Besides providing moments of powerful drama, Lugosi also invests his role with an effective subtlety that makes Anton Lorenzen one of the most realistic—and human—characterizations of his cinematic career. Gone are the broad, theatrical gestures and grandiose inflections that so often comprise a Lugosi performance, replaced here by evocative expressions and subtle tones. Lorenzen's initial meeting with his old friend Jack Sampson provides a perfect opportunity for Lugosi to shine. When Jack demands, "What happened?!" Lugosi's weary face hardens as he answers through clenched teeth, "Shanghaied," his voice low and hard, the solitary word obviously leaving a bitter taste in his throat. When Jack recalls, "Why, you were a fine, high-kicking buck," one side of Lugosi's mouth momentarily turns upwards in a weary parody of a half-smile, but it quickly droops again into a mask of dissolute fatigue. When Sampson finally finishes, Lugosi looks at him and pleads, "Jack, let me sleep here." Lugosi swallows hard and gives a hint of a bitter smile and slight shake of his head as he explains, "That's all I want." His eyes close and he lifts his chin as he concludes, almost to himself, "sleep," like a man too weary to hold his head level. Through subtle facial expressions, Lugosi runs the gamut from anger to wistfulness to resigned weariness, bringing his character alive and immediately establishing a sympathetic link with the viewer. These scenes and Lugosi's performance in general demonstrate that he was much more versatile than his critics and film assignments generally allowed. Unlike so many of Lugosi's films, *The Mystery of the Mary Celeste* affords us a rare glimpse of Lugosi the actor rather than Lugosi the personality.

"A virile, hefty bunch of men have been chosen for the crew," noted *Variety*. They certainly fit the profile of "the toughest mugs I ever laid eyes on" much better than the crew of the S. S. Venture (who inspired this quote from a timid theatrical agent in *King Kong*). Not only was this bunch "hefty," but they could act as well, and Lugosi was fortunate to receive the support of such an impressive array of veteran British character actors.

Arthur Margetson (Captain Briggs) left his job as a stock-broker's clerk for the footlights of the English stage where he quickly became a popular supporting player. He entered films in 1930 and appeared in two dozen British productions (including *Juggernaut* [1936] starring Boris Karloff) over the course of the decade. In 1940 he came to Hollywood where he made a handful of films before abandoning motion pictures in 1943 for the Broadway stage, finding great success in such plays as *Life with Father* and *The Play's the Thing*. Margetson's final film was the Rathbone/Bruce entry, *Sherlock Holmes Faces Death* (1943), in which he joined *Mary Celeste* alumnus Dennis Hoey (a regular in the Holmes series). Margetson died in 1951 (of a "prolonged illness") at age 54.

Edmund Willard (Toby Bilson), also a well known stage actor, began his thespian career in 1900, eventually touring the U.S. theater circuit a total of six times. During World War II, Willard played Jonathan Brewster in the London production of *Arsenic and Old Lace*, the role Boris Karloff made famous on Broadway.

Dennis Hoey (the lecherous Tom Goodschard), like Arthur Margetson, also worked on the London Stock Exchange before turning to acting. On stage from 1918, Hoey began acting in British films in 1927, appearing (like Margetson) in about two dozen features (including Tod Slaughter's screen debut, *Maria Marten* or *Murder in the Red Barn*) before coming to the U.S. about the same time as his Mary Celeste colleague. In Hollywood, Hoey began a busy two-decade career, beginning with the prestigious *How Green Was My Valley* (1941). Undoubtedly, Hoey's most famous role is that of Inspector Lestrade, who was one-upped time and time again by Basil Rathbone's Sherlock Holmes in half-a-dozen Holmes features starting with *Sherlock Holmes and the Secret Weapon* (1942) and including *The Spider Woman* (with Gale Sondergaard) and *Pearl of Death* (with Rondo Hatton). Hoey also appeared (as a police inspector, naturally) in *Frankenstein Meets the Wolfman* (1943).

Ben Soutten (sometimes billed as Graham Ben Soutten or B. Graham Soutten), who appeared in the brief but memorable role of Jack Sampson, also acted in two other British horror (or near-horror) pictures, both starring Tod Slaughter ("The Horror Man of Europe"). Soutten played "the Beadle" in *Sweeney Todd, the Demon Barber of Fleet Street* (1936) and "Nathaniel" in *The Crimes of Stephen Hawke* (1936). Soutten also worked behind the camera on occasion, including serving as assistant director on *The Secret of the Loch* (1934), Britain's early contribution to dinosaur cinema. Aside from his professional versatility, Soutten also possessed an unusual physical characteristic—he was missing a leg. In films he often wore an artificial appendage to disguise this handicap (as he did in *Mary Celeste*).

Though generally well-acted, *The Mystery of the Mary Celeste* could not entirely escape its temporal origins. The early scenes involving the love triangle of Sarah, Briggs, and Morehead ring with theatricality as each of the three players stretch themselves a bit too taut in their melodramatic histrionics. This should come as no great surprise, however, since the film is, after all, a British melodrama from the 1930s enacted by a cadre of stage actors. One should just be thankful that most of the mawkish melodramatics were left onshore when the Mary Celeste finally put to sea.

Apart from a few early moments of overly theatrical thesping, *The Mystery of the Mary Celeste* also suffers from some ill-advised expediency in its storytelling. It is a great pity that scripter/director Denison Clift decided to so cavalierly gloss over the fates of Briggs and his wife Sarah—two pivotal characters. Sarah, in fact, quickly becomes the audience focus figure as she, along with the viewer, questions the wanton brutality of this hard life. To settle her fate with a simple throw-away line (to the effect that the killer "got her") rings hollow.

As an interesting footnote, *The Mystery of the Mary Celeste* contains two lines of dialogue unusual for a production of 1935 (particularly one from the prim and proper British Isles). The first occurs when the Captain scares up a crew in a sleazy waterfront bar. The proprietor states, "And here's your cook," pointing to a small white man in a dirty bowler hat. "If you don't like the look of his face I'll get you a chink or a nigger." Though filmed over sixty years ago, such a blatantly racist comment was shocking even by 1935 film standards. The second 'scandalous' bit of dialogue comes when the Captain, after having some trouble with the crew, orders his Mate to "Find out what the hell is happening"—and this a full four years before Clark Gable shocked the industry with his "Frankly, my dear..." exclamation.

The Mystery of the Mary Celeste generally fared well with the critics, as did Lugosi. *Variety* (December 4,1935) called the film "very strong stuff for those who like tragic entertainment" while noting that "outstanding role is played by Bela Lugosi." *Daily Film Renter* called it "pretty grim fare... with sudden deaths and disasters galore... Bela Lugosi has a part after his own heart as the bleary-eyed, one-armed Lorenzen, who stalks the decks like a sinister portent."

Lugosi was so well-received for his return to a more straight dramatic role in *The Mystery of the Mary Celeste* that British Independent Pictures offered him a two-picture contract at $12,500 per film (a proposed remake of *The Cabinet of Dr. Caligari* was bandied about in the trades about this time). However, when the actor learned that his four prized dogs would have to be quarantined for six months before they would be allowed to join him in England (due to that country's strict animal import laws), he turned down the offer and returned to Universal to ultimately work on *The Invisible Ray* (1936). One can only wonder at the turn his career might have taken had he not been such a dedicated dog lover.

Ever looking to escape his role of Dracula and break out of the horror mold, Lugosi was encouraged by his success in *The Mystery of the Mary Celeste* to make plans to start his own independent production company. The actor made no secret of his dissatisfaction in being passed over for non-horror parts, telling Eleanor Barnes of the *Illustrated Daily News* (Sept. 1935): "Every time I get my thoughts centered on a role that I believe fits me, some other actor—always a great actor—gets there first. So what am I to do? I'll finance my own company and star in pictures that I want to play in." Cagliostro (a tale of an eighteenth-century Wizard) was to be the first production of his new company, but the project (and the company) never fully materialized (nor did his longed-for escape from horror roles). An amusing remark made by Robert Montgomery (related by actress Audrey Totter in Doug McClelland's *Forties Film Talk)* illustrates Lugosi's inescapable image: "One day while filming *The Saxon Charm* [1948] we were in the [Universal] commissary and Bela Lugosi was there, with a young boy [probably Bela, Jr.]. Bob Montgomery said, in a melodramatic voice, 'I see that Bela Lugosi is having a small boy for lunch!'"

Though far from a recognized classic, and not really a "horror film" per se (yet containing isolated moments of terror), *The Mystery of the Mary Celeste* remains noteworthy for its realistic settings and ship, the air of dread laced with horrific undertones hanging over the doomed vessel, and most of all, for the rare opportunity it afforded the most charismatic horror star of the Golden Age. No Lugosi fan should miss this boat.

Poster courtesy Ronald V. Borst/Hollywood Movie Posters

THE DARK EYES OF LONDON (1939)

by Dennis Fischer

CREDITS: Director: Walter Summers; Producer: John Argyle; Screenplay: Patrick Kirwan, J.F. Argyle, and Walter Summers based on *Dark Eyes of London* by Edgar Wallace; Director of Photography: Bryan Langley; Art Director: Duncan Sutherland; Editor: E. G. Richards; Music: Guy Jones; An Argyle Productions Ltd. Production; Released in the U.K. by Pathé and in the U.S. by Monogram as *Human Monster*, 1939, 76 Minutes

CAST: Bela Lugosi...Dr. Orloff, Hugh Williams...Inspector Holt, Greta Gynt...Diana Stuart, Edmond Ryan...Lt. O'Reilly, Wilfred Walter...Jake, Alexander Field...Grogan, Arthur E. Owen...Lew, Julie Suedo...Secretary, Gerald Pring...Henry Stuart, Bryan Herbert...Walsh, May Hallatt...Policewoman, Charles Penrose...Drunk

1938 had been a disastrous year for Bela as the horror market dried up and job offers dwindled to nothing. In the process, the star lost his mansion and big automobiles, and Actors Relief had to help him pay for the birth of his son, Bela Lugosi, Jr. Fortunately for Bela, Universal found a gold mine in re-releasing *Dracula* and *Frankenstein* as a double bill and immediately ordered that *Son of Frankenstein* be made with both Karloff and Lugosi appearing in it.

Knowing Lugosi's financial straits, Universal got him at a cut-rate price of $500 a week and only intended to use him for one week. Director Rowland V. Lee got wind of the plans and rewrote the script as he was filming, expanding Lugosi's part in the process. Soon 20th Century-Fox opted to use Lugosi as a red herring in the Ritz Brothers comedy *The Gorilla* while Universal cast him in his last serial, *The Phantom Creeps*, with Lugosi as the evil Dr. Zorka. Ernst Lubitsch also took pity on the actor, casting him in *Ninotchka*, one of the greatest comedies ever made, which demonstrated how well Lugosi could handle non-horror fare. Bela was back in business!

In April 1939, Bela Lugosi returned to England, where he had shot *The Mystery of the Mary Celeste* (aka *Phantom Ship*) in 1935, to make his last and best British film, *The Dark Eyes of London*, which was shot at Welwyn Studios. The film became the first British film to earn the recently designated "H" certificate.

The film was based on a book by Edgar Wallace, an extremely prolific pulp crime novelist who dictated two or three novels a month for years. Wallace was born Richard Horatio Wallace in 1875, and died in 1932. While primarily known for his imaginative crime thrillers, Wallace also wrote science fiction including the "future war" novels *Private Selby* (1909) and *1925: The Story of a Fatal Peace* (1915), and stories of mind control in *The Door With Seven Locks* (1926), world catastrophe in *The Fourth Plague* (1913), *The Green Rust* (1919), and *The Day of Uniting* (1921), and of a counter Earth in *Planetoid 127* (1924). He also tried his hand at weird fiction, including the novel *Captains of Souls* (1922) and scripted the obscure horror film *The Table*.

Wallace's work was frequently adapted for the cinema in Great Britain in the '30s and included such titles as *The Case of the Frightened Lady*(1930 and '40), *The Calendar* (1932 and '48), *The Crimson Circle* (1930, '37, and '61), *The Terror* (1928 and '39), *Kate Plus Ten* (1938), *Sanders of the River* (1935), *The Squeaker* (1937), *The Ringer* (1932 and '52), etc.

Wallace's crime stories later enjoyed a revival and would form the basis of the popular

German film and book genre of *krimis* (literally "crime stories") and a plethora of Wallace's work was remade in Germany during the early '60s. Wallace's last credit was a co-story credit for the classic *King Kong*; however, he died before any story was really finalized and the actual story was concocted by female scriptwriter Ruth Rose.

Our favorite hardworking Hungarian shines with a great double role in the film, as the nefarious Dr. Orloff (no relation to the Jesus Franco series) and the kindly Mr. Dearborn (with long, drooping mustache, white hair, and blindman glasses completing the transformation). Dearborn's voice was dubbed by O.B. Clarence, a British actor noted for playing benevolent, doddering roles, in order to prevent the deception from becoming too obvious. The dubbing is of fairly good quality and is greatly aided and abetted by Lugosi's performance as Dearborn. He demonstrates that a blind character would move his body very differently than a sighted one, and so alters his motions in contrast to those of the more overbearing Dr. Orloff, whose evil relish is more typical of Lugosi's florid style.

The film begins moodily enough with a shot of Tower Bridge over which Lugosi's mesmerizing eyes and the credits are superimposed, followed by a montage sequence showing a body floating down the river Thames and then washed ashore, the latest victim of a mysterious serial murderer.

At Scotland Yard, the commissioner of the Criminal Investigations Department, feeling pressure from the home office, briefs his men that five insured people have drowned in the last eight months, apparently not concerned with any uninsured ones. (Working class stiffs don't count, no doubt).

Inspector Larry Holt (Hugh Williams) is called aside and informed that a Chicago detective, Lt. O'Reilly (Edmond Ryan), is accompanying Grogan, an extradited forger, and wishes to study the English police's "antiquated" methods. "I'll attach him to you, then he won't learn anything," the Commissioner notes drily.

Meanwhile, in the Greenwich insurance office of Dr. Feodor Orloff (Lugosi), Mr. Henry Stuart (Gerald Pring) is borrowing a sum of money from the broker in order to finance an invention. Uncertain what type of collateral to offer for the loan, Orloff suggests that he sign over his life insurance to Orloff. Stuart reveals that he is uninsured and so signs a promissory note instead.

Orloff is known for his charity, and indeed quotes the Bible's admonition that "The greatest of these is charity." Told that he is a good man by Stuart, Orloff replies, "I want to be, Stuart. I wanted to devote my life to the healing of mankind. I wanted to be a doctor. But they got together—those narrow-minded, prejudiced medical men—to see how they could ruin me. Brilliant but unbalanced, that was the verdict. And so, I serve the blind."

Indeed, everyone is blind to Orloff's true intentions. Lugosi hits the proper note of pathos with this speech, indicating that he is another in a long line of sufferers at the hands of a dull-witted medical establishment. Of course, while such men as Galileo, Copernicus, Kepler, and Pasteur were told by scientific experts that they were crazy, the same was also said of a great many who were truly crazy, and Dr. Orloff proves to be one of the latter.

Orloff explains that a friend of his, a Mr. Dearborn, operates a home for blind vagrants in London, and after fixing him with a hypnotic stare, suggests that if Stuart wishes to express his gratitude, he should pay a visit there tomorrow evening. Stuart assents and departs.

Orloff's secretary (Julie Suedo) comes in and is informed to pay the bail of Grogan, the forger, as soon as it is posted. Orloff writes out a message in braille, rolls it up, and tosses it to Lew, a blind violin player who waits below and acts as Orloff's early warning system.

Inspector Holt arrives and identifies himself as an inspector from Scotland Yard and informs him that they are making a check on all recently insured persons. Orloff indicates that he will be only too willing to assist if he can. Holt inquires about a specific case of a person named Ingol who was found drowned and left a mysterious woman £20,000. Orloff tells him, "I can give you an address, but I have a notion she went abroad." Ursula Sable, another of Orloff's clients, was also found drowned, and Holt is told that the beneficiary, Carl Hasher, was a Romanian whose last address was a Manchester hotel. Holt promises he will look into the matter, which, as it is a blind alley, is conveniently ignored from then on.

Stuart arrives at Dearborn's Home for the Destitute Blind, where moments before Dearborn is shown delivering a sermon, reading from a braille bible. Orloff greets him, explains that Dearborn has been called away and offers to show him around personally. Orloff registers surprise and rage when Stuart mentions having a daughter, but nevertheless steers Stuart toward some rickety stairs as he expresses his desire to show him his special department upstairs, a supposed medical clinic.

At the top of the stairs, Orloff opens the door to reveal Jake, Orloff's monstrous henchmen (played by Shakespearean actor and playwright Wilfred Walter, who is said to have had a hand in designing his own makeup, which effectively conveys the impression of a lumbering, dull-witted behemoth with a barrelchest and protruding teeth). Jake holds a straitjacket and menacingly approaches the kindly inventor as Orloff slams the door shut.

From this horrific moment, the film indulges in some lame comic relief as Holt is attracted to a young lady at the train station, who later proves to be Diana Stuart (Greta Gynt), Henry Stuart's daughter now returning from America, whose foot he inadvertently trods on. There he meets the brash Lt. O'Reilly, who jokingly slaps handcuffs on him only to remember that the key which opens the cuffs is back in Chicago. The unrestrained Grogan climbs into the police patrol wagon, and, of course, a constable arrives and assumes that the detectives are escaped criminals and so they have to ride back to Scotland Yard in the patrol wagon as well.

Once there, they receive a stern lecture from the commissioner. While the commissioner harangues, a phone call comes in. There's been another drowning victim. Holt and O'Reilly immediately set off to the crime scene. (Quick, the commissioner must be thinking, put our least competent men on it right away).

The victim is revealed to be Henry Stuart, and the corpse is missing half of one of its cufflinks. O'Reilly loses a presentation cigar case as he leans over the body and it falls into the muddy river. The cinematography by Bryan Langley is appropriately moody and murky. A thorough examination of the body also yields a message written in braille.

An autopsy is conducted, and Holt demands that the quality of the water in the dead man's lungs be checked. There are no signs of violence on the body, giving credence to the idea that the victim had an accident or committed suicide. (The straitjacket preventes Orloff's victims from being able to defend themselves when they are drowned).

The relative who comes to identify the body is Diana, who once more makes Holt's acquaintance. O'Reilly is impressed with the idea that the British have policewomen, an innovation that hadn't reached Chicago as yet; however, the dour matron (May Hallatt) he encounters informs him that she is responsible for looking after public morality after Holt jestingly insinuates that O'Reilly had hopes that the policewomen would be assigned for the aid and comfort of the policemen.

A boisterous drunken fop (Charles Penrose) is placed in Grogan's cell, and Grogan relieves him of his newspaper. He then sees a coded message in the personal column of the paper. The drunk is later revealed to be an undercover policeman who reports to Holt on Grogan's activities. O'Reilly takes out a rubber tube and suggests that he can make Grogan talk by giving him the third degree; however, Holt insists that the British use more civilized methods such as becoming the crook's friend, a sly dig at America's tough guy reputation and reputed brutality.

Holt learns that the water found in Stuart's stomach was clear tapwater and not the muddy water of the Thames. The partial message found in Stuart's pocket are the letters "MUR." Holt agrees to allow Grogan to be released on bail, but instructs that he be tailed.

Grogan signs Stuart's signature to some papers in Orloff's office and leaves just as the police arrive. When Holt warns him about Grogan, Orloff replies, "Yes, I know all about Grogan, Inspector. My volunteer activities include the vice presidentship of the Prisoners Relief Association. Grogan was asking my help for his defense."

Holt mentions Stuart's murder and inquires if Orloff has heard of him. Orloff admits that his company insured Stuart and that he had loaned Stuart money. When Holt asks how he could afford insurance, Orloff explains that he had paid for the last two premiums on Stuart's policy himself. Holt asks who benefits by the policy, Orloff replies, "I am the beneficiary. You see, Stuart made over the policy to me when he couldn't meet the premiums in return for the loan of £2,000. This is the policy and this is the receipt for the loan. Suspecting a forgery, Inspector?"

Lugosi portrays Orloff as a man quite taken with his own fiendish cleverness. We can clearly see the motivation for this string of murders is Orloff's desire to bilk the insurance company he brokers for out of its money at the cost of others' lives.

Holt pretends to be satisfied and leaves. Orloff calls in his secretary to obtain a list of the underwriters for Stuart's policy which he expects to cash in as soon as possible. He then seeks out the phone number for Diana Stuart.

That night Grogan is singing merrily in his bath when the lights in his room go off and Jake makes an unexpected appearance and silences him beneath the suds. (Hey, what happened to Grogan's police tail? Must have had the night off). Jake no sooner departs when the police arrive, discover the body, and Holt calls the Yard to learn that Diana has gone to visit Orloff.

Orloff pretends concern for Diana's welfare and asks her what she intends to do. She stoutly insists that she shall find the man who killed her father. Orloff advises her, "Of course, but don't let your sorrow dwell on your mind. Work would help to heal it. Now, I have a very dear friend who runs a home for the blind, he himself is blind, who needs a secretary who can see to help him."

Diana is grateful for this new opportunity and Orloff speaks to Dearborn. Orloff tells Diana not to worry about the salary and tells her, "My man has a taxi waiting for you. Now, don't brood on the past. Think of the future." Orloff has been making his fortune on other people's futures, or rather the lack of them.

Conveniently, Diana's taxi driver turns out to be Inspector Holt, who informs her about Grogan. She tells him about her new position and Holt promises to keep an eye out for her.

At the home for the homeless and blind, white-haired, bespectacled, mustachioed Dr. Dearborn (a largely unrecognizable Lugosi) shows her around. Dearborn introduces her to the residents who are surprised that she can see (as if the blind assumed that everyone simultaneously lost their sight when they did). He even shows her the clinic upstairs where Lew is being tended to by Jake.

Holt arrives and asks Dearborn to translate the braille message. Dearborn informs him that the first initial is "M," but that the rest is indecipherable.

Shortly after Holt leaves, Orloff enters the clinic and confronts the prostrate Lew: "You have been very foolish, Lew. You have been writing on little bits of paper. The police have been here. They might come back, Lew. They might ask you questions. You're blind and you can't speak, but you can hear, and that will never do."

To remedy the situation, Orloff applies two electrodes to Lew's ears and proceeds to fry Lew's hearing with a strong jolt of electricity.

Diana meanwhile searches Dearborn's office and finds proof that her father is linked to the whole seamy set-up, though why she expects Dearborn to have some connection isn't clear. Orloff enters, sees what she is doing, and decides to alert her to his presence. She quickly replaces everything and leaves. Orloff turns to Jake and tells him, "You know where the young lady lives, Jake. She's a difficult young woman, Jake. Perhaps you'd better see her safely home," in a meaningful way that does not bode well for Diana's safety.

At headquarters, Holt reveals, "I've been checking up on that nice doctor guy. Doctor, I thought he was bogus, but it isn't. He'd be a practicing physician today if a megalomanic streak hadn't got him into trouble years ago. Now he runs the insurance company. He takes out bogus policies, forges the signatures of carefully selected people, he waits a reasonable time in paying the premiums, and everything is safe and above board."

In *The Dark Eyes of London*, Lugosi portrays a character who indulges two distinct personalities... the kindly Mr. Dearborn and the evil Dr. Orloff (pictured above). This British film shot at Welwyn Studios became the first British film to earn the recently designated "H" certificate.

"Then neatly bumps them off," says O'Reilly in amazement, slow on the uptake as usual.

"Collects the money from the underwriters, makes a fictitious entry in his books saying the money has been paid out to people who don't exist," Holt concludes.

Diana calls to tell them of her discovery. The lights go out in her flat and Jake shuffles across the room *a la* Rondo Hatton. Still, Diana is too quick for the slow moving monster and locks herself in another room. He is about to break down the door when the police burst in and Jake flees by way of the fire escape.

Holt persuades Diana to return to her job to gather more evidence despite her obvious danger and shaken nerves. They decide to go together first to Orloff's office and search that. Despite a lack of incriminating evidence, Holt orders Orloff's arrest for murder.

Diana reads about it to Dearborn as Holt and O'Reilly arrive at the home to continue their investigation. Dearborn shows Holt upstairs where Holt attempts vainly to communicate with mute Lew. When Holts asks Dearborn what the purpose of a large iron tank in the room is, Dearborn replies that only Dr. Orloff would know. Holt gives Dearborn a list of questions to transcribe into braille in hopes that Lew can answer them.

Dearborn gives Diana the key to the cupboard where the braille machine is kept and returns upstairs. As Diana is taking the machine out, she sees her father's cufflink in the corner of the cupboard, a very obvious piece of evidence left carelessly strewn about by the otherwise meticulous Orloff. She then decides to ask Dearborn about it.

"This belonged to my father," she tells him. "How did it get into this house?"

"I don't recollect ever seeing it before," replies Dearborn.

Diana pounces on the obvious slip. "Seeing it? How could you see it, Mr. Dearborn? Blind. No more blind than I am. You're a fake and you're shielding the man who killed my father."

"Since you're so interested, I'll tell you," says Orloff, divesting himself of his Dearborn disguise, and altering his voice back to normal. "Yes, I am the man who disposed of your father, for the same reason that I must now dispose of that poor fool on the bed—both got in my way."

Orloff straps Diana into a straitjacket and gloats. "That stupid policeman, he stood there and asked me what the tank was used for. Now, I will show you."

He then unstraps the struggling Lew from his bed and drowns him in the tank, then continues his explanation: "This building was once a warehouse and the floor we're on now overhangs the river. Below there are mud flats which shall prove most useful. Eventually the tide reduces them and the rest you will understand. In your father's case, unfortunately, we couldn't follow procedure. Jake carried him to the river."

With that, Orloff disposes of Lew's now inert corpse. Diana tries to argue that Holt will soon be there and the men in the home will know. "The men downstairs know nothing," Orloff responds. "They are blind. Who else will be alive to tell them?" He calls for Jake.

The police head for Dearborn's home, but Jake soon has Diana and starts to carry out Orloff's orders. Then she hits upon an idea. "Jake, where's Lew?" she asks, telling him, "He's gone, Jake! Orloff got rid of him like he got rid of all the others. Out of this window into the river."

The bereaved Jake stops what he's doing and begins tearing the room apart looking for Lew. Furious, Orloff returns upstairs, and demands, "Jake, what are you waiting for! Do as I told you!" However, the brute advances on Orloff instead, who shoots him.

"I shall have to settle with you myself," he informs Diana. He hears the police break in downstairs. He dashes to confront them, throwing down a flask which sends up billows of gas and smoke while he takes aim. Bang. He's shot in the arm.

Deciding that discretion is the better part of valor, he retreats, but before he can escape up the ladder to the roof, Jake grabs hold of his ankle and the two grapple back and forth in desperate battle. Jake manages to dump Orloff into the mud flats below where he slowly sinks into the slime, a somewhat appropriate end.

Jake dies of his bullet wound as Holt and O'Reilly break in the door and free Diana. Holt and Diana plan their marriage while O'Reilly looks forward to returning to America.

The film's co-scripter and director, Walter Summers, was born in Barnstaple, England in 1896 and he passed away in 1973. His parents were in show business and he started on the stage as a boy, becoming an assistant director at the ripe young age of 17. By 1918, he was writing screenplays for director Cecil Hepworth, becoming a director himself five years later with *I Pagliacci* (1923).

Summers worked on several documentaries including *Ypres, The Battle of Mons,* and *The Battles of Coronel and Falkland Islands*. His other films include *The Lost Patrol* (1929), *Chamber of Horrors* (1929) [not to be confused with the 1940 British film *Chamber of Horrors* directed by Norman Lee based on Edgar Wallace's *The Door With Seven Locks*]; *Suspense* (1930), *The Man From Chicago* (1930), *The Flying Fool* (1931), *Deeds Men Do* (1932), *The Return of Bulldog Drummond* (1934), and others. His son, Jeremy Summers, also became a director of low-budget British thrillers (e.g. *Vengeance of Fu Manchu; House of a Thousand Dolls*).

Producer and co-scripter John F. Argyle was both a producer and director, producing the 1940 version of *Chamber of Horrors* mentioned above as well as *Tower of Terror* (1941) [in which a lighthouse keeper becomes convinced that a woman is the reincarnation of the wife he killed], *Mutiny on the Elsinore* (1936), and *Once a Sinner* (1950) and directing such films as *Paradise Alley* (1931), *Smiling Along* (1931), and *Send for Paul Temple* (1946).

The film was released in the U.S. in 1940 by Monogram Pictures Corporation under the title *The Human Monster* and was by far the best of the Lugosi Monograms, the others all being actual Monogram productions. When the film was submitted to the New York-based National Motion Picture League, it prompted the following outraged response from Adele Woodard, the League's president, who wrote to the company regarding the film, stating:

"Judging all pictures from a moral and psychological standpoint, the National Motion Picture League regrets that the Monogram picture, entitled, *The Human Monster*, featuring Bela Lugosi, Hugh Williams, and Greta Gynt, from the book by Edgar Wallace, cannot receive an endorsement.

"OUR REASON FOR NON-ENDORSEMENT:

"Dead man's body floating in water, five murders, trickery, espionage, drowning blind people in tank to get insurance, instruction in criminal methods, drinking, blind man's home a camouflage for gangster's evil deeds, horrible screams, crime made exciting and alluring, many views of drowned bodies lying in slimy water, drunkenness, drowning man in big tank, joking about tragedy, coarse language, tattooed arm, horrible face, harrowing details of straping (sic) blind mute in bed and making him blind, horrible screams as eyes are operated upon to make him blind, forgeries, bogus insurance policies, horrible screams as girl is chased, maniacle (sic) sounds, choking girl in preparation for drowning her, faking blindness, drowned bodies thrown out window into river, many views of drowned bodies, murder by shooting, throwing vials of gas at people, shooting, taking law into one's own hands, publicity states 'If you are weak don't come. For the strong only.'

"REMARKS:

"This picture is a disgrace. Monogram Pictures deserve (sic) the censure of every patriotic citizen for producing such an unwholesome film."

In response, Monogram general sales manager, Edward A. Golden, wrote back to Mrs. Woodard telling her, "We have your endorsement of our picture, *The Human Monster*, dated April 11, and are sending a copy of same to each one of our sales offices. Thanks for your cooperation."

Film collector and scribe (and long-time Lugosiphile) Ron Borst commented in *Garden Ghouls Gazette* #20, that *The Human Monster*"is one of Bela Lugosi's top ten films. I do not believe that I have ever seen another of his films in which he has portrayed such an inhuman character.... [T]here is, in addition to the obvious crimes committed by Orloff, the added evil of a past sprinkled with various medical transgressions. This adds greatly to the overall effect of evil which Orloff creates."

While the film clearly belongs to Bela who performs unmitigatedly malevolent characters better than anyone, Hugh Williams and Greta Gynt do provide staunch support as the incorruptible hero and heroine. Edmond Ryan is one of the liveliest of the film's performers; however, his brash personification of an Irish-American is distracting without being amusing and comes off as a noisy intrusion. He mostly stands around asking obvious questions or appreciating Holt's brilliance. Wilfred Walter does inject an effective note of pathos to the role of Jake in the scenes where he looks after the helpless Lew, who indeed proves the brute's only friend.

The film was remade as *Dead Eyes of London* (original title: *Die Toten Augen von London*) in 1961 as part of the German Edgar Wallace *krimi* series. The remake starred Joachim Fuchsberger, Karin Baal, Dieter Borsche, Wolfgang Lukschy, Ann Savo, and Ady Berber and was directed by Alfred Vohrer.

Nevertheless, it is still the Lugosi version that remains the most memorable, especially for Lugosi limning one of his most ruthless and heartless characters as well as his impressive impersonation of the seemingly mild-mannered Dearborn. Sadly, the great Hungarian actor would not find any subsequent roles as worthy of his talents, though he tackled them with equal aplomb and relish rendering several otherwise unwatchable efforts with their only saving grace notes as Lugosi vehicles.

Proud poppa Bela Lugosi with his son Bela, Jr. on the set of *Son of Frankenstein.*

Son of Frankenstein

(1939)

by Susan Svehla

CREDITS: A Rowland V. Lee Production; Producer/Director: Rowland V. Lee; Original Screenplay: Willis Cooper; Director of Photography: George Robinson; Art Director: Jack Otterson; Assistant Art Director: Richard H. Reidel; Musical Director: Charles Previn; Musical Score: Frank Skinner; Musical Director: Charles Previn; Music Arranged by Hans J. Salter; Assistant Director: Fred Frank; Set Decorations: Russell A. Gausman; Editor: Ted Kent; Makeup: Jack P. Pierce; Sound Director: Bernard Brown; Technician: William Hedgcock; Costumes: Vera West; Special Effects: John P. Fulton; Universal Studios, Released January 13, 1939; 94 Minutes

CAST: Basil Rathbone...Baron Wolf von Frankenstein, Boris Karloff...The Monster, Bela Lugosi...Ygor, Lionel Atwill...Inspector Krogh, Josephine Hutchinson...Elsa von Frankenstein, Donnie Dunagan...Peter von Frankenstein, Edgar Norton...Thomas Benson, Emma Dunn...Amelia, with Perry Ivins, Lawrence Grant, Michael Mark, Lionel Belmore, Gustav von Seyffertitz, Lorimer Johnson, Tom Ricketts, Caroline Cooke, Clarence Wilson, Ward Bond, Harry Cording, Bud Wolfe, Betty Chay, Jack Harris

The premiere Hollywood Monster Factory was no more. After *Dracula's Daughter* in 1936, the fathers of horror, Carl Laemmle Sr. and Jr. in a bizarre corporate takeover, departed Universal Studios leaving it in the extremely incapable hands of Charles R. Rogers who bore no love for the horror genre. Production of horror films screeched to a halt leaving the Universal horror film masters adrift in the Hollywood Hills. James Whale, *persona non grata* to the new Universal regime due to his flamboyant lifestyle, would be relegated to directing two lesser films at Universal, while Karloff signed a multi-picture deal with Warner Bros. Lugosi eagerly looked forward to getting back to dramatic roles, putting the horrific Count to rest. Unfortunately, thanks to *Dracula*, the great Hungarian actor was to be forever typecast as a fiend. The phone never rang with those "normal" job offers; in fact, it didn't ring at all.

Under Rogers' mismanagement Universal lost three million dollars during his two-year tenure. At the beginning of 1938 he was replaced by Nathan Blumberg, formerly of RKO. RKO had scored big with its megahit *King Kong* in 1933; perhaps with Blumberg at the helm, there was still hope for the dearly departed horror film.

It was during the summer of 1938 a down-on-its luck Hollywood theater rented three older, cheaper films for play. This triple threat of horror—*Dracula, Frankenstein*, and *Son of Kong*—proved the adage, "if you show it, they will come." The story could almost have been dreamt up by Hollywood screenwriters looking for a new version of the backstage musical.... Hey, I've got a theater, let's put on a horror show! The little theater, not to mention the horror film genre, was saved. People lined up around the block to once again face the terror of the horrifying Monster, the deadly seductive Count, and the King of Beasts.

Universal quickly realized the profit potential of the "monsters" and stuck new prints, re-releasing *Dracula* and *Frankenstein* wide, and, in the process, breaking box office records throughout the country.

The Universal Monster Factory was back in production! Universal quickly put into motion plans for a Frankenstein sequel, *Son of Frankenstein.* Rowland V. Lee, coming off a successful film for Universal, *Service De Luxe* (1938), was given the coveted Producer/Director position. A script was quickly churned out by Willis Cooper, a writer for the radio series *Lights Out,* a script that was to be radically changed by Lee.

The original Cooper script had Wolf von Frankenstein, the son of Frankenstein, discover the remains of the lab and the bride, but no monster. Later in the story the monster kidnaps the young son of Frankenstein, planning to implant the child's brain into himself, a plot device that was recycled for *Ghost of Frankenstein* in 1942. Lugosi was slated for the Inspector role, in this version called Neumuller. Ygor was nowhere to be found.

Universal, backing the film in a big way, released to *Variety* a cast list including Peter Lorre, Boris Karloff, and Bela Lugosi. Unfortunately the script hadn't even been completed at this time.

Several theories abound as to why Lorre didn't appear in the film; either he had no interest in the role and turned it down or Lee nixed the casting of Lorre as Baron Wolf von Frankenstein. Either way, it was probably for the best. It would be difficult to picture Lorre, the portrayer of characters who were usually delightfully weird and kinky, as the stiff-upper-lipped doctor and family man.

Lee held out for dashing Basil Rathbone as the leading man. Rathbone had made his mark in *Romeo and Juliet* (1936), after which he portrayed a series of despicable villains in films such as *David Copperfield* (1935), *Anna Karenina* (1935), and *The Adventures of Robin Hood* (1938). *Son of Frankenstein* offered him the rare opportunity to play a dedicated father, scholar, and hero.

Karloff was once again to play the tragic Monster. He agreed to second billing under Rathbone, providing the Monster did not speak. The script was changed to accommodate him.

Lionel Atwill, most known to horror fans for his deviant roles in *Mystery of the Wax Museum* (1933) and *Murders in the Zoo* (1933), was signed for the role of the Inspector, leaving no part for horror icon Bela Lugosi. Lee and screenwriter Willis Cooper quickly rectified this oversight, creating the character of Ygor specifically for Lugosi, a role many people consider to be his very best work. Director Lee gave Lugosi free reign in creating the character of Ygor and Lugosi played the part to the hilt.

The studio, never known for its overwhelming generosity and knowing the financial bind Lugosi was in, reportedly cut the typical salary of Lugosi in half. Upon learning of this, Lee did everything he could to keep Lugosi working the entire shooting schedule of 46 days. As you watch the film you will notice many brief appearances by Ygor as well as numerous closeups of him during lab sequences that have little to do with the action on screen but much to do with the thoughtfulness of director Lee.

Josephine Hutchinson was cast in the role of Elsa von Frankenstein and four-year old cutie Donnie Dunagan was cast as Peter von Frankenstein; he wasn't the best child actor in the world, but he was adorable.

Technicolor test footage of *Son of Frankenstein* was filmed, but after seeing the monster in color, thankfully, these plans were scraped. The visual imagery of light and shadows as well as the amazing set decoration make *Son of Frankenstein* a truly remarkable film. The filmmakers carefully created a stunning black and white atmosphere that color would have destroyed.

It is obvious Art Director Jack Otterson and Cinematographer George Robinson were vastly influenced by the German Expressionistic artists and filmmakers of the silent era such as Paul Wegener (*The Golem*, 1920), Fritz Lang (*Metropolis*, 1926), and F.W. Murnau (*Nosferatu*, 1922) as well as Danish filmmaker Carl Dreyer whose use of light and shade in *Vampyr* (1931) certainly inspired the creators of *Son of Frankenstein*. The amazing aura created by the talents of Otterson and Robinson are at their best in scenes such as the one in the laboratory when Frankenstein first learns the Monster is active. The Monster, followed by Ygor, rises from the lower level of the lab, the vapors of the sulphur pit rising behind him; he approaches the Baron and slowly places a hand on his shoulder. A remarkably chilling moment.

Production on the film began Nov. 9, 1938, with a tentative budget of $250,000 which Lee rapidly pushed to $300,000. The budget would reach $420,000 by the end of the picture, not a great deal more than *Bride of Frankenstein* whose final budget was $397,023. *Bride* was also completed in 46 days.

Lee tossed out the old script and began filming with basically no script at all, often handing the actors their lines just minutes before shooting began.

The makeup and special effects for *Son of Frankenstein* were quite elaborate causing Karloff and Lugosi to spend many hours in Jack Pierce's makeup chair. The Ygor makeup took four hours to apply and consisted mostly of yak hair. Lugosi loved the character remarking, "God, he was *cute*!"

The basic story that finally emerged is well known to all horror film lovers. The Frankenstein family moves to the village of Frankenstein. The villagers sullenly voice their objections, soon becoming an angry mob. Ygor, a blacksmith hanged for bodysnatching, has guarded the Monster and used him for revenge upon the jury that condemned him. The Monster is stuck by lightening and falls into a coma, as Ygor explains to Frankenstein. The Baron, hoping to restore his father's good name, agrees to bring the Monster out of the coma. Needless to say, havoc ensues.

As the film opens the first shot is of the damaged Frankenstein castle gatehouse. A sad haunted face peers out a broken window. He watches village women hide their faces as they rush past the cursed castle. Two young boys, feigning macho bravado, speak brashly of not being afraid of Ygor but bolt frantically when they notice him at the window. The villagers lament, "We live in the black shadow of that cursed place up on the hill that only that crazy Ygor with his broken neck dares to stay!" The village scenes are dark and stormy, the landscape desolate and dreary. The viewer immediately feels the curse upon this hamlet.

In direct contract to the first scene, the introduction of the Frankensteins— Wolf, Elsa, and little Peter—shows a warm, loving family. They are taking the train to their new home, the ancestral home of the Frankensteins. The cozy security of the little family as Peter is tucked into his bed is directly contrasted by the grim scenery outside the train windows. Bare, crooked trees reach eerily toward a dark, rain-soaked sky. Baron Frankenstein appears unaffected by the locale. "It's exciting, isn't it?! Out there in the darkness a new life looms before us." One can almost physically feel the warmth of the coach diminish when gazing at this frigid landscape.

Frankenstein displays a hint of his obsession with his father and his father's work when he tells his wife, "It wasn't my father's fault that the being he created became a senseless murdering monster. He was right. It was the unforeseen blunder of a stupid assistant that gave his creation the brain of a killer instead of a normal one. How my father was made to suffer for that mistake."

The family is greeted by a milling crowd outside the train station. The Baron tries to apologize for his father's mistake, but the crowd angrily departs, leaving a lone policeman standing in the deserted street.

A tremendous rain storm rages as the Frankensteins arrive at their new home. The interior of the Castle Frankenstein is huge but cold and barren. The large fireplace throws little warmth or light into the massive downstairs room. The coldness of the room aptly reflects the hatred felt for the Frankensteins by the villagers.

The main hallway was designed with a winding wooden staircase that leads to the bedrooms upstairs. The diagonal shadows of the stairs create a feeling of apprehension in Elsa as well as the audience. A feeling all is not well here.

The library, like the rest of the castle, is full of angles and curves, it is the room where Frankenstein will begin to see his cozy safe existence take many strange turns, erratic turns that will threaten his sanity and the safety of his family.

The library is dominated by a portrait of Wolf's notorious father and this room will see many clever exchanges take place between Baron Frankenstein and Inspector Krogh. The Baron opens a box given him by the Burgomeister and reads a letter from his father. "You have inherited the fortune of the Frankensteins. I trust you will not have inherited their fate."

The music takes on an ominous tone and heavy lightening bolts erupt in the rainy night. A soggy Ygor pulls himself up outside the library window. He ducks down quickly before being noticed by the Baron and and his butler, Benson (Edgar Norton in another noteworthy performance by the wonderful character actor). Filler scenes like this one kept Lugosi working the entire picture.

Lionel Atwill as Inspector Krogh arrives to warn the Baron of the burden he carries along with the Frankenstein name. When the Inspector enters the castle to offer his protection, it is difficult to take his character seriously in this as well as his many other scenes throughout the film. Scenes such as when he uses his left hand to raise his wooden arm and polish his monocle are difficult to watch without a chuckle today. The passage of years, as well as Mel Brook's *Young Frankenstein,* is partly responsible for this reaction.

When Frankenstein insists the stories of the monster are exaggerations and asks the Inspector if he has ever seen the monster, he is shocked by the answer. Krogh tells of how when he was a small boy, about Peter's age, the monster broke into his home and grabbed him by the arm. "One doesn't easily forget, Herr Baron, an arm torn out by the roots." The story forces the audience to face the fact the monster is a vicious killer, not just a misunderstood creature searching for his creator father as in the original film.

Atwill's character is perhaps the most defined and interesting in the film. The Inspector displays a sense of sadness as he explains it was always his dream to be a great soldier, but because of the Monster he is forced to command his small police force. Even though he has more reason than most to hate the Baron, his sense of honor and duty compels him to offer protection to the Frankensteins. Atwill is very good in this role, especially when you get past the wooden arm theatrics.

It is at this point the six unsolved murders in the village are mentioned. Six prominent men have been killed, their hearts burst. Even the great Scotland Yard has not been able to solve the mystery.

An establishing shot has Ygor moving aside a secret panel and staring at the Peter sleeping angelically. This secret panel will play an important part later in the film.

The next day, Frankenstein, looking very much the proper English gentleman, visits the destroyed laboratory of his father. The lab is a two-story affair of corridors, ladders, bubbling sulphur pit, and secret rooms. As in the original *Frankenstein*, Kenneth Strickfadden provided the electrical apparatus for *Son of Frankenstein.*

At this point in the film Lugosi's Ygor finally has more to do than stare at other cast members. A stark shot of a hole in the wall of the laboratory, a huge boulder, and a beam with a chain hides Ygor as he spies on the interloper. Suddenly, Ygor pushes the boulder toward the unsuspecting Baron Frankenstein. It misses, and pointing his rifle at Ygor, the Baron demands the stranger come down. Ygor grabs the heavy chain and lowers himself to the ground. "Why did you try to kill me?" asks the Baron. "I thought you came here to kill me," Ygor croaks, his head bent to one side. One is barely able to distinguish the suave tone of the infamous Hungarian Count Dracula in the pathetic voice of this creature. Ygor explains he was hung as a bodysnatcher and declared dead; this is the reason for his crippled appearance.

Lugosi sinks his teeth into this basically supporting role. He imbues Ygor with a sly personality bordering on madness. He gleefully scurries through the part with his neck bent to one side, his right shoulder raised, croaking his rudimentary dialogue. As you watch him in the role, you notice Lugosi move his entire body when he speaks, playing on the fact the character's broken neck will not move. He will turn his whole body toward a speaker, or use his hands in a way that reminds us of his deformity. His movements as Ygor are an amazing accomplishment and are one of the reasons this performance is considered by many to be his *tour de force.*

Ygor leads the Baron through a hidden passageway to the crypt of his father and grandfather. Once again we see the influence of silent filmmakers as the actors traverse the passageway. Light and shadows are used impressively as the Baron and Ygor make their way down

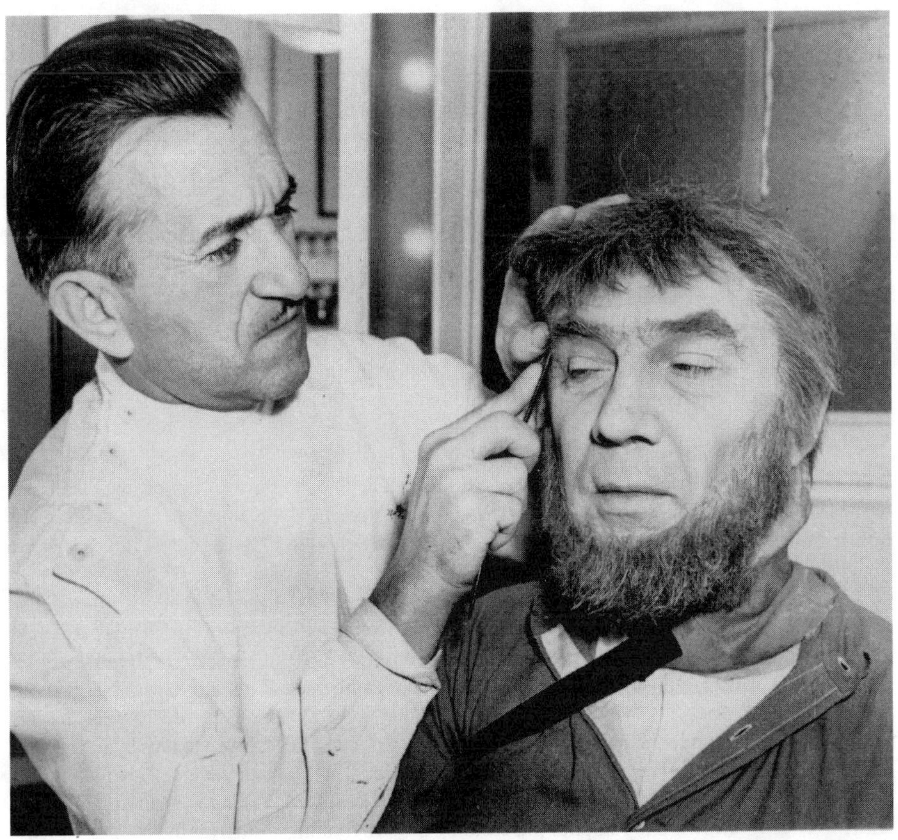

Makeup wizard Jack P. Pierce applies complicated Ygor makeup on a patient Bela Lugosi.

an incline in shadow to the burial chamber of the Frankensteins.

Ygor watches closely as Frankenstein first sees the Monster lying on a slab. In a clever tribute to the original film and Colin Clive, the Baron touches the huge hand of the monster and jumps back shouting, "He's alive!"

Lugosi grins with lunacy as he tells the Baron, "He's my friend; he does things for me." Reportedly during the filming of this scene the sight of Karloff lying prone on the slab and Lugosi uttering this double entendre broke up the entire film crew, a sight many of us would loved to have seen.

Frankenstein agrees to try to bring the Monster out of his coma. During these lab scenes, director Lee gives Lugosi numerous closeups, seemingly delighting in the freakish character Lugosi has created.

The town council decides to bring Ygor in for questioning, another fine scene for Lugosi. "Tell us the truth or we'll hang you again and make a better job of it next time."

"No you no can hang me again." Ygor cries, beseeching the judge. What follows is bizarre black comedy as the council argues whether Ygor can be hanged again, since he has already been declared dead once. Lugosi's eyes sparkle with delight during this scene. During the course of the questioning it is brought out that eight jurors convicted Ygor, and six of them are now dead. The villagers suspect Ygor, but he always has an alibi, having been heard playing his mournful songs on his horn. Ygor, slyly displaying his loathing for one of the remaining jurors who convicted him, begins to cough as he leaves the witness stand, and leaning close to the juror, spits in his face. "I'm sorry I cough. You see, bone gets stuck in my throat."

Back at the lab, Ygor is the only one who can control the now mobile monster. Lugosi seems to take devilish delight in ordering his old nemesis, the silent Karloff, around. He leads the monster to the next juror who is about to meet his maker. Lugosi plays his horn as the Monster knocks the man down and then proceeds to run his cart over him, a fairly shocking scene for the time. As the man dies, Ygor grins in triumph.

The mad Ygor then plays his horn while taunting the irate village mob gathering outside the Frankenstein gate. Frankenstein, realizing the Monster has been responsible for the village murders, rushes to the lab, and picking up a boulder, tries to crush the sleeping Monster. Ygor stops him.

In between these trips back and forth between the castle and lab, Frankenstein has been dueling verbally with Inspector Krogh, at one point indulging in a strange game of darts. The Inspector sticks the darts in his wooden arm, another scene Mel Brooks has ruined for us, although hilariously.

Frankenstein, descending deeper into madness each passing moment (or what some refer to as serious overacting on the part of Rathbone), decides to throw Ygor off the estate. He dashes wildly to the laboratory and orders the equally deranged Ygor from the castle. Ygor picks up a hammer and throws it at the Baron who responds by shooting Ygor. Lugosi falls slowly to the ground.

The Monster finds his only friend dead. He notices blood on his hand (Ygor's blood) and lets out a piercing scream of agony. Karloff, who basically had only to walk through this part, plays this scene for all it is worth. The relationship between Ygor and the Monster, while that of user and victim, is still a friendship between misfits. Two creatures, dead but alive, who have no one else in which to turn. The Monster, now totally alone, goes on a rampage destroying the lab, throwing equipment into the bubbling sulphur pit. He picks up a book given to him by little Peter, and one can see the idea of revenge slowly dawn on his face. The Monster traverses a hallway filled with frightening angles and shadows to enter to room of the child. Taking the trusting little boy with him, he heads toward the sulphur pit. Holding the still trusting child over the pit, the Monster cannot destroy the only other creature who has been kind to him. The Inspector and Frankenstein arrive at the lab and battle the Monster; in the process the Inspector once again sees his arm torn out, fortunately, this time, it is the wooden one. The Monster places little Peter under his huge foot; Frankenstein, in a swashbuckling bit of derring-do, swings on a chain and knocks the Monster into the pit.

As the Frankensteins leave the village on the train, the townspeople cheer the Baron for ridding them of the Monster. Light is once again used to create an emotion, as the scene is lit brightly, signifying an end to the dark curse over the village of Frankenstein, at least until *Ghost of Frankenstein.*

Seemingly Lugosi and Karloff had their best working relationship ever working on this film. Photos of the cast having a surprise birthday party for Karloff show the two grinning and eating cake. That day, Karloff had another pleasant surprise, the birth of his first child, Sarah. The two new fathers, Karloff at 51 and Lugosi at 50, had much to talk about. Bela brought 10-month-old Bela, Jr. to the set, although the sight of Mr. Karloff in monster makeup frightened the baby, at least photos show him ready to cry when posing with Boris.

The advertising campaign for the film featured one-sheet posters proclaiming, "The Screen's Most Fearsome Three!... in a stark... terrifying drama of shadowy lives!" The all important shadows even making their way into the advertising materials. Many of the posters focused on Rathbone with Karloff's and Lugosi's images displayed much smaller although their names were the same size... Rathbone, Karloff, Lugosi. Other versions and sizes of posters proclaimed, "A new juggernaut of destruction loosed upon the world!... Transformed terror... dormant for 20 years... suddenly unleashed by this half-man half-demon... plagued by the mania of his father... the Monster Maker!" Another poster screams, "Is he man or monster! Human... warm...normal... until sinister shadows of the past stir the dread heritage in his blood.

The pressbook for *Son of Frankenstein* offers articles for newspapers that focused on the casting of Karloff and Lugosi. "Aimed to surpass all former entries in the field of bloodchilling shockers, Universal's *Son of Frankenstein* achieves that mark through the sheer force of its eerie drama. Karloff, as the halfhuman Frankenstein creation, and Lugosi, as the broken-necked peasant, top their grim characterizations of the former *Frankenstein* and *Dracula* thrillers." The pressbook, in an astonishingly ahead-of-its-time attitude, tried to appeal to the female audience with the following:

"Women have long been considered the weaker sex. Some man with a genius for labels fastened that one on them and it has stuck ever since. The popular belief is that women can't stand this, that, or the other, mentally or physically. In contradiction, most of the requests for permission to visit the *Son of Frankenstein* stages while the picture was being filmed at Universal Studios came from women.

"These were women who had seen the first *Frankenstein* on the screen and they were eager to glimpse Boris Karloff once again in his revolting make-up, and Bela Lugosi as Karloff's misshapen prisoner, as the two famous actors will appear in the new *Son of Frankenstein.*

"One of the things women are supposed not to be able to stomach is the sight of blood. Yet seventy-five years ago, 1854, to be exact, Florence Nightingale plunged herself body and soul into the thick of the bloody horrors of the Crimean War, setting a heroic nursing standard which has subsequently been followed by millions of her sex.

"And 125 years ago, when it was the fashion of women to have 'vapors,' faint daintily at the sight of a mouse, and otherwise give every reason to be called the weaker sex, a woman created the most horrible monster in literature, and set the pattern for all future literary effort in which such creatures of horror were depicted.

"...It is a fair conclusion that as much woman interest will be centered in *Son of Frankenstein* because of Boris Karloff and Bela Lugosi, as will be given to Basil Rathbone and Lionel Atwill, admittedly two of the handsomest men on the screen."

Son of Frankenstein debuted in Hollywood at the Pantages Theatre in January 1939, Friday the 13th to be exact. Reviews were excellent.

Variety..."Picture is well mounted, nicely directed, and includes cast of capable artists."

Motion Picture Herald: "Histrionically, the picture is outstanding because of the manner in which Basil Rathbone, Boris Karloff, Bela Lugosi, and Lionel Atwill... sink their teeth into their roles."

The Hollywood Reporter: "Bela Lugosi is quite horrible and very impressive as the living dead man, Ygor."

New York Daily Mirror: "...The Messrs. Lugosi and Karloff vie with each other in being horrible and it is touch-and-go all the way..."

Audiences flocked to see the film, breaking box office records and being held over in many cities. The success of the film revived the horror film genre as well as the career of Lugosi. Karloff went on to many other films while Lugosi signed a contract at Universal. His first project under that contract was the 12- chapter serial *The Phantom Creeps*, directed by Ford Beebe and starring Lugosi and Regis Toomey.

In 1942 Lugosi would once again bring the character of Ygor to life in *The Ghost of Frankenstein* directed by Erle C. Kenton and starring Lugosi, Lon Chaney, Cedric Hardwicke, Ralph Bellamy, and Lionel Atwill. In this outing, the second son of Frankenstein meets his destiny with the Monster and Ygor. The misshapen Ygor manages to have his brain transfered into the Monster.

Today *Son of Frankenstein* is highly regarded by film historians as well as film fans. Ygor is but a small role, but a role that Bela Lugosi made his own. A performance that will forever endear Lugosi to fans of film as well as fans of finely crafted acting.

As many writers have noted in this volume dedicated to the work of Bela Lugosi, his later career would, basically, be a sad end for a regal actor. However, in studying the real horrors of Hollywood we find Bela was not alone in his fate. The Hollywood powers that be, whether in the '30s or through the '90s, are a merciless lot. Many fine actors have been rudely cast aside as they aged or, in the case of women, began to lose their looks. The dashing Errol Flynn who thrilled audiences with his heroic adventures in films such as *The Adventures of Robin Hood* (1938) ended his career with the abysmal *Assault of the Rebel Girls* made on a nonexistent budget in 1959. The stunning Bette Davis who dominated every film she appeared in, especially *All About Eve* (1950), ended her career in the terrible *The Wicked Stepmother* (1989). Perennial character actor John Carradine appeared in films such as *Drums Along the Mohawk* (1939) but ended his long and noteworthy career in independent films such as *Vampire Hookers* (1979). Jose Ferrer who won an Academy Award for his performance in *Cyrano De Bergerac* (1950) also made *Zoltan—Hound of Dracula* in 1977. Beginning in the 1950s musicals were unable to compete with the advent of television, and the stars who kept MGM afloat, talents such as Jane Powell, June Allyson, Esther Williams, Van Johnson, Vera-Ellen, and many others were unceremoniously let out of their contracts. Kirk Douglas, who starred in the great *Gunfight at the OK Corral* (1957), appeared in *Holocaust 2000* (1978) later in his career. I think if Bela and his horror cohorts had been around in the '70s they would have been appearing on the *Love Boat* Halloween special.

While these low-budget, independent schlock films are regarded either as high camp, exercises in bad filmmaking, or worshiped by a new type of film fan—those who revel in bad taste, they do serve an important function. Independent horror films and their directors have kept Hollywood icons employed and in front of the cameras long after these great stars have been forgotten by the omnipotent Hollywood Dream Factory. Film fans, whether they respect directors such as Ed Wood or not, truly own these Hollywood mavericks a debt of gratitude for enabling film buffs to watch these wonderful actors, troupers such as Bela Lugosi, once again weave their charismatic spells.

Karloff and Lugosi together again in Unviersal's *Son of Frankenstein*.

Island of Lost Souls
Ninotchka
Fantasia

by Dennis Fischer

ISLAND OF LOST SOULS (1932)

CREDITS: Director: Erle C. Kenton; Screenplay: Waldemar Young, Philip Wylie from *The Island of Dr. Moreau* by H.G. Wells; Director of Photography: Karl Struss; Makeup: Wally Westmore; Paramount 1932, 72 minutes

CAST: Charles Laughton...Dr. Moreau, Bela Lugosi...Sayer of the Law, Richard Arlen...Edward Parker, Leila Hyams...Ruth Walker, Kathleen Burke...Lota, the Panther Woman, Arthur Hohl...Montgomery, Stanley Fields...Captain Davies, Robert Kortman...Hogan, Tetsu Komai...M'Ling, Hans Steinke...Ouran, Harry Ekezian...Gola, Rosemary Grimes...Samoan Girl, Paul Hurst...Donahue, George Irving...American Consul

NINOTCHKA (1939)

CREDITS: Director: Ernst Lubitsch; Script: Charles Brackett, Billy Wilder, Walter Reisch, based on a story by Melchior Lengyel; Photography: William Daniels; Sets: Cedric Gibbons, Randall Duell, Edwin B. Willis; Costumes: Adrian; Music: Werner Heymann; Editor: Gene Ruggiero; Makeup: Jack Dawn; MGM 1939, 110 minutes

CAST: Greta Garbo...Ninotchka, Melvyn Douglas...Leon, Claire Swana...Ina, Bela Lugosi...Razinin, Sig Rumann...Iranoff, Felix Bressart...Buljanoff, Alexander Granach...Kopalski, Gregory Gaye...Rakonin, Rolfe Sedan...Hotel Manager, Edwin Maxwell...Mercier, Richard Carle...Gaston

FANTASIA (1939)

CREDITS: Production Supervisor: Ben Sharpsteen; Story direction: Joe Grant, Dick Huemer; Music Director: Edward H. Plumb; Musical Film Editor: Stephen Csillag; *Toccata and Fugue in D Minor* by Johann Sebastian Bach segment directed by Samuel Armstrong; *The Nutcracker Suite* by Piotr Ilich Tchaikovsky segment directed by Samuel Armstrong; *The Sorcerer's Apprentice* by Paul Dukas segment directed by James Algar; *The Rite of Spring* by Igor Stravinsky segment directed by Bill Roberts and Paul Satterfield; *Pastoral Symphony* by Ludwig van Beethoven segment directed by Hamilton Luske, Jim Handley, and Ford Beebe; *Dance of the Hours* by Amilcare Ponchielli segment directed by T. Hee and Norman Ferguson; *Night on Bald Mountain* by Modest Mussorgsky and *Ave Maria* by Franz Schubert segment directed by Wilfred Jackson; Animation supervision: Vladimir Tytla; Disney 1940; Production released by RKO Pictures, 120 minutes

CAST: Leopold Stokowski and the Philadelphia Orchestra, Deems Taylor, Ballet Russe (including Roman Jasinsky, Tatiana Riabouchinska, and Irina Baranova), Bela Lugosi

There is a difference between Bela Lugosi's best films and the best Lugosi films. Lugosi was an actor who established himself as a horror star and spent most of his career headlining

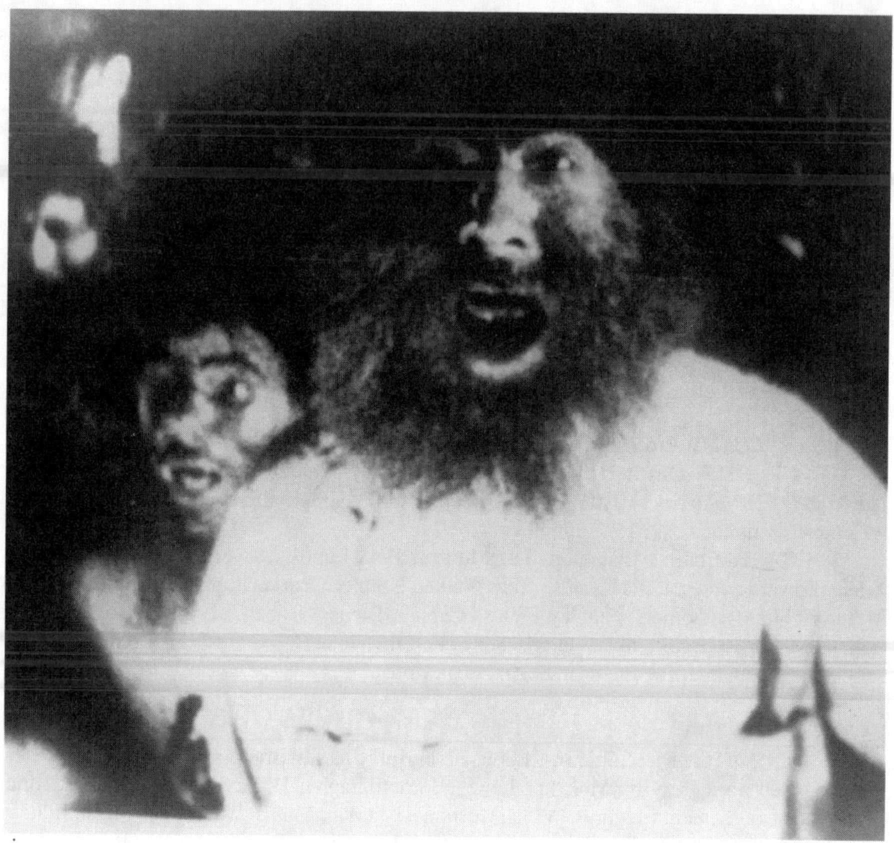

Bela Lugosi portrays the Sayer of the Law in *Island of Lost Souls.*

substandard vehicles, so it remains an ironic aspect of his career that in the greatest films he made, Lugosi was relegated to extremely minor roles, albeit expertly performed, while in the films that really showcased his talents, Lugosi's performances tend to be the only quality of the film meriting interest.

The controversial *Dracula* aside (with critics today still debating the film's merits or lack of them), what of Lugosi's other major films? True, *Son of Frankenstein* proves that Lugosi could steal a film away from Boris Karloff while Karloff was assaying one of his greatest roles (or from Lon Chaney, Jr. in the sequel for that matter), though the part of the fiendish Ygor with his pitifully hunched back and macabre delight in his dastardly doings easily upstages the Monster when it is reduced to an automaton; however, apart from its magnificent sets, what interest does *White Zombie* hold apart from Lugosi's magnificently malevolent Murder Legendre and his delightfully arch line readings? *Mark of the Vampire* efficaciously employs Lugosi as a horror icon arrayed resplendently in atmospheric photography but comes up with nothing interesting for him to say or do. I think part of the reason that audiences cheer Lugosi on to bump off the other cast members in *The Raven* is that the rest of the crew is so dreadfully dull in comparison, and the less said about his impoverished Monogram productions the better.

Nevertheless, such "showcases" illustrate Lugosi's admittedly limited range at the top of its form and that is the reason we are grateful for their existence. Still, the true cinéastes must admit that none of these movies will find a place among the greatest films ever made, but there are some films Lugosi acted in that do achieve the pinnacle of greatness: namely, *Island of Lost*

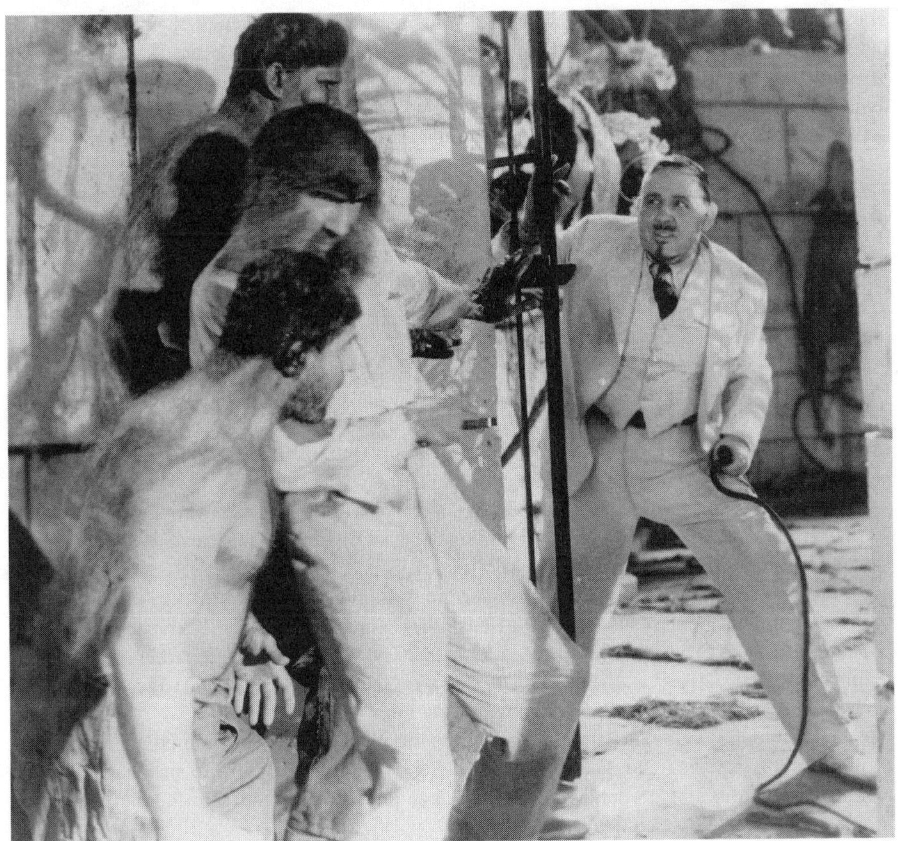

Moreau (Charles Laughton) clearly delights in playing God over his less fortunate fellow creatures from *Island of Lost Souls.*

Souls, Ninotchka, and Walt Disney's *Fantasia*.

In *Island of Lost Souls*, Lugosi only appears in a few scenes as the hairy faced Sayer of the Law, but he nevertheless leaves a lasting impression. Lugosi's performance is indelible as he brings a feral intensity to the part that is suggestive of a tortured, animalistic being who has been the object of the sadistic attentions of Laughton's depraved mad doctor. Who can forget his recitation of the chant "Not to go on all Fours: that is the Law. Are we not Men?" (Certainly not the rock band Devo who used the last four words as the title and catchphrase for their first album).

Island Of Lost Souls, adapted from H. G. Wells' great anti-vivisectionist novel *The Island of Dr. Moreau*, features a superb and slyly naughty performance from Charles Laughton as the mad Dr. Moreau, who through a series of painful operations transforms animals into men and hopes to prove his findings by having one of his creations mate with a shipwrecked sailor (Richard Arlen).

Laughton knew Wells personally. According to his wife Elsa Lanchester, he was "more or less subservient to people like Wells and his friends. He was impressed and quiet, absorbing and drawing upon their words of wisdom, which he later was not above using himself. Wells, stuttering but effective, had the great art of simplicity that always seemed to elude Charles when he later became an imposing figure himself with listeners at his feet."

Wells' work has since its initial release often been dismissed as a simple thrilling adventure story, but a close examination of the novel reveals that Wells' intentions are somewhat grander. It is true that most of Wells' work lacks characters, replacing them with mouthpieces who outline a particular point of view the author wishes to examine. However, *The Island of Dr. Moreau* only has three human beings—Moreau, the devilish/divine scientist; Montgomery, his assistant, a drunken doctor in disgrace; and Prendick, the common man and narrator—and they serve symbolic roles so this fault does not obtrude as it does in other of Wells' works.

Moreau owes something to both Swift's *Gulliver's Travels* and Shakespeare's *The Tempest*, only this Prospero's island is populated only by Calibans. Like Gulliver, Prendick is a common man who is shipwrecked and becomes troubled by the close kinship between human beings and animals.

In the novel, Prendick initially suspects that Moreau is experimenting on human beings to beastialize them. The film's Prendick is Edward Parker, who never has this suspicion and is initially grateful to Moreau after running afoul of Captain Davies (Stanley Fields, a former prizefighter who specialized in Wallace Beery type roles) whose passenger Montgomery (Arthur Hohl) arranged to have Parker rescued while Davies was drunk. When Davies abuses the unfortunate servant M'Ling (Tetsu Komai), Parker decks him, so when transferring cargo to Moreau's ship, Davies arranges to have Parker thrown overboard, in effect stranding him there on an uncharted island away from the main shipping lanes.

The film also includes a fiancée, Ruth Walker (Leila Hyams), who anxiously awaits word from her man in Apía and who, after finding out what Davies has done, arranges with Captain Donahue (Paul Hurst) to be transported to Moreau's island.

As a test of his achievement in transforming animals into men, Moreau is anxious to see how successful his greatest success, Lota the Panther Woman (newcomer Kathleen Burke), will be accepted as human by his visitor. Indeed, Lota quickly is quite taken with Parker and he begins to find himself attracted as well, but when he discovers that her fingernails are suggestive of cats' claws, he heads for Moreau demanding an explanation.

Moreau points out that some of the exotic plants around his compound are greatly evolved familiar species, and that he has been using his discovery of how to speed up evolution to transform various animals that Montgomery has acquired for him into semi-human shapes and forms using vivisection techniques.

(At the turn of the century in England, there was a great outcry from some quarters against conducting scientific experiments on animals for any purpose, much like the People for the Ethical Treatment of Animals and other animal rights groups today who oppose any kind of testing on lower species regardless of the potential benefit to humanity. Both Wells and George Bernard Shaw were part of a group known as the Fabians who opposed vivisection and promoted socialism).

Many incidents from the novel are dropped in the film. In the novel, Moreau dies after a female puma on which he is operating escapes and he is overcome by his creations halfway into the story, with Prendick taking a shaky control from then on only to have Montgomery get drunk and get done in himself. Eventually the Beast People forget the language they have learned and lapse back into natural savagery.

The key to understanding Wells' intent is to notice that in the novel, the nature of the island's population is a central, and that when the Beast People are at their most human, they reveal the animal; at their most animal, the human. Consider this passage where Prendick encounters a "Horse-Rhinoceros":

> "It may seem a strange contradiction in me—I cannot explain the fact—but now, seeing the creature there in a perfectly animal attitude, with the light gleaming in its eyes, and its imperfectly human face distorted in terror, I realised again the fact of its humanity. In another moment others of its pursuers would see it, and it would be overpowered and captured, to experience once more the horrible tortures of the enclosure. Abruptly I slipped out my revolver, aimed between his terror-struck eyes and fired."

Wells' Law which the Beasts chant is deliberately meant to suggest the liturgical chant

"For His Mercy Is On Them That Fear Him: Throughout All Generations." The film version eliminates some of the more satirical passages: "Not to suck up Drink: that is the Law. Are we not Men? Not to eat Fish or Flesh," etc. However, the religious implication is clear in Lugosi's Sayer's tortured declaration: "*His* is the hand that makes! *His* is the hand that heals! *His* is the House... of... *Pain!*"

Wells himself labelled the novel "an exercise in youthful blasphemy," indicating clearly that for Wells, Moreau is not just god-like and Promethean but actually symbolizes God, and furthermore, that Wells isn't too impressed with Him. When God is dead, the island's population reverts to savagery, though Moreau's spirit hovers invisible above the island. (Pendrick says, "For a time you will not see him. He is there—pointing upward—where he can watch you. You cannot see him. But he can see you.").

The blame for the Beast People's misery is set squarely on Moreau's shoulders: "Before they had been beasts, their instincts fitly adapted to their surroundings, and happy as living things may be. Now they stumbled in the shackles of humanity, lived in a fear that never died, fretted by a law they could not understand." Obviously, this is meant as a metaphor for the lot of the human race.

Additionally, Moreau declares that he can "see into their very souls, and see there nothing but the souls of beasts, beasts that perish—anger, and the lusts to live and gratify themselves." Wells saw the same conditions in the lower classes of England (who can forget the fearsome, flesh-eating Morlocks in *The Time Machine* or his warnings of the dangers of the mob in *Things To Come*?).

Nor are Montgomery or Prendick, the remaining humans, any more sympathetic, as both lack understanding for each other or empathy for the plight of the Beast People.

Wells believed in evolution and accepted the idea that regardless of religious cant man is an animal. He underscores this idea at the end by having Prendick return to civilization and feeling no different: "I could not persuade myself that the men and women I met were not also another, still passably human, Beast People, animals half-wrought into the image of human souls; and that they would presently begin to revert, to show first this bestial mark and then that." Everywhere he looks, Prendick sees evidence of man's inescapable animal nature. In doing so, Wells expands his vision from one small island to include the great world outside where beast mentality is everywhere and the vast, pitiless mechanism of blind fate cuts and shapes the fabric of existence.

The screenplay for *Island of Lost Souls* retains much of the original's perversity, power, and blasphemy. In its finely wrought images, the film creates a symbolism of its own. Parker coming out from the sea and traveling through a tunnel to reach Moreau's domain suggests a rebirth. The dark jungle with its creepers and vines gives rise to a notion of dangerous fecundity. Here nature is dangerous and out of control.

Moreau's compound is made of stone and iron bars and is highly suggestive of a prison. Deciding that it would be advantageous to his experiment for Parker to stay, Moreau arranges to have his own yacht sunk, thereby trapping Parker.

Unlike the censored "I know what it feels like to be God" speech from *Frankenstein*, Moreau clearly delights in playing God over his less fortunate fellow creatures, consequences be damned, and says as much. However, he too is trapped by his own rules when he violates his law "not to spill blood" (the operations conducted on the Beast People without benefit of anesthetic being an easily overlooked exception) and orders Ouran (Hans Steinke), apparently an orangutan-man, to kill Donahue.

In the early days of sound, directors were hired to direct the actors' performances, and directors of photography were often the ones who figured out where to set-up and/or move the camera as well as control the lighting for a shot. *Island of Lost Souls* was fortunate to have the great Karl Struss as its director of photography.

Struss' work includes some of the best and a little of the worst cinematography in

Hollywood history. He won the very first Academy Award for cinematography for his work on *Sunrise*, and would later photograph such films as the Fredric March version of *Dr. Jekyll and Mr. Hyde, The Sign of the Cross, The Great Dictator, Journey Into Fear, Rocketship X-M*, the execrable *Mesa of the Lost Women, The Alligator People,* and the Kurt Neumann version of *The Fly*.

To emphasize Moreau's powerful command of his island, Struss shot Laughton from low angles to emphasize his dominance of the scene, but at the finale, he is pulled from the top of the frame to below it, an unseen carved up carcass cut by his own surgical instruments of torture wielded by the vengeful Beast People who give Moreau a sample of the House of Pain's specialty.

A love scene between Parker and Lota is framed on the reflections of the figures in a pool rather than the figures themselves to emphasize that their attraction is illusory. This is further emphasized by having their images in the water break up, symbolizing the shattering of this idyllic scene as soon as it comes into contact with the reality of Lota's true nature.

Karl Struss' gleaming photography is best appreciated in MCA's digital laserdisc transfer from an excellent print that is a far cry from the dupey or foggy prints one often encountered in the past.

The script for the film is by Philip Wylie in collaboration with Waldemar Young. Wylie's numerous contributions to science fiction, both literary and visual, often are overlooked or are not discussed. In addition to this film, they include the novel *The Murderer Invisible* which provided inspiration for Whale's adaptation of *The Invisible Man*, of which Wylie did an early draft; he also scripted the films *The Savage Gentleman, The King Of The Jungle*, and the memorable *Murders In The Zoo*, provided the source novels for the films *Gladiator* and *When Worlds Collide*, and the script for *Los Angeles A.D. 2017*, Steven Spielberg's science fictional episode of the TV series *The Name Of The Game*. His novel *The Disappearance*, about how men and women suddenly find themselves in different parallel universes, was optioned by George Pal and was announced as a film shortly before the filmmaker's demise.

Laughton's performance turns Wells' Moreau into a sweating sadist, something which Wells strenuously objected to (Wells approved of the movie being banned in Britain, such was his dislike of the final results), but Laughton's intimations of sexual perversity is part of what makes the film so eminently watchable today. He plays the part as a slightly paunchy, primly bearded pervert with a effeminate fussy manner and a luminous ice cream suit that stands out against the oppressive darkness of the surrounding jungle.

Laughton had recently made his first film in America, James Whale's rarely screened classic *The Old Dark House*, and made an unforgettably decadent Nero in *Sign of the Cross*. It was right after completing *Island of Lost Souls* that he achieved his breakthrough role in *The Private Life of Henry VIII*, which won him an Oscar and stardom. (Laughton would play the role again years later in George Sidney's *Young Bess*). While most film fans remember him best for his performances in *The Barretts of Wimpole Street, Ruggles of Red Gap, Les Misérables*, the 1935 *Mutiny on the Bounty* (in which he created a historically inaccurate but unforgettable Captain Bligh), *The Big Clock, Witness for the Prosecution, Spartacus,* and as crafty Senator Seab Cooley in Preminger's *Advise and Consent*, genre fans will most remember him as *The Hunchback of Notre Dame, The Canterville Ghost*, and the director of *Night of the Hunter*.

For Laughton, *Island of Lost Souls* was not a happy experience. He was annoyed with director Kenton for dressing in an identical white suit and hat and then demonstrating how he wanted Laughton to act and even how to handle a whip. An animal lover, he felt disgusted by the story. He claimed that he was never able to enjoy a zoo again because the smell of caged animals reminded him of the picture and made him sick.

To get the caged animals to react, men dressed in monkey skins were made to prod them, which resulted in tragedy when a tiger lashed out and tore one man's arm from his socket. Shot on a trip from Los Angeles to nearby Santa Catalina Island, the seas proved rough and caused the animals to become sick and vomit.

According to Richard Bojarski in *The Films of Bela Lugosi*, several directors including Dan Venturini and Norman Taurog were considered by Paramount before they finally settled on Erle C. Kenton. Kenton was an experienced director whose work extends back into the silent era, but he had never made a horror film before *Island*. Later, he came to be considered something of a specialist in them, helming such classic efforts as *The Ghost of Frankenstein, House of Frankenstein, House of Dracula*, and *The Cat Creeps*.

Kenton's best film remains *Island of Lost Souls*, for which he not only extracted one of Laughton's best performances but also created an atmosphere of oppressive terror. While lines about "the natives are restless" are clichéd now, the film still evokes a kind of primordial fear of something hairy, feral, and fearsome coming out of the darkness with malevolent intentions to do us harm.

Wally Westmore and his makeup crew deserve high praise for their creation of the Beast People using myriad designs. Struss' photography reveals telling details, giving us hints of each creature's origins, but keeps the masses of Beast People in darkness so that our imaginations have to flesh out the horrific suggestions of the various forms.

Actors Randolph Scott, Buster Crabbe, Joe Bonomo, and Alan Ladd have long been rumored to be among the disciples of Lugosi's Sayer of the Law under Wally Westmore's hirsute makeup designs. Laughton himself recalled, "I remember each horror and monster had more hair than the one before. Hair was all over the place. I was dreaming of hair. I even thought I had hair in my food."

Footage of Lugosi as the Sayer of the Law from this film also turned up in Edgar Ulmer's *Beyond the Time Barrier* and in Joe Dante's "Reckless Youth" addendum at the end of *Amazon Women on the Moon*, a parody of Dwain Esper-type social commentary movies (try explaining that to a mass audience) in which Paul Bartel's doctor introduces Carrie Fisher's Mary Brown to "Pete Jones," (Lugosi footage) who was transformed into a hirsute beast by smoking cigarettes and drinking beer.

Though the story has also been filmed under the titles *Ilé D'epouvante, Terror Is A Man, Twilight People*, and *The Island Of Dr. Moreau* (Don Taylor's dull 1977 remake starring Burt Lancaster), this 1932 Paramount production remains the best film adaptation of Wells' entertaining yarn.

Lugosi appeared in very few "straight" films after his success in *Dracula.* He was in *Broadminded* (1931) for Mervyn LeRoy and *Women of All Nations* (1931) for Raoul Walsh, but his best venture into the world of mundane movies was Ernst Lubitsch's *Ninotchka*, which was nominated for best film and best screenplay in the banner year of 1939 (losing out to *Gone With the Wind*).

Ernst Lubitsch had wanted to shoot a film with Garbo for years, but never got the chance until 1939 when he filmed one of his greatest comedies, *Ninotchka*, in two months at Metro-Goldwyn-Mayer, finishing on July 27, 1939.

The film came about when Garbo's close friend Salka Viertel met with Hungarian writer Melchior Lengyel at the Brown Derby and told him that MGM producer Bernie Hyman wanted to make a comedy with Garbo that could be advertised with the slogan "Garbo Laughs," and did Lengyel have a story?

Lengyel came over to Garbo's house the next day while she was swimming naked in the pool and told her, "Russian girl saturated with Bolshevist ideals goes to fearful, capitalistic, monopolistic Paris. She meets romance and has an uproarious good time. Capitalism not so bad, after all." MGM paid him $15,000 for those sentences.

Initially, Gottfried Reinhardt was assigned to direct and Viertel and Lengyel tried to write it. After Jacques Deval also failed, it was turned over to S.N. Behrman, who concocted an amusing love story about a lady commissar and a French gigolo who came to Paris to make a deal for the ore in a Siberian nickel mine.

Garbo liked the script and asked for Lubitsch, who liked the dialogue in Behrman's script but felt the plotting was too loose and that nickel ore was uncinematic, preferring diamonds for their romance and visual appeal. He wanted Walter Reisch to work on it. (Walter Reisch's later films as screenwriter include *Comrade X* [an Academy Award nominee], *Titanic* for which he shared an Academy Award, *That Hamilton Woman, The Girl in the Red Velvet Swing*, and *Journey to the Center of the Earth*).

Behrman refused to collaborate with Reisch and so left the project, at which point Charles Brackett and Billy Wilder joined the team. Brackett and Wilder were one of Hollywood's greatest comedy writing teams, crafting the films *Bluebeard's Eighth Wife, Midnight, Arise My Love, Ball of Fire, Five Graves to Cairo*, and *Sunset Boulevard* together among others. (Additionally, Brackett was the producer of that ghostly gem *The Uninvited* and was the cowriter-producer of *Journey to the Center of the Earth*). Wilder went on to become one of the greatest directors of all time, creating the classics *Sunset Boulevard* and *Some Like It Hot* among many other fine films.

In *Ninotchka*, Garbo plays a dour female Soviet commissar sent to supervise a trio of bumbling agents entrusted by the Soviet government to sell certain crown jewels for badly needed foreign currency. The setting is Paris and under the seductive ministrations of Melvyn Douglas' corrupt Leon d'Algout, Comrade Nina Yukushova becomes Ninotchka, "dear little Nina."

The comic idea behind *Ninotchka* was to take a good-hearted, satirical look at the mores of the Soviet Union by exposing three well-intentioned representatives of the Soviet Board of Trade to the hitherto unexperienced luxuries of capitalism. Lubitsch perfectly cast the parts with expert character actors from Hollywood's large pool of such experienced performers.

Sig Rumann, whose work includes *To Be Or Not To Be, House of Frankenstein, A Night at the Opera, Nothing Sacred, It Happened Tomorrow,* and *Only Angels Have Wings,* and who specialized in playing pompous Prussians, plays Iranoff. Felix Bressart, whose work includes *To Be Or Not To Be, Shop Around the Corner*, and *Portrait of Jennie*, plays the amiable, whimsical Buljanoff. Polish actor Alexander Granach, whose work includes *There Goes An Actor, Hangmen Also Die*, and *For Whom the Bell Tolls*, rounds out the comic trio playing Kopalski.

The film is very unusual in a number of ways. For one thing, it deftly mixes politics and romance. It has a strong, female protagonist who is a serious, dedicated member of the Communist party, who is also an attractive, intelligent, sympathetic good person. She is not a caricature of a woman, but the real thing, who fervently believes in the dictatorship of the proletariat and the class struggle and is allowed to argue her viewpoint with intelligence. (Such strong female characterizations were rare back then and seem even rarer now).

The comic irony of the story is that she falls in love with her polar opposite, a Parisian gentleman who is a parasitic gigolo, who is dedicated to nothing but his own pleasures, albeit a man possessed of humor, intelligence, and taste. Together, each learns something from the other and comes out the better for it. They confront each other as equals, as the wounded in love Ninotchka (she kissed a Polish lancer before he died), who has been leading the way for others as a way of losing herself, re-embraces life after a persuasive kiss from Leon. Individualism triumphs over the collective.

The film is rife with wonderfully comic lines and performances, which I have no wish to spoil for those who haven't seen it as yet. Garbo proves herself a master of deadpan humor, as when Buljanoff asks how things are in Moscow and she replies, "Very good. The last mass trials were a great success. There are going to be fewer but better Russians."

Lugosi has the minor part of Razinin, the Commissar on the Board of Trade to whom Ninotchka must return to report on the progress the three comic protagonists have made. Razinin complains that he sent them to Constantinople on an important fur deal solely on the strength of Ninotchka's Paris report on these gentlemen; however, the three comrades have not only failed to sell a single piece of fur, but are dragging the good name of Russia through every café and nightclub in Constantinople.

Lugosi reads, "How can the Bolshevik cause gain respect among the Moslems if your three representatives, Buljanoff, Iranoff, and Kopalski, get so drunk that they throw a carpet out of their hotel window and complain to the management that it doesn't fly?"

Ninotchka must repress a smile and asks if Razinin is certain that the report is correct. "It gives details which couldn't be invented," Lugosi observes drily. "Naturally I want to verify it and that's why I need you."

Ninotchka begs Razinin figuratively not to throw her in that briar patch, but he austerely informs her: "That is for me to decide, Comrade Yakushova" and "Please don't waste my time, Comrade. Do your duty. Good-by."

Naturally, this proves the impetus needed to get all the main characters together for the happy ending. Lugosi makes for a very convincing serious Russian official and performs his minor part well. He is given third billing, above Rumann, Bressart, and Granach who are central characters throughout the film. Director Lubitsch explained, "People are so accustomed to him as Dracula that I thought a sympathetic moment would surprise audiences as much as it did him."

The film has been remade twice, first as *The Iron Petticoat* with Katharine Hepburn and then as the musical *Silk Stockings* with Cyd Charisse and Fred Astaire. Neither come close to matching the charm and appeal of the original.

Lugosi's uncredited contribution to *Fantasia* is seldom mentioned or noted, but nevertheless I feel it was a very important one that helps this animated classic to achieve its artistic climax.

Fantasia grew out of a meeting Leopold Stokowski had with Walt Disney where the famous conductor expressed an interest in working together on something. Disney wished to do something which would restore Mickey Mouse to his former level of popularity and it was felt that Paul Dukas' *The Sorcerer's Apprentice* might do the trick. Stokowski agreed to conduct and wondered why Disney planned to stop at a short subject, why not a full length film with several other musical works that suggest "the mood, the coloring, the design, the speed, the character of motion of what is seen on the screen," as Stokowski later expressed it. In short, a fantasia, which means a free development of a given theme.

It was decided to open the film with Stokowski's own orchestral transcription of Bach's *Toccata and Fugue in D Minor*, which was complemented by visual detailing suggestive of falling asleep at the orchestra. Recalled Disney, "All I can see is violin tips and bow tips—like when you're half asleep at a concert," apparently a not uncommon occurrence for the easily bored studio exec.

(In preparing for *Fantasia*, Disney subscribed to a box at the Hollywood Bowl where, he told a co-worker, he invariably fell asleep, lulled by the music and the warmth of the polo coat he liked to wrap himself in. There is also a story that he ridiculed an animator on the film as being homosexual for taking a music appreciation class in preparation for the project).

The final film is in many ways a glorious wedding of sound and image, but one that is not without its faults. Oskar Fischinger, an avant garde painter who worked with Fritz Lang on the special effects for *Frau im Mond* (aka *Woman in the Moon*), helped design the opening sequence, but his designs were considered too abstract by the literal-minded Disney and so he was denied credit and his designs altered.

Bach is best experienced with the original instrumentation and not a bombastic transcription for full orchestra. Igor Stravinsky's *Rite of Spring* has its music seriously distorted under Stokowsky's baton. (Disney offered the composer $5,000 for his work and pointed out that since Stravinsky's work was copyrighted in Russia, and as the U.S. had not signed the Berne copyright agreement, he could simply pirate the music anyway). Beethoven's *Pastoral Symphony* was truncated, a problem exacerbated later when a pickininny centaur was excised from the film on subsequent reissues as being in poor taste. The female centaurs in that sequence were originally all bare-breasted, but the Hayes office insisted that discreet garlands be hung around their necks.

Other aspects of the film remain perpetually pleasing. The design on the *Nutcracker* excerpts is delightful, *The Sorcerer's Apprentice* is inventive and amusing, and the ostrich and hippopotamus send-up of *The Dance of the Hours* is a wonderfully comic lampooning of the pretensions of high culture.

Still, the highpoint of the film remains *A Night on Bald Mountain*, with its gargoyles, demons, and other creatures of the night. The spirits of the night rise from the local graveyard and travel to Bald Mountain for a celebration of Evil, a ritualistic bow to Tchernobog, the Black God. The flames become dancers, then animals, then lizards, at the whim of the great Black God, who revels in the passionate exhibition. However, as morning approaches and church bells are rung, the Black God recoils in horror and is driven back until he is vanquished as the music segues to Schubert's *Ave Maria*, which Schubert scored for solo voice, but is given a choral treatment here with new lyrics by Rachel Field; it bombasts the crescendo of magnificent malevolence that precedes it out of existence.

Bela Lugosi's important contribution to the film was portraying the figure of Tchernobog. He was photographed miming the actions the character would do (and Lugosi's expressions on the character's face are unmistakable). Lugosi's work was then rotoscoped and animated by Vladimir Tytla, one of Disney's greatest master animators.*

Tytla ended up leaving Disney after the famous Disney strike of 1941, brought on by Disney's refusal to allow a union. Tytla went to work for UPA, directed Little Lulu cartoons, and became director of Paramount's Famous Studios cartoon branch for six years beginning in the mid-'40s, where his talent was sadly wasted on trite material, and he ended up as a freelance director-animator for Terrytoons working on "Deputy Dawg" and "Hector Heathcoate" cartoons.

Despite Ralph Bakshi's claim of rotoscoping as an important new innovation in the '70s, Disney had been rotoscoping live action figures as guides to animation as far back as *Snow White*. Indeed. members of the Ballet Russe, notably Roman Jasinsky, Tatiana Riabouchinska, and Irina Baranova modeled for the elephants, hippos, and ostriches (respectively) in the *Dance of the Hours* sequence.

Disney had wanted to shoot the film in widescreen and offer it on a reserved seat basis before giving it a wide release; however, his bankers objected and the only innovation Disney was able to offer was "Fantasound," an early stereo process which was available in only a few theatres.

The film fared badly in initial release, when it was trimmed to 88 minutes, though it was critically well received; however, it more than recouped its costs (about $2,250,000) with subsequent releases and until its release on video was one of the Disney theatrical perennials. Unfortunately for Disney, he had just spent a fortune building his dream studio and World War II shut down his foreign market and a significant portion of his revenues so that the banks closed off his line of credit in 1940 and he was forced to offer stock to the public for the first time.

Nevertheless, Disney and *Fantasia* both survived, with the latter achieving classic status. One of Disney's incipient ideas for the project was to periodically re-release it with the order and selection of musical programs altered. Such tunes as Debussy's *Clair de Lune*, Weber's *Invitation to the Waltz, Humoresque*, Sibelius' *Swan of Tuonela*, Wagner's *Ride of the Valkries*, and Prokofiev's *Peter and the Wolf* were considered for insertion into future releases (with only the last one reaching the animation stage in Disney's lifetime as a fairy tale with music for the film *Make Mine Music*).

This plan will now be put into action by the current owners of the Disney studios, and if *Bald Mountain* is retained in the line-up, then *Fantasia* cinemagoers can once more savor Lugosi's important contribution to this film on the big screen where it was intended to be seen.

Any true film fan or Lugosiphile would be well advised to check out all three of these movies, the best that Lugosi ever made.

* Whether Bela Lugosi was actually the model used in the final segment of *Fantasia* is open to debate. In the book *Disney Animation: Illusion of Life* by Thomas & Johnson, animator Tytla stated that he was unhappy with Lugosi's performance, filmed by assistant Wilfred Jackson. After Lugosi left and received his check, even unknown to Walt Disney, Tytla asked Jackson to remove his shirt and model for the character. More recent sources even claim that character actor Nestor Paiva was the actual model used for the rotoscoping. The truth may never be known.

The Devil Bat

(1940)

by Gary J. Svehla

CREDITS: Producer: Jack Gallagher; Director: Jean Yarborough (aka Yarbrough); Associate Producer: Guy V. Thayer, Jr.; Executive Producer: Sigmund Neufeld; Screenplay: John Thomas Neville; Original Story: George Bricker; Director of Photography: Arthur Martinelli; Sound Engineer: Farrell Redd; Art Director: Paul Palmentola; Musical Director: David Chudnow; Production Manager: Melville De Lay; Film Editor: Holbrook N. Todd; Released December 13, 1940 by PRC, 68 minutes

CAST: Bela Lugosi...Dr. Paul Carruthers, Suzanne Kaaren...Mary Heath, Dave O'Brien...Johnny Layton, Guy Usher...Henry Morton, Yolande Mallott (aka Donlan)...Maxine, Donald Kerr..."One-Shot" McGuire, Edward Mortimer...Martin Heath, Gene O'Donnell...Don Morton, Alan Baldwin...Tommy Heath, John Ellis...Roy Heath, Arthur G. Bryan...Joe McGinty, Hal Price...Police Chief Wilkins, John Davidson...Prof. Raines, Wally Rairdon...Walter King

"Imbecile...bombastic ignoramus!" These words of anger, frustration, and superiority fly from the lips of the downtrodden Bela Lugosi, as Dr. Paul Carruthers, in the 1940 PRC release of *The Devil Bat*. Lugosi's star hadn't exactly fallen out of the sky as of yet, but instead of being a big fish at the star-studded Universal pond (he would now be reduced to performing supporting roles at the studio palace he had helped maintain a decade earlier), he was soon to become horror king of poverty row, most especially at Monogram Pictures where he starred in a slew of wonderful little "B" romps most distinguished by efforts such as *The Invisible Ghost* and *The Corpse Vanishes*. However, Bela Lugosi was to first make one memorable nasty for bottom-of-the-barrel PRC, the much aligned *The Devil Bat*, but as we will see, Lugosi's performance here was marvelous and a credit to his craft. While the film never tried to be any more than exactly what it was—a low-budget "B" programmer—it still manages, even today, to entertain.

Perhaps Bela Lugosi's pride would never allow him to recognize the fact that being king of Monogram and PRC was pretty pathetic compared to his glory days at Universal, but our love for the man and his talent is stronger today because of Bela's failure to wake up and smell the coffee. Just as Peter Cushing demonstrated at Hammer Film Productions, a professional Shakespearean style performance could elevate even the lowest of product-minded Hammer productions (*Evil of Frankenstein, Frankenstein Created Woman*, etc.). Peter Cushing's star has risen to incredible heights not because his films are worthy of Academy Award attention but simply because he approached all his films and all his performances as though his reputation were on the line each and every time. He had no inclination to think and pause and say this film is bottom-drawer so I shall give only 60% of myself. Cushing thought of his fans, of his personal dedication to his craft, and always gave 100 per cent even when he realized the film certainly was not worthy of his talents. That dedication to his craft is what earned Cushing kudos throughout his productive career and such praise will continue to mushroom after his recent death.

Unfortunately, for Boris Karloff, the same cannot be said. To me, Karloff has always been the king of horror, the archetypal bogeyman icon that essayed some of the most memorable performances in the annals of the horror film genre: his Monster in both *Frankenstein* and *Bride of Frankenstein*, his Imhotep in *The Mummy*, his Ellman in *The Walking Dead*, his Poelzig in

"It's a shaving lotion... smell it. Rub it on the tender part of your neck."

The Black Cat, his Gray in *The Body Snatcher*, etc. When Karloff was thrown into the midst of an excellent production with a first-rate script and imaginative director, no one could surpass his cinematic talents. But what about the Karloff of *The Climax* or of *Abbott and Costello Meet Dr. Jekyll and Mr. Hyde*? How about the Karloff of *Voodoo Island*? Even when performing the stereotypical mad doctor in *House of Frankenstein*, Karloff is good but he is coasting, certainly not stretching, and this performance becomes competent and adequate at best. But the point here is that Karloff sometimes cakewalked through a performance, was satisfied to deliver less than 100 per cent, that he approached certain films as being beneath his talent, and that his disdain was clearly etched in some of his performances.

For better or worse, Bela, like Peter Cushing, approached every movie as though each film and performance was as important as the one before. Good films, bad films; good characterizations, cliche roles simply were not part of Lugosi's vocabulary. The only thing that seemingly mattered was the next film and the next performance. Approach the current film as being the ultimate chance to display your talents and perhaps you would have the opportunity to act again. Or, to state the philosophy more succinctly, an actor is only as good as his last film.

Thus, being king of the Monogram/PRC mountain still meant being the king and having the starring role. If Lugosi's critical sense-of-being had kicked in and told poor Bela that his talents was being exploited, that these films were far beneath his talent, and that he should simply collect the money, turn in a cursory performance, and try to get better roles in more prestigious properties, Bela Lugosi might have become a fifth or sixth billed *prestige* supporting/character performer in Warner Bros. or MGM "A" productions; he may have maintained a sense of pride, but he would never have become the horror film icon that decades of "B" exploitative moviemaking produced. True, all Lugosi fans relish his starring roles in superb, classic Universal Pictures such as *Dracula,*

The Raven, The Black Cat, etc. but his career, personality, and reputation are perhaps most clearly established by his decades of performances in these cheesy Monogram and PRC productions. To be honest, these "poverty row horrors", as writer Tom Weaver so intuitively defined them in his superb work of the same name, are so much fun to watch and rewatch and the primary reason for this is in the strength of Bela Lugosi's performances. Even when all else around him is going to seed, Lugosi imbues each and every performance as though this were the film to put him back on top.

Put another performer in the Lugosi starring role (such as George Zucco in *Fog Island*, John Carradine in *Face of Marble*, George Zucco in *The Flying Serpent*, George Zucco in *The Mad Monster*, or John Carradine in *Revenge of the Zombies*, etc.) and see how easily forgotten these poverty-row horrors become. But films such as *Voodoo Man, The Ape Man, Return of the Ape Man*, and especially, *The Invisible Ghost* which star Lugosi become a different type of schlock classic primarily because of Lugosi's performance. How many times can a buff watch *Dead Men Walk* (with George Zucco) compared to any of the Lugosi Monograms or *The Devil Bat*? Simply stated, Bela Lugosi becomes the primary focus and reason for these films' longevity and closeness to the heart.

So while many film fans admit to loving films such as *The Devil Bat* with an air of embarrassment and guilty pleasure, Bela Lugosi approached these movies with the same creative gusto that he approached Vollin in *The Raven*. Lugosi's pride and ego would never allow him to see the truth, thus, we as fans should not be embarrassed for Lugosi because generally his poverty-row performances are not embarrassing, and if the quality of the films themselves seems to compromise the great actor's talents, we can appreciate Lugosi's talents that much more in that his presence made a silk purse out of a sow's ear.

A close examination of *The Devil Bat* reveals the simple fact that Bela Lugosi is having so much fun enacting an energetic performance in a god-awful movie. But fortunately, Lugosi's starring length role (unlike many actors today, Lugosi does not submit a cameo performance and warrant star billing) truly dominates the screen with a performance that places him in the majority of the scenes, many with a ridiculous rubber prop as his acting foil, allowing him the latitude to truly command the audience's attention. In *The Devil Bat*, the viewer not only gets superb Lugosi, but the viewer gets plenty of superb Lugosi (something not so in his meager Universal supporting performances of the 1940s).

First of all, the script of *The Devil Bat* places the action in an almost fairy-tale land of Heathville, an idyllic "village" that could have come directly from Capra's *It's A Wonderful Life* mold. The film's printed foreword attempts to create such a Camelot: "All Heathville loved Paul Carruthers, their kindly village doctor. No one suspected that in his home laboratory on a hillside overlooking the magnificent estate of Martin Heath, the doctor found time to conduct certain private experiments—weird, terrifying experiments."

Enter Bela Lugosi, our star!

The laboratory, heavy stone bricks form the back wall, features bubbling beakers and flasks. A deadly serious Dr. Carruthers, wearing a suit and tie no less, opens a hidden passageway behind a cabinet wall. Passing through a strange cellar area, the doctor opens another hidden entrance leading to a strange stairway, leading up to the attic room where he keeps his bats!

"Ah, my friend! Our theory of glandular stimulation through electrical process was correct. A few days ago you were as small as your companion. And now, look at you!!!" Smiling, the doctor carries the giant, sleeping bat (a no-frills rubber prop in medium/long shot becomes an upside-down stock footage of an actual bat in closeup) on what looks like a metal clothes hanger through the recesses of his home, back down into his lab whereby he hangs the monster bat onto electrical apparatus preparing to give the animal its daily zap of energy.

Carruthers goes outside the electrical room closing the door which has a glass window allowing the doctor to observe his experiments from a safe distance. Putting on protective goggles, a somber Carruther watches from outside as electrical charges feed into the bat's body. As the energy apparatus is turned off, Carruthers patiently and intently observes for any sign of life. He clinches his fist from anticipation and smiles as the bat's wings fluctuate. The doctor listens to the bat's heart beat and is interrupted by a phone call. Protesting he is too busy working on his secret formula "for a new shaving lotion" to accept a dinner invitation from his benefactors, he reluctantly gives in telling them he will attend (when in reality he has no such intention).

Returning to the laboratory, he uses tongs to saturate a swab in a vial of liquid and thrusts the chemical smell into the bat's face. The bat awakens and emits a shriek. "You have not forgotten... you hate this strange oriental fragrance—even while you sleep, just as you did before I made you big and strong. Now, if you detect the fragrance tonight when you're fully awake—you will strike! Yes, you will strike—to kill!!!"

What has Lugosi to work with here? A no-frills laboratory with cheap electrical cast-offs from Ken Strickfadden or an imitator. Lugosi does not even have the benefit of a lab coat but instead wears a suit and tie. He delivers all his lines to the silliest rubber bat prop ever conceived, but Lugosi delivers these lines as though his life depended on it. In a silly environment speaking to a silly prop on an ordinary wire clothes hanger, this great actor suspends not just his disbelief but the viewer's as well delivering a monologue of intensity and power that transcends the entire budget limitation of such a poverty-row production.

Now the so-called plot.

Faithful and dedicated scientist Carruthers invented a greaseless cold cream and was given the choice of door #1 (a check for $10,000) or door #2 (partial cash but a share in future business payoffs). Carruthers chose door #1 while the investors Morton and Heath made millions. The reason for their telephone call was to invite Carruthers to dinner to offer the dedicated doctor a bonus check of $5,000. When Carruthers ignores the invitation because he is too busy working on his shaving lotion formula (Lugosi's deadpan delivery is akin to how a girl might turn down a guy for a date because she is too busy washing her hair!), Roy Heath volunteers to hand deliver the check to the doctor's home.

Pouring some of his formula into a smaller bottle, Carruthers puts Roy off, "I'll be right with you," standing a few feet away. After Carruther's cursory apologies, Roy presents the doctor with his surprise. "Let's see what it is—$5,000, I see, a bonus," the doctor mutters matter-of-factly as though Roy just delivered to him the proverbial Christmas fruitcake. "It's awfully nice. I will thank them tomorrow."

Then Carruther's expression changes as he becomes excited. "But aren't you curious in my new formula!??? It's a shaving lotion... smell it."

"Pretty strong!"

"No, no, the scent evaporates. Use it. Now, rub it on the *tender* part of your neck. Soothing, isn't it? Good... bye—Roy!" The ambiguity in Lugosi's voice is of course campy but the double-entendre is crystal clear and cleverly delivered to boot.

Again alone, Lugosi stares at the meaningless check and in voice-over narration delivers another powerful monologue as only Lugosi could deliver. "Lovely check, isn't it doctor! They are wealthy, because of *you*! *You* made them rich, doctor, it was *you* and your formula. Tonight they gave you $5,000 and wanted you to come down to their house and *thank* them for it. That was *your* money they gave *you*—like a bone tossed to a faithful dog."

Carruthers laughs hysterically. "*You* should be very grateful, doctor, very grateful. They are rich and happy thanks to *you*. But what have *you* got, doctor?"

Putting the check in his pocket, with a determined stare, Carruthers returns to his bat room. "Tonight you have work to do. It's time you were on your way." Suddenly, in a shot repeated numerous times throughout the production, we are outside the doctor's attic window whereby the window is slowly raised with a rope and numerous small bats fly outside. Then, after the normal-sized bats are free, the gigantic devil bat exits on its mission of destruction.

In standard shots repeated for every murder, the giant devil bat is seen swooping down above the trees in a small wooded area before swooping down near its intended victim, in this case

Lugosi as deadly serious Dr. Paul Carruthers, wearing a suit and tie no less, working with his bubbling beakers and flasks in his secret laboratory, perfects his deadly shaving lotion.

Roy, as he returns home by automobile. The bat always attacks by first swooping down, then the victim is accorded one shot registering holy terror as the bat swoops down a second time, attaching itself to the person's neck, severing their jugular vein. Roy succumbs in this very manner.

Second brother Tommy is set up in much the same way. "This is the first time I've ever been invited anywhere and asked not to shave until after I get there," the jovial Tommy explains to Doc Carruthers.

"I want this lotion to be perfect before I turn it over to you to be marketed," Carruthers explains, pouring some lotion into his hands.

The oft-repeated "it's a little strong" complaint is followed by the encouraging "it will make customers think they're getting their money's worth... it feels great, very soothing" as Tommy sees another million-selling product.

In his best double-entendre delivery, Carruthers solemnly states, "I don't think you'll ever use anything else!" At this moment Tommy attempts to sprinkle some of the lotion on Doc's hand, but Carruthers pulls his hand away grimacing in a fury. "I have a violent dislike for perfumes... good-bye... Tommy!" Interesting enough, Lugosi then extends his hand to shake Tommy's, the same hand that is permeated with the concoction. As soon as Tommy exits, the doctor takes his jacket off and throws it down in a huff, as though some of the formula may have found its way to his clothing. Momentarily, the attic window again opens. The devil bat realizes what it must do!

Donald Morton is sent a bottle of the lotion as a sample, quickly tries some, and dies off camera.

After ace-reporter Johnny Layton and his photographer One-Shot McGuire see the devil bat strike down Tommy, Layton has One-Shot approach the local village taxidermist to have him create a mock-up of the actual devil bat so a photo can be faked claiming to be the actual devil bat in action. When McGuire slips up and leaves a "made in Japan" tag visible at high magnification, the two reporters are quickly fired by hotshot editor Joe McGinty. When Carruthers learns that the dismissed Layton plans to continue his investigations of the devil bat working with Chief (of Police) Wilkins, the doctor offers Layton a sample bottle of his formula. Out in the garden after midnight, Layton and McGuire are ready for the devil bat's attack and manage to kill the fiend. However, Carruthers simply "transforms" another regular bat to create a new devil bat. "You will be even greater than your unfortunate predecessor," Carruthers smiles with demented delight. His next target... Henry Morton himself, one of the two men to whom the doctor sold his formula. "Tonight, I shall call on Henry Morton; you shall strike him down," the Doc rants and raves to his favorite rubber prop.

Latter, calling upon Morton at Heath Cosmetics, Ltd., Carruthers announces, "Henry, the lotion has turned out to be better than I hoped. I want you to try it."

"Isn't it too strong," is voiced once again by Morton.

Countering, the doctor explains, "No, no! The application quickly tones it down to the right scent. Just a little—*here*. The texture of the skin *there* is always very delicate!"

"I smell to high heavens, " Morton protests.

"Perhaps that will be the secret of its success!" Carruthers declares.

Then Morton "rubs" Carruthers. "Net profits of over one million dollars; a mere $10,000 for your formula. You shouldn't have demanded all cash, doc. You should have ridden along with us and you'd be rich too! Then, you had a lot of fun in your laboratory, with your experiments. Dreaming up something new. You're a dreamer, doc (Lugosi, at this time, is just seething with bitterness and anger but manages to remain silent). Too much money is bad for dreamers."

Carruthers can bite his tongue no longer. "So you try to pay me in flattery, trying to tell me I'm a dreamer. Well, I do dream. Dreams that you could never guess... Your brain is too feeble to conceive what I accomplished. When you find out, Henry, it will be too late!"

Puzzled, Morton states, "You can't control a man's destiny."

Gleefully, Doc replies, "I've already proved it—three times! Good... bye, Henry!"

Carruthers having tipped his hat to Morton too obviously, Morton phones the Heaths and states he has figured out the mystery and will be over the house immediately. Of course, Lugosi is one step ahead storing the devil bat in his trunk, which he releases before Henry Morton arrives. As Carruthers is being entertained in the Heath parlor, we hear Morton's car arrive. Suddenly we hear the grating shriek of the devil bat, and Lugosi registers the most perfect "little-boy-with-egg-on-his-face" expression which changes to a devilish smile when Morton screams in a horrible death agony. Arriving at the front door, Henry takes one step and dies. The over-the-top performance of Lugosi in this sequence is right on the money and it is a delight to see the subtlety inherent in even broad acting gestures. Lugosi is truly a master and subtly shines here.

After reporter Johnny Layton visits Carruther's home when the doctor is visiting the Heath home, Layton pretty well has the pieces of the puzzle put together. The film's climax shows how Layton cleverly tricks Lugosi into revealing his guilt.

First, he calls on Carruthers. "I heard you were out, stalking the devil bat. Any success?" the doctor inquires.

"I thought you may be able to help me. You can give me some more of that new concoction of yours, that shaving lotion... I still have a crazy idea if I douse myself with it, it might attract the killer," Layton reveals.

"I don't see how you can connect the two. But there is a bottle of the lotion on the table." When Layton rubs the lotion on his cheek and neck, Carruther's eyes light up in anticipation. The Doc breathes a sigh of relief when Layton tells him that he plans to wait all night in the garden for the killer to strike. "Layton, I'm afraid all these killings have affected your mind," Carruthers grimly announces.

"Maybe you'd like to come along and be an eyewitness," Layton invites. Carruthers, realizing he would be safe since he is not wearing the lotion, agrees: "I'm sure it would be a waste of time, but I'd be glad to watch your experiment."

However, sitting alone in the solitary gloom of the garden in darkness, the doctor hastily changes his mind. "I tell you Layton, expecting a bat to be attracted by the scent of a lotion, it's all foolishness. I'd better run along!"

"Ah, sit down doc! You're not very chummy tonight. I'd thought you didn't want to be sitting too close to me in case the devil bat shows up," Layton starts toying with the doctor. Fear and dread are written across Lugosi's face.

"According to your theory, the killer wouldn't attack me. I haven't any of that lotion on me," Carruthers states.

In response, Layton throws a stream of the lotion across the Doc's face and shoulder. Shocked, insulted, Carruthers rises to his feet, outraged. Suddenly fear breaks through his arrogance. "Why did you do that," the pathetic doctor asks.

"Not so funny when it's your own jugular vein that's in danger," Layton responds. "Maybe you made a mistake when you let that devil bat of yours out of the attic tonight. Don't worry about the bat killing you tonight... I'm saving you for the hangman. Tell me doc, how did you develop a monster bat like that?"

Paul Carruthers, now sweating profusely, chimes back, "You wouldn't understand scientific theories."

Suddenly the bat makes an appearance, and Carruthers tries to wrestle a gun away from Layton. They struggle and roll around on the ground near the garden bench. Chief Wilkins fires and misses but the commotion allows time for the doc to flee into the woods surrounding the garden. Swooping up love interest Mary Heath, Carruthers is still struck down by his own devil bat and dies as the beast tears at his neck.

As proclaimed earlier, the world inherent in *The Devil Bat* is a fantasy world that only resembles the actual, real one. However, in this fantasy world, good does not necessarily win out over evil. Doctor Paul Carruthers, the well-loved village doctor whom even Chief Wilkens states was above suspicion for any of these crimes, is a very sympathetic madman. Once again Hollywood deals with a creative man who is exploited by big-money interests, in this case entrepreneurs Morton and Heath. Carruthers is mocked by his Heath-Morton masters who do in fact throw him a bone of a bonus of $5,000 most likely out of a feeling of guilt. Since Lugosi sold his interest for money instead of riding along with his benefactors, and since the net profits from his formula total over one million dollars a year, the businessmen can certainly afford to do better by Carruthers than give him a mere one-time check for $5,000.

Thus, many of the common folk moviegoers out there can truly sympathize with the exploited Carruthers and secretly enjoy his methodical plan for revenge. In a perverse sense, even though the Heaths and Mortons certainly do not deserve to die such horrible deaths, the audience does derive pleasure from seeing cold-hearted businessmen and their heirs receive an equally cold punishment for their insensitivity. Even Chief Wilkins suspects a "disgruntled factory employee" as being the fiend who plotted to wipe-out the Heaths and Mortons.

Similarly, the relationship between Layton and McGuire being so quickly fired from the *Chicago Register* by editor McGinty parallels the relationship between Carruthers and the Heaths/Mortons. Though the first mockup of the devil bat was bogus, the team actually did see the actual devil bat in action and only wanted to validate the facts. And the movie audience can support

McGuire's claim to his boss that "when I find that bat, I'll bring it on in myself and stuff it down your throat!" Later when the bat is again seen by the journalists as One-Shot ducks, and the first bat is shot dead, he screams, "I'll cook that bird myself and stuff 'em for McGinty!"

Thus, at the heart of this "B" programmer is the constant conflict of creative people, talented "doers," and honest workers who are unfairly squeezed by insensitive and money/power driven exploiters.

And Bela Lugosi's performance in this PRC release delivers. Logic and self-esteem would seem to dictate to the proud Lugosi that he should have simply taken the check and phoned in his performance, but such was never the case for Bela. His Paul Carruthers is both sympathetic and maniacal, both devil and victim. What actor could remain so focused when delivering lines to a silly rubber prop hanging upside down on a metal clothes hanger? But Lugosi almost makes his audience forget these poverty-row sets and props. Since Lugosi takes this all so seriously, so do we! He makes the development of a new shaving lotion seem as revolutionary and important as the creation of the atomic bomb or a cure for AIDS.

And Lugosi does not deliver a one-note performance either. Yes, he is focused, broad, larger-than-life, but he does much more than simply rant and rave his outrage to his friend the devil bat. Like a cat, he has fun with his intended victims. He offers them a bottle of his formula, tells each intended victim to put a dab on the tender part of their throat, and when they protest the strong odor, he placates them by telling them its application controls the scent. And he devilishly, usually with a sly, twisted smile, gives each victim their final kiss-off: "Good... bye, Mr. ...!" delivered in such a manner that the audience and Lugosi are both in on the secret. We as the viewer cannot help but laugh at some of Lugosi's antics throughout the movie, and for the most part, we are supposed to laugh at such dramatic irony. It is a perfect case of laughing with Lugosi and not at him. The viewer can certainly trash the cliche riddled script, the broad performances (with the exception of Lugosi and perhaps a few other performances), and the pathetic props and effects, but Bela Lugosi's performance stands tall and remains a credit to his reputation.

It is far easier for an actor to look his best when he is working with an ensemble of performers who share his talent and enthusiasm, when he is being creatively inspired by an expensive, well-mounted production, a talented director, a well-written and creative script, etc. But shouldn't Bela Lugosi deserve much *more* credit here because he is the only inspiring element in an entire production brimming over with mediocrity and cheapness. The simple fact that Lugosi can create such a memorable character through an intense delivery of such standard dialogue drivel is testimony to his talent and how he and he alone made all these poverty-row productions—be they PRC, Monogram, or Edward D. Wood, Jr. movies—memorable simply due to his presence and talents. Who would have imagined that many horror film buffs would be watching and rewatching Lugosi's nadir fifty years after their speedy, low-budget conception, that such movies would be made available in the 1990s on deluxe laserdisc double and triple feature packages.

Thankfully, Bela Lugosi never understood the difference between starring in a PRC/ Monogram or in a MGM or Universal picture. He only knew that star billing meant giving the audience the best performance possible (and personal illnesses, sciatic nerve pain, and addiction were never excuses for failing to give any less than 100 per cent). Thus, the irony of a gifted performer being reduced to poverty-row productions and approaching them as though each one were a diamond in the rough attests to the legend of one Bela Lugosi. Mainly through a close examination of these inferior duds can we truly appreciate the man's talent and dedication to his craft.

The Ape Man

(1943)

by Mark A. Miller

CREDITS: Associate Producer: Barney A. Sarecky; Producer: Sam Katzman and Jack Dietz (Banner Productions); Director: William Beaudine; Original Screenplay: Barney A. Sarecky; Original Story: (*They Creep By Night*): Karl Brown; Director of Photography: Mack Stengler; Assistant Director: Arthur Hammond; Film Editor: Carl Pierson; Art Director: David Milton; Sound: Glen Glenn; Musical Director: Edward Kay; Released March 19, 1943, Monogram Pictures, 64 minutes.

CAST: Bela Lugosi...Dr. James Brewster, Louise Currie...Billie Mason, Wallace Ford...Jeff Carter, Henry Hall...Dr. George Randall, Minerva Urecal...Agatha Brewster, Emil Van Horn...The Ape, J. Farrell MacDonald...Police Captain, Wheeler Oakman...Brady, Ralph Littlefield...Zippo, Jack Mulhall...Reporter, Charles Jordan...O'Toole, George Kirby...Townsend, the Bulter, Charles Hall...Barney, the Photographer, Ray Miller...Detective, Sunshine Sammy Morrison...Office Boy.

In Rod Serling's poignant *Requiem for a Heavyweight* (1962), Mountain Rivera (Anthony Quinn), once a champion boxer, is reduced to prostituting his profession through his participation in a wrestling charade. He does so to the best of his ability, despite the personal degradation. Fortunately for Anthony Quinn, when the role was over he could return home and glance at his two Academy Awards on the mantel. Bela Lugosi's similar degradation—starring in *The Ape Man*—was, sadly, one of real life, not a part in a movie. In it, he played a monkey and shared most of his scenes with another man wearing a silly looking gorilla suit. Never before or after was Lugosi cast in so demeaning a role.

The early 1940s should have begun a revival of Bela Lugosi's screen career. In 1939 he practically kidnapped director Rowland V. Lee's *The Son of Frankenstein* from Basil Rathbone and Boris Karloff with his portrayal of Ygor. His gravelly voice, rag costume, and twisted neck contributed to a scene-stealing performance that managed to chill and escape the shadow of Dracula at the same time. Also, in England, Lugosi starred in *The Dark Eyes of London,* a well-made, atmospheric Edgar Wallace crime-drama that allowed him to display his versatility in a dual role. A small but straight part that same year in a prestigious MGM Greta Garbo film, *Ninotchka,* directed by Ernst Lubitsch, suggests that, with good professional guidance and careful selection, Lugosi might have settled into some of the hundreds of solid ethnic parts the various Hollywood studios cast every year. Given good direction and rehearsal time, Lugosi's pronunciation remained interestingly exotic but within the bounds of an audience's acceptance. Moreover, his screen presence could still be formidable when directors, such as Lee and Lubitsch, encouraged him to take a more subtle than usual approach.

Adding to this optimism was the fact that Lugosi's personal life seemed to have been happy and productive in the early '40s. He gave generously of his time and energy to the War effort and was happily married to Lillian, his wife since 1933. They lived in his favorite Hollywood home, at 10841 Whipple Street in North Hollywood.

Bolstering Lugosi's professional prestige in the early '40s was his often overlooked stage work. In 1943 he once again toured in a revival of Hamilton Deane and John L. Balderston's

Dracula, and although this didn't help him escape his iconoclastic typecasting, his performances were warmly received by audiences and critics.

Much more important, though, were the tremendous critical plaudits Lugosi earned for *Arsenic and Old Lace* after the *Dracula* revival. Producer Joseph Blumenfield had to persuade Lugosi to accept the role of Jonathan Brewster because playwright Joseph Kesselring had specifically written the part for Boris Karloff. Karloff's great success in the role on Broadway and on tour made Lugosi reluctant to take the part when Karloff left the show. He knew comparisons between Hollywood's two famous horror stars would be inevitable. Revealing tremendous confidence and courage, however, Lugosi accepted the role and parlayed it into an unqualified triumph. Some reviewers commented that Lugosi's performance was superior to Karloff's.

Unfortunately, during this period, Lugosi's respectable film roles and theatrical kudos (and some impressive radio performances) were all undermined by disastrous decisions that spelled career suicide. In 1940, Lugosi starred in PRC's *The Devil Bat,* a hopelessly absurd Poverty Row horror film in which he hands out shaving lotion to his enemies so that his giant bat will detect the smell and kill them. Evidently the terrible script and ultra cheap production values did not raise a red flag for Lugosi (as *The Ape* [Monogram 1940] had probably done for Karloff) because that same year he signed with Banner Productions, operated by producers Sam Katzman and Jack Dietz, as a sort of bargain basement unit at Monogram, another Poverty Row studio. Between 1941 and 1944, Lugosi starred in no fewer than nine disastrously terrible films for the company. The result? With the exceptions of *Zombies on Broadway* (RKO 1945) and *Abbott and Costello Meet Frankenstein* (Universal-International 1948), Lugosi never again received a starring role from a major studio. He secured parts in only a paltry twelve movies after his last Monogram picture, three of them Ed Wood, Jr., pictures that are now famous for all the wrong reasons. Between films, Lugosi struggled to make a living.

When a part from a major studio did come along for Lugosi in the early '40s, it was usually a minor, lackluster one, such as Eduardo the caretaker in *The Black Cat* (Universal 1941), although a reprisal of his Ygor in *Ghost of Frankenstein* (Universal 1942) certainly gave cause for optimism. Yet after returning to one of his best screen characterizations, Lugosi still headed back to 4376 Sunset Drive for three more horrible— instead of horrifying—Monogram pictures.[1] Did lack of major studio promotion force Lugosi to slum it at Monogram, or did slumming at Monogram make major producers reluctant to promote Lugosi?

After having proved himself so ably and memorably in films of 1939 and then enjoying conspicuous, successful stage work in the early '40s, Lugosi probably cut his own throat for ready cash and a chance to rule at least somewhere (Poverty Row) in horror films. At a time when juicy character parts should have been offered to Lugosi, almost every producer in his right mind was reluctant to cast the star of something like Monogram's *Spooks Run Wild,* which only played in small towns or grind houses in metropolitan areas. Lugosi had made his name synonymous with low-quality, old-fashioned productions that could not be taken seriously on any level. He was a great actor with even greater qualities of sheer presence on the screen, but the poorest of visionaries in making career choices. Watching his Monogram pictures is to witness a Rolls Royce cruise through a city dump.

Of Lugosi's nine Monogram films, the sixth is the saddest of them all. Lugosi had just finished playing the Monster in Universal's *Frankenstein Meets the Wolf Man* when he began filming *The Ape Man* in the winter of 1942. As though an omen of catastrophe, editors cut most of Lugosi's part from the Frankenstein film; as a result, viewers had no idea why his Monster seemed so clumsy because all mention of his blindness was missing, as was all of his dialogue spoken in Ygor's voice. (The Monster had been given Ygor's brain in the previous film.) Still, next to *The Ape Man, Frankenstein Meets the Wolf Man* looks brilliant.

In *The Ape Man,* Lugosi plays Dr. James Brewster, a scientist who, according to his assistant, Dr. George Randall (Henry Hall), six months before "made an astounding discovery. It was so far in advance of anything that's been done to date that Jim decided to be the guinea pig

Bela Lugosi as Dr. James Brewster is conforted by his sister Agatha (Minerva Urecal) after injecting himself with his own serum.

for this experiment himself. Unfortunately, it was a great success." As a result of this "great success," Brewster gained certain physical and behavioral traits of an ape after injecting himself with simian spinal fluid.

Although Lugosi made a terrible choice of movies, to his credit his performance in *The Ape Man* never even hints of anything other than utter seriousness, intensity, and sincerity—even under the worst of circumstances, as when he gesticulates and articulates like a monkey. His co-star, actress Louise Currie, remembers that "Lugosi was very into it. He really was living the part of becoming an ape. He was a serious actor, studious and concentrated, just as eager to make this a good picture as he would have been had he been playing it at MGM. He made that part believable because he was a fine actor. Otherwise, it would have been a farce. He made the part seem real and quite legitimate."

With no time for rehearsals or retakes, and lacking the benefit of quality direction, Lugosi was on his own in a nightmarish fiasco conceived to exploit his name, not his talent. He convincingly assumes the gait of a gorilla, lumbering from side to side as he walks, his back bent and his arms dropped to his sides. Lugosi even considers such details as how a monkey would sit in a chair: First he leans on the chair's arms with the backs of his hands. When Lugosi's lab gorilla starts a ruckus, he backs it into a cage by growling at it menacingly (in what is presumedly gorilla language) and by raising his arms straight up in war-like defiance. Afterwards, he collapses, weeping, and laments to his sister, "What a mess I've made of things." The awful irony of the line is uncanny in retrospect.

Lugosi infuses his preposterous role with realism through his mood swings. One moment he is gentle toward his faithful sister, Agatha (Minerva Urecal), but in the next he regresses into a growling, threatening animal that even attempts to strangle her when she questions his actions. Lugosi is completely convincing as someone who loves his sister but cannot keep a check on the line that separates man from beast. Louise Currie points out that "Lugosi was way beyond playing this kind of role, of course, but yet if he hadn't been a serious, good actor, the film would have been just forgotten years ago. It wouldn't have been any good at all."

The undoing of Lugosi's skillful, mercurial performance is his monkey talk, demanded by the script. He has several conversations with his gorilla, played by Emil Van Horn in a bad monkey suit that seemed much more apropos when Van Horn wore it in wacky comedies starring W.C. Fields (*Never Give a Sucker an Even Break* [1941]) and Abbott and Costello (*Keep 'Em Flying* [1941]). At one point, Lugosi leans out a window and orders his hairy friend hiding in a bush to climb in and commit a murder—the entire communication accomplished in unintentionally hilarious grunts and growls. Such moments render Lugosi's performance beyond redemption. Even worse, Lugosi sometimes falls into his Ygor voice, which turns the role into a humiliating mockery of one of his best portrayals.

Two of the film's assets are Wallace Ford and Louise Currie, playing the newspaper reporter and photographer who eventually expose Lugosi as a murderer. Ford's wisecracking Jeff Carter is somewhat amusing—and Ford's small facial reactions say much when the script fails him. He affably beams dismay, skepticism, and confusion to liven up the dull proceedings. Louise Currie affectionately recalls Ford as a "very nice man and a good actor. It was so easy working with him. He was breezy and casual and he made everything fun." Ford's hard-earned reputation as a solid, colorful supporting actor made it possible for him to appear in something like *The Ape Man* and Alfred Hitchcock's *Shadow of a Doubt* in the same year.

Louis Currie was called the "Katherine Hepburn of Monogram" by Sam Katzman, and this beautiful, slender woman did resemble Hepburn and was always a bright spot in Monogram pictures. Her acting career spanned almost ten years and included approximately fifty movies, most produced at Monogram, Republic, and RKO. (According to Currie, her part in *Citizen Kane* as a reporter, alongside Alan Ladd, was cut, even though it took enough time to shoot it as five or six Monogram pictures.[2]) She was cast in two great Republic serials (*Adventures of Captain Marvel* [1940] and *The Masked Marvel* [1943]), and worked with Lugosi in two other films, *You'll Find Out* (RKO 1940) and *Voodoo Man* (Monogram 1944). She acquits herself honorably in *The Ape Man,* all things considered. Her repartee with Ford certainly lacks the wit of Cary Grant's and Rosalind Russell's in *His Girl Friday* (1940), which, of course, is no surprise at all, but she *is* spunky and believable.

What, in part, gives *The Ape Man* an anachronistic ambiance of an early talkie is the performance of Minerva Urecal as Lugosi's sister, Agatha Brewster. Urecal's dated acting style includes wildly popping her eyes while talking of ghosts and haunted houses to Ford. Her exaggerated reaction to her brother's ape-like appearance harks back even further, to the silent cinema, as she pops her eyes, throws up her arms, and screams in such a melodramatic fashion that one expects to see a title card next. Yet, inexplicably, when Lugosi tells her that he has some human spinal fluid for his needed injection, she shows no reaction whatsoever to the fact that he had to murder to obtain it.

Knowing that Karl Brown penned the original story (*They Creep in the Dark*) for *The Ape Man* before one actually sees the film raises a certain sense of false optimism. Brown worked on the screenplays and stories for Boris Karloff's "Mad Scientist" Columbia films, *The Man They Could Not Hang* (1939), *The Man With Nine Lives* (1940), and *Before I Hang* (1940). Although these films are not remembered as Karloff's best, they are solid entertainment and certainly enhanced Karloff's reputation as a horror star.

Associate producer Barney A. Sarecky adapted Brown's story into a script (originally titled *The Gorilla Strikes*) that is a stink bomb. How bad the story smelled before Sarecky wrote the script is anyone's guess. Borrowing elements from *Murders in the Rue Morgue* (Universal 1932), which starred Lugosi, and *The Ape,* Sarecky doesn't consider logic and character motivation as necessary elements. The purpose of Lugosi's experiment evidently is to turn a human being into an ape man. Why anyone would seek poor posture, a hairy face, and regressions into monkey behavior is never explained. To counteract the effects of the simian spinal fluid, Lugosi needs spinal fluid from a living human being (which will kill the donor). The first injection of spinal fluid (from Randall's butler, Townsend) cures Lugosi—for all of five and a half minutes. This indicates that Lugosi will need hundreds of gallons of spinal fluid to achieve a lasting effect.

Lugosi does, in fact, bear the brunt of the terrible script. In one breath he tells his sister that he wisely locks himself up with his gorilla whenever he fears "he might do something terrible," but in the next he passionately whines that Randall will not help him murder for the spinal fluid he needs for a cure. (The switch that opens the gorilla cage, by the way, is well within the reach of anyone inside!)

In addition, Lugosi's relationship with his lab gorilla is wildly inconsistent. In an unintentionally funny sequence, Lugosi is seen curled up asleep with it in its cage. The gorilla wakes up first, then nudges Lugosi awake in a scene oddly resembling a wife getting her husband up for work. Soon, however, Lugosi aggressively growls at his simian friend and threatens it with a whip. They seem to have an inexplicably volatile domestic relationship, at best. When Lugosi needs the gorilla to walk the city streets with him in search of unwilling spinal fluid donors, the beast is all cooperation. Yet, at the end of the film, the gorilla breaks Lugosi's back because he is chasing Louise Currie around the lab. As in most of Monogram's horror films, motivation succumbs to plot convenience.

Throughout it all, Lugosi never has an opportunity to earn audience sympathy for his plight, because he selfishly and gleefully murders others to attempt his cure. This normally would not matter, given that the actor is often at his best as a completely unsympathetic, demonic prince of sorts (as in *The Raven,* Universal 1935). Unfortunately, in *The Ape Man* he is a monkey, not a prince.

Perhaps the script's greatest injustice to Lugosi, however, is the inclusion of a tall, stooped, skinny actor (Ralph Littlefield) who, wearing a comical hat, pops up throughout the movie as a mysterious, omniscient character. In the beginning of the film, at a boat dock, he slinks over to Jeff Carter (Ford) to tip him off that Agatha Brewster—sister of the missing scientist, James Brewster—is about to step off the ship just seen in stock footage. With unconvincing enthusiasm, he advises Carter, "Good story, a great story, it's a pip!"

Throughout the rest of the film, Littlefield is seen almost everywhere, with no explanation of his identify. His reaction shots, cut into the film at what should be dramatically important moments, almost seem designed to ridicule Lugosi. For instance, in Lugosi's basement lab, when Dr. Randall is giving him a human spinal fluid injection for the first time, the film cuts to Littlefield outside, watching the proceedings through a window, as he smiles and winks to the viewer. Then, after the injection, Lugosi nervously paces and tries to straighten his back, hoping he is cured. This is one of the few opportunities for Lugosi to have a dramatic moment, but his pantomime is performed in vain because the sequence includes an insert of Littlefield apparently laughing to himself as he watches.

Littlefield becomes a spectator, like the film's audience, encouraging all to laugh at Lugosi, who is fervently trying, in all sincerity, to make something of his self-deprecating role. By the film's conclusion, when Littlefield reveals, "Oh, I'm the author of the story. Screwy idea, wasn't it?" the cheap and unfunny joke is finally revealed—at Lugosi's expense. As Samuel Johnson humbly and sarcastically put it in his famous letter to Lord Chesterfield, "I had done all that I could; and no man is well pleased to have his all neglected, be it ever so little."

Considering that Monogram pictures of this period were shot in an average of seven to

Dr Brewster (Lugosi) uses the gorilla to help him murder unwilling spinal fluid donors, the only thing that will help cure his affliction. Lugosi smiles and makes the best of his poor script in *The Ape Man.*

ten days, it is hardly surprising that director William "One Shot" Beaudine gave no time to such trifles as directing actors and fixing bad scripts, when he was expected to race each shot into the can as quickly and economically as possible. Currie confirms that "Beaudine had to get the picture in under the budget and on schedule, and he couldn't spend a lot of time with the actors. He expected the actors they hired to know what to do already and to learn their dialogue. Once in a while we had to do a retake if something technical went wrong, but normally we just shot it." Each morning the cast reported to work, wearing their own clothes as costumes, and were expected to march through each scene in one take, flubs be damned. They were virtually on their own in interpreting their roles because Beaudine simply did not have the time to give. Currie remembers that "the director had to figure out the next shot, and he was so busy telling the cameraman how to set it up, he just had to feel that the actors knew what to do. We *had* to play mostly on our own." Knowledge of this predicament gives the viewer a new sense of respect for Ford and Currie who, in one shot, had over a minute of continuous dialogue. They had to get it right the first time.

Beaudine broke into films at the very bottom as a 17-year-old errand boy/janitor at Biograph in 1909. Fifteen years later he was directing Mary Pickford in *Sparrows* (1926). Before he died in 1970, he had directed some 150-175 features, 300-325 one and two reel comedies, and approximately 350 television episodes. At Monogram (later called Allied Artists), he directed 76 films between 1942 and 1957. He fit into the Monogram mold perfectly—work fast and under budget and remain adequate if not good. Louise Currie liked to work with Beaudine, even though he could offer her little actual direction, because he was pleasant and kept everyone relaxed, despite the breakneck speed.

Because Beaudine lacked time, money, and all other big-studio resources, he was forced to use fewer set-ups. As a result, the film has an antiquated, stagey quality. Beaudine tried to disguise this problem by panning and dollying, to give his frame some movement, but he is only partially successful. At the end of the film, he crosscuts among three characters (Lugosi, Currie, and Wallace), which is ambitious for a Monogram picture. For all his effort, though, the sequence does not build much suspense.

Reviews of *The Ape Man* would make any major Hollywood producer think twice about giving Lugosi intelligent supporting or starring roles. The *Daily News* remarked, "Monogram's writer didn't have to wipe the dust from Bela Lugosi's *Ape Man*; he had to rake the mould off." *Variety* chimed, "*The Ape Man* [is] good for laughs which aren't in the script... Bela Lugosi, rigged out in a shaggy beard and formal morning attire, ambling like an ape and sharing a cage with a gorilla, scares nobody..." *The Hollywood Reporter* echoed the same sentiments that Lugosi and the film were outdated and ineffective: "Those who scream easily when a sliding panel moves aside, and when a gent arrayed in an ape's fur coat carries off the heroine, will probably find this just their dish of horror gruel. Others will concede it to be hilarious burlesque."

Seven years after *The Ape Man*'s release, when Lugosi was reduced to hosting midnight spook shows to pay his rent, he would open his program climbing out of his coffin on stage, followed by several live acts described in ads as "the bloody guillotine, the bat man and the monster in a death struggle, beautiful girl burned alive, [and] vampire maidens and assorted voodoo apparitions." Then, without shame, Lugosi would end the show with a screening of *They Creep in the Dark,* a retitled print of *The Ape Man.*

Recently, film historian Tom Weaver wrote warmly of Lugosi in *Poverty Row Horrors!:* "Lugosi will always have his detractors, but it's tough to imagine who would have filled the bill in movies like *The Ape Man* if Lugosi hadn't been around to do them. Even when he's not at his best, he gives these quickies a great deal of color; the roles are tailor-made for his sinister personality, and few other actors had what it takes to elevate these measly pictures the way Lugosi did." This, of course, is undoubtedly true. Despite their ruinous effects on Lugosi's career, had these Monogram pictures been made without him, they would not merit discussion today.

Other contemporary film historians have often divorced Lugosi's Monogram pictures from their negative effects on his career and defended them as quality movies. Some enthusiasts also argue that Lugosi's Monogram performances are much more fascinating to watch than his small, uninteresting parts during the same period, such as that of the servant Rolf in *Night Monster* (Universal 1942), a film in which Lugosi receives top billing for only a minor role as a red herring. True, the Monograms give viewers more Lugosi for their money, but some Lugosi fans prefer quality to quantity and dismiss the Monograms as beneath the great actor's dignity. Lugosi's many, well-deserved fans will probably never come to any kind of consensus on these issues.

A quick study of Lugosi's American filmography, however, does reveal a remarkable fact: With the exception of *The Raven,* Lugosi does not headline a single film that simultaneously possesses a good script, good supporting players, good production values, and good direction. These qualities are all present in films boasting some of his best supporting roles, but in the purely Lugosi canon not a single film stands out except *The Raven.* Why, then, do fans and film historians rush to Lugosi's defense? Why, among horror stars, is he so often singled out as memorable when it is next to impossible to watch even his most famous horror film, *Dracula* (Universal 1931), in its entirety without dozing off?

The answer may be that even though no truly outstanding horror films that star Bela

Lugosi exist (excluding *The Raven*), all films that star Bela Lugosi, no matter how mediocre or awful, feature at least one unforgettably brilliant Lugosi moment that only he, with his deliciously odd accent and mannerisms, could have pulled off.

For instance, although *Dracula* seems to move in slow motion once the location switches to London, the first reel at Dracula's castle contains some of Lugosi's finest moments in any movie. His lines to Renfield (Dwight Frye) are delivered with a menacing, magnetic majesty that aptly mirrors the decay and hidden horrors of the fantastic, Gothic castle. "I am —Dracula...I bid you welcome." In retrospect, Lugosi seems to be welcoming audiences to the beginning of the golden age of sound horror films. His friendly smile, however, does not fit comfortably on his face. It is a grimace emitting a sinister lie that promises safety. Then, reacting to a blood-chilling wolf's howl, Lugosi issues his famous line: "Listen to them. Children of the night. What music they make." His quiet merriment, conveyed with an odd inflection on the word *they*, so that it sounds like his tongue is having a love affair with the word, grants him a unique brand of decadence that has never been duplicated on screen.

His most memorable line, of course, is "I never drink—wine." Lugosi shares these words with us like an inside joke from Hell. Finally, with his simple "Good night, Mr. Renfield," Lugosi displays his singular power to make "Good night" sound like "You've had it!" Throughout, Lugosi's pauses and inflections are given dire significance by his unnatural physical stillness that effectively mocks death. Lugosi is not the screen's best Dracula, but he is still the icon of the Count over sixty years later. This is a fantastic tribute to the actor that even *The Ape Man* and his eight other awful Monogram films cannot diminish.

Universal handed Lugosi and director Robert Florey *Murders In the Rue Morgue* (1932) as a substitute for *Frankenstein* (1931), the classic film that Florey lost to James Whale, who offered Karloff the career-pivoting, monster role Lugosi did not wish to play. Instead, *Murders In The Rue Morgue* introduced Lugosi in a part he would repeat many times, the unrelenting, fabulously insane scientist. Unlike Karloff and later Christopher Lee, Lugosi seldom if ever humanized his madmen or monsters. They are pure evil—raving, gleeful maniacs who alienate themselves from audience sympathy. "The loneliness of evil," a phrase coined by Lee, never applies to Lugosi in such roles. In fact, not even a hint of desire for moral redemption exists in Lugosi's mad scientists. Each is John Milton's fallen angel, uncompromisingly at war with Heaven.

Lugosi's first sequence in *Murders in the Rue Morgue* is his best in the film and promises great things to come—but they never arrive. As Dr. Mirakle, who finances his experiments with a carnival sideshow featuring his ape named Erik, Lugosi rants broadly and magnificently about Darwin's theory of evolution as onlookers react with fear and anger. Soon, however, it becomes obvious that the direction and cinematography are the real stars of this film, not Lugosi. He loses to Florey and Karl Freund's approach that eventually turns the film into an exercise in style over substance. Sadly, Lugosi's ability to communicate with his ape in this film presages this inherently ridiculous talent that is later exploited to a hilarious proportion in *The Ape Man.*

In spite of all this, Lugosi's opening segment is wonderfully chilling. He would have to wait until *The Raven* in 1935, however, to cut loose with his best mad scientist in ideal circumstances: a good, tailor-made script that provides room for Lugosi's over-the-top performance; solid supporting players; an adequate budget; and sure, competent direction.

Equal to, or perhaps surpassing, his role as Dracula is Lugosi's performance as zombie master Murder Legendre in *White Zombie,* made on a tiny budget by brothers Victor and Edward Halperin in 1932. Lugosi's nuances and delivery are polished, evil gems. In his best sequence, while he nonchalantly carves a wax voodoo doll, Lugosi watches with mild interest his rival for the virginal Madeline Short (Madge Bellamy) convulse and implore mercy as he slowly turns into a zombie. One of Lugosi's lines is classic: When actor John Harron spies Lugosi and his army of approaching zombies and fearfully asks, "Who are you? And what are they?" Lugosi answers melodiously, "For you, my friend, they are the angels of death." Lugosi's rendition of the line is

Dr. Brewster threatens photographer Louise Currie who will eventually be saved by the love-struck gorilla.

tinged with a revelatory madness that climaxes the film's horror.

Unfortunately, the film suffers from the same snail-like pacing that plagues *Dracula.* Compounding this problem are absolutely terrible performances from John Harron and Joseph Cawthorn that are so distracting that they almost bury the film's positive aspects. Nevertheless, each Lugosi moment stands out like a large, October full moon, breaking through dark clouds of ineptitude with the most sinister of transcending rays.

Dracula, Murders In The Rue Morgue, White Zombie, and *The Raven* are the only horror films of the 1930s in which Lugosi is clearly the star and main attraction even though he is not necessarily billed first—and only *The Raven* is not seriously flawed. Then, after Lugosi's unexpected and promising year of 1939, the burnout of his career began on Poverty Row. Yet even these terrible films offer Lugosi moments that rise above his squalid surroundings, as a look at a few of them will reveal.

For instance, in *The Devil Bat* (1940) Lugosi kills his employers one by one because they have become millionaires off his greaseless cold cream formula—after he sold it outright to them, instead of accepting a percentage of the profits. Lugosi's memorable moments come as he gives

Bela Lugosi as he appeared in *The Corpse Vanishes* hoping to restore life to his wife, never allowing the death of innocent victims to stand in his way.

each of his intended victims a bottle of a shaving lotion that will attract his giant killer bat. "Try a few drops," he amiably suggests to one doomed man. "Now rub it on the tender part of your neck," he adds with a broad, delighted smile, pointing to his own neck. At least four times during the film, he concludes such conversations with "Good-bye, Mr. [whoever]" in a wonderfully ironic tone that becomes increasingly less disguised and more mocking in its sarcasm as victims leave his home smelling like bat food. Unfortunately, in the context of the tacky production and preposterous script, this line's kinship with Lugosi's "Good night, Mr. Renfield" from *Dracula* taints *The Devil Bat* with a melancholy reminder of Lugosi's better days.

Invisible Ghost (Monogram 1941) almost does not look like a Lugosi Monogram picture. Director Joseph H. Lewis's camera angles and shot selection reveal much more skill and purpose than the perfunctory, indifferent work of other Monogram directors, namely William Beaudine. Lugosi benefits from this careful direction and gives an appropriately reserved, sympathetic performance. He plays kindly Charles Kessler, a tragic victim of a personality disorder—and of another moronic script. Nevertheless, some of the images in the film are memorable. For example, Lewis gives Lugosi a wonderful close-up after he has spotted his supposedly dead wife staring at him through a rain-streaked window. In the shot, Lugosi at first

In *Voodoo Man* Lugosi once again plays a distraught husband hoping to restore his wife from a zombie-like trance. The real difference, though, is Lugosi's sympathetic, extremely low-key interpretation of Dr. Marlowe.

looks startled. Then his expression softens and evolves into anguish and, finally, into anger and madness. Lugosi achieves this emotional metamorphosis subtly and convincingly, using only his eyes and facial muscles, in a few seconds that serve as a sad example that this actor had a much neglected refinement seldom tapped by filmmakers.

In *The Corpse Vanishes* (Monogram 1942), Lugosi is Dr. Lorenz, back to his mad scientist's business as usual, this time distributing orchids, instead of shaving lotion, the aroma of which turns young brides into sleeping Juliets for Lugosi to kidnap. He needs their body fluids to restore youth to his wife (Elizabeth Russell). The film's one notable Lugosi moment is his explanation to reporter Patricia Hunter (Luana Walters) of why he and his wife sleep in coffins. In a gentle, grandfatherly manner, he expounds, "I find the coffin much more comfortable than a bed. Many people do so, my dear." Here, Lugosi fuses morbidity with normality, as though Patricia (and the viewer) is the most naive person in the world for not knowing that "many people" sleep in coffins. Most of the rest of the film consists of Lugosi giving secret, malicious looks around corners and through door cracks, as he contends with another logic-defying script and the mechanical, impersonal direction of Wallace Fox.

Lugosi almost repeats his Dr. Lorenz role in *Voodoo Man* (Monogram 1944), as he kidnaps young, female motorists (instead of brides) and again uses them to restore his wife, this time from a zombielike trance. The real difference, though, is Lugosi's sympathetic, extremely low-key interpretation of Dr. Marlowe. His best moment is an extremely emotional one during which his wife (Ellen Hall) momentarily is brought out of her trance in a voodoo ritual and acknowledges her husband. Lugosi's elation quickly turns into despair, however, as she lapses back into a cataleptic state. He sinks to the floor, begging her not to leave him. Lugosi handles the emotional extremes of this scene with believable restraint, so that he convinces the viewer that his character genuinely loves his wife. The scene is strangely touching, and Lugosi reveals—much as he did in *Invisible Ghost*—that his acting was not limited to bombast.

As in all of Lugosi's Monogram pictures, however, the true villain is again the script—and also, in this case, the performance of John Carradine, who so overplays his role as Lugosi's servant that his portrayal is embarrassing and works against Lugosi's restraint.

In *Return of the Ape Man* (Monogram 1944), Lugosi freezes a man alive, then restores him, travels to the Arctic to find a frozen-alive prehistoric man (and does), paralyzes a colleague (John Carradine) with electrical current, and performs a brain transplant. And all of these incredible accomplishments occur within the picture's first 40 minutes! *Return of the Ape Man* (not a sequel to *The Ape Man*) crowds together enough preposterous pseudo-science for several horror films. It also marks Lugosi's last ruinous Monogram movie. He has one good moment, however: At a dinner party, relaxing in a chair with a cigar, Lugosi is obviously in a contemplative mood as he ponders where he will find a brain for his ape man. A guest walks over to him and comments, "You look very quiet, Professor." "Yes, I was thinking. I enjoy studying people," Lugosi responds in a sarcastic tone. "You know," he adds imperiously, as he gazes at the sundry guests, "some people's brains would never be missed." His critical comment, coming as it does in his last Monogram picture, makes one wonder if Lugosi was not really speaking of Monogram's screenwriters.

Even Lugosi's last few depressing films in the 1950s offer occasional Lugosi moments. The most notable of these occurs in Ed Wood's *Bride of the Monster* (Rolling M Productions, 1955). This is Lugosi's last mad scientist, a role he had essayed for over twenty years on the screen. From an armchair, speaking to Professor Strowski (George Bacwar), the underweight, aged Lugosi delivers his lines with the same intense spark of madness that he had exhibited as Dr. Mirakle in *Murders in the Rue Morgue* twenty-three years earlier. "I was declared as a Madman, a charlatan," Lugosi declares, eyes ablaze. "Outlawed in the world of science which previously honored me as a genius. Now, here, in this forsaken jungle hell, I have proven that I am all right." In the "jungle hell" of independent, bottom-of-the-barrel cinematic offal, Lugosi did prove himself to be "all right," even to the last.

Plagued by poor career decisions and the formidable odds of lousy scripts, impoverished production values, poor or hurried direction, and impossible shooting schedules, Lugosi had to earn his lasting fame the hard way. No other actor achieved so much out of so little. And for many today, these accomplished, unforgettable Lugosi moments make sitting through even his worst films worth the bother. Is there a single Lugosi horror topliner that does not contain such a moment? Yes. Only *The Ape Man.* However, it presents a poignant illustration of the actor's unflappable professionalism in the face of absurdity, and, as such, the film will always have an audience of Lugosi admirers.

Chapter Notes

1. *The Ape Man* did frighten at least one person. Louise Currie took her six-year-old son to see the film when it was released. "He was absolutely terrified," Currie remembers. "I didn't realize he would take it so literally. He told me later that he had nightmares for many years of Bela Lugosi being an ape and almost catching his mother. I was with him when he saw it, and he knew it was make-believe, but he got carried away with the picture. That was how realistic Bela Lugosi

seemed."

2. Louise Currie acted in a skit with W.C. Fields in his last film, *Sensations of 1945* (United Artists, 1944). She recalls that the short sequence "took almost as long as doing a whole movie because W.C. Fields could not remember any lines. They'd have prompters and they'd have big cue cards up, but he'd forget to look at the card or couldn't hear the prompter. We'd do take after take after take, which almost drove me wild because I wasn't used to that. I was used just to doing one or two takes, and that was it. It was still fun working with him. He was a wonderful character, wonderful."

Special thanks to Paul M. Jensen, Louise Currie, Tom Johnson, and Tom Weaver.

In *Return of the Ape Man* (not a sequel to *The Ape Man*) Lugosi freezes a man alive, finds a prehistoric man, paralyzes a colleague, and performs a brain transplant in his last film for Monogram.

Bela Lugosi, in his Frankenstein Monster makeup for *Frankenstein Meets the Wolf Man*, appears anguished. Perhaps he could see into the future where all his dialogue would be cut making the film and his performance an incomprehensible mess.

Frankenstein Meets the Wolf Man (1943)

by Don G. Smith

CREDITS: Director: Roy William Neill; Producer: George Waggner; Screenplay: Curt Siodmak; Director of Photography: George Robinson; Art Director: John B. Goodman; Assistant Art Director: Martin Obzina; Director of Sound: Bernard B. Brown; Set Decorator: Russell A. Gausman; Associate: Edward R. Robinson; Film Editor: Edward Curtiss; Gowns by Vera West; Musical Director: Hans J. Salter; Assistant Director: Melville Shyer; Special Photographic Effects: John P. Fulton; Makeup: Jack P. Pierce; Released March 5, 1943, 72 minutes, Universal Pictures

CAST: Lon Chaney...Lawrence Talbot, Ilona Massey...Baroness Elsa Frankenstein, Patric Knowles...Dr. Frank Mannering, Lionel Atwill... Mayor, Bela Lugosi...the Frankenstein Monster, Maria Ouspenskaya... Maleva, Dennis Hoey...Police Inspector Owen, Don Barclay...Franzec, Rex Evans...Vazec, Dwight Frye...Rudi

STORY:

When graverobbers disturb the crypt of Larry Talbot, the man turned into a werewolf by a Gypsy curse, he is resurrected by the light of the full moon. He commits several murders, wants to die in order to end the curse, and travels to Europe to find Maleva, the old Gypsy whose son turned him into a Wolf Man. Maleva agrees to help him die by taking him to Vasaria, the home of Dr. Frankenstein, whose diary contains the secrets of life and death.

After Maleva and Larry arrive in Vasaria, the young man again turns into the Wolf Man and kills the innkeeper's daughter. While trying to escape, he finds and befriends the Frankenstein Monster. Larry then returns to the village and, after disingenuously offering to buy her property, tries to persuade Baroness Frankenstein to give him her father's diary. The Baroness refuses to sell the land and discounts the existence of such a diary.

Meanwhile, Dr. Frank Mannering arrives in Vasaria and tries to persuade Talbot to return to England for treatment. Talbot refuses, after which the Frankenstein Monster enters the village looking for his friend. Larry and the Monster escape, Baroness Frankenstein agrees to give Larry the diary, and Mannering accompanies her to the castle. Mannering promises to help Larry die, but, obsessed with the idea of seeing the Monster at full strength, changes his mind at the last minute. As Mannering revitalizes the Monster, Larry turns into the Wolf Man and grapples with the newly empowered creature. When one of the villagers dynamites the dam, flood waters crash over the castle, sweeping away the Wolf Man and the Monster. Apparently, only Mannering and Baroness Frankenstein escape.

PRODUCTION AND MARKETING:

Given the nature of the movie industry, *Frankenstein Meets the Wolf Man* was inevitable. Universal's *The Wolf Man* had turned a huge profit in 1941, and *The Ghost of Frankenstein* was a financial success in 1942. So when author Curt Siodmak wittily remarked to George Waggner that Universal should make "Frankenstein Wolfs the Meat Man—I mean Frankenstein Meets the Wolf Man," Waggner did not smile. Instead he assigned Siodmak to write the screenplay.

Since Lon Chaney had played both Larry Talbot in *The Wolf Man* and the Frankenstein Monster in *The Ghost of Frankenstein*, the initial plan was to have the actor play both Wolf Man and Monster in the sequel. When the logistics became too difficult, Universal wisely decided to let Chaney play Talbot only. But who would play The Monster? Boris Karloff, who had essayed the role in *Frankenstein* (1931), *The Bride of Frankenstein* (1935), and *The Son of Frankenstein* (1939) had expressed his preference never to rise again as The Monster. Anyway, he was just beginning a 66-week national tour in *Arsenic and Old Lace*.

For a variety of reasons, in October of 1942, Universal offered the role of the Monster to Bela Lugosi. Probably foremost in Universal's mind was the public's identification of Lugosi with horror. After all, he *was* Dracula, and he had turned in a splendid performance in *The Black Cat* (1934). Also, at the end of *The Ghost of Frankenstein*, the Monster has both Ygor's brain and voice. Lugosi in the role would therefore provide some continuity.

Of course, Bela turned down the Monster's role in 1931 because it had no dialogue. In considering himself above the role, he allowed Boris Karloff to step in and overshadow him as filmdom's top horror man in the early thirties. Now, almost ten years later, Lugosi was desperate for *any* work he could get. Having struggled though 1937 and 1938 with virtually no work, he made a brief comeback with Universal in 1939 as Ygor in *The Son of Frankenstein*, a role he also successfully reprised in *The Ghost of Frankenstein*. Apparently according Lugosi little credit for those successes, however, the studio insisted on wasting him thereafter in small roles in *Black Friday* (1940), *The Black Cat* (1941), and *Night Monster* (1942).

Universal did use him to advantage, however, in *The Wolf Man* (1941). As Bela the Gypsy, Lugosi played the fortune teller consulted by Jenny, the doomed friend of Lon Chaney and Evelyn Ankers. As he looks into the young woman's palm he sees the sign of the pentagram, which appears on a werewolf's next victim. As Bela is a werewolf, he knows that the poor girl is soon to die at his hand. Exuding all the weariness and moral despair that accompanies the werewolf condition, he rushes the frightened girl out of his tent, and stands alone in the night, face in hands. Moments later we hear the cry of a wolf!

While relegated to largely second-rate parts at Universal, Lugosi undertook starring roles in such Monogram quickies as *The Devil Bat* (1940), *The Invisible Ghost* (1941), *Spooks Run Wild* (1941), *Black Dragons* (1942), *The Corpse Vanishes* (1942), and *Bowery at Midnight* (1942). Unfortunately, the general quality of most of those films was such that they failed to enhance his reputation.

Still, the casting of Lugosi was probably not a wise move for Universal. The sixty-year-old actor was bitter about his career and physically ill. Since the role was physically demanding, stuntmen Eddie Parker and Gil Perkins had to stand in for Lugosi during several key scenes.

After shooting, an additional problem arose when the production staff watched the finished product and concluded that the Monster's dialogue was ludicrous and laugh-producing. Their remedy was to cut the scenes in which the Monster speaks, even though that meant excising explanations crucial to an understanding of the Monster's motivations. After all, he was supposed to be half-blind and weak. The result was a performance in which the Monster staggers about ineffectually for no apparent reason.

When the film went out to theaters, Ilona Massey's name topped the credits, followed by co-star Patric Knowles. Massey's only other foray into the horror genre was her starring performance in *The Invisible Agent* (1942, with Peter Lorre). Though Massey expressed a love for horror films and a desire to be in *Frankenstein Meets the Wolf Man*, Knowles later made known his displeasure at being in another horror.

Lon Chaney, of course, played Larry Talbot. Chaney was now Universal's top horror star, having rung the cash registers with *The Wolf Man* (1941), *Man Made Monster* (1941), *The Ghost of Frankenstein* (1942), and *The Mummy's Tomb* (1942).

Returning in her role as Maleva the Gypsy woman from *The Wolf Man* was Maria Ouspenskaya. Other memorable cast members were Lionel Atwill and Dwight Frye. Atwill, who had turned in fine performances in such films as *Dr. X* (1932), *Mystery of the Wax Museum* (1933), *Murders in the Zoo* (1933), *Nana* (1934), *The Mark of the Vampire* (1935, with Lugosi), *The Devil is a Woman* (1935), *The Hound of the Baskervilles* (1939), *Son of Frankenstein* (1939, with Lugosi), *Man Made Monster* (1941), and *The Ghost of Frankenstein* (1942, with Lugosi) had been professionally brought down by a sex scandal. In *Frankenstein Meets the Wolf Man* he played the genteel mayor of Vasaria. Dwight Frye, known to horror film aficionados as Fritz in *Frankenstein* and Renfield in *Dracula*, made his last appearance for Universal in *Frankenstein Meets the Wolf Man*, which was released several months after his death.

An impressive pressbook and ad campaign accompanied the film's release. Posters featured art of the Frankenstein Monster and the Wolf Man in mortal combat (though neither of the depictions much resembled Chaney or Lugosi). A reclining, seductively clad Ilona Massey also featured prominently in the poster art. Pressbook ads hyped the many hours that Chaney and Lugosi endured at the hands of makeup man Jack Pierce. One Lugosi ad claimed the following:

"The old-fashioned milkman, who got up at 3 a.m. to make deliveries, had nothing on Bela Lugosi. Recently Bela had to get up at 2:30 a.m. to prepare himself for his strenuous role as the monster...

"His early morning preparations included a hot bath, then a rubdown, and a half-hour rest. This was followed by massaging of cream on his face, neck, chest, hands, and arms so that the ingredients used in his monster makeup would not burn or blister him.

"Then came four to five hours in the hands of Jack Pierce, Universal's veteran makeup artist, to have the actor's head 'built' up into the hideous features of the monster.

"Next his legs were weighted heavily and geared to give that mechanical walking effect."

Another ad, titled "Monster Strikes Blow at Enemies," related that:

"The enemy powers have more to fear in the monster, played by Bela Lugosi... than will the moviegoers who wish to be thrilled by the gruesome scenes.

"Lugosi, while the picture was being filmed, organized the 10,000 Hungarians in Los Angeles area into the American Hungarian Defense Federation for the battle against the so-called 'new-order.'

"The Los Angeles Hungarians donated over $1600 to the Red Cross, bought $65,000 in war bonds in one day, and have raised funds to buy and completely equip an ambulance for the American forces."

While pressbook ads are often notoriously inaccurate, Lugosi did undergo much at the hands of Jack Pierce, and he was a distinguished figure in the Hungarian community's war effort. Among other activities, he did, on one evening alone, raise $10,030 to aid Hungarian freedom fighters, and he did deliver the keynote address at an anti-Nazi rally at the Riverside Breakfast Club in Los Angeles.

Actually, Lugosi fared well in the advertising: two pressbook ads were devoted solely to Lugosi, while Lon Chaney, the film's real star, garnered only three solo ads. Of course, many of the ads hyped the "Titans of Terror! Clashing in Mortal Combat!"

CRITIQUE:

Upon release, *Frankenstein Meets the Wolf Man* unsurprisingly received its share of negative reviews. Showmen's Trade Review wrote:

"Universal has turned out the horror-of-horrors for the... chiller-diller fans in this latest picture in which the Frankenstein Monster is resurrected to meet the Wolf Man. It would be difficult to imagine the customers who go for this... stuff finding a more suitable vehicle of entertainment. Has been well-produced by George Waggner and skillfully directed by Roy William Neill, with most of the cast turning in swell performances. Especially good are Lon Chaney, Jr. as the Wolf Man seeking to die to end his impulses to kill, and Bela Lugosi as the Monster seeking to regain his power."

Frankenstein's Monster is examined by Dr. Frank Mannering (Patric Knowles), Baroness Frankenstein (Ilona Massey), and Larry Talbot (Lon Chaney).

Predictably, *The New York Times* panned the film and sarcastically suggested that Universal and Monogram join forces to produce "Wolf Man and Monster Meet the East Side Kids!" Interestingly, the *Times*' review had nothing to say about the acting performances of Chaney and Lugosi.

Frankenstein Meets the Wolf Man still receives mixed reviews today. While elements of the film garner kind words, many revile it as the first of the monster jamborees, in which, two, three, or more Universal monsters combine to spice up the tired proceedings:

"Here is a film that is important only because it marks the signal decline in the film of the compelling Frankenstein idea. If the film proves anything it is that one cannot make a fine horror movie simply throwing great old horror regulars together."—Leonard Wolf, *The Ultimate Frankenstein*, 1991.

"Curt Siodmak's pen brought two of Universal's best known creatures together in a film of ludicrous dimensions... Almost as funny as *Abbott and Costello Meet* anybody."—Ed Naha, *Horrors from Screen to Scream*, 1975.

"Arguably the nadir of Universal's Frankenstein series—hard to say if it's worse as a Frankenstein or as a Wolf Man movie. Patric Knowles is Frank Mannering, a doctor very unconvincingly infused with the Frankenstein spirit... And this is Lon Chaney, Jr.'s most annoying stint at Larry Talbot... As in *Ghost...*, Lugosi and Atwill are wasted. Even the music and art direction are uneven. (Special effects) combine to make the justly-renowned opening sequence satisfyingly atmospheric, though there is an embarrassing pause for poetry ('Even a man...") in a crypt."—Donald C. Willis, *Horror and Science Fiction Films II*, 1982.

"It's great to see Lon Chaney, Jr. back as Larry Talbot and Maria Ouspenskaya as Maleva the Gypsy, but casting Bela Lugosi as the Frankenstein Monster was a big mistake."—Michael Weldon, *Psychotronic Encyclopedia of Film*, 1983.

"... this is one of Lugosi's worst performances, not helped by the fact that he was now ill and stuntman Eddie Parker had to double for him through much of the film. The fact that the film was cut before release may explain at least part of the performance's embarrassing inadequacy... Competently directed (especially the beginning) but basically an unimaginative rehash, the film is definitely sunk by Lugosi's performance."—*The Encyclopedia of Horror Movies*, 1986.

Though its reputation hasn't improved much in the years since its release, many knowledgeable critics tend to treat the film more favorably than most Universal horror films of the forties.

"*Frankenstein Meets the Wolf Man* is a far better product than its audience required; what should have been only an exploitative horror film with its accent on monsters and action is also a well-crafted production with fine attention to detail. The film boasts the best-ever Wolf Man scenes and gives us one last real look at the Monster before he becomes a lowly prop in the *House* films... a brisk pace, a plot filled with incident, and Roy William Neill's artistry place it a cut above all the other '40s sequels "—Michael Brunas, John Brunas, and Tom Weaver, *Universal Horrors*, 1990.

In my view, aside from the inconsistency of trying to reconcile the time periods of the Frankenstein Monster and the Wolf Man, and aside from problems arising from casting Lugosi as the Monster, *Frankenstein Meets the Wolf Man* is a thoroughly enjoyable film. First of all, no fair-minded critic can substantiate the criticism of Lon Chaney's performance as the Wolf Man. As Brunas, Brunas, and Weaver correctly note:

"Chaney dominates the film; forlorn but no longer whiny, desperate but not as panic-stricken, he brings some new dimensions to the melancholy Larry Talbot and evokes yet-greater sympathy as he searches vainly for the secret of death.

"*Frankenstein Meets the Wolf Man* also boasts some of the best Wolf Man scenes from any of the character's five movies: the opening scene in the crypt, his vicious attack on the Cardiff bobby, the posse in Vasaria, and ultimately the roof-raising brawl with Lugosi's Frankenstein Monster."

In his book *It's Alive!*, Gregory William Mank agrees: "It is Lon Chaney... who carries *Frankenstein Meets the Wolf Man*. His performance is the best of his Universal sojourns, and he creates and sustains a pathos that conveys the tragedy, and not just the melodrama, of the lycanthropic Talbot."

Chaney elicits great empathy in his hospital scenes as he gestures for help, knowing who he is, but not yet remembering what he is. A very athletic and bestial Chaney attacks the Cardiff policeman who earlier discovered him unconscious in the streets and whistled for help. Unlike in *The Wolf Man*, this is a Talbot who has learned from experience, a Talbot who is both cunning and purposeful.

Additionally, Ilona Massey is the strongest and best of all the Frankenstein series heroines, and Patric Knowles is a better leading man/love interest than he was in *The Wolf Man*. Together they substantially raise the quality of the film. Though he falls far short of his classic portrayal of Inspector Krogh in *Son of Frankenstein*, Lionel Atwill is charming as the affable but rather puffed-up mayor of Vasaria. Maria Ouspenskaya is every bit as good in *Frankenstein Meets the Wolf Man* as she was in her most memorable *The Wolf Man*. Her line in reference to Talbot, "He simply wants to die," is a profound echo of Karloff's "We belong dead," the most poignant line in *Bride of Frankenstein*, and of Lugosi's immortal lines from *Dracula*, "To die, to be really dead—that would be glorious."

The opening credits, which form from the vapors of a test tube, are the best of any Universal horror film, and the atmospheric opening scene in which the grave robbers enter the crypt of Lawrence Talbot is also one of their best efforts. The festival of the new wine and the song sung by Adia Kuznetzoff is the best "light relief" in any Universal horror film, especially since the singer's last stanza brings Talbot's frustrations to light among the villagers. Additionally, the comic relief is thematically integrated with the film's main ideas.

While *Frankenstein Meets the Wolf Man* is certainly not a good Frankenstein film, it is a top-notch werewolf film, ranking with *The Wolf Man* and *Son of Dracula* as one of Universal's top two or three horror films of the forties. Largely because Chaney's performance as the Wolf Man successfully rivals that of Karloff as the Frankenstein Monster (I disagree with Brunas, Brunas, and Weaver in that regard), *Frankenstein Meets the Wolf Man* must be considered one of Universal's finest efforts.

Before turning to Lugosi's performance as the Monster, I wish to briefly discuss another reason why *Frankenstein Meets the Wolf Man* is such a memorable film: Curt Siodmak's screenplay. A theme that has never been mentioned in regard to the film is the Blakeian journey from childhood and innocence to experience. As Baroness Frankenstein wistfully remarks when hearing the first strains of music from the festival of the new wine, "It takes me back to my childhood." The words of Kuznetzoff's song, "For life is short, but death is long," is certainly a theme of adult experience explored in literature by Blake, Emily Dickinson, and many others. The mutability of life leads the more sentimental among us to become disciples in the cult of memory, to take a bitter-sweet pleasure in reflecting upon the golden days that are no more. While Talbot is not intellectual enough to appreciate such things, Siodmak certainly is, and he infuses the screenplay with many references to the Balkeian journey. This leads us to reconsider Talbot's journey from care-free youth to death-cursed maturity, a journey we all must face. The Romantic desire to return to a younger, more idealistic past, symbolized by the journey to Vasaria and the festival of the new wine, is shared in the film by Talbot, the Monster, Baroness Frankenstein, and certainly the villagers of Vasaria, who would obviously like nothing better than to return to a time of peace and prosperity, free of wolf men, monsters, and violent death. As Patric Knowles wrote in response to my inquiries, "After forty years, I'm afraid my memory of *The Wolf Man* and *Frankenstein Meets the Wolf Man* is rather vague. I'm sure we all had a marvelous time together—we were so young!" These are themes that will touch the heart of the Romantic and raise the film to even greater heights of artistry for such a personality.

Freud's death instinct is also a related theme that Siodmak weaves through the character motivation—particularly that of Talbot. The well-read, well-educated Siodmak endowed *The Wolf Man* and *Frankenstein Meets the Wolf Man* with philosophical, psychological, and literary themes that deserve even greater scrutiny than they have already received. Likewise, maybe *Frankenstein Meets the Wolf Man* will eventually receive the critical respect that it deserves.

The remainder of this chapter will be devoted to a critique of Lugosi's performance as the Frankenstein Monster. First of all, it is impossible to evaluate a performance that ends up on the cutting room floor. Still, knowing what we now know about the clipped scenes (and clipped character motivation), I will attempt to evaluate Lugosi's performance from the standpoint of what finds its say into the final theatrical version, with some attention to the type of direction he must have received from Neill, who was directing a half-blind/weak monster—a fact unknown to the audience as a result of those final cuts.

We first see the Monster when Chaney exposes its face in the ice. The face we see, however, in not Lugosi's but that of stunt man Eddie Parker. Parker is also the Monster that Chaney eventually lifts out of the ice.

The cave scenes immediately following the Monster's emergence from the ice were cut. Therein, Chaney and Lugosi converse about their plight. Among Lugosi's excised lines were the following: "Where are you? I can hardly see... Help me to get up. I once had the strength of a hundred men... It's gone... I'm sick." These lines would have established the Monster as ill and half blind, accounting for Lugosi's interpretation of the Monster as stiff and unsure.

After Lugosi and Chaney agree to join forces against those "futile little mortals" better known in horror films as villagers, the Monster agrees to lead Talbot to Frankenstein's laboratory. The film picks up again at this point with Chaney leading Lugosi, who walks with outstretched arms as though blind. Uttering a growl, Lugosi pushes over a piece of timber blocking his path. The screenplay describes the action: "Larry pushes the debris out of his way—the monster follows him, half-blind, groping his way with both hands, touching the wall."

The Monster's growl exhibits anger and frustration as much as anything else, a frustration lacking motivation due to the editing. Also snipped was the motivation for Lugosi's groping performance, all of which renders the Monster's actions puzzling and strikingly non-frightening.

Universal then cut scenes during which Chaney and Lugosi discuss the relative merits of life and death, Chaney concluding that death is preferable if one is a werewolf, and Lugosi opining that a monster's life is worth preserving if only the restoration of sight and strength were possible. The film picks up as Lugosi leads Chaney to a box reputedly containing the diary. When Chaney is dejected at finding the box empty, Lugosi simply utters the world, "gone." Unfortunately for Lugosi, while Universal allowed the scene to remain, it removed the sound of Lugosi's voice, making the Monster's silent, flapping mouth appear ludicrous.

The screenplay describes the later scene in which the Monster disrupts the Festival of the New Wine: "Toward the square—out of the night—walks the Monster, half-blind, groping its way toward the lights. As it comes nearer, SHOUTS ARE HEARD." When Chaney reaches Lugosi, "The monster recognizes him—it's Larry he was looking for—and with a smile on his ungainly face, he turns clumsily. Larry pushes him toward the truck." In these scenes, Lugosi is most ineffectual as the Monster, at least as audiences without knowledge of the cut scenes would conclude. He stands, arms at his sides like a "wind-up doll," as Chaney goes into action to save their skins. Though stuntman Eddie Parker rolls barrels out of the back of the fleeing "truck" to stall the villagers' pursuit, the Monster appears a bumbling Stan Laurel to Chaney's exasperated Oliver Hardy.

One can only consider Universal correct in its decision to cut Lugosi's dialogue (and Chaney's too in this case) as Talbot admonishes the Monster for showing itself in the village:

Larry (bitterly): "You think you're so clever—Frankenstein gave you a stunning brain, did he? But you're dumb! You've spoiled our only chance. (Dr. Mannering [named Harley in the screenplay] calls for Talbot).

Monster: "Don't leave me—don't go! I'm weak... They'll catch me and bury me alive!"

The film picks up as the Monster, responding to Dr. Mannering's voice, walks away from the cave mouth and lifts a log in defiance, growling a warning to anyone who enters. Again, Chaney steadies him to allow Knowles and Massey to enter. Though Lugosi is adequate in this scene, he looks incredibly old through the makeup, and his stature is again diminished by his reinforced status as Chaney's burden.

Universal then cut scenes in which Lugosi explains to Knowles that he wants to be made well again. Knowles pays great attention to Lugosi's opinions at this point, and for once someone else's motivations are weakened for the viewing audience by the cuts. Later, when Knowles decides to revive the Monster, he does so with little apparent motivation.

Later, a scene features Lugosi repeating his desire to rule the world. Shortly afterward, the film picks up with the appearance of Ouspenskaya. She and Chaney talk as Lugosi takes a few steps backward and stiffens as a statue at the sound of water turning the turbines. In this scene, his receding into the background into a statuesque stance almost tends to reinforce the impression that he is indeed a fixture in the film rather than an integral character.

Interestingly, the film's finale gives Lugosi his only chance to play a revived, physically restored Frankenstein Monster—and he makes the most of it, providing one of the most chillingly effective moments in the Monster's long cinematic history. That scene occurs as Knowles changes his plans and decides to revitalize Frankenstein's creation. Lugosi, strapped to a lab table, first twitches his face as the welcome lifeforce courses through his body. Then his eyes open and his mouth executes an evil grin of recognition and expectation. Perhaps if Lugosi had been able to re-shoot his motivation-defining dialogue scenes to Universal's satisfaction, this scene might have haunted the nightmares of audience members for decades to come. As it is, the scene is still powerful, making one wonder how a younger, physically fit Lugosi might have portrayed the Frankenstein Monster under more propitious circumstances.

In the final scenes in which the Frankenstein Monster and Wolf Man engage each other in mortal combat, stuntmen handle all of Lugosi's physically demanding moments. Bela does get to open his arms wide, his face ablaze with expectation, as he invited Chaney to do his worst! The waters from the exploded dam then wash the monsters away, sending the audiences safely home, but leaving room for yet another sequel.

So how do we evaluate Bela Lugosi as the Frankenstein Monster in *Frankenstein Meets the Wolf Man*? Ultimately, if we go by what we see, the idea of Lugosi as the Monster was misguided from the start. Bela is simply miscast—period!

While Lugosi might have fulfilled the height requirement, his body was sick and tired. The weighted shoes might indeed have accounted for the stiff walk that has become stereotypical of the Frankenstein Monster. But was the effect intended by Universal, or were Lugosi's tired legs simply unable to adequately carry the weight?

Would an uncut release of the film enhance Lugosi's performance? In some ways yes, for the audience would understand why the actor staggered about as though blind. I suspect, however, that Lugosi's dialogue would have killed the film. The Monster delivering lines that might have brought laughter to whoever said them—and in an Hungarian accent no less—probably would have damaged the film far more than the cuts do. The fact that, despite all the problems, *Frankenstein Meets the Wolf Man* still emerges as one of the best horror films of the forties is a testament to how outstanding it otherwise is.

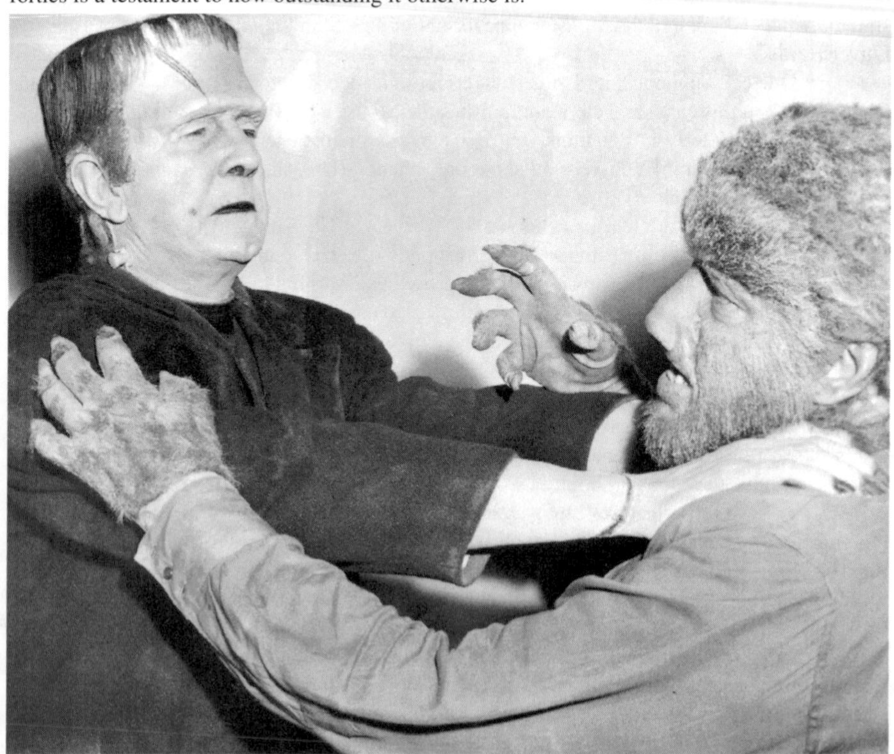

A posed publicity shot featuring the horrific battle of the century!

Return of the Vampire

(1943)

by Don Leifert

CREDITS: Director: Lew Landers; Producer: Sam White; Story and Screenplay: Griffin Jay, Kurt Neumann, Randall Faye; Photography: John Stumar, L. W. O'Connell; Makeup: Clay Campbell; Music: Mario C. Tedesco; Art Director: Lionel Banks; Special Effects: Aaron Nadley

CAST: Bela Lugosi...Armand Tesla, Nina Foch...Nicki Saunders, Frieda Inescort ...Lady Jane Ainsley, Roland Varno...John Ainsley, Matt Willis...Andreas Obry, Miles Mander...Sir Frederick Fleet, Gilbert Emery...Professor Saunders, William C.P. Austin...Gannet, Ottola Nesmith...Elsa, Leslie Denison...Lynch, George McKay, Shirlee Collier, Billy Bevan, Donald Dewar, Jeanne Bates

It's safe to say that quite a few bottles of Hungarian wine were downed when Bela Lugosi learned that Universal Studios had snubbed him and cast the new kid on the block, Lon Chaney, as Dracula in its upcoming production of *Son of Dracula*. Lugosi certainly must have questioned how the studio could have possibly overlooked his old-world charm in favor of a stocky Oklahoman with a flat midwestern accent and a rather limited acting range. It was a classic case of ingratitude to the actor who had helped raise Universal's finances from the dead when he starred in *Dracula* for the studio back in 1931.

By 1943, however, Lugosi's star had fallen, but he was still a working actor who received top billing whenever he performed on the Monogram lot. And, he continued to give good performances in whatever projects he undertook despite the poverty row status of many of the studios that hired him. Yet, Universal's latest casting decision must have been a particularly painful one for Lugosi. He wanted the Dracula role in the upcoming production, and he felt he deserved it. Meanwhile, Columbia's Harry Cohn must have gleefully watched the situation from afar in his studio office, prompting him to offer Lugosi the leading role in an upcoming horror film about vampirism.

The proposed cast, which included Frieda Inescort, Nina Foch, Matt Willis, and Miles Mander, was an interesting blend of seasoned pros like Lugosi and Mander and newcomers such as Foch and Jeanne Bates, which resulted in some rather disparate acting styles. It was an odd mix, but *The Return of the Vampire*'s cast didn't seem to notice. Nina Foch, who was slated to play the ingenue who falls under Lugosi's hypnotic spell, also starred in *Cry of the Werewolf* (Columbia, 1942) as the title creature. In a recent interview, she recalled her work in *The Return of the Vampire* and *Cry of the Werewolf* rather unenthusiastically: "I'll tell you the best thing about playing a "werewolf," she offered. "You get to rest while the wolf works. I was also in *The Return of the Vampire* for Columbia. Those films do not rank high in my life's work. I'm not amused by horror pictures."

Nor was she amused by the inconsistent treatment she was receiving from Harry Cohn and company at Columbia when she appeared in *The Return of the Vampire*: "I didn't belong at Columbia at all," she continued. "I was too young, and I'd come from nice schools in New York. The language on the sets was generally shocking. It was all very coarse. And they kept telling me, 'you can act, but it's a shame you're not pretty and you have no sex appeal at all.' Shortly afterward, I went to New York and did a play. The New York press said I was sexy and beautiful, so Columbia

Bela Lugosi as Armand Tesla, posing as Dr. Hugo Bruckner, visits the home of Lady Jane Ainsley (Frieda Inescourt).

changed their attitude toward me. I never did have the looks they liked in that period of fat lips, tiny noses, and apple cheeks. Before the option of my contract came up, I went to Cohn and said, 'I'll be a second-rate actress if I stay here. I'd be better served if I could go to New York and learn my craft.' Cohn agreed and let me go."

Despite Foch's rather obvious displeasure with Columbia, Lugosi certainly had the studio to thank for taking his mind off Universal's casting snub. Cohn arranged to pay Lugosi $3,500 for a four-week shooting schedule, and even better, Lugosi was given top billing and a sizeable role in a reputable production. His most recent outings at Universal found him fifth-billed under first-billed Lon Chaney in *Frankenstein Meets the Wolf Man* (1943), and the once-in-demand Hungarian bogeyman knew that Universal had become Chaney's playground in the forties.

But Columbia Studios had a surprise card up its corporate sleeve. If Lugosi couldn't get an invitation to play a vampire at his old studio, why not shoot *The Return of the Vampire* in the style of a Universal horror film? And it's amazing how completely this mission was accomplished. The finished film bore an uncanny resemblance to the somewhat generic horror films being cranked out with machine-like precision by Universal, while, ironically, *Son of Dracula* (1943) defied the Universal mold and continues to be cited as the studios' most original and stylish forties entry in the horror genre. Columbia had no such artistic pretensions, however, and *The Return of the Vampire* looks like it was shot at the Universal monster factory.

Louis Diage's atmospheric sets were reminiscent of the graveyard scenes in *Frankenstein Meets the Wolf Man*, but Diage's expressionistic, mist-laden cemetery with its gnarled trees and twisted tombstones seemed claustrophobic, giving the viewer the impression that if the camera tilted slightly to the left or right it would capture a napping grip or a gaffer downing his coffee. It

The vampire Tesla enslaves the soul of Andreas (Matt Willis), the cursed werewolf, in Lew Landers' *Return of the Vampire*.

is interesting to note that Diage's Priory Cemetery set was constructed and shot at Fine Arts Studio because Columbia was cramped for space during *The Return of the Vampire*'s shooting schedule. Regardless of the oddly claustrophobic feel of the outdoor sets, they certainly evoke an atmosphere suited to Lugosi's nocturnal mayhem, provided he didn't miss his mark and take too many steps to the left or right.

In addition to the *Frankenstein Meets the Wolf Man* inspired sets, there are also some elements inspired by *Dracula's Daughter* (Universal, 1936), the studio's first Lugosi-less sequel to *Dracula.* Comparisons are inevitable between the scene in which *Dracula's Daughter* star Otto Kruger fails to save a bedridden victim (Nan Gray) of vampire Gloria Holden and *Return of the Vampire*'s scene in which Gilbert Emery and Frieda Inescort question a bedridden Jeanne Bates, who dies of fright while recalling her encounter with Lugosi.

The impression that the film was produced by Universal was furthered when Harry Cohn secured the services of screenwriter Griffin Jay, who had composed the screenplays for *The Mummy's Hand* (Universal, 1940), *The Mummy's Tomb* (Universal, 1942), and *Captive Wild Woman* (Universal, 1943) before penning the script for *Vampires of London* which ultimately became *The Return of the Vampire*. The finished product incorporated elements from the popular

Wolf Man and Dracula films, but added a unique World War II setting.

The film opens with a pre-credit sequence in which the vampire, Armand Tesla (Lugosi), confronts a woman (Jeanne Bates) on a foggy street. She screams and the screen explodes into a blast of fog which signals the upcoming credits. (In a 1994 interview with Tom Weaver for *Comics Scene*, Ms. Bates revealed that she never met Lugosi. A stand-in was used for the scene.)

The action continues as a werewolf (Matt Willis) lumbers into a graveyard and awakens his vampire master, Armand Tesla, to set out on his nightly search for blood. The camera then pans across the estate of Lady Jane Ainsley (Inescort) where she and fellow scientist Professor Saunders (Gilbert Emery) try to determine the condition of a woman (Jeanne Bates) found "practically bloodless" and brought to Ainsley's estate. While being questioned by the concerned scientists, she dies of fright.

As Professor Saunders reads a book about vampirism, the fiendish Tesla steals into the room of his granddaughter Nicki (Shirlee Collins) who becomes Tesla's latest victim.

The following morning, Professor Saunders finds two small punctures in the neck of his weakened granddaughter. Recalling his knowledge of vampire lore, he gives the child a blood transfusion and sets out, with Lady Jane by his side, to drive a stake through the vampire's heart. They find Tesla's daytime resting place, and as they drive the stake home, the vampire's slavish werewolf appears and assumes human form.

The action shifts to 1943. Andreas, the former werewolf, is now one of Lady Ainsley's lab assistants in her combination research facility/hospital. Nicki (Nina Foch) is now in her early twenties and engaged to Lady Ainsley's son (Roland Varno, whose son Martin penned the screenplay for American International Pictures' *Night of the Blood Beast* in 1958). Their peace of mind is suddenly destroyed when an Axis bomb disturbs Armand Tesla's crypt, where Professor Saunders and Lady Jane destroyed him years earlier.

A British worker (Billy Bevan) assigned to find corpses disturbed by the bomb blast searches the local graveyard where he finds Tesla. Mistaking the stake in Tesla's chest for a bomb splint, he removes it.

Revived, Tesla poses as Dr. Hugo Bruckner and plans to enslave Andreas' soul once again. He accomplishes his mission, turning Andreas into a wolf man at will, and sets out to reacquaint himself with Nicki's neck. Meanwhile, Ainsley is on to Tesla's fiendish deeds, but spends a substantial portion of the film's 69-minute running time trying to persuade Sir Frederick Fleet (Miles Mander) that there is a vampire terrorizing her home.

Ainsley finally persuades Sir Frederick to follow Nicki during one of her nocturnal walks, during which she appears entranced. They follow her to a graveyard where Tesla rests by day, but their hope to rescue Nicki is thwarted when an Axis bomb explodes in the graveyard. Andreas, during the confusion, drags the now-unconscious Nicki into Telsa's crypt.

When Tesla denies the wounded Andreas' plea for eternal life, the wolf man (in a rather silly voice over) hears the words of Lady Jane ("You are saved Andreas because I have taught you the meaning of goodness...") and assumes his human form. He confronts Tesla with a crucifix, but a bomb blast interrupts the struggle. When the smoke clears, Andreas drags the unconscious Tesla into the sunlight where he melts (literally!). Lady Jane arrives as the recovering Nicki is removed from the scene by stretcher. Sir Frederick, who still disbelieves in the existence of vampires, turns to two subordinates (Leslie Denison, William C.P. Austin) and asks, "Say, you fellows don't believe in this vampire business, do you?"

They reply, "Yes sir, we do!"

Sir Frederick, in a painfully awkward moment, looks directly into the camera and asks, "And do you people?"

The film premiered at the Rialto on January 28, 1944. Griffin Jay's screenplay (which was based on an idea by Kurt Neumann, who was originally slated to direct) appealed to 1944 audiences who couldn't get enough wartime fare at the boxoffice. While the film's WWII setting exists in the background during most of the film's running time, there is a key scene in which Axis bombs inadvertently lead to the vampire's resurrection.

Lew Landers assumed directorial duties when the intended director, Kurt Neumann, left to direct *The Unknown Guest* at Monogram. Landers was a reliable action director who had previously worked with Lugosi in *The Raven* (Universal, 1935), which contains one of the actor's finest performances. He directed *The Raven* under the name Louis Friedlander, but subsequently shortened his name to Lew Landers. In addition to *The Return of the Vampire*, he helmed over fifty films, including *The Boogie Man Will Get You* (Columbia, 1942) and *Mystery Ship* (Columbia, 1941). Landers also directed *Man in the Dark* (Columbia, 1953), a remake of the studio's *The Man Who Lived Twice* (1936). He is best remembered, however, for the exciting pace he achieved through editing and cinematography in *The Raven*, yet Lander's ability to sustain an involving rhythm is hardly evident in *The Return of the Vampire*, which would have benefited measurably from a less leisurely pace.

The film's musical score was written by Mario Castelnuvo-Tedesco (billed as Mario C. Tedesco), a composer widely known during the 1920s. While best known for composing two Shakespearean operas, *The Merchant of Venice* (1961) and *All's Well That Ends Well* (1957), he has also written violin concertos, a cello concerto, and overtures to twelve plays by William Shakespeare. Unfortunately, none of his musical genius was in evidence when he composed the score for *The Return of the Vampire*. Much of the incidental music seems inappropriate and intrusive; the visually impressive scenes in the mist-shrouded graveyard are almost ruined by Tedesco's rather abrasive "mood" music (which subsequently turned up in 1957 in Columbia's *Zombies of Mora Tau*); and by way of comparison, Tedesco was no match for Universal's Hans Salter when it came to composing scores for horror films.

These flaws aside, *The Return of the Vampire* scores passing marks in some departments, notably the performance turned in by Frieda Inescort who assumed the Van Helsing role in the person of Lady Jane Ainsley, a research scientist whose household is jeopardized by the undead Armand Tesla (Lugosi). In essence, Inescort, a very capably British actress, forms the moral center of the film and manages to turn in one of *Return*'s best performances. It is interesting to note that her short-lived career in the horror genre almost extended beyond *The Return of the Vampire* when Monogram producers Sam Katzman and Jack Dietz planned to showcase Inescort, Lugosi, John Carradine, and George Zucco in *Voodoo Man* (1944) and *Return of the Ape Man* (1944). Despite Dietz and Katzman's plans, she failed to appear in either of these horror offerings.

While Inescort gives the film a much-needed boost, veteran character actor Miles Mander turns in *The Return of the Vampire*'s worst performance as Sir Frederick Fleet, the stock skeptic who refuses to acknowledge the existence of vampires despite the signs that surround him. Generally a first-rate performer, Mander's whining delivery is downright grating and far below the actor's usual standards in productions such as *Wuthering Heights* (Goldwyn, 1939) and *Stanley and Livingston* (Fox, 1939). This time around, he appears ill at ease throughout his performance and his sharp exchanges with Frieda Inescort over the existence of vampires seem like nasty overreactions to her beliefs.

Makeup man Clay Campbell's original werewolf design for Matt Willis is effective, but somewhat inconsistent from scene to scene. Campbell duplicated the makeup to better effect over a decade later for Steven Ritch in *The Werewolf* (Columbia, 1956). Actor Matt Willis, who tends to be a scenery chewer, is unintentionally amusing as the talking werewolf. This is best summed up by Tom Weaver in an article for *Filmfax*: "Less effective (than Lugosi) despite a good performance, is Matt Willis' werewolf. Little more than a Man Friday who happens to have hair on his face, the werewolf talks, fistfights his way out of trouble, and wears a doglike makeup that's actually rather cute."

Silent film comedian Billy Bevan (who also appeared in *Dracula's Daughter*) plays a frightened worker assigned graveyard cleanup duty after a bomb strikes Priory Cemetery. He basically reprises the stock frightened character he performed in the earlier film and only appears

on screen for a few minutes. It's the kind of tired humor that tends to slow down the pace of a film without being even marginally amusing.

As for Lugosi, *The Return of the Vampire* may have been a mere one-picture deal, but it was certainly a good career move, as it afforded him the opportunity to return to the role that earned him fame. The final results, however, are a disappointment. The aristocratic charm and animal magnetism are nowhere to be found in the Columbia offering, nor does Lugosi seem to be having as much fun with the role as he did in *Abbott and Costello Meet Frankenstein*

(Universal-International, 1948). In fact, Lugosi, who appears tired in many of his scenes, would have benefited from an hour or two with makeup man Clay Campbell, who apparently became so preoccupied with Matt Willis' lycanthrope that he forgot to apply cosmetics to the title creature. Gone is the black, slicked-back hair that topped Lugosi's Count in *Dracula* and *Abbott and Costello Meet Frankenstein*. In fact, Lugosi looks more like someone's favorite grandfather than the erotic Count of 1931 fame, especially in those scenes in which Armand Tesla assumes the identity of Dr. Hugo Bruckner. At times, he even seems uncomfortable moving on the set, a case in point being the scene in which he is introduced to Lady Jane's guests at a formal party. Lugosi awkwardly descends a single step in such a way that he appears fearful of missing his mark or falling. It's a small moment, but a surprisingly awkward one for an actor who seemed more high-spirited in his films for Monogram during the same time period.

Lugosi's full-blooded, melodramatic style does manage to surface, however, in the climactic struggle with Matt Willis, during which he mugs deliciously as he attempts to avoid contact with a crucifix. Interestingly enough, this rather theatrical scene is evocative of the stage appearances Lugosi would be making years later, in which he would appear before a restless crowd of moviegoers, some of whom had never heard of Lugosi, and perform a horror skit, often involving an actor in a gorilla suit. While Lugosi brings the proper level of histrionics to *The Return of the Vampire*'s climactic confrontation, the confining crypt set and his broad reactions have the "feel" of one of those demeaning road shows to which the actor would be subjected years later.

Nonetheless, the film was a financial success and a sequel, *Vampires Over London,* was in the works, but the project eventually evolved into *Cry of the Werewolf* (1944), causing Lugosi to lose out on another opportunity to play a vampire. This was a sad state of affairs indeed from a studio that had recently offered Boris Karloff a 5-picture deal, which consisted of *The Man They Could Not Hang* (1939), *The Man With Nine Lives* (1940), *Before I Hang* (1940), *The Devil Commands* (1941), and *The Boogie Man Will Get You* (1942). Meanwhile, Lugosi had to be contented with Cohn's single-picture deal.

The critics have been mixed over the film's relative merits. *Variety* felt "Developments are telegraphed in advance," but went on to say that "Lew Landers managed nicely on his direction." As for Lugosi, *Variety* reported that "Lugosi's villainy remains standard for him and Frieda Inescort, as one who saves the life of a vampire victim and helps trap Lugosi, contributes the outstanding portrayal." Richard Bojarski, in *The Complete Films of Bela Lugosi*, recalled that despite favorable press in America, British censors felt some scenes were too intense for English audiences and snipped the climactic shot in which Armand Tesla's head melts (an effect achieved by melting a hollow version of Lugosi's life mask). Tom Weaver apparently wished the entire film should melt when he wrote in *Poverty Row Horrors* that "Columbia's *The Return of the Vampire* was a derivative hack job." James J. Mulay is much more generous. In *The Horror Film*, he shares that "Bela Lugosi, who played a phony vampire in Tod Browning's *Mark of the Vampire* (MGM, 1935), essays the real thing here for the first time since *Dracula* (1931), though the famous count's name couldn't be used because Universal owned the rights to it." He goes on to say, "Lugosi is properly menacing as the vampire, and Lew Lander's atmospheric direction makes this a fairly memorable, although minor, horror venture."

And how have the critics treated *Return of the Vampire*'s nemesis from the Universal lot? Robert Siodmak's *Son of Dracula* has fared exceptionally well with the critics; in fact, Lugosi's absence doesn't seem to faze reviewers, most of whom have been quite enthusiastic about the picture. *Variety*, in a favorable review, felt that "after (the) usual series of suspenseful episodes, Robert Paige is able to kill vampirish forms of both Chaney and Louise Albritton for fadeout; it's a cinch the Dracula strain will be revived again for further cinematic adventures." More recent critics have been even more enthusiastic, citing Siodmak's direction as the most stylish in a forties' Universal horror film. William K. Everson, in *More Classics of the Horror Film*, goes so far as to say, "On virtually every level, from its impressive credits to its downbeat ending, *Son of Dracula* is a beauty of a film."

Universal revived Dracula yet again in *House of Frankenstein* in December of 1944 starring John Carradine as the undead Count, a role he reprised to good effect the following year in *House of Dracula*. Once again, Lugosi wasn't even invited to the party.

While *The Return of the Vampire* hasn't received the critical kudos *Son of Dracula* has garnered, it was a box-office moneymaker. And despite *Son of Dracula*'s warm reception, Chaney's horror career was about to take a dip with some pretty awful *Inner Sanctum* mysteries such as *Calling Dr. Death* (1944) and *Dead Man's Eyes* (1944), but his distinctly American persona allowed him to branch out into crime pictures and westerns in the years to come. Lugosi had no such options. He wasn't commanding the salaries of either Chaney or Boris Karloff, and his work in *The Return of the Vampire*, while reputable, would hardly change the downward spiral his career had taken. *Voodoo Man* followed for Monogram in 1944, and by 1947 he was relegated to dreck such as *Scared to Death* (Screen Guild).

From a total career perspective, *The Return of the Vampire* pales in comparison to Lugosi's golden-age ventures such as *The Black Cat* (Universal, 1934), or *The Raven* (Universal, 1935). It can't even compare to the actor's work in films such as *The Wolf Man* (Universal, 1941), in which he practically steals the film in a brilliant cameo, or *The Ghost of Frankenstein* (Universal, 1942), in which he played the broken-necked Ygor to wonderful effect. Yet, *The Return of the Vampire* remains a mildly entertaining little thriller that provided Lugosi another opportunity to don the familiar top hat and cape. As such, it's worth a visit, but unlike the film's title creature, you won't want to return.

The vampire Tesla's fate is sealed not by a crucifix but by a World War II bomb enabling his enemy to drag him into the deadly sunlight.

Zombies on Broadway
Genius at Work
(1945-46)

by John Soister

Zombies on Broadway
CREDITS: Director: Gordon Douglas; Producer: Ben Stoloff; Executive Producer: Sid Rogell; Screenplay: Laurence Kimble; Original Story: Robert Faber, Charles Newman; Adaptation: Robert E. Kent; Make-up: Maurice Seiderman; Art Direction: Albert S. D'Agostino, Walter E. Keller; Set Decoration; Darrell Silvera, Al Greenwood; Recorded by Richard Van Hessen; Rerecorded by Terry Kellum; Assistant Director: Sam Ruman; Gowns: Edward Stevenson; Music: Roy Webb; Music Director: C.K. Bakaleinikoff; Editor: Philip Martin, Jr.; Dance Director: Charles O'Curran; An RKO Radio Picture; released April, 1945; Released in Great Britain as *Loonies on Broadway;* US running time: 68 minutes

CAST: Bela Lugosi...Dr. Renault, Wally Brown...Jerry Miles, Alan Carney... Mike Strager, Anne Jeffreys...Jean, Sheldon Leonard...Ace Miller, Joseph Vitale...Joseph, Ian Wolfe...Prof. Hopkins, Frank Jenks...Gus, Russell Hopton...Benny, Darby Jones...Kolaga, Louis Jean Heydt...Douglas Walker, Sir Lancelot...Calypso singer

Genius At Work
CREDITS: Director: Leslie Goodwins; Producer: Herman Schlom; Executive Producer: Sid Rogell; Screenplay: Robert E. Kent, Monte Brice; Music Direction: C.K. Bakaleinikoff; Photography: Robert de Grasse, ASC; Special Effects: Vernon L. Walker, ASC; Art Direction: Albert S. D'Agostino, Ralph Berger; Set Decoration: Darrell Silvera; Sound Recording: Robert Van Hessen, Roy Granville; Editor: Marvin Coil; Gowns: Renie; Assistant Director: Harry D'Arcy; An RKO Radio Picture; released August, 1946; Released in Great Britain as *Master Minds;* US running time: 61 minutes

CAST: Bela Lugosi...Stone, Lionel Atwill...Latimer Marsh/The Cobra, Wally Brown...Jerry Miles, Alan Carney...Mike Strager, Anne Jeffreys...Ellen Brent, Marc Cramer...Lt. Rick Campbell, Ralph Dunn...Lt. Gilley, with Robert Clarke, Forbes Murray, Eddie Borden, Phil Warren

Some years ago, Ed Koch, the then-mayor of New York City, proposed a city-wide boycott of all movies in order to protest rising ticket prices. The boycott, albeit brief, was successful enough to merit a response from the studios, which claimed that expensive technology and astronomic salaries were the underlying reasons for the increased admission costs. If only, sighed the suits, we could return to the old system of studio contracts, salaries would be more reasonable, and movies more affordable. Sure, and if pigs had wings...

For actors around long enough to remember exclusive studio contracts, reminiscences vary from pleasant to horrific. While belonging to a particular studio *could* mean constant work (especially for superstars or character people), it could also mean long periods of unemployment (for any of a variety of reasons), with no chance to keep the wolf away from the door by appearing elsewhere.

In reality, the whole policy was nothing more than a highstakes crapshoot. The constant release of product starring "hot" personalities could provide either incredible profits and ever-soaring popularity, or overexposure. (It was more the latter than behind-the-scenes squabbling or changing comedic tastes that lead to Abbott and Costello's wearing out their welcome at Universal.)

Many of the really big names had clauses in their contracts permitting them to work at other studios under certain conditions. At the whim of the studio executives, however, just about anyone could be loaned out, even against his or her will. (At times, this policy backfired dramatically. Both Claudette Colbert and Clark Gable were "banished" to Columbia in 1934 as punishment for their uncooperative behavior at their home studios. The resulting effort—*It Happened One Night*—netted them both major Oscars, and saw lowly Columbia snag the top award for best picture as well.)

Before *Frankenstein,* Boris Karloff owed allegiance to no one studio; he freelanced, and was happy to get what work he could. Some 18 months after *Frankenstein,* however, he walked off the Universal lot when the Laemmles fudged on scheduled pay raises to the now-celebrated star. Boris' renegotiated Universal contract allowed him to work elsewhere on *his* own terms, and not on those of a chastened Uncle Carl.

Then there was Bela Lugosi. Bela had been involved with several studios (chiefly Fox) during the late silent era; the English language as set forth on title cards held no terror for the Hungarian. As sound pictures became the norm, Bela's accent and phonetic stage English allowed him such "foreign" parts as an Austrian nightclub owner, an expatriated police inspector, a singing teacher, and a Marabout (again, chiefly at Fox). Prior to *Dracula,* his involvement with Universal was limited to vocal work (either dubbing or serving as "interlocutor") for Hungarian release versions of American films, and to a bit in the silent feature, *How to Handle Women.*

After *Dracula* hit the mother lode, Bela was signed to do a second, similar film: *Frankenstein.* Posturing and temperament resulted in his move over to yet another horror project, *Murders in the Rue Morgue,* as infighting and betrayal did to erstwhile *Frankenstein* director, Robert Florey. Escaping a mute role (and getting his teeth into the rococo dialogue of Dr. Mirakle) was a personal triumph for Bela, if not for the disappointed and bitter Florey. For Universal, however, *Murders in the Rue Morgue* was a financial disaster, barely recovering costs.

With an eye on the astounding receipts of James Whale's *Frankenstein,* the Laemmles decided that Universal had seen the last of Monsieur Florey. (In fact, the French director was conspicuous in his absence from the lot for over 15 years. When Universal merged with International Pictures in 1946, and studio heads Leo Spitz (former president of RKO) and William Goetz announced that only "A" features would henceforth be filmed, it was only a matter of time before Florey (who had built something of a reputation at the other studios) was recalled. His only feature for UI was 1948's *Rogue's Regiment,* a Dick Powell potboiler about the French Foreign Legion. After that one, Florey disappeared from Universal for good.)

As for the aggravating Mr. Lugosi, he would never be top horror man in any Universal film as long as they owned the studio (nor, tragically, would Lugosi appear as sole genre villain again for Universal under any subsequent ownership).

For the few films remaining under his *Black Cat* contract (with the exception of the tepid and quickly forgotten *Postal Inspector*), Bela would be forced to share (disproportionately) the spotlight with Boris Karloff, the monster *he* had helped create. (Throughout the course of his career after *Postal Inspector,* Lugosi would return to Universal for eight more features. He would receive top billing only once, as a red herring in *Night Monster.*) To keep the roof above his head, Bela continued to "branch out," as he had always done, and offered his services to any and all takers.

Monogram is the *second* studio that comes to mind when one thinks of Bela Lugosi (although, in terms of volume, Fox Studios—in any and all of its corporate identities—must pull rank on the poverty row company). Shot on a one-picture deal, Bela's *Mysterious Mr. Wong* (1935) was one of the last films produced by the old Monogram, before it merged with other independents to form Republic Pictures. The bloom was off the rose a year after the merger papers were signed, though, as W. Ray Johnston and Trem Carr pulled out of Republic and worked at reviving Monogram; by spring of 1937, the studio was back in business. It wasn't until the early forties, however, that the company thought to employ "that Dracula man" again. (Republic's only offerings to Lugosi would be a feature, *House of a Thousand Candles,* from which he would withdraw due to illness, and *S.O.S. Coastguard,* an above-average chapterplay with serial mega-star, Ralph Byrd. The former proved to be a critical and financial success, and might have led to additional, non-genre employment. The latter provided the actor with several of the very few bucks he made in films between horror cycles.)

Next in line, after Monogram, must come Bela's various features for RKO. The feisty studio had built a comfortable niche for itself during the thirties; just about anybody who was anybody—from Fred Astaire to Fay Wray—made an appearance or two for the smallest "major" in the industry. Genre-wise, the eighth wonder of the world—*King Kong*—had brought monster-sized revenue to the studio in 1933, and Charles Laughton's marvelous portrayal of Quasimodo had capped the decade off quite profitably.

Only weeks before the thirties passed into history, Bela was offering support to suave villain George Sanders, while being pursued by suave detective George Sanders, in *The Saint's Double Trouble.* Released in February, 1940, *Double Trouble* was a decent addition to the popular detective series and gave Bela virtually his last role in a non-horror film. Lugosi was billed fourth (primarily for name-value), a "cheat" felt keenly by his many fans, who expected to see their favorite heavy do his thing in his own inimitable style. If he expected the "straight" role to lead to other, similar ventures, Lugosi was as disappointed with the part as his fans were.

In July of that same year, though, Bela signed on to play Prince Saliano in RKO's *You'll Find Out,* a "mystery-musical" featuring the big band eccentricities of Kay Kyser and his College of Musical Knowledge. That was the good news; the bad news was that, once again, Bela would be appearing opposite Boris Karloff. It was one thing to have Karloff dog his steps at Universal (the two had just co-starred with Stanley Ridges there in *Black Friday*): for RKO to arrange the same thing, however... And any hopes that Peter Lorre, a fellow Hungarian, might prove an ally or provide a respite from the Englishman's maddening tea breaks were quickly dashed: Lorre and Karloff hit it off like old school chums. Their friendship was to endure to the end of the diminutive Lorre's life.

(And no matter how much grumbling goes on nowadays about the unimaginative plot or the wasted opportunity, *You'll Find Out* drew huge crowds and made a pile. Horror fans can't even take consolation in that it was the presence of their "boys" that tipped the revenue scales: Kyser's earlier film—*That's Right, You're Wrong*—was an even bigger grosser than the spook show.)

1944 may have been a busy year for Lugosi, but in terms of gross income, he was making the Hollywood equivalent of minimum wage. By the time Columbia's *Return of the Vampire* had been released in January, Bela was scrambling for cash. Some was forthcoming, as two more Monogram specials (*Voodoo Man* and *Return of the Ape Man)* were in postproduction (whatever that meant over at Monogram), awaiting release, and Paramount's *One Body Too Many* was ready to shoot.

For almost any other leading actor, a film currently in release, two in the can, and one ready to go—all within six months—would have spelled financial security. Almost any other leading actor, though, would have displayed more business savvy (in terms of compensation, billing, and publicity) than Bela. His constant financial plight had been a matter of record since his filing for bankruptcy in the early thirties, and his lack of tact or diplomacy in his dealings with studio personnel was also public knowledge.

In his hands, a bottle of rare and crucial zombifying element; in his eyes: hope, doubt, fear, and resolve—the moment of truth for Dr. Renault.

In order, then, to get the money necessary to facilitate his family's return (Lillian and his son had left him to his drugs and boilermakers earlier that year), Bela accepted a part which, for all its brevity, would represent some of his most subtle work in films. Still, he found himself in a miniscule role, on a one week contract, appearing (again) with Karloff. The fact that his part was created expressly for him *was* a bit of a lift, as was his billing (second), but his being "burked" by Karloff (and a subsequent scene requiring him to lie submerged in a vat of "brine") took the edge off that pretty quick. On the other hand, Val Lewton's subdued horror films were the talk of Hollywood at the moment, and *The Body Snatcher* promised to be (and ultimately was) one of the best.

Again, for "poor Bela," the result was both too little and too late. *The Body Snatcher* wouldn't hit theaters until spring of 1945, frustrating any close-in possibilities for work as a result of good notices. While Lillian and Bela, Jr. *would* return, their financial future was in no way assured through Bela's efforts alone. The "Dracula house" on Whipple Street would soon be lost. There was the occasional stock production of *Dracula,* but the aging Lugosi's film roles dwindled, not only as a result of the end of the second horror cycle, but also because most studios lost interest in an alcoholic, narrowly-typed character actor whose best years were clearly behind him.

Lugosi spent a bit more time at RKO than the above account indicates, however. Unlike Karloff, Bela's association with Val Lewton would not lead to an extremely lucrative three-picture contract. His sole experience with the gifted producer was shot between halves of an existing two-picture deal, while he was supporting RKO's answer to Abbott and Costello: Alan Carney and Wally Brown. Although grateful for the work, Bela cannot have been amused. As the second of his two assignments—*Genius at Work*—also turned out to be the last of the mediocre team's efforts, apparently audiences weren't amused, either.

The first of his two assignments (the comedians' sixth feature together) was *Zombies on Broadway.*

Zombies had been popping up on the screen since 1932, when their particular menace was exploited by the Halperin Brothers in *White Zombie* (starring a younger, but still poorly compensated Bela Lugosi.) The word "zombie" had been introduced to North American theater-goers earlier that same year by Kenneth Webb, the author of a not-long-for-this-world melodrama entitled (what else?), *Zombie.* (In an incredible display of '90s' aggressiveness, Webb tried to enjoin the Halperins from using the "Z" word. Juries must have been made of sterner stuff in those days; the suit disappeared without leaving an aftertaste.)

Unique in that they had some tenuous ties to reality (several impoverished Caribbean countries—notably Haiti—supposedly employed them to work the sugar cane or tobacco plantations), zombies were always to be the monsters-of-choice for poverty row film makers; they neither had supernatural powers nor underwent physical transformations (requiring expensive special effects), they were unmistakably human in appearance (saving extensive and costly make-up applications), and they were invariably mute (extras cost *so* much less than featured players).

Some four years after their initial success, the Halperins tried to rake in more money with *Revolt of the Zombies.* Despite having moved the locale from the (supposed) Caribbean to the (supposed) Orient, the brothers couldn't match the thrill (or the box office take) of the earlier film. Probably more germane to the film's failure than the setting was the casting; for all his histrionics, Dean Jagger's Zombie-master couldn't hold a (carved) candle to Bela Lugosi's Murder Legendre. Following a brief but extremely effective zombie cameo (by genre favorite Noble Johnson) in Paramount's 1940 *The Ghost Breakers,* and a decent shot by Monogram (*King of the Zombies,* which *was* to have starred Bela), RKO picked up the ball for the next bout with that particular branch of the undead. In a move that presaged James H. Nicholson's and Sam Arkoff's later practice (at AIP) of creating a title, and *then* writing a story, Val Lewton crafted an eerie, almost poetic tale to fit *I Walked With a Zombie* (1943).

The RKO spooker hit the box office before the next Monogram "B" (*Revenge of the Zombies,* the greatest asset of which was the farcical comic relief of Mantan Moreland), and a later Republic effort (*Valley of the Zombies,* whose greatest assets were Ian Keith's barnstorming performance and a short running time). Lewton's gentle chiller, however, was considered by many to be the definitive (forties) treatment of the subject. Whether or not one agrees with this assessment, the importance of *I Walked With a Zombie* with respect to *Zombies on Broadway* can't be overemphasized. The later film draws its mythos, its location, its Calypso narrator, and its native bogeyman (renamed Kolaga from Carrefour) from Lewton's minor masterpiece. The fact that the Lugosi picture is a spoof of and not a sequel to the earlier film, is a reflection of the changing tastes of the post-war audiences.

Zombies on Broadway opens some several thousand feet above the Great White Way, as handfuls of leaflets advertising the opening of a new nightclub, "The Zombie Hut," are tossed into the air by the pilot of a small plane. (If the amount of falling paper seen in the stock footage is any indication, the plane should have been a Flying Fortress.) Ace Miller (Sheldon Leonard), ex-gangster and owner of The Zombie Hut, is all smiles at the aerial bombardment and at an enormous "Grand Opening" sign being hauled around town by a truck equipped with a loud-speaker.

Moments later, however, Ace's joy turns to concern when he discovers that his publicists' *piece du resistance*—a live zombie—is nothing more than a brazen (and fraudulent) scheme. The two publicity flacks, Mike Strager (Alan Carney) and Jerry Miles (Wally Brown), almost win Ace over to their way of thinking (Since no one's ever seen a real zombie, who's to know that Sam, a second-rate boxer, isn't the genuine article?), when they let it slip that they've even made contact with famed radio debunker, Douglas Walker.

Walker appears as if on cue, and promises Ace a ton of publicity—all of it terrible—if the nightclub owner fails to deliver on his promise of a "live" zombie. Ace has his back to the nightclub wall; Gus (Frank Jenks), one of his lieutenants, suggests that the notoriety of the two PR men "committing suicide" would take the heat off the zombie business. Ace decides to give Jerry and Mike a chance to make good: "You either produce a real zombie for me on opening night, or I'll take Gus' idea."

The boys make for the International Museum, only to find it closed, as the place has shorter hours than most banks. Pulling some double talk on Wellington, the janitor (Stepin Fetchit clone Nicodemus, who would find a more extensive but no less demeaning role as Lightning (the janitor) on TV's *Amos and Andy* during the fifties), they end up in a basement conference with Professor Hopkins, the curator.

Hopkins (Ian Wolfe) knows nothing himself about zombies, but, amid some pedestrian schtick involving a wildly improbable stuffed ape and an even less credible mummy, advises them that he knows of someone who might be able to help them out. "A chap I went to school with many, many years ago made a great study of them." The chap, a Dr. Renault (Bela Lugosi), may still be alive on Saint Sebastian Island ("one of the smaller Virgin Islands"), but no one has heard from him for the past twenty-five years.

Jerry and Mike are all for bailing out at this point, and they return to their hotel room to pack. Ace had them followed to the museum, though, knows their plans, and is waiting for the boys with two tickets to Saint Sebastian Island and a revolver which will ultimately prove capable of firing eight shots without reloading. Gus and fellow henchman, Benny (Russell Hopton), see the boys off at dockside; Mike and Jerry trade quips despondently, as the nameless ship moves out to sea.

Following five seconds of nautical stock footage and a dismal exchange with the captain ("Is [Saint Sebastian] a nice place?" "To an undertaker, a cemetery is a nice place."), the two nervous zombie hunters arrive at the island. Scarcely have they disembarked, when they are approached by a calypso singer (Sir Lancelot, performing the same narrative function he did in *I Walked with a Zombie,* and even adapting one of the same tunes—*Fort Holland*—that had been prominently featured in the earlier source movie). To their faces, the singer strums his guitar and melodically bids them welcome. As the boys wander off, however, Sir Lancelot's ditty takes on a more menacing tone:

"But the visitors would not so happy be,
If they could see what's behind the tree.

Bela glowers and Wally Brown cowers for the still photographer. In the film, Wally's character—Jerry Miles—more than holds his own against the larger (and armed!) Dr. Renault; one of the more far-fetched situations in *Zombies on Broadway.*

If they could see the eyes which are watching them,
They would leave this island of evil men.
But if they wait till the full moon comes
To shine on the hands on the voodoo drums,
The chance to leave may come too late,
And blood on the ground will mark their fate.

By a marvelous coincidence, that very night will see the full moon. Joseph (Joseph Vitale), Dr. Renault's righthand man (and the fellow referred to—rather ungrammatically—as "what's behind the tree"), pays the calypso singer to keep an eye on the new arrivals.

Joseph rides back to the castle, where he delivers to the intently busy Dr. Renault a container of some nefarious substance from criminal sources back in the States; it's just what the doctor ordered. Renault's experiments haven't been going well lately; two servants are burying the remains of the latest out back. "What is wrong? What is wrong?" moans Renault. "How can the natives do with their silly voodoo what I cannot accomplish by scientific means?" Refusing to be consoled by Joseph, the doctor keeps on kvetching: "You've seen me create a zombie. If only I could keep them (sic) in that state! If only they didn't die, or return to normal in a short period."

But, with the new chemical at hand, brighter times are ahead. In a genuinely chilling scene, Renault activates a sliding door; behind it is another, lower, sliding door. As this second door opens, a casket noiselessly moves out from within the wall. The lid swings up on its own, and the gaunt zombie, Kolaga (Darby Jones), sits bolt upright, before arising and walking directly into the camera. Kolaga is both Renault's servant and a mute testament to his scientific failures: "Look at Kolaga here. Nearly twenty years ago, I took him away from the natives, and *still* no sign of disintegration whatsoever." The undead islander is dispatched to obtain new subjects ("...not natives"), and off he plods.

Jerry and Mike, meanwhile, have pulled up a table at the Cafe San Sebastian (only moments before Kolaga hies himself up to a convenient window: the dead *do* travel fast), and begin to quiz the help on zombies. The vivacious entertainer, Jean (Anne Jeffreys), overhears their conversation and strikes a bargain: passage on their ship when it returns in exchange for her leading the two men to a nearby voodoo ceremony. Having very little choice, the boys agree to the deal, and the singer leaves to don her civvies.

In less time than it takes to read this phrase, Jean has changed from her costume to something more practical, and heads out the dressing-room door. In a scene similar to the one played later (and more effectively) by Lou Costello and a lurking, hirsute Lon Chaney in *Abbott and Costello Meet Frankenstein,* the heroine reopens the door to the darkened room, but exits again before she can be nabbed by the grasping arms of the determined zombie.

Jean and the two publicists head off into the nearby jungle, following the beat of the drums, and being followed by Kolaga. After Mike literally stumbles into a couple of voodoo warning signs, he becomes separated from Jerry who, in turn, becomes separated from Jean. Although both men interact with the zombie, only Mike and Jean (who faints into its outstretched arms) see it. Jerry, of course, refuses to believe his partner.

As Kolaga carries the unconscious girl back to the castle, the boys become embroiled in the voodoo ceremony. They dive for cover within a handy, unattended hut. Mike hides behind a curtain where, with foresight (and not a little bit of scripted racism), he dabs some soot onto his face and hands. Jerry jumps into a basket, which is promptly carried out of the hut and into the midst of the ceremony by a couple of burly natives.

During the ceremony, the natives frenziedly jab the basket with spears until Jerry, along with a little monkey with which he shares the basket (and which will ultimately prove to be an enormously crucial plot contrivance), rears up and runs off into the jungle, basket and all. While the natives give chase, Mike, back at the bonfire, is frightened by the appearance of another zombie (this time, a white man in blackface, sans Kolaga-like eye make-up), and takes off in the same general direction.

The boys run into each other and end up at Dr. Renault's castle, where they are discovered by Joseph. Unbeknownst to them, their timely arrival has prevented Dr. Renault from trying his new formula on Jean, who is gagged and strapped to an operating table in the castle basement. Although Joseph tells them that the doctor has been studying banana blight (and not zombies), the boys can't contain their relief at Renault's still being alive. (Lugosi gets the closest thing to a real chuckle in the film, moments later; he tells Mike and Jerry that he's devoted his studies to coconut blight. When they tell him that Joseph mentioned banana blight, Bela shrugs and quips, "Ahhh, Joseph's colorblind." Trust me; it plays better than it reads.)

Before turning in for the evening, the boys are kept busy digging what looks suspiciously like their own graves. Hitting a catch with his shovel, Mike falls through the bottom of the hole and into the basement of the castle. As he watches in horror, Kolaga's casket slides forth, and the zombie sits erect, looking the frightened publicist right in the eye. Mike runs up some stairs and through a door, only to tumble back into the grave he's just dug. Once again, he can't convince Jerry of what he's seen.

Dr. Renault, concerned lest word get back to the USA that he's still alive and working, decides to use the two new men as his latest guinea pigs, leaving the girl for last. As the boys are preparing for bed, Kolaga is sent off to their room via a secret passageway, and is seen (yet again) by Mike, but not by Jerry. While Jerry goes on and on about zombies from within the recesses of the closet, Kolaga sweeps the chubby Mike into his arms and carries him off. (No mean feat for the emaciated Darby Jones!)

Jerry hits the sack (rather casually, considering he's noticed that his new pal, the monkey, has replaced as bunkmate his old pal, the idiot). Mike, meanwhile, has been injected by Renault, and has become zombified. The doctor is pleased—so far —with the results of his new formula: "Good...good; no pulse whatsoever. It works faster than any I have used before. I hope it lasts." Mike, bearing the same protruding eyes and stiff carriage as Kolaga, heads back to his room, as the now-believing Jerry is trundled off into the basement.

Downstairs, Joseph is making some kind of adjustment to Kolaga's sliding casket when Jean, having freed herself from her bonds, brains him with a pipewrench. (A pipewrench to fix a casket?) Renault is not faring much better, as the monkey has snatched a loaded hypodermic and is evading the doctor's efforts to capture him via that old comedy chestnut, the confusing chest of drawers. (A chest of drawers in a laboratory?) Jean unties Jerry, who pauses to get into a fistfight with Renault. A monkey-tossed skull inadvertently downs the hero, but Jean upends the operating table on the mad scientist, giving her (and the monkey and Jerry) another chance at getting out of there.

The scuffling isn't over yet. Renault, pistol in hand, follows everyone upstairs and takes charge once more as Jean, in another old comedy chestnut, whacks Jerry over the head with a bottle. While the mad doctor pauses to wax villainously, however, Jean manages to revive Jerry with some seltzer, and the good guy and bad guy go at it again. Somehow, Jerry manages to get the gun away from Renault, who then pulls his trump card; he summons the murderous zombie telepathically.

Spade in hand (*everyone* spends his spare time digging in this film), Kolaga appears, in answer to the mental command. In what Strother Martin would later refer to as a "failure to communicate," the mindless zombie interprets Renault's cries ("Kill, Kolaga, kill!") rather narrowly, and dispatches the *scientist* with a blow of the shovel. As Kolaga carries off the late Dr. Renault, Jerry, Jean, and the monkey take the opportunity to round up Mike and to head for the pier.

Between the ship and the good guys, however, is that group of spear-toting natives, still teed off and spoiling for a fight. Zombified Mike shuffles into view, giving the natives a fright, and also giving his pal and the gal (and the monkey) an idea; arms akimbo, they all shuffle past the natives to the safety of the boat. On board, Jerry wires Ace to expect a zombie and a sensational girl singer in time for the opening.

Met at the dock by Benny and Gus, the trio (and the you-know-what) are driven to the nightclub. In the car, Mike is proven to be insensitive to pain, the hallmark of a true zombie. At the club, however, Dr. Renault's serum wears off, and Mike returns to what passes for normal.

Left zombie-less, and facing ruin from Walker, who's sitting out front with two zombie "experts," one of whom is Professor Hopkins(!?), Ace runs out of patience and starts shooting. While a half-dozen or so shots ring out, Jean (who has appropriated the zombie-serum hypo from the monkey) turns out the lights and commences injecting.

Inside the club proper, the band leader reacts to the gunshots ("That's our cue!"), and strikes up the entrance music, as four chunky extras carry in a sedan chair. When the curtains part, a zombified Ace Miller rises stiffly to the gasps of the audience and to the approval of Walker's experts. Backstage, Jerry starts to put the moves on Jean, but sits on that ubiquitous hypo. As the music swells, the publicist turns, eye make-up and all, to face the camera for the final fade out.

Zombies on Broadway is a shameless, low-budget "B", but it's also an undemanding good time. The sets may be slapdash, the plot recycled, and the humor sparse (and grasping), but director Gordon Douglas keeps things moving at a fast enough pace to forestall any complaints.

Douglas had been a comedy writer before he had taken up directing, and had worked with classic comedians Laurel and Hardy in their last feature at Hal Roach's "Lot of Fun," *Saps at Sea* (1940). His life's work ran the gamut from noirs to oaters, with stops for just about everything else in between. An effective (if undistinguished) career journeyman, he retained an affinity for comedy—that, if anything, being his specialty—but professed a personal liking for mystery/horror/science fiction. Be that as it may, Doulgas' career was singularly lacking in titles of interest to genre fans (unless *In Like Flint* and the like are included). His most notable effort was 1954's *Them!,* grandfather and prototype of all giant bug films.

Zombies on Broadway, unlike *Them!,* was designed for the bottom half of a double bill, and was both penned and lensed with the understanding that humor would have a major role. Responsible for inserting some lighter elements in the later giant ant epic, Douglas gets the credit for keeping the humor more focused here than is usually the case with a comedy-spooker. Working in tandem with cinematographer Jack Mackenzie, Douglas is attentive to the pacing, the lighting and, most importantly, the integrity of the horror sequences.

(Allowing the "monsters" to work within their special realm of unreality, yet, at the same time, in the *real* world, is the mark of an effective horror pastiche (cf. Bob Hope's *The Ghost Breakers*). Allowing them to be made ridiculous at the hands of imbecilic comic leads is not (cf. *You'll Find Out)*. Supernatural/super-human/super-scientific villains should receive their come-uppance due to a logical consequence of the legend or dramatic basis to which they owe their existence; they should not fall victim to stupidity, inadvertence, or comedies of errors. Menace should be overcome by knowledge, not by ignorance.)

Most of the verbal humor just doesn't come off, a fault which must be shared both by scripters Lawrence Kimble and Robert Kent, and by the two nominal stars, Brown and Carney. In all fairness to the writers, the comedians clearly didn't have the delivery of an Abbott and Costello; to be fair to the comics, even Abbott and Costello would have had a heck of a time with the mediocre gags they were handed. (A longer gander at RKO's #1 comedy team follows below.)

As Renault, Bela displays his old panache; Darby Jones may be more grotesque, and Joseph Vitale more physically threatening, but there's no doubt here as to who's the boss. Lugosi shows little sign of the slowing down that would mark his final years; (in *The Body Snatcher,* shot almost immediately after the zombie spoof, Bela appears sluggish and uncertain. Strangely enough, he seems more in control and self-assured in the subsequent *Genius at Work.* Perhaps the dynamic of the role, or the trauma of appearing opposite Karloff again contributed more to his unease than did his addiction to morphine.) In *Zombies on Broadway,* however, Bela is a *vigorous* villain, giving (the surprisingly apt) Jerry as good as he gets in their various tussles.

Joseph Vitale made a career out of playing henchmen in comedies, mysteries, and comedy-mysteries throughout the forties and fifties. Typically second in command to the lead villain, his character's strong point was seldom intelligence (although he was usually in better mental shape than the hero), but rather the capacity for violence. Hopping from studio to studio, Vitale offered his unique brand of supporting mayhem to such audience favorites as Bing Crosby (in *A Connecticut Yankee in King Arthur's Court*), Bob Hope (in *The Paleface*), Bing Crosby and Bob Hope (in *The Road to Rio*), and Martin and Lewis (in *My Friend Irma Goes West*).

Ian Wolfe had been around for years when *Zombies on Broadway* was shot, and he was still active almost forty years later, appearing in Warren Beatty's costly epic, *Reds.* Born in 1896, he enhanced over 200 films (by his own count), including Universal's 1935 teaming of Karloff and Lugosi, *The Raven.*

Apart from scads of westerns, "women's pictures," and nondescript whodunits, Wolfe shared the screen with just about every genre notable there was. The year before *Zombies* was released, Wolfe had been seen in the company of Basil Rathbone, Nigel Bruce, and Rondo Hatton (in the excellent Sherlock Holmes tale, *The Pearl of Death*), as well as with Jon Hall and John Carradine in *The Invisible Man's Revenge.* The year after *Zombies,* he would play, again opposite Karloff, in Val Lewton's atmospheric *Bedlam.* He worked for pompous genius, Alfred Hitchcock (in 1942's *Saboteur*), was in one of Claude Rains' few real turkeys (Irwin Allen's *The Lost World,*

1960), and brought up the rear (in the company of no one in particular) in Universal's musical remake/mistake, *Murder in the Blue Room* (1944). Having "done it all," Ian Wolfe took his last bow in 1993.

Sheldon Leonard is probably as familiar as a TV sitcom producer (ranging from the fondly remembered *Danny Thomas Show*(s) to the justifiably obscure *Big Eddie*), as for his perennial Damon Runyonish screen persona. He portrayed a slightly offbeat, ponderously precise thug in dozens of serious crime dramas and noirs (like 1948's *The Gangster*), and in about as many not-so-serious potboilers, almost simultaneously. That characterization reached its apex in *Guys and Dolls,* and it wasn't long after that Leonard abandoned the silver screen for television. In addition to his behind-the-scenes executive work, he never hesitated to spoof his stock-in-trade; his racetrack tout, for example, was a semi-regular on Jack Benny's long-running TV show.

In all honesty, it was *Genius at Work* and not *The Saint's Double Trouble* that was Bela Lugosi's last "straight" role. Despite the presence of perennial horror favorite Lionel Atwill and assorted colorful trappings (torture chamber, wax figures, secret panels, eccentric criminal mastermind), *Genius at Work* remains a rather mundane mystery. Exploiting audience interest in show business "backstage" life (a formula popular since before the coming of sound), the film is a combined update of RKO's earlier *Super Sleuth* (1937), and a liberal reworking of Abbott and Costello's superior *Who Done It?*

The film's credits show, once again, how the mighty had fallen. Whereas Lugosi had shared the title card with Brown and Carney (and, of course, the title) in *Zombies on Broadway,* he is relegated to the second slate here, and is billed third, after Atwill and heroine Anne Jeffreys. While the pecking order in an obvious "B" may have taken a back seat to cash on the barrelhead for Bela at this point, the fact that his two-film contract permitted such disparate billing terms indicates either the woeful business sense mentioned above, or, more likely, his total lack of clout.

The working title was *The Masterminds,* but whether the original reference was to the heroes or the heavies is moot. While Bela's character is an active participant in the mayhem (even giving some good advice that's heeded more than once), he's clearly depicted as Marsh's servant and factotum. Nevertheless, apart from a spate of uncomfortable "Sirs" (and an awkward dressing down from Atwill), it's apparent that in spirit, if not in name, the two veteran bogeyman are true partners in crime.

The opening scene shows the pair working like a well-oiled machine under C.K. Bakaleinikoff's moody title music: one man creating a diversion, the other committing an assault. Knocked unconscious and carried off is John Tippett Saunders, a local tycoon with enough money to warrant three names. A succession of newspaper banners identify master criminal "The Cobra" as holding his victim for ransom.

Over at the offices of Station SBS, Mike Strager (Alan Carney) and Jerry Miles (Wally Brown) are acting out the latest installment of their continuing radio show, "Crime of the Week." Sitting in on the rehearsal is Ellen Brent (Anne Jeffreys), whose job description at the station seems to shift from headwriter to program manager to public relations expert to police liaison, all the while pulling double duty as love interest and amateur detective. Also present is Latimer Marsh (Lionel Atwill), criminologist, author, and the brains behind the program. The nominal stars do what they do best—bicker and bluster—while reading through the copy for that night's broadcast: a dramatic representation of Saunders' kidnapping by the Cobra.

A cut and a moment later, as the studio organist noodles ominously, the actual broadcast begins. At Marsh Manor, the famed crime expert, in the company of his manservant, Stone (Lugosi), and a bound and gagged Saunders, tunes in the transmission. Stone is aghast at how close the reenacted account of the kidnapping is to the real thing. Marsh denies providing much information; the girl, Brent, he maintains, is clever at adding up details. Besides, he brags, his ransom notes are "merely red herrings to mislead the very stupid police. I'm merely holding Mr.

While Lattimer Marsh and John Tippett Saunders exchange steely glances, Stone appears to be caught with his glare down. ***Genius at Work.***

Saunders until I've determined upon some interesting way to affect his demise."

Back at the studio, two plainclothes cops walk in on the broadcast, catching Mike's and Jerry's prediction that "...within twenty-four hours, the body of John Saunders will be found, murdered!" After the audience leaves, Lieutenants Campbell (Marc Cramer) and Gilly (Ralph Dunn) wander up to the microphone, looking to learn where the radio stars get their information (Brent: "Maybe I'm just psychic."), and to demand an apology for on-the-air remarks made about the police. Ellen refuses to divulge Marsh as her source, and she and Campbell (on their way to being an item) leave the studio together.

"Saunders Found Murdered!

Miles and Strager, Radio Detectives, Predicted Saunders' Death!"

In the safety of his home, Marsh scans these headlines, as his aide-de-camp continues to grouse about the wisdom of the whole radio set-up. The Cobra agrees with Stone, and together they formulate how to throw a scare into the boys, a scare "that will make them drop this Cobra case from now on." Calling the boys, Marsh makes an appointment to meet them and Miss Brent at "Club Oriental."

"Club Oriental" must have been renamed in the interim, for Jerry and Mike show up at the "Oriental Cafe," where they join Marsh at his table. With Stone sitting unnoticed across the room, Marsh suggests that they all lay off the Cobra, lest they fall victims to his anger. Nervous already, Mike reacts hysterically upon finding that (in what is arguably the most budget-conscious display of menace in "B" movies) the Cobra has stamped his name and image on the menus. Mike is frightened further when a knife, thrown expertly by Stone, sails past his nose and into an ornamental screen. Marsh unfolds a note, impaled on the blade: "Marsh, Miles & Strager—this is your last Warning! Get off the Cobra's trail or take the Consequence. The Cobra."

The note, bearing letters cut from newspapers and another impression from the Cobra's personal rubber stamp, is all that it takes; the three, along with most of the other customers, pile out the door.

Ellen, however, refuses to withdraw from the case. Although the police are annoyed with the radio team, and the mayor is threatening to bar them from the air, the courageous young lady vows that "we'll catch the Cobra ourselves." Before doing that, though, she and the boys will throw a party for the cops, and formally apologize to them.

At the station house, the two loonies are being briefed on a woman's footprint, found near Saunders' body. A plaster cast has been made from the impression, but neither Campbell nor Gilly lets Ellen in on the clue when she shows up to invite them to the gastronomic act of penance. (For all their mutual attraction, apparently Campbell hasn't made up his mind about the beautiful writer.)

Ellen and the boys head out to Marsh Manor, eager to go over the criminologist's file on the Cobra. While they are enroute, Marsh is giving Stone hell for not having cleaned the mud from the shoes of "Lady Guinevere," one of a pair of osculating wax figures from his collection. Stone doesn't have a chance to make good at the moment, though; the three radio detectives are already at the front door.

Marsh shows off his "hobby room," which contains a pillory, stocks, at least two guillotines, an iron maiden, and enough maces and axes to arm the cast of *Richard III.* The boys pick up a copy of the author's latest work, *Torture and Murder Can Be Fun*, and are left to amuse themselves while Ellen goes through the Cobra files. Within moments (in what turns out to be a hamfisted attempt at foreshadowing), Mike and Jerry have to be rescued from a medieval bone-crusher.

The three sleuths leave, but Ellen suspects their benefactor of hiding something. Waiting until dark, she and the boys return secretly to Marsh Manor. Doing their best to stay out of the way are Marsh and Stone, who knew darn well earlier what was going to happen. "Curiosity killed the cat, Stone, and it will very likely kill Miss Brent."

With the usual, expected silliness (Mike bumping into and breaking a vase, a bout of loud "sssshhhhhing," etc.), the three sneak back into the manorhouse. Again, *pro forma,* Jean and Jerry leave the low comic to stand watch, while they make for the file cabinet. Stone, from within an adjacent secret passage, keeps his eye on Mike, who wanders about aimlessly, until he comes upon the waxen Lady Guinevere. In a necessary but completely unbelievable plot wrinkle, the cosmically dense Mike is able to determine that there's something peculiar about mud on the shoes of a wax figure. Running to tell Jerry, he bumps into Stone (who has removed the shoes through a secret panel), and then into Marsh.

The two heavies and the featherweight then intrude on Jean and Jerry, who are about to use an antique blunderbuss to blow open the locked file drawer. Marsh smugly uses his key on the file drawer, revealing a cache of liquor bottles. Ellen is embarrassed and oxymoronized: "Liquor is Stone's strongest weakness." After a bit of venerable slapstick involving Mike and the front-loader, the forces of righteousness are hustled out the door.

Ellen still thinks that Marsh might be the Cobra; "Why else would he have all that information about Saunders?" (Her obnoxious persistence is an annoying chink in the logical chain here. At the outset of the film, Marsh's fame as criminologist and author are clearly established, as is the pivotal role he plays in providing background information and analysis for Ellen and the two boys. Why wouldn't he have files on *any and all* timely criminal activities, if this is the source of his bread and butter? Ellen's nagging doubts serve only to turn a necessary dramatic corner at this particular point in the unspooling.)

Anyhow, the little "I'm sorry" party for the cops has transmogrified into a "banquet" honoring the entire police force, and the sinister pair are in attendance, albeit hidden in a fan room off the rear stairwell. A disconnected piece of ductwork provides them with a bird's-eye view of the studio, and a handy phone (inside the fan room!) allows them to have Ellen paged to answer *another* handy phone, providentially only yards from the stairwell door.

Stone chloroforms the gal as Marsh fires a poisoned dart (from a blowgun he carries in his walking stick) at Mike. Klutzy Mike bends over to retrieve a page he's dropped, and the poor schlemiel of a sound man is killed by mistake. As Marsh and Stone scram down the freight elevator, broadcast and apology are abruptly terminated, and the cops discover a groggy and disoriented Ellen by the stairwell phone, clutching the exotic murder weapon. The fact that Ellen is undeniably female ties in with the woman's footprints found by Saunders' corpse, so the lovely writer is hauled down to the stationhouse.

Campbell, however, is a better cop than he's been given credit for, and eliminates his honey in two shakes: her feet are the wrong size for the footprints, and her propensity for getting lipstick all over cops and cigarette butts (but not blowguns) seems to indicate that it wasn't her mouth that provided the lethal breath. The last barrier down between them, Ellen tells her lieutenant that she feels Marsh is the Cobra. A moment later, she receives a note from the boys—they're heading out to Marsh Manor with some suspicions of their own. Ellen and the cops ride to the rescue.

The boys initially ask Marsh to help them prove Ellen's innocence, but a casual mention of "footprints" sets Mike off. (The plot now demands an awesome suspension of disbelief on the part of the audience, who are asked to swallow a *second* (and even less credible) demonstration of applied thought for the intellectually-challenged Mike). "Those footprints were made by Mr. Marsh to fool the police. I saw the muddy shoes in his workshop. Muddy shoes. *He* [Stone] hid them, and *he* [Marsh] is the Cobra!"

Stone pulls a gun, giving the villains the upper hand; the boys pull the rug out from under Stone, giving them the gun, and the advantage. Jerry again leaves his partner on watch (doesn't this guy *ever* learn?), while he goes off in search of rope with which to tie them up. Marsh convinces the once again thick-as-a-plank Mike that Jerry means to take all the credit for the capture of the Cobra; why doesn't Mike fire some shots through Marsh's smoking jacket, to give an heroic aura to the affair? Naturally, Mike empties the gun into the jacket, and both he and (the returned and understandably miffed) Jerry end up back in the medieval bone-crusher. Once again, Marsh and Stone make their getaway.

Ellen and the men in blue arrive in time to release the boys before the bone-crusher can do the villains (and the audience) a favor. Campbell maintains that the only evidence against Marsh is circumstantial; they need to catch him in the act. Ellen has an idea: "Marsh thinks they're dead. When he finds out they're not..." Without much enthusiasm, the boys complete the sentence: "...he'll come back to kill us again."

"Cobra Eludes Police! Radio Actors Key to Cobra's Identity! Radio Sleuths to Expose Cobra! Murderer Will Be Named On Radio Tonight!"

As Stone reads these headlines aloud, his boss is shaving off his natty little moustache in preparation for his latest plot. At the station, just prior to the broadcast, Stone (sporting spectacles and an impressive Van Dyke) and Marsh (in drag as a wheelchaired dowager), are being turned away; there are no seats left. Mike and Jerry, unaware (as always) of what they're doing, slip the couple some passes, and send them upstairs in the freight elevator. The heavies make for the fanroom (which is still unguarded), remove the ductwork (which had been replaced; didn't anyone check the trajectory of that first dart?), and prepare to fire poisoned darts with *another*

In last-ditch attempt at killing Miles and Strager, the Cobra prepares to don high drag; holding the latest in cross-dresses is partner-in-crime, Stone.

blowgun they've brought with them.

The lights are lowered, the organ grumbles, and the broadcast begins. Standing in front of a curtain are the shadowy figures of Mike and Jerry. As the radio detectives wend their verbose way toward the exposure of the Cobra, the villain fires a dart into one of the figures; nothing happens. Again and again, one dart after another is fired, with the same result: nothing. Desperate and frustrated, The Cobra whips out his trusty revolver. Over Stone's protests that they'll be heard and their position located, Marsh pumps a couple of shots into the boys. As the cops swarm all over the studio, the announcer reveals that Miles and Strager are unhurt; they've been *behind* the curtain, while the darts and bullets have struck two wax statues out front.

Although Marsh and Stone split up, during exchanges of gunfire with the cops both end up on a window ledge outside the studio. Naturally, Mike and Jerry, in seeking to get the hell out of the line of fire, have also crept out onto the ledge, and are menaced not only by the killers, but by police bullets as well. Both Marsh and Stone are gunned down by the cops, and fall off the ledge (and out of frame) to their demises. Jerry ends up on the roof whence, by mistake, he manages to launch his partner into space with a two-by-four. All ends happily, however, as the camera reveals a transparent, but otherwise still breathing Mike, hanging from a flagpole.

Genius at Work is seldom seen nowadays, but whether that's due to the hesitancy of most TV stations to access either older "B" or black and white films, or to the fact that the movie *never* got much exposure, is hard to say. As neither it, nor the earlier *Zombies on Broadway* are in the public domain (as are so many of Bela's forties features), marginally substantial rental expenses might also mitigate against its being shown. Perhaps, however, it all boils down to the fact that *Genius at Work* isn't a very good movie.

It's certainly not helped by an indecisiveness concerning the character of Marsh. With the murder of Saunders, the Cobra is depicted as a coldblooded killer, but the script neglects to provide him with motive. While the newspapers scream ransom, and indicate that this is but the latest in a series of Cobra kidnapings, Marsh kills the industrialist for a lark. On this basis, Atwill's Cobra is far more loathesome than any of his other fiends: Ivan Igor, Professor Moriarty, Otto von Neimann—the crimes by *these* monsters were motivated by revenge, reward, or research. The Cobra is calculating, merciless, unfathomable.

On the other hand, having Marsh author a book with so preposterous a title as *Murder and Torture Can Be Fun* tips the scales towards spoof. Is this criminal so schizophrenic that he commits haphazard mayhem one moment and pontificates on the same in print the next? Having the character both ways is more an indication that screenwriters Robert E. Kent and Monte Brice were uncomfortable with the mystery/comedy meld, than that they took a stab at giving the totally black-hearted villain a multi-dimensional personality.

Wonderful old Lionel Atwill played his swan song as Latimer Marsh, and he deserved a better-etched role for his last feature. Any credibility the character has is due to Atwill's efforts, and it's sad to see him (and Bela) expending so much energy in such uninspired surroundings. For all its lack of depth though, *Genius at Work* must have possessed some sort of cosmetic therapeutic value, at least where the two horror stars were concerned. As was stated above, the addicted Lugosi looks positively hale and hearty when compared the image captured by Robert de Grasse's camera in *The Body Snatcher.* (de Grasse also lensed *Genius at Work.*) Atwill, too, although dying of bronchial cancer, seems more composed and less tired than he appeared to be in his previous work, PRC's *Fog Island.*

On another note, the difference his pencil-line moustache makes in terms of his appearance is remarkable; the clean-shaven visage glaring daggers at the absent radio sleuths might be that of the Atwill of the early thirties. Appearances were deceiving, though. Atwill wouldn't live to complete his next assignment—Universal's serial, *Lost City of the Jungle.* He died on April 22, 1946, some four months before *Genius at Work* finally was released.

Anne Jeffreys was one of the brightest contract starlets at RKO, which was renowned for making most of its films with personnel borrowed from other studios. Singing and dancing reasonably well, she brought a wholesome beauty to wartime movie audiences, and soon worked her way up from bit parts in early-forties "Bs" to leads in late-forties "Bs." The most regular of the Carney/Brown heroines (besides *Genius at Work* and *Zombies on Broadway,* she shared the pain with them in 1944's *Step Lively,* wherein she gave Frank Sinatra his first screen kiss), Jeffreys was featured as Tess Trueheart opposite Morgan Conway in both *Dick Tracy* (1946) and *Dick*

Tracy Vs. Cueball (1947).

To this day, Anne Jeffreys remains most firmly associated with the role of Marian Kirby ("The ghostess with the mostest")—her husband, Robert Sterling, played her husband, George Kirby—in Hal Roach's hit TV series, *Topper.*

The team of Wally Brown and Alan Carney was wholly manufactured by RKO Studios, which was looking for a piece of the Abbott and Costello action. The ex-vaudevillians already held separate contracts with the studio, and had played bits in any number of features (straight-man Wally Brown had been in Val Lewton's *The Seventh Victim*), prior to making *Adventures of a Rookie* in 1943. Finding their service comedy a winner, the team encored with *Rookies in Burma.* The two mystery-comedies under discussion capped off the eight features they made together.

Wally Brown and Alan Carney really weren't all that bad; their main fault lay in the fact that they weren't Abbott and Costello. Capable comics, both, they were never given the chance to follow their own impulses; they were hired to ape the most popular comic formula of the decade, and not to develop a chemistry of their own.

The assembly line was the governing force of the early to mid-forties. While our boys were overseas, Rosie the Riveter and her sisters stepped in and handled mass production of everything from bullets to bombers. Their increased output was made possible by standardized sizing: there was one mold, one model, one prototype, and all the machinery of war and peace was copied from that. In the interests of conservation (and profit), and to attract audiences who had already demonstrated what they liked, wartime movie studios seized onto standardized themes; find that one desirable prototype, and copy the hell out of it.

Whereas the thirties had produced a broad array of comic teams, each had had its own personality, its own area of concentration. Laurel and Hardy, for example, were two child-like fellows, trying desperately (but usually unsuccessfully) to keep abreast of the world around them. The Marx Brothers spent their career trying to destroy that same world, puncturing holes in every sacred cow from higher education to grand opera. Wheeler and Woolsey, Olsen and Johnson, The Ritz Brothers: these and others resisted the impulse to clone another team's style, to imitate another team's schtick.

Wally Brown and Alan Carney had appeared in vaudeville, individually; they brought no background in team comedy to their features. While RKO was billing them as a comic duo, the studio insisted that each man continue to appear separately in various assigned productions. This Jekyll/Hyde behavior on the part of the studio heads did little more than undermine any effort to create audience awareness of the *team* Wally Brown and Alan Carney. So far as ticket-buyers knew, Brown and Carney were nothing but two contract players, occasionally appearing together.

(The team offered *one* unique element, though: Brown and Carney portrayed the same characters throughout their career as a team. While not a major deal, using the same character names gave some stability, some identity to the team throughout its existence. Laurel and Hardy had always used the same names—their own—after 1928, and this allowed audiences to feel familiar and comfortable with the comedians. Abbott and Costello's characters' names varied from picture to picture, but as they essentially remained Abbott and Costello regardless, picturegoers knew what to expect. Only Brown and Carney maintained stable "other" identities—Jerry Miles and Mike Strager—for the body of their more popular features.)

In *Zombies on Broadway,* Brown and Carney don't benefit much from strong verbal humor, but they interact well physically with the familiar horror situation. Despite their buffoonishness, they are actively involved in both the overthrow of the villain, and the dramatic irony of the ending. In *Genius at Work,* however, Carney's profound stupidity is more annoying rather than amusing, and the boys are denied even a modicum of heroism, as both Atwill and Lugosi are dispatched without any assistance from them whatsoever. To be fair, by the time they were being menaced by Bela Lugosi, the team had seen the spray-painting on the wall.

To judge them on the originality of their efforts, or the quality of their jokes, or the freshness of their scripts would be cruel. For a large percentage of the public, for whom a joke was a joke, no matter from whom or how old, Brown and Carney delivered the goods. The body of their work together may not merit a "retrospective," but among their eight features there are more than a few isolated good moments, where the comedians were able to rise above their material.

At the end of the forties, Wally Brown and Alan Carney moved from RKO to freelance both in films and on TV. No longer required to follow in someone else's footsteps, they both settled in to offer their own brands of support for the rest of their careers. A familiar face to Baby Boomers, thanks to countless parts on (now) vintage TV shows, Wally Brown died in 1961. Alan Carney added his touch of madness to a number of Disney films (including hits *The Absent-Minded Professor,* and *Son of Flubber*), and enjoyed an excellent cameo (along with every other still-breathing classic comic in the USA) in Stanley Kramer's near-mythic *It's a Mad, Mad, Mad, Mad World* (1963). Mike Strager—partner to Jerry Miles in eight undistinguished but amusing little "Bs"—passed away in 1973.

Playing a bit in the film was Robert Clarke, who had just rubbed elbows with Bela, Boris, and Henry Daniell in *The Body Snatcher.* (He would also be featured in the later Lewton/Karloff *Bedlam.*) Fans of fifties' science fiction films know Clarke chiefly from *The Man from Planet X, Captive Women, The Hideous Sun Demon,* and *The Astounding She-Monster,* among others. Most recently, Clarke has announced plans for a '90's sequel to *The Hideous Sun Demon.*

For Bela Lugosi, neither *Zombies on Broadway* nor *Genius at Work* delivered more than the contractual fees. Of the two, however, *Zombies* had to be a more comfortable fit. For one thing, it afforded Bela a turn on familiar turf; he had just played a Zombie-master for Monogram (in *Voodoo Man,* 1944), and that he knew his beakers from his retorts could be chalked up to his recent *Return of the Ape Man.*

More apropos than theme, however, was status. *Zombies* offered Bela the part of the Big Cheese; he was as firmly in control on Sol Lesser's jungle set as he was in the cardboard dungeons at Monogram. *Zombies on Broadway* was a continuation of the low-budget grandeur to which he had become accustomed during the course of the forties; whether snatching poisoned brides, gesturing hypnotically at Huntz Hall, reviving fruit-of-the-loom-sporting Neanderthals, or strangling occidentalized Nipponese saboteurs, Bela was the apotheosis of screen villainy. At Monogram (and in RKO's *Zombies on Broadway*), Bela Lugosi was no man's menial.

Genius at Work, on the other hand, was a throw-back to all those demeaning butler roles, in which Lugosi's participation would be limited to serving coffee, taking coats, or announcing late arrivals. Even though here he was the butler who *did* do it, there was a valuable opportunity lost in not having Bela's Stone the manipulative equal of the Cobra.

Genius hasn't the tightness of the earlier Brown & Carney film; while both films get things going from frame one, *Genius*'s script sags at times, especially in terms of reaction shots. During the rather protracted scene wherein Marsh unlocks the mysterious file cabinet, Bela is given little to do (and *nothing* to say), even when the weighty blunderbuss is dropped on his foot. The Monogram Lugosi would have at least postured menacingly, or glowered magnificently; the latter-RKO Lugosi gasps and bears it.

After *Genius at Work,* UI's *Abbott and Costello Meet Frankenstein* was the only major-league deal remaining for Lugosi. He returned to the role which had both brought him fame and denied him employment, and he made it his own again. In the company of other familiar grotesques, Bela's Dracula moved comfortably and well. The film was a success; his performance was acknowledged. Would his fortunes *finally* take a turn for the better?

As the audiences threw money at their feet, and as the critics thumped them on the back, the UI bigwigs beheld a new formula, ripe for exploitation: *Abbott and Costello Meet the Contractual Monsters.* Promised (relatively) high budgets and (reasonably) good production values, Universal's Kings of Comedy were back. The Invisible Man would meet them. The Mummy would meet them. Even Boris Karloff would meet them. Twice.

But Dracula had already had his crack at the big money; Bela Lugosi would meet a Brooklyn Gorilla.

ABBOTT AND COSTELLO MEET FRANKENSTEIN (1948)

by David J. Hogan

CREDITS: Released August 1948; filmed February and March 1948; Producer: Robert Arthur; Director: Charles T. Barton; Screenplay: Robert Lees & Frederic I. Rinaldo, and John Grant; Cinematography: Charles Van Enger; Special Cinematography: David S. Horsley and Jerome H. Ash; Music: Frank Skinner; Makeup supervisor: Bud Westmore; Black and white; Universal Pictures; Running time: 83 minutes

CAST: Bud Abbott...Chick Young, Lou Costello...Wilbur Gray, Lon Chaney... Larry Talbot, Bela Lugosi...Count Dracula, Lenore Aubert...Dr. Sandra Mornay, Jane Randolph...Joan Raymond, Glenn Strange...Frankenstein's Monster, Frank Ferguson...McDougal, Charles Bradstreet...Dr. Stevens, Vincent Price...Voice of the Invisible Man

When Bela Lugosi co-starred as Dracula in *Abbott and Costello Meet Frankenstein* in 1948, he was 66 years old and looked every day of it. His 15-year marriage to the former Lillian Arch was foundering and his career had been dashed upon the rocks many years before. To Hollywood, a town known around the world for splashy, big-budget motion pictures, Lugosi was little more than a shadow with a name by the time the Abbott and Costello film started shooting in February 1948. He had become a denizen of Hollywood's grimy netherworld of six-day shooting schedules, five-figure budgets, and cramped sound stages hidden on narrow side streets off Hollywood and Santa Monica boulevards.

Abbott and Costello Meet Frankenstein was in no sense a prestige picture (the comedy team had slipped out of the boxoffice Top Ten a few years before, and their films had never enjoyed much critical box-office acceptance), but it was the product of respected professionals working at a reasonably important studio. And for Bela, it was an enormous step up from the six films he made prior to it: *Return of the Ape Man, One Body Too Many, The Body Snatcher, Zombies on Broadway, Genius at Work,* and *Scared to Death.*

Of this group, only *The Body Snatcher* (produced at RKO by Val Lewton and directed by Robert Wise) was a picture of consequence, but Lugosi's role was small and clearly subordinate to that of his longtime rival, Boris Karloff. Most of the five other films are foolish and completely trivial, and one, Christy Cabanne's *Scared to Death,* is so wretched as to be unwatchable, despite being the only Lugosi vehicle shot in color.

A&C Meet Frankenstein returned Bela to Universal, the "minor major" where he had achieved world fame seventeen years before as star of Tod Browning's *Dracula.* He co-starred not merely with Bud and Lou, but with Lon Chaney, Jr. (playing the Wolf Man), Glenn Strange (Frankenstein's Monster), and a talented supporting cast.

With all this, one might reasonably assume that Lugosi's high-profile involvement in *A&C Meet Frankenstein* would have jump-started his career and returned him to the ranks of Hollywood's most popular stars. As events proved, that didn't happen. To the contrary, Lugosi's professional and personal declines were only hastened. Consider the six films he made *after* the Abbott & Costello picture: *Mother Riley Meets the Vampire, Bela Lugosi Meets a Brooklyn*

A behind-the-scenes shot on the set of *A & C Meet Frankenstein.*

Gorilla, Glen or Glenda, Bride of the Monster, The Black Sleep, and *Plan 9 From Outer Space*. Although every one of these films is endlessly fascinating, the fascination is the sort experienced by the witness to a gruesome auto crash or a wildly destructive natural disaster. *Brooklyn Gorilla*—a soundstage jungle cheapie starring Martin & Lewis knockoffs Duke Mitchell and Sammy Petrillo—is the best of the bunch, and that's faint praise indeed.

Mother Riley turned out to be the swan song of British music hall comic Arthur Lucan, whose impersonation of Irish washerwoman Mother Riley unfailingly brought howls of laughter for decades from the yobs in the provinces. *The Black Sleep*?—a write-off for Lugosi fans, who cringe at his token role as a slack-jawed mute in support of a dissipated Basil Rathbone.

The remaining three films of Lugosi's final six were productions of Edward D. Wood, Jr., perhaps the most eccentric character in Hollywood. Although personally ambitious and inventive, Wood's main talent seems to have been an ability to convince people to work for him. As has been documented (sometimes cruelly) elsewhere, he had little flair for direction and even less for writing. Predictably, then, Wood felt compelled to write nearly all the pictures he directed. His professional association with Lugosi led to a genuine friendship, which was splendid, but which had very little positive impact on Bela's career. Lugosi enjoyed a good, solid role in Wood's

Wilbur Gray (Costello) and Chick Young (Abbott) take delivery of a pair of large crates addressed to McDougal's House of Horrors. Soon they discover the occupants are the real thing.

entertaining but poverty-stricken *Bride of the Monster* but was mere window dressing in the *auteur*'s transparently autobiographical *Glen or Glenda.* And Lugosi didn't really "star" in *Plan 9* at all, for he died a month before Wood began principal photography in September 1956; Lugosi's "scenes" are little more than scraps of film that Wood had shot without sound earlier in the summer, just days before Lugosi's death.

So that he and Lillian could eat, Lugosi devoted much of the last dozen years of his life to personal appearances, which ranged from a successful 1954 run at Las Vegas's Silver Slipper (cut short because of Bela's fatigue) to embarrassments like his participation at the 1953 Hollywood opening of *House of Wax,* where he showed up with a "gorilla" on a chain.

Also on Lugosi's agenda were a few television appearances (most notably a disastrous 1953 run-in with a madly ad-libbing Red Skelton) and ragged touring productions of *Arsenic And Old Lace* and *Dracula*, the latter often featuring a game Lillian Lugosi as one of the Count's victims. Worse, Lugosi found himself making soul-killing appearances at local "spook shows," sometimes as a solo and sometimes as part of acts headlined by illusionists such as Bill Neff; this for the entertainment of Atomic-Age kids who found Bela's gothic posturing more laughable than scary.

Lugosi's agent in the late forties was a man named Don Marlowe. For many years afterward, Marlowe claimed that he had had to literally beg Universal-International production chief William Goetz to cast his client in the Abbott and Costello film. The claim was perpetuated by other writers, including Lugosi biographer Robert Cremer. According to Marlowe's version of events, the studio was determined to cast character actor Ian Keith as Dracula and had no interest in giving the job to Bela. But Marlowe ultimately appealed to Goetz's sense of fairness—and box office—and secured the part for his client.

A good story but a dubious one, for historian Gregory William Mank has cited studio records suggesting that Bela was penciled in for the Dracula role when the project was in development and titled *The Brain of Frankenstein.* U-I may have idly considered Ian Keith, but the role was apparently designed for Bela from the start.

Clearly, *Abbott and Costello Meet Frankenstein* is the professional highlight of the last twelve years of Lugosi's life. Arguably, it is also the best picture Bud Abbott and Lou Costello made (some A&C aficionados will make the case for *Buck Privates, Buck Privates Come Home,* and *Hold That Ghost*). Regardless, *A&C Meet Frankenstein* came along at a propitious moment, not just for Lugosi, but for Universal-International and Bud and Lou; by 1948, all of these players needed a hit badly.

Bud Abbott and Lou Costello climbed to motion-picture stardom the hard way, via the burlesque stage. Abbott's early work in this vigorous show-biz arena was as a manager and producer, and later as a straight man to his wife, Betty, and for a variety of other comics.

Costello began his career in Hollywood, where he worked as an extra and stuntman beginning in 1927. Eventually, like Abbott, he worked the New York burlesque circuit. He had a chance meeting with Abbott in 1933 and the two teamed up early in 1936. Their snappy patter and carefully crafted personae—Lou as the befuddled innocent, Bud as the abrasive father figure—won them considerable popularity.

Burlesque was on its last legs, however, and the boys jumped onto the vaudeville circuit in early 1937. There, they were seen by Ted Collins, the manager of singer Kate Smith. In February 1938 Abbott and Costello made their radio debut on *The Kate Smith Hour.* At that juncture, the pair had no intention of giving up stage work; although they were skilled verbal comics, they realized that a large measure of their appeal arose from slapstick and their physical differences.

After a slow start, they caught on with radio audiences, and in 1940 began to be courted by Hollywood. The pair made their film debut as supporting players in Universal's *One Night in the Tropics*, released late in 1940. Their second picture, *Buck Privates* (1941), was designed around them and was a smash. Abbott and Costello soon established themselves not simply as skilled screen comics, but as "one" of the Top Ten moneymakers in Hollywood. At their peak in 1942, A&C earned nearly $790,000, a fabulous sum at a time when memories of the Great Depression were still strong.

The team remained among the top Hollywood moneymakers throughout the first half of the forties, but became perhaps too familiar to audiences, as Universal kept them on a killing pace (sometimes via loan-outs to other studios) that saw 24 Abbott and Costello films (excluding *One Night in the Tropics*) released from 1940 through 1949; four A&C vehicles were released in both 1941 and 1942, and no year in the period saw the release of fewer than two new A&C pictures. The team's output would have been even greater had not a bout with rheumatic fever sidelined Costello from the summer of 1943 until the summer of '44.

Despite his illness, and despite the tragic drowning of his infant son late in 1944, Costello maintained his on-screen brightness. Abbott, too, worked hard to keep the patter as fresh as possible. But A&C's box-office dipped, in part because of such experiments as *Little Giant* and *The Time of Their Lives* (both 1946), which deviated from the team's established formula. Audiences may have grown weary of the familiar sort of Abbott and Costello picture but were apparently little interested in "novel" A&C comedies; in effect, Abbott and Costello had become victims of their own success.

Fortunately, they worked for a studio that had been forced by events to become visionary. By 1948, Universal had achieved considerably more industry clout than it had wielded during Lugosi's short-lived tenure as one of the studio's most bankable stars in the early thirties. A 1946 merger with small but prestigious International Pictures created an entity called Universal-International. Moneymen J. Cheever Cowdin and Nate Blumberg handed production control to executives Leo Spitz and the aforementioned William Goetz (the latter the son-in-law of MGM chief Louis B. Mayer, and founder of International Pictures). Early attempts to upgrade the U-I product (notably the deal that allowed the studio to release Laurence Olivier's *Hamlet*) were financially disastrous, and Spitz and Goetz were ousted (though Goetz remained on the lot) and replaced by Edward Muhl, who had been studio plant manager since the twenties.

Muhl recognized the threat posed by television and the increasing independence of stars. He decided not to pursue the high road and risk precious assets on a short slate of pricey prestige productions, but to follow the less-risky low road, spreading the studio's resources among many second features. The assembly-line style of production that had served the studio well in the thirties and early forties saved its bacon again. A loss for fiscal-year 1948 was nearly cleaned up in 1949, and for the next eight years U-I was consistently profitable.

Even better, Universal finally had an advantage over its larger competitors: In May 1948, when federal courts forced the studios to give up their theater holdings (thus breaking the majors' cost-effective but monopolistic stranglehold on exhibition), Universal wasn't rattled for it owned few theaters of which to divest itself. It thus had no reason to significantly restructure its methods of distribution and exhibition. It also had no reason to panic, and so was able to stride confidently into Hollywood's postwar era.

U-I diversified throughout the fifties, building the momentum that would vault it to prominence as one of Hollywood's indisputable powerhouses and make it a leader not just in film production but in television and music, as well. By the mid-fifties, the bread-and-butter U-I release was a brisk genre picture, slickly shot in black and white and starring young, modestly remunerated contract players. The uplevel releases might be classed as B-plus productions, shot in color and sometimes CinemaScope (perhaps the studio's only visible acknowledgement of the threat posed by TV).

Of all the major studios, Universal had the greatest affinity for "formula" pictures, having profited wildly from them during the thirties and early forties with vehicles designed around Deanna Durbin and Abbott and Costello. The fifties would bring further refinements—and more profit—as witness the successful Francis the Talking Mule and Ma and Pa Kettle comedies, a seemingly endless succession of entertaining westerns with Jeff Chandler and Audie Murphy, and the fabulously well-crafted romantic melodramas directed by Douglas Sirk.

If a formula worked once, Universal was quick to put it to work again. And when a formula worked no longer, the studio was sufficiently canny to combine it with something else. So the timing of staff producer Robert Arthur's idea to team Abbott and Costello with the studio's monsters (who had been inactive since *House of Dracula* in 1945) was impeccable.

"Spook comedies" had been a longtime staple of Hollywood features and shorts, with a history nearly as long as that of film itself. Comic actors of all stripes—from Bob Hope to the Three Stooges, Lupe Velez to Mantan Moreland—had done their duty in haunted houses. (That the phenomenon continued into the fifties and nearly to the present day—remember *Haunted Honeymoon*?—indicates the inherent durability of the form.)

Among the chief architects of the studio's transformation was the aforementioned Robert Arthur, who understood audiences and the bottom line. (Four other staff producers joined Arthur as key players in U-I's postwar rise: Ross Hunter, William Alland, Albert Zugsmith, and Aaron Rosenberg.) Arthur prospered as a producer for more than twenty years via such pictures as *The Big Heat*, *Man of a Thousand Faces*, *A Time to Love and a Time to Die*, *That Touch of Mink*, and *Sweet Charity*.

Prior to 1948, Arthur had produced a pair of Abbott and Costello pictures, *Buck Privates Come Home* and *The Wistful Widow of Wagon Gap*, thus positioning himself to do the same on *A&C Meet Frankenstein*. When Arthur approached Bill Goetz with the idea of teaming the boys

In 1948, 17 years after *Dracula*, Lugosi's charimatic Count can still charm the ladies, in this case Jane Randolph.

with the studio's monsters, he was allowed to develop a script. Despite modest pre-production travail, the shoot was efficient and routine. The finished picture was a high point of film comedy, a personal triumph for Lugosi, and, unexpectedly, a delicious footnote to the history of horror cinema.

Perhaps the most fascinating aspect of *A&C Meet Frankenstein* is Costello's initial unwillingness to make it. According to *Abbott and Costello in Hollywood,* a splendid book by Bob Furmanek and Ron Palumbo, the initial story treatment was assigned to writer Oscar Brodney. His treatment (now lost) was superseded by one written by Bertram Milhauser, a veteran contributor to Universal's successful Sherlock Holmes series. Milhauser sketched out a chase thriller with absurd comic elements, such as a sequence in which Costello shrinks the monsters to pocket size!

Screenwriters Robert Lees and Frederic I. Rinaldo took over, scrapping most of Milhauser's ideas and coming up with a finished script entitled *The Brain of Frankenstein.* The pair were longtime collaborators who had written *The Invisible Woman, The Black Cat* (1941 version), *Crazy House,* and numerous A&C comedies including *Hold That Ghost* and *Hit the Ice.* Later, they would write one of Dean Martin and Jerry Lewis's better vehicles, *Jumping Jacks.*

As they set to work on *The Brain of Frankenstein,* Lees and Rinaldo took their cue from Walt DeLeon's script for George Marshall's *The Ghost Breakers,* making a point to keep the script's "spook" elements genuinely scary. Although Abbott and Costello and the monsters would interact, the latter would remain in character—that is, menacing and deadly.

Unfortunately, Lou Costello hated *The Brain of Frankenstein* and called it "a piece of junk." Furmanek and Palumbo suggest that Lou's negative reaction arose from the fact that the script's comic "business" was all new, except for a moving candle gag (suggested by Robert Arthur) that had brought the house down in *Hold That Ghost.* Costello, the authors suggest, felt nervous in the face of so much material that was not tried-and-true.

The assumption is reasonable enough, although one wonders if Costello was simply worried by the prospect of being upstaged by Universal's monsters, three of the most notorious scene-stealers in Hollywood.

At any rate, Costello was mollified by the addition of longtime A&C contributor John Grant to the creative team. Less a screenwriter than a gag man, Grant had an unerring instinct for gags that would get laughs. Because he had worked with A&C in radio, his contributions to their film work were more verbal than visual, and that's fine, given that the boys always relied heavily on verbal humor. The down side to this was that Grant's "patter-style" bits could interrupt the flow of a film (*A&C Meet Frankenstein* has a couple of notable instances). Still, the routines seldom failed to bring laughs from audiences.

Because Goetz had no interest in Abbott and Costello other than as cash cows, and because he trusted Robert Arthur, no major executive from the front office ever visited the set. However, Goetz did intervene when the studio sales department voiced concern about the project's title, noting that *The Brain of Frankenstein* suggested nothing of the story's comic underpinnings. Goetz ordered a title test, and when the instincts of the sales department were proved correct, Goetz insisted that the title be changed.

Abbott and Costello Meet Frankenstein was shot over a six-week period in February and March of 1948. Originally budgeted at just under $760,000, it ran one week over schedule and some $33,000 over budget. Charles Barton was assigned to direct, and hindsight suggests he was the ideal choice. A diminutive man with a gamin's face, Barton began his career as a performer on the vaudeville stage. His early film activity included on-camera work as well as "gofer" chores behind the scenes. Barton eventually became a protege of director William Wellman, and directed his first film, *Wagon Wheels,* in 1934. Although few of his pictures rose above the routine (he was given the unenviable task, for instance, of directing the mercifully short-lived *Five Little Peppers* series), Barton proved himself an effective storyteller and a director who was mindful of schedules and budgets. He was prolific, too: In one year alone, 1942, he directed nine films.

An association with the Disney organization late in Barton's career led to *The Shaggy Dog,* a box-office smash in 1959, and the less successful *Toby Tyler.* He directed his last feature (an atrocious Tommy Noonan/Peter Marshall comedy called *Swinging Along*) in 1962. The remainder of Barton's professional activity was as a television director, where he had already found considerable success as producer and director of *Amos and Andy* (1951-53). His latter-day TV work included directorial assignments on *Hazel, Dennis the Menace, McHale's Navy,* and other situation comedies. He died in 1981.

Barton began his association with Abbott and Costello in 1946, when he was assigned to direct *The Time of Their Lives* and *Buck Privates Come Home.* Other A&C/Barton collaborations are *The Wistful Widow of Wagon Gap; The Noose Hangs High; Hayride; Africa Screams; Abbott and Costello Meet the Killer, Boris Karloff*; and the team's last, *Dance With Me Henry.*

Cinematographer Charles Van Enger had had prior experience with horror, having shot the Lon Chaney version of *The Phantom of the Opera* in 1925. Most of his other credits are routine (and include other A&C vehicles), but there's no denying the importance of his contribution to *A&C Meet Frankenstein.* His lighting inside the film's impressive mansion sets and on ornate sound stages used for "exteriors" makes marvelous use of contrasts between black and white and achieves subtle gradations of tone and mood. Familiar visual "tricks" like backlit mist and steam seem fresh and are creepily evocative rather than stale.

The imposing sets (decorated by Russell A. Gausman and Oliver Emert, and art directed by Bernard Herzbrun and Hilyard Brown) appear solid and substantial. Although Van Enger shot much of the film in low light, every setup reveals the sets' depth and detail.

Camera effects, including laboriously shot lap dissolves of Chaney's transformations to the Wolf Man, were handled by special cinematographers David S. Horsley and Jerome H. Ash. Cartoon animation used for Dracula's man-to-bat transformations, and for the film's inventive opening titles, was likely executed by Grim Natwick and/or James "Shamus" Culhane; accounts differ. (Because animator Walter Lantz had severed his relationship with U-I in 1947, his involvement in the movie's cartoon sequences seems unlikely.)

Composer Frank Skinner's association with Universal began in the thirties and continued into the sixties. Like most staff composers, he was facile and versatile, and comfortable with a variety of genres. Skinner's credits include *Son of Frankenstein, Destry Rides Again, Saboteur, The Egg and I, Francis*, and *Imitation of Life*. He earned Academy Award nominations for his contributions to *Back Street, Arabian Nights*, and others. Skinner's score for *A& C Meet Frankenstein* achieves a perfect balance of ominousness and whimsy. And he pulled off the ultimate challenge—to bounce between both qualities in single scenes—perfectly.

Makeup genius Jack Pierce, who created the world-famous visage of Frankenstein's Monster in 1931 and the Wolf Man's ten years later, had been unceremoniously dismissed by Universal two years before *A&C Meet Frankenstein* started production. His reportedly imperious attitude did not endear him to studio heads, nor did his time-consuming working methods win him any points. So it was that the special makeups on the Abbott and Costello picture were handled by a department headed by Bud Westmore and (anonymously) staffed by Chris Mueller, Emile LaVigne, Jack Kevan, and others. For *A&C Meet Frankenstein,* Mueller sculpted foam-rubber head and facial appliances that could be quickly fitted to Chaney and Strange, and removed with far less fuss than Pierce's complex, layered designs. But it is more to the credit of Pierce's original conceptions than to Westmore's multi-piece masks that the makeups are strikingly believable.

As scripted by Lees and Rinaldo, *Abbott and Costello Meet Frankenstein* is a clever blend of belly laughs and genuine scares. While working as clerks at a Florida express office, Wilbur Gray (Costello) and Chick Young (Abbott) take delivery of a pair of large crates addressed to McDougal's House of Horrors, a "spook house" for gullible tourists. Wilbur soon discovers that the occupants of the crates—Dracula (Lugosi) and Frankenstein's Monster (Strange)—are the real thing. Worse, they are very much alive and make their escape after Dracula hypnotizes Wilbur into insensibility .

Chick, of course, is convinced that Wilbur is loony—never mind that Wilbur's gorgeous girlfriend Sandra (Lenore Aubert) believes him. Mr. McDougal (Frank Ferguson) is just plain furious, and threatens the boys with a whopping lawsuit unless his "exhibits" are returned.

Someone other than McDougal wants to locate the monsters: Larry Talbot (Chaney), who phones the express office from London to warn Wilbur that great danger is afoot. True enough, and there's danger in London, as well, for when the moon rises over the Thames, Talbot drops the phone and is transformed into the Wolf Man.

Meanwhile, Dracula and the logy, partially revived Monster make their way to the Florida coast and an enormous mansion, where they are greeted by Sandra—in reality Dr. Sandra Mornay, an unscrupulous scientist in league with Dracula to return the Monster to full strength via a new brain. But Dracula has learned from the mistakes of the past: "And about the brain," the Count intones. "I don't want to repeat Frankenstein's mistake and revive a vicious, unmanageable brute. This time the Monster must have no will of his own. No fiendish intellect to oppose his master."

Sandra smiles and gives a sinister nod. "There, my Count, I believe I have exceeded your fondest wishes. The new brain I have chosen for the Monster is so simple, so pliable, he will obey you like a trained dog."

It is clear, of course, that the brain in question belongs to Wilbur. From this point, *Abbott*

Count Dracula needs a new brain for the Monster, a brain "so simple, so pliable, he will obey you like a trained dog." Wilbur fits the bill.

and Costello Meet Frankenstein becomes a glorious chase thriller, as Chick and Wilbur frantically dodge not only Dracula and the Monster, but the Wolf Man (by now in Florida), the incensed McDougal, Sandra, a clever insurance investigator (Jane Randolph), and the police.

The climax inside the shadowy mansion is a lengthy, brilliantly executed sequence that expertly combines laughs and scares, and that brings Dracula, the Monster, and the Wolf Man together in a clash that is a fitting conclusion to Universal's horror cycle.

A&C Meet Frankenstein has a lot going for it, but one of its biggest assets, its pacing, is nearly subliminal. Aspiring screenwriters should look to the picture as a model of construction, time compression, and narrative economy and logic. Examples are numerous. For instance, after McDougal accepts delivery of his crates at the freight office, one might reasonably wonder how (and why) Wilbur and Chick will continue to figure in the story. After all, McDougal has his merchandise and is on his way with them to his place of business. Writers Lees and Rinaldo solved this neatly, and in a way perfectly in keeping with Costello's persona, by establishing that Wilbur has banged the crates around so much while unloading them that McDougal insists that the boys accompany him to his House of Horrors to await an insurance investigator who will determine if the merchandise has been damaged.

Once at the House of Horrors, Wilbur reads aloud from display placards McDougal has prepared for his exhibit, summing up the backgrounds of Dracula and Frankenstein's Monster, and thus bringing up to speed audience members unfamiliar with the characters (an unlikely happenstance, but a possible one, nonetheless).

***A & C Meet Frankenstein* returned Bela to Universal where he had achieved world fame years before as star of Tod Browning's *Dracula*. He co-starred not merely with Bud and Lou but with Glenn Strange and Lenore Aubert.**

Dracula's remarks to Sandra about not wanting to revive "a vicious, unmanageable brute" not only provided Lugosi with some deliciously emphatic dialogue, but establish Dracula's central dilemma, and, by way of Sandra's reply, the solution to it.

After Dracula and the Monster escape the House of Horrors, brief dialogue in the following scene establishes that Wilbur and Chick have spent a day and a night in jail, before being bailed out by a beautiful woman. There are no scenes of the boys' time behind bars, not even a montage—merely expository dialogue that explains what has happened. With marvelous economy, then, Lees and Rinaldo provided a rationale for the introduction of the insurance investigator, Joan Raymond (who, we later learn, has posted the boys' bond). More importantly, the dialogue compresses twenty-four hours into a few moments, allowing Larry Talbot sufficient time to have traveled from London to Florida, where he soon links up with Wilbur and Chick.

With all the major players in place, the narrative steams ahead via a series of clever, vividly presented set pieces:

—Talbot insists that Wilbur lock him in his hotel room at night, and although Wilbur obeys, he repeatedly returns to the room (he's guilty about a piece of purloined fruit), unaware that Talbot has become the Wolf Man.

—At the mansion, Wilbur stumbles through a secret panel and discovers an enormous underground river and dock, and comes face to face with Dracula.

—In a dimly lit dungeon, Wilbur unknowingly sits in the Monster's lap and plays a creepy—and hilarious—game of "handsy," smacking the Monster's gigantic mitt, hoping against hope that it somehow is one of his own.

—Wilbur meets Dr. Lejos (the incognito Dracula), and thinks he's a swell guy.

—At an outdoor costume ball, the Wolf Man stalks Wilbur and nearly kills McDougal; Chick is blamed.

—Wilbur is mesmerized by Dracula and pilloried in the dungeon to await the brain transfer.

—Chick and Talbot elude an angry posse and burst into the mansion's operating room just as Sandra is about to open up Wilbur's skull.

—Dracula and the Wolf Man battle to the death in the laboratory and surrounding corridors.

—The Monster stalks Chick and Wilbur outside and is burned to death on a gasoline-soaked dock.

—The boys, apparently safe in a rowboat, have one final, unexpected visitor before the fadeout.

It's no surprise, of course, that *Abbott and Costello Meet Frankenstein* is dominated by Abbott and Costello. The picture was designed expressly for them, and their combined salary of $105,000 was the production's major above-the-line expense. Yet the film would not have nearly the force it does if an actor other than Lugosi had played Dracula. As in most of their pictures, Abbott and Costello do not instigate the action; rather, they react—in this case, to events set in motion by Dracula. For this reason, the Count, although not the story's major character, is its linchpin. Everything of consequence that occurs during the film's eighty-three minutes is set into motion by him.

Although aging and in ill health because of his addiction to morphine (and, some sources claim, methadone, as well), Lugosi summoned every ounce of power and regalness the Dracula character deserves. Ghostly white pancake makeup not only obscures Lugosi's age, but adds a suitably ghostly pallor and a peculiar, Old-World sort of dignity. And his lips, a deeper hue than when he played the part in 1931, suggest an increased appetite for blood.

Bela excelled at the grand gestures called for by the script: the cape over the face, the mesmeric hand gestures levied against Wilbur and others, Dracula's aggressiveness during the climactic battle with the Wolf Man. But Bela shone in more subtle moments, too, as when Dracula revives the Monster to a semi-comatose state. "Master," the Monster says weakly. Dracula smiles and looks down at his pawn. "Yes...," he whispers, bringing to that single word the sibilance of an undead evil, and a dark anticipation of the horror he proposes to unleash. Later, when he shouts to Mornay, "I am accustomed to having my orders obeyed!" one is compelled to believe him. Mornay learns this the hard way moments later, when she is forced to gaze into Dracula's eyes. Helpless, her head falls back and Dracula pierces her throat.

Perhaps the most impressive aspect of Lugosi's performance is the vigor he brought to the physically challenging climax, in which the Wolf Man pursues Dracula around the laboratory, into the labyrinth of corridors outside, and onto a balcony overlooking the sea. Although of course not filmed non-stop, the action that dominates individual setups is nevertheless strenuous and would have been impossible for many men of Lugosi's age. Yet on screen Lugosi betrays no hint of fatigue or timorousness. Whether winding up and flinging a flower pot at the Wolf Man's head, wielding a gurney like a weapon, or dodging about in corridors, Lugosi's Dracula seems a creature of immense agility and vigor. The actor may have been exhausted when the cameras stopped rolling but on the screen, where it counted, Lugosi was (as he remains) the greatest Count Dracula.

Bela's contract to do the picture was strictly a one-shot deal promising no options and no subsequent work. He was offered four weeks and a day of employment at $2000 a week—good money in 1948 but a pittance in Hollywood and particularly paltry when one considers that Bela did not work again in film for four years. Unfortunately, Lugosi did not have Dracula's option of self-imposed "hibernation" during dry spells. What little money he earned in his declining years had to be stretched more dramatically than Silly Putty.

If Bela Lugosi was the logical choice to play Dracula, no one but Lon Chaney, Jr. (by this time billed as simply Lon Chaney) could have played the Wolf Man. As the son of one of the greatest movie character stars of all time, the younger Chaney was regarded by Hollywood as having big shoes to fill. That he did not manage the feat doesn't matter, if only because his career lasted considerably longer than his father's, and, in his time, he became nearly as well known. The title role in *The Wolf Man* (1941) was an obvious high point of Chaney's career. As with so many other horror stars, though, his success as the tormented Larry Talbot typecast him—not to the degree as in Lugosi's case, but enough so that he rarely broke out of the B-picture arena, and when he did (as in *High Noon*), it was in small roles only.

A large man with a passive, somnolent acting style, Chaney nevertheless brought conviction to the Talbot role each of the five times he played it on the big screen. His interpretation of the part in *A&C Meet Frankenstein,* in fact, is second only to his first one.

Veteran cowboy actor Glenn Strange first played Frankenstein's Monster in *House of Frankenstein* in 1944. To many fans (this writer included) his interpretation of the Monster is surpassed only by Karloff's—and is wholly different. The sympathetic nature inherent in Karloff's portrayal is well known. Strange, a far less accomplished actor, nevertheless brought a new quality to the Monster: homicidal dementia. With his enormous frame, red slash of a mouth, and lantern jaw, Strange conveyed lunacy and an unsubtle sort of physical intimidation. There's no reasoning with *this* Monster, which adds to the fun and sense of menace of *A&C Meet Frankenstein.*

Yugoslavian actress Lenore Aubert, cast as the scheming Dr. Mornay, is one of the film's perpetually unsung assets. Her dark good looks and European accent make her immediately intriguing, and she underplayed her nicely written role in dead-serious style. Her film career began in 1938 and apparently ended with her 1948 appearances in *Abbott and Costello Meet the Killer, Boris Karloff* and *Barbary Coast.*

Blonde Jane Randolph, who played insurance investigator Joan Raymond, had a career that was even more brief than Aubert's, stretching only from 1942 through 1948; the Abbott and Costello picture was her last before her retirement at age 30. Randolph was suitably urban and cynical as Joan, yet sufficiently feminine to appeal both to Costello and to the audience.

The acting profession was good to Frank Ferguson, perfectly irascible as McDougal, and a scowling presence in comedy (*The Good Humor Man*) and drama (*Johnny Guitar*) on film and television for nearly thirty years. Invariably cast as an ill-tempered cop, businessman, or petty official, he was rather like a "real world" version of Laurel and Hardy's perennial antagonist, actor Jimmy Finlayson. Like Fin, Ferguson was a master of the squint and sputter, and his anger could grow to similarly apocalyptic proportions. Ferguson's McDougal fills a vital role in *A&C Meet Frankenstein* because the character's persona—comically exaggerated but not wildly so—is the bridge that connects Bud and Lou's comic style with the grimness offered by Lugosi and the others.

Finally, if there is a "forgotten" actor in the film, it's blandly handsome Charles Bradstreet, cast in the peripheral and completely thankless role of Dr. Stevens, a well-meaning young scientist whose equipment is exploited by Mornay and Dracula. Bradstreet apparently never rose above small parts, and only one other credit—1947's *The Unfinished Dance*—could be found for him.

A&C Meet Frankenstein was filmed on an amiable, antic set that typified Bud and Lou's preferred way of working. Marathon card games were interrupted only for the chore of a quick read-through of the next scene or lining up for a take. Abbott, fearful of his chronic epilepsy, began to drink in the afternoons, and mildly suggested to Barton that he get in the can what he could before four o'clock. Props that appealed to Costello invariably went home with him. And, as always, comic actor Bobby Barber was kept around (and on the studio payroll) to provide on-set laughs and encourage Costello's practical jokes. Seltzer ambushes and pie fights were not uncommon.

Director Barton kept as tight a rein on Costello as possible, discouraging excessive ad-libbing or physical gags that were not in the script. Sometimes, when Barton was convinced he was right, he would humor Costello by shooting an alternate take incorporating an idea dreamed up on the spot by Lou, secure in the knowledge that Lou would concede after looking at rushes. (Still, one suspects that some of Costello's inventions did make the final cut, as when Wilbur screws up his face and barks at a matron's fox fur, and when he blithely dabs at his mouth with Chick's tie after momentarily gaining the upper hand, girl-wise.)

Lugosi was a friendly and convivial on-set presence, but steered clear of Barber's squirting seltzer and other nonsense, preferring instead to chat quietly with less manic cast members, or simply to relax in a corner with a cigar and a good book.

It was a great day when Lugosi's son, Bela Lugosi, Jr. (today an attorney in Los Angeles), impressively attired in the uniform of the military school he attended near his parents' home at Lake Elsinore, visited the set. Photographs of the visit reveal Bela as a beaming, proud papa, his son happy to be there and impressed with his father and the rest of the cast.

Despite a great deal of physical action (running, things being thrown about, Lou's always-funny dashes into walls, and so forth), only one notable injury occurred during the shoot. The script called for the enraged Monster to lift Dr. Mornay in his arms at the climax and toss her to her death through a high laboratory window. Glenn Strange expertly hefted stuntwoman Helen Thurston (hooked to wires and doubling Lenore Aubert), but the fake glass did not break when Thurston was flung against it. Instead of crashing through, she rebounded onto Strange, breaking his ankle. The sequence was completed when Chaney (who had played the Monster in *The Ghost of Frankenstein*), donned the costume and foam-rubber appliances and successfully propelled Thurston through the re-engineered window. Strange played the remainder of his scenes wearing an ankle brace.

The initial box-office success of *Abbott and Costello Meet Frankenstein*—a worldwide gross of $3.2 million—was tremendous, propelling Bud and Lou back onto the Top Ten moneymakers list (where they would stay through 1951) and allowing U-I to take a big step closer to profitability. Predictably, the picture inspired a raft of lesser "Abbott and Costello Meet" films that range from acceptable (*A&C Meet the Invisible Man*) to weak indeed (*A&C Meet Captain Kidd,* co-starring Charles Laughton!) Inevitably, television beckoned, and the boys reprised their most venerable routines in a successful, low-budget series, *The Abbott and Costello Show,* that aired in syndication from 1951 to 1953.

The team's final picture for U-I, *Abbott and Costello Meet the Mummy,* was released in 1955. By that time, Bud and Lou's style of patter (which had superseded Laurel and Hardy's gentler brand of comedy in the early forties), had itself been superseded by the wilder, more surreal approach of Dean Martin and Jerry Lewis, who had established themselves as box-office kings in the early fifties. Bud and Lou's swan song, the execrable *Dance With Me Henry,* was released by United Artists in 1956.

Fatigue and Abbott's drinking precipitated the team's split late in 1956. Costello did a solo film comedy, *The 30-Foot Bride of Candy Rock,* in 1959, made the rounds of TV talk shows, and gave some effective dramatic performances on TV anthology shows. He died of heart failure in 1959.

In 1961 Abbott briefly teamed with stocky comic Candy Candido, worked a bit in episodic television, then retired with wife Betty to a comfortable life that would have been more comfortable still had it not been for enormous tax bills that wiped out many of his assets. He came out of retirement in 1967 to provide "his own" voice for a series of limited-animation Abbott and Costello cartoon shorts. He passed away in 1974.

As with nearly any movie project, the cast members of *A&C Meet Frankenstein* went their separate ways when the shooting wrapped. But a special moment came in 1950, when Abbott and Costello were joined by Lugosi, Chaney, and Strange for a reenactment of moments from their best film on NBC television's *The Colgate Comedy Hour.*

Lillian Lugosi stuck it out with her husband for a few more years before divorcing him in 1953. Fed up with his diminished earning power, his maddening jealousy, and a peculiar alteration of role that found her functioning more as Bela's mother, keeper, and chauffeur (Bela never learned to drive) than as his wife, she wanted out.

Bela conquered his twenty-year drug habit in just four months in 1955 after voluntarily committing himself to the Los Angeles County Hospital. A sickly skeleton when admitted, he appeared healthy and bright-eyed upon release. He was anxious to return to work and completed Ed Wood's *Bride of the Monster* and Reginald LeBorg's *The Black Sleep* before succumbing to a heart attack in his modest Harold Way apartment in Hollywood. His fifth wife, the former Hope Lininger (a woman thirty years Bela's junior who had sent him adoring, supportive letters while he was in the hospital) was at the grocery store at the time. Death came as Lugosi was reading a script.

Today, most film buffs regard *A&C Meet Frankenstein* as a first-rate low comedy featuring a clutch of legendary performers. Upon the picture's initial release, however, many "legitimate" reviews were less than kind. *The New York Times* stiffly remarked, "Most of the comic invention in *Abbott and Costello Meet Frankenstein* is embraced in the title." The *Chicago Sun Times* called the film "a considerable bore" and the *Los Angeles Examiner* bemoaned the boys' "familiar routine."

Assessments offered by industry trade papers were more sanguine. The *Hollywood Reporter* said the film "spells out showmanship right down the line"; *Variety* called it "a happy combination both for chills and laughs" and noted that Lugosi and the other horror stars "bulwark the chills and thrills."

A particularly insightful review came from the *New York Star,* which said, "It's heartwarming to see all our favorite monsters once more, each inexorably expressing his individuality, all at the same time. It's kind of like a class reunion.... a broad, friendly comedy, good to see. It's real American folklore; look at it that way."

Given what has passed for screen comedy (and horror, for that matter) since the seventies, one is astonished to discover that *A&C Meet Frankenstein* continues to inspire antipathy in some critics and historians. John Flynn, in *Cinematic Vampires* (a book rife with errors), claims that *A&C Meet Frankenstein* is "lacking originality and imagination." David Pirie, in his scholarly *The Vampire Cinema,* calls the film a "bastardization" of Universal's classic monsters and describes Lugosi as a "stooge" for Abbott and Costello. And the film is omitted by virtue of format from Tom Weaver's otherwise complete *Universal Horrors: The Studio's Classic Films, 1931-1946.*

Still, the shifting critical tide that has inspired reevaluations of such directors as Joseph H. Lewis and Phil Karlson has also "rehabilitated" Lugosi and *A&C Meet Frankenstein.* Leonard Maltin's superb, best-selling *Movie and Video Guide* awards the film three-and-a-half stars and calls it an "All-time great horror-comedy...." The enthusiastic and perceptive historian Danny Peary, in his *Guide for the Film Fanatic,* says, "In one of the few films to deftly combine horror and comedy, the monsters are treated with respect and affection.... Horror fans [will] appreciate the nifty special effects and make-up, [and] will find the monsters appropriately frightening."

Of course, the particular pleasures of *Abbott and Costello Meet Frankenstein* have been there all along. The film never needed a critic's validation. It was good when it was released nearly fifty years ago, and it's still good today.

And yet, for decades the common assumption was that the Universal horror cycle ended in 1945 with *House of Dracula.* To many eyes, *A&C Meet Frankenstein* was beneath contempt, a foolish burlesque that demeaned the studio's classic monsters while promoting a pair of unsubtle, low-brow comics. In fact, the film is an apt conclusion to Universal's horror series and a splendid showcase for the beloved monsters, all of whom are better served here than in either *House* thriller, and even *Frankenstein Meets the Wolf Man.* And by allowing Abbott and Costello their best-ever showcase, the film isn't just the proverbial "laff riot," but an invaluable record of two comics who for many years were, like the film itself, criminally underrated.

For Bela Lugosi, *Abbott and Costello Meet Frankenstein* was the official return to the character that had paradoxically given him fame and a one-way ticket to professional oblivion. By rights, he should have hated and loathed Dracula, for he knew as well as anybody that the Count had played a part in his undoing. Yet publicly, at least, Lugosi professed a fondness for Dracula. "No, no, Dracula never ends," he smiled to a British interviewer in the early fifties, "it never ends."

The statement was more true than even Lugosi could have dreamed, for he, along with Dracula, has achieved the sort of immortality that has eluded most of his contemporaries, as it will elude most of the stars working in film today. Lugosi, like John Wayne and Marilyn Monroe, is one of Hollywood's Great Originals, and his performance in the enjoyable diversion called *Abbott and Costello Meet Frankenstein* is the last truly fine one of his career. Although he gave his all in the handful of films that followed, Lugosi never again enjoyed the right combination of role, script, co-stars, director, and budget.

When Charles Van Enger's camera looks closely into Lugosi's eyes as Dracula mesmerizes Lenore Aubert's Dr. Mornay, we're watching more than a good moment in a wonderful film. We're witnessing the forceful, proud good-bye of one of the screen's imperishable personalities.

Lugosi enjoys a behind-the-scenes chat with co-star Lenore Aubert.

When producer Richard Gordon met Bela during the late 1940s, Lugosi was hoping to do a stage version of *Dracula* to put him back on top. Here is a rare portrait of Lugosi from a stage version of *Dracula*.

AN APPRECIATION OF BELA LUGOSI

by Richard Gordon

August, 1948. Bela Lugosi was starring in a Summer stock production of *Arsenic and Old Lace* that toured the United States. In the listings of Summer stock plays and in paid advertisements, the New York newspapers proclaimed that Bela would be appearing in this revival at Sea Cliff, Long Island.

My brother Alex and I had emigrated from England to the United States on November 1, 1947. This was a period when wartime restrictions had been eased but not yet abolished in our home country, and we felt that it was a necessary career move. Both of us had been released from military service not much earlier but had gained jobs in the film industry in London while waiting for the emigration formalities to be completed. Alex had obtained a position as publicity manager of George Minter's Renown Pictures, an independent distributor which several years later became an important producer. I was employed as an assistant to the publicity manager of Pathe Pictures, a major company that was the distribution arm of Associated British which owned a studio as well as the largest chain of cinemas in the country.

For many years, we had already been active in various activities connected with films. At college, Alex became involved with a film society. We started fan clubs for Gene Autry and Buster Crabbe. During my service in the Royal Navy, I organized film shows for the entertainment of enlisted men. We had also started to write articles and reviews for the fan magazines which proliferated in England as soon as the war was over, limited only by shortages in paper supplies and other necessary elements.

We arrived in New York with a mandate from several magazines to send home articles about the film industry in America. They were especially interested in interviews with well-known personalities, and they were prepared to pay for them although the fees were modest. Because wartime exchange control restrictions had not yet been lifted, the money could not even be freely transferred to the United States. Reimbursement of expenses was not even considered. Hence we found ourselves in the position of being able to request interviews only with stars who were visiting New York or appearing in local theaters since we had no money to travel to Hollywood or elsewhere. One of our first interviews was with William "Hopalong Cassidy" Boyd who came to New York for television.

Summer stock was a boon to our activities because Hollywood stars who were no longer in demand for worthwhile film roles regularly toured in plays which were usually revivals of Broadway stage hits. We were lucky to meet such personalities as Kay Francis, Chester Morris, and Richard Arlen, but when the announcement of Bela Lugosi's arrival appeared, it was the most exciting moment of all.

Horror films, along with westerns, had become our favorite genre when we were growing up. Seeing them, however, presented serious problems. While westerns did not play extensively in English cinemas during the war, there were always the Saturday morning children's matinees which could be counted upon to show a seemingly endless supply of cowboy adventure stories, accompanied by an exciting serial. Horror films, on the other hand, while shown in regular release, had censorship problems that were not easily circumvented.

In the early 1930's, England had its two principal censorship categories, the "A" (for

Adult) certificate that prohibited anyone under 16 from attending the cinema unless accompanied by a parent or guardian, and the "U" (for Universal) certificate which had no such restrictions. However, the British Board of Film Censors also administered a little-known third category which was called "Adults Only" which meant that persons under 16 could not be admitted at all. This was used for the occasional sex film but more often for horror films that the Board deplored.

When the international success of the classic horror films in the early '30's resulted in a significant increase in the number of such pictures to arrive in England, the "H" (for Horror) certificate was created. The first film to be released in this category was MGM's 1936 remake of *The Thirteenth Chair*, an earlier 1929 version of which had starred Bela Lugosi. Sometimes the Censor Board also took it upon itself to ban from showing altogether certain films that the Board considered particularly undesirable, such as Paramount's *Island of Lost Souls*, in which Lugosi played a character role, and MGM's *Freaks*. These pictures were not publicly exhibited in England until some thirty years later when the floodgates opened in the permissive age of the "X" certificate which by then had replaced the "H" and encompassed sex and violence as well as horror.

Thus Alex and I grew up on a starvation diet of the horror films we craved to see, and our first exposure to the Kings of Horror were in films of other genres in which they occasionally appeared. We first "met" Bela Lugosi on the screen in such diverse pictures as *Postal Inspector*, *The Gorilla*, *Ninotchka*, and the two serials *Shadows of Chinatown* and *S.O.S. Coastguard* while thirsting to see their Universal horror classics. The first time we saw Boris Karloff was in *The House of Rothschild*. There was a moment of supreme excitement when a revival showing of *The Invisible Ray* allowed us to see Lugosi and Karloff together as this film somehow escaped the "H" certificate and could be seen when accompanied by an adult.

Our parents were avid moviegoers but hardly devotees of the horror film so even the "A" certificate required a modicum of ingenuity. It became common practice for children under 16 to hang around the vicinity of the cinema until a sympathetic-appearing adult arrived who could be approached with a request to be taken into the show. This mostly but not always worked. Sometimes the request would be sternly rejected with a lecture on the immorality of trying to circumvent the law. The mind boggles today at the thought of children soliciting a total stranger to take them into a place of entertainment.

Therefore, it was not until the wildly successful reissue of *Frankenstein* and *Dracula* in 1939 that we finally caught up with the Universal horror classics starring Bela Lugosi and Boris Karloff. When *Son of Frankenstein* was released, there was not only a renaissance of horror film production but they began to flood onto the screens of England to such an extent that the Censor Board over-reacted. Claiming that we were surrounded by too much real-life horror because of the war, they proclaimed to Hollywood that horror pictures would hereafter be banned altogether. Just another good reason to emigrate to the United States as soon as possible, we told our skeptical parents!

Sea Cliff, 1948. We presented ourselves at the Summer stock playhouse to see *Arsenic and Old Lace* and to interview Bela Lugosi for our English fan magazines. The thrill of seeing Bela in person, and the prospect of meeting him off-stage, eclipsed any possible critical appreciation of the play but I remember it as a good production in which Bela acted very well and seemed to enjoy playing a role which, after all, was a humorous take-off on Boris Karloff. The important memory is of how Bela received us back-stage after the performance—tired but in a good mood, genuinely appreciative that we had not only come to see him perform but to interview him for England, and full of enthusiasm for what the future might hold.

Instead of giving us a few minutes of his time, he generously invited us to join him and his wife for dinner at a nearby restaurant where we spent several hours together and started a friendship that lasted until his tragic death. Everyone in the restaurant was aware of his presence and occasionally someone would dare to approach our table and request an autograph, always receiving a sincere and characteristically warm reception. At the same time, Bela could not resist a flamboyantly dramatic moment such as, when ordering a bottle of red wine for the table, he

Portrait of a young Bela Lugosi.

sampled a glass, holding it to the light and remarking in a voice which not surprisingly carried to most of the nearby tables, "I drink only red wine—I like it because it is the color of blood".

During the course of the evening, we discovered that Bela at that time had no agent. He was living in New York between his travels and he had a manager whom he thought we should meet, a young man who was unfortunately more of an admirer than a professional, but from whom he expected great things. He spoke mostly of his hopes for the future, especially for a Broadway revival of *Dracula*. Since we were interviewing him for an article to be published in England, he recalled with pleasure his trips to London to make *The Mystery of the Marie Celeste* (which was released in America as *The Phantom Ship*) and especially the production of the famous Edgar Wallace thriller, *The Dark Eyes of London* (re-titled *The Human Monster* in USA). He remarked that his greatest thrill would be an opportunity to return to England for a West End production of *Dracula* on the London stage.

We left each other with the promise to meet again at the end of his Summer tour.

In 1949, I founded Gordon Films, Inc. to act as an independent agent for producers overseas, primarily in England, to sell their films for exhibition in North America. George Minter of Renown Pictures, where Alex had been publicity manager several years earlier, had become an important producer and gave me my first break when he offered me the opportunity to represent his company.

Bela and his wife Lillian were now living in a residential hotel on the Westside of New York. Bela was making personal appearances at cinemas throughout the city, generally accompanying the showing of one of his films which unfortunately were mostly from his Monogram series. The exhibitors thought that they did not need to spend any extra money to book his better films so long as the marquees proclaimed that Bela Lugosi was appearing in person. His stage act consisted either of short scenes from *Dracula* with a suitable female, or sometimes a skit involving a rather phoney-looking ape on a chain.

Towards the end of 1949, he obtained a starring role in a live television adaptation of Edgar Allan Poe's *The Cask of Amontillado* for a TV series called *Suspense*. His co-star was Romney Brent, a distinguished English stage and screen actor who was in New York to do a Broadway play. Alex and I accompanied Bela to the studio to watch the production. He gave an excellent performance but the low budget for live half-hour television shows made it extremely difficult. For a longish scene of his character descending several flights of stairs to the cellar of a sinister mansion, there was only one set of stairs to be photographed and Bela had to keep walking down the same flight until he was exhausted. Nevertheless, he made a powerful impression on the small screen.

After the show, we accompanied him with his wife to one of his favorite Hungarian restaurants, the Tokay, on the Eastside of New York, where he entertained everyone lavishly with food and drink, probably spending the entire salary he had been paid for the evening's work. Such was his generosity throughout his life that whenever he had what he considered a windfall, he insisted on sharing it not only with his friends but also any strangers of the moment whom he encountered.

On another occasion, Bela was engaged to be a guest star on Milton Berle's hugely successful *Comedy Hour* television programme. He was given lines to learn and, on the evening of his appearance, fortified with a somewhat excessive amount of alcohol, appeared at the studio. This was, of course, also live and not filmed television. His sketch portrayed him as an evil scientist but Berle was accustomed to ad-libbing instead of sticking to the script and Bela became confused. He was not ready for such repartee and, being somewhat hard of hearing, had trouble with responding to Berle's throwaway lines.

Alex and I were then still too inexperienced to do him much good but nevertheless he asked me, perhaps because he knew that I was in contact with many film producers, especially overseas, if I would take over the management of his affairs. I had great reservations because I had become devoted to him as a friend and did not want to let him down; on the other hand, it was a challenge and no one else was then showing much interest in his activities. Bela was never a person who could "sell" himself.

By this time, Alex and I had also met and interviewed Boris Karloff who had appeared on Broadway in two plays, both unfortunately with no great success. The first was *The Linden Tree* in which he played a kindly professor. It was written by J. B. Priestley whose novel *Benighted* in the early 1930's had been the basis of one of Karloff's biggest horror films, James Whale's *The*

Old Dark House. The other was an English thriller by Edward Percy called *The Shop at Sly Corner* which had already been filmed in London with Oscar Homolka. It was released in America as *Code of Scotland Yard* and its only claim to fame today is that it included the screen debut of Diana Dors in a bit part.

Boris had a small apartment at the Dakota in New York where I occasionally visited him when he was in town. Another resident of the Dakota was Zachary Scott with whom I later made two films. Much later, the Dakota was made famous as the setting of *Rosemary's Baby* and then infamous as the scene of John Lennon's tragic death.

In my office in the old General Motors building, I had covered the walls with autographed photos of the stars whom we had met. I discovered quickly that when Bela Lugosi came for an appointment and saw his picture hanging next to that of Boris Karloff, the idea upset him! After that, whenever he was expected, I removed Karloff's picture and substituted someone else, replacing it after Lugosi left.

At that time, my main efforts on behalf of Bela were directed towards setting up a revival of *Dracula* on the stage in England. I had tried, and failed, to interest my film producers to use him in their pictures. Finally, near the end of 1950, a London management firm named Routledge & White offered to do *Dracula* with a tour of the English provinces that would culminate in a West End production in London.

With my lack of experience, especially in the theatre, I allowed them to work out everything without the proper supervision. They undertook to raise the financing, promote the play, and become the limited partners. Finally, in 1951, came the day when all the agreements were signed and the production became a reality. Bela and Lillian sailed to England, full of enthusiasm with dreams of a great comeback. Their luggage included Bela's personal satin-lined Dracula coffin, his cape, and other props for the play.

Before their departure, Bela had come to me with what he thought was a brilliant idea. Somewhere he had read that, in the 1930's, Tom Mix had made headline news in England when, upon his arrival for a personal appearance tour, he jumped with his horse Tony from ship to shore. Bela wanted to have himself carried off the ship in his coffin in which the Customs people would discover him "sleeping" when it was opened for inspection. I had a hard time persuading him that in post-World War II in England, His Majesty's Customs Service would not be amused to become the unwitting participants in a publicity stunt, and it could not be done. Nevertheless, Bela's arrival was greeted with a blaze of publicity on radio and in the newspapers, giving him a new lease on life.

What we did not know was that Routledge & White had had the greatest difficulty in raising the money for the production and were counting so strongly on Bela's name to carry the show that they had skimped horribly on every other aspect of the tour. Sets, costumes, and the supporting cast smacked of "poverty row." The disappointment of finding himself surrounded by such amateurish elements crushed Bela's hopes and reduced him to desperation. Nevertheless, being the trouper that he was, and with Lillian's support, he determined to make the best of it and struggled gamely to overcome the handicaps. He fought for improvements to the best of his ability but was out-maneouvered by Routledge & White at every turn. They were either too stupid or too greedy to realize that they were digging their own graves and burying Bela with them. Every few days, I received long reports from Lillian at my office in New York but I was unable to be of material help.

The provincial tour was delayed as last-minute changes were nevertheless made. Finally, *Dracula* was set to open at the Theatre Royal in Brighton, the scene of many a try-out for plays destined to be shown in the West End of London. Although Lugosi fans came from everywhere to see their idol in person, it was a disaster. Bela of course was word perfect in a role that he had committed to memory over the years as much as any Shakespearean actor knows his *Hamlet*. The rest of the cast, too inexperienced to do otherwise, had not mastered their lines. Perhaps they were also intimidated by his presence. Bela, who by then was almost deaf in one ear, did not hear it when they missed a cue and spoke his dialogue when his turn came. The result dismayed the audience and the press.

It was not enough that the fans flocked to his dressing-room or mobbed him at the stage door, pleading for autographs which he signed in his favorite "color of blood." He became demoralized and depressed, and often turned to drink for solace. The long provincial tour never materialized and the production was shut down by Routledge & White who declared bankruptcy, leaving behind them not only a trail of unpaid bills but also the unpaid salary of Bela who had been engaged for a weekly fee of one thousand dollars. The Lugosis found themselves stranded without even the fare to return to America in a civilized manner.

At this point, I was able to come to their rescue. I still represented George Minter's Renown Pictures which a few years earlier had taken over the production of a continuing series of English comedies starring a well-known vaudeville team known as "Old Mother Riley and her Daughter Kitty." George was preparing a new episode when I approached him with the suggestion to co-star Bela Lugosi with Mother Riley and make a film that might have success in America where Mother Riley was unknown.

George was quick to see the possibilities. The risk was small since the presence of Mother Riley guaranteed the English market. Bela's salary would be modest and there was not the necessity of paying the cost to bring an American actor to London. We agreed a fee of five thousand dollars for four weeks' work during which the living expenses of the Lugosis were also to be paid. The existing script for the new film was scrapped and a new screenplay to take full advantage of Bela's presence was commissioned from writer Val Valentine. For lack of a better idea, and because of the pressure of time, Valentine shamelessly plagiarized *Abbott and Costello Meet Frankenstein* which had been a huge success in England. The film was to be made as *Mother Riley Meets the Vampire,* but at my insistence, an alternate title *Vampire Over London* was agreed for international sales. I had previously tried out an earlier Mother Riley film in New York by changing its title to *A Wild Irish Night* although without success. Daughter Kitty was eliminated from the script to give Bela greater prominence as Mother Riley's co-star. John Gilling was engaged to direct the film which went into production at the Nettlefold Studios on the outskirts of London with some exterior shooting in the city. Six years later, when the studio had been renamed Walton Studios, I shot *The Haunted Strangler* and *Fiend Without A Face* there.

Old Mother Riley was the brain-child of Arthur Lucan, a famous English vaudeville performer who was born in 1885. He started touring in England and Ireland at a very young age, often playing a "dame" in pantomime. At the age of 18, he married Kitty McShane in Dublin and she became a part of his act. During a successful tour of Australia, Arthur developed a sketch which they were invited to perform at the Royal Variety Command Performance of 1934 in London. This was the beginning of "Old Mother Riley and her Daughter Kitty," the popularity of which led to a series of films that were hugely successful in the British Isles. By 1951, the act was beginning to show signs of old age and their domestic life had become unhappy. They had a son who was grown up and had become a doctor. Kitty was not much younger than Arthur and had increasing difficulties to play his daughter. Their continuous battles on and off the set led George Minter to welcome the opportunity of writing Kitty out of the script and, in fact, she was barred from coming to the set during the shooting of *Mother Riley Meets the Vampire.*

Both Arthur and Kitty drank heavily and, in fact, the Lugosi film became Lucan's final screen appearance. Two years later, during a stage appearance in Yorkshire, he collapsed with a severe hemorrhage and died in his dressing room without regaining consciousness. Kitty unsuccessfully tried to continue her career with other partners. She died ten years later in 1964 and their son died in 1975, ending the last link of Mother Riley's chain. In Hull's Eastern Cemetery where loyal fans of Lucan still come to place flowers on his grave, the inscription reads "Arthur Lucan, better known to millions of children as Old Mother Riley."

Arthur Lucan had the habit, when he was filming, of always putting on his costume at home and arriving at the studios in full make-up. Likewise, at the end of the day's shooting, he

Dracula dines with his daughter. Bela Lugosi shares a bite with Gloria Holden, star of Universal's Dracula's Daughter. "I never drink... wine."

would depart in his chauffeured limousine without removing the make-up or costume until he arrived at home. Thus very few people were familiar with his real-life persona and he could generally appear in public in his free time without being recognized and approached by his fans.

On the first day of shooting of *Mother Riley Meets the Vampire*, I accompanied Bela to the studio to meet the cast and crew. Bela, always the optimist, looked forward to making his first film in England since *Dark Eyes of London*. Having read the script, he was quick to recognize its resemblance to *Abbott and Costello Meet Frankenstein* in which he had scored a great personal success. He would model his performance on his appearance as Dracula in that film. He knew nothing of Arthur Lucan or Mother Riley except what was in the script which told the story of an old cleaning lady who becomes a prisoner in the house of a "mad scientist" and wreaks havoc wherever she goes. Since the closing of the *Dracula* play, events had moved so quickly that he had no time to concern himself with anything else.

Bela immediately won the affection of George Minter and the entire crew with his old-world courtesy, his enthusiasm, and his happiness at the opportunity to work with them. He was determined to give it his best shot as he had always done throughout his career. Most of the crew had previously worked with Arthur Lucan and looked forward to witnessing the first meeting of Old Mother Riley and Count Dracula! Bela rose to the occasion, embraced Lucan warmly as if he were a grand lady, and treated him with all the charm that he could muster. Later, he admitted to me that he hardly understood Lucan's Lancashire accent and had begun to wonder whether Mother Riley was really a man in drag or a woman.

During the ensuing weeks, the relationship unfortunately soured because of the recurring problem in Bela's life which I had witnessed in his encounter with Milton Berle. Lucan was used to ad-libbing much of his role when he played Mother Riley and coming up with bits of comedic physical action on the spur of the moment. Bela was used to working with a prepared script and, whenever possible, rehearsals before shooting started. In his scenes with Mother Riley, he never knew what Lucan might do next and suffered a great deal of physical discomfort at the other man's expense. Nevertheless, he gave a superb performance and, especially in the scenes where he was not upstaged by Lucan, he had all the power of his best Hollywood films. Cast and crew silently applauded him on many occasions and even Lucan learned to admire and respect him although it did not alter his comic capers.

Immediately after the filming was over, and without waiting to see a rough-cut of the picture, Bela and Lillian returned to America, gave up their residence in New York, and moved back to Hollywood. Unfortunately, I never saw him again but Alex, who had meanwhile left New York to start on his career as a Hollywood producer, was there to renew their friendship and stayed with him until his tragic death.

George Minter released *Mother Riley Meets the Vampire* in England towards the end of 1952. It enjoyed only a moderate success because the public had become tired of the character. Bela's fans resented seeing him ridiculed and preferred the reissues of his Hollywood successes. I received the finished film as *Vampire Over London* but found that the Lugosi name was not sufficient to overcome the handicap of Arthur Lucan whom nobody knew and most Americans could not understand. It was impossible to find a theatrical distributor. Alex had the ingenious idea to write a new story around Bela's scenes, eliminate as much of Mother Riley from the film as possible, and make a new film with additional shooting by Lugosi in Hollywood; but the necessary finance could not be raised.

Eventually, we sold the film to Jack Harris, an independent producer/distributor who made the original film of *The Blob* with Steve McQueen. Jack tried to release the film as *Carry On Vampire* to cash in on the great success of the *Carry On* series of British comedies produced by Nat Cohen, but Nat's company obtained an injunction against the use of his title. Harris then changed it to *My Son The Vampire* which was quite meaningless and the film never had a proper theatrical release. It now plays from time to time on late-night cable television and is available on home video under one or another of its titles.

My experience of working with Bela Lugosi was relatively short—it was not much more than three years from our initial meeting to the last time I saw him—but it had a profound effect on my ambitions to become my own producer of horror films. I learned never again to set up a production without being in control of the financing as well as the creative side, and never again to hire an actor and then leave him to his own devices.

About four years later, Boris Karloff gave me a unique opportunity when he brought a story called *Stranglehold* to my attention and offered to star in it if I could set up the financing and the production of the film in England. In the interim, I had learned a great deal more about production by making seven action pictures in England as co-productions with established independent companies, and bringing to them such Hollywood players as Zachary Scott, Pat O'Brien, Wayne Morris, Rod Cameron, and Richard Denning. Alex, who had meanwhile become a successful producer at American International Pictures, gave me invaluable assistance and the benefit of his experiences in working with Sam Arkoff, Jim Nicholson, and Roger Corman, but I learned the most important lessons from Bela Lugosi—to approach each new project with great enthusiasm and, no matter how it developed, to give it my "all" and treat it with the same respect as any other project that might have seemed more important.

Bela once said to me, "When you sign on the dotted line, it becomes the most important project of your life." He was, of course, referring to himself as an actor but it most certainly holds true also for a producer.

Many falsehoods and much malicious gossip have been written about Bela Lugosi in the years since his death. He has been accused of having been unfriendly and reclusive towards his fellow actors during the making of his films. It resulted from his unfamiliarity with the English language at the start of his Hollywood career and his innate shyness when confronted with situations that he could not understand. His so-called drug addiction has been totally misrepresented, perhaps partly due to his own fault when he publicly announced it in his desperate need for financial assistance. Bela suffered from ill-health all his life and from pains which were sometimes so severe that doctors prescribed morphine long before its addictive nature was established. Lillian had been a registered nurse and was by his side when he needed it because the pain had become unbearable.

His drinking habits have also been grossly exaggerated. Certainly he was fond of alcohol and sometimes he took too much but he never allowed it to interfere with his work. He was capable of consuming huge amounts of whiskey and beer before a performance but the moment he stepped out on to a stage or in front of a camera, he was in complete command of himself, the sign of the true professional. He was an aristocrat by nature. His old-world charm and courtesy, his extraordinary sense of humor when he was in a happy mood, and his warmth and generosity towards everyone with whom he came in contact were lifelong attributes and he never became cheap or coarse. He would no more use the language attributed to him in Martin Landau's portrayal in Tim Burton's *Ed Wood* than he would physically abuse another person. He loved his family, his home, and his friends. Alex and I spent many happy and memorable evenings in his company. Like many other accomplished artists, however, he could be intolerant and become difficult when he was forced to be with people who he felt did not know their jobs or were jealous of his success.

Millions of young people have unfortunately been given a totally false impression of what Bela Lugosi was all about, due to the insensitivity with which he was portrayed in *Ed Wood*, an otherwise very entertaining film about the dark side of Hollywood independent filmmaking fifty years ago.

Moreover, certain writers have recently begun to take a revisionist approach when describing his career and his films, even going so far as to downgrade his performance in the original *Dracula* in favor of Christopher Lee's stereotyped interpretation.

Lastly, it's time to set the record straight about the relationship between Bela Lugosi and Boris Karloff. It has become common knowledge that, after the success of *Dracula*, Bela was offered the Monster role in *Frankenstein* which he declined to accept. No one would deny that it was arguably his greatest career mistake. Nevertheless, he could hardly be blamed for James Whale's choice of Boris Karloff to replace him, and he was too intelligent not to realize that it was really his own fault. When Universal co-starred Lugosi and Karloff in several great horror films, they enjoyed a good relationship, even if they did not become personal friends because their private interests were so different. When Bela's fortunes declined while those of Boris prospered, Bela naturally envied the other man's success but his only real resentment was towards Universal who, he rightfully felt, did not make the same efforts on his behalf as they were making for Karloff. The Laemmles shamelessly forced Bela into increasingly inferior roles at less money than they dared to offer Boris and I sometimes wondered if this was their way of "punishing" Bela for rejecting *Frankenstein* although it makes no sense since the fortunes they earned from *Frankenstein* and its sequels far outstripped their returns on *Dracula*..

Time has rendered the motives unimportant. Today, Bela Lugosi is as great and important a star in the Hollywood history of horror films as Boris Karloff, and—before them—the great Lon Chaney. Every other actor who has since followed in their footsteps knows that these three giants made it all possible.

Bela Lugosi could play comedy very well, if only by capitalizing on his imperious visage, and not necessarily by relying on audiences' memory of his turns as the master vampire. Bela's comedy roles are usually given short shrift in his filmographies, but they do deserve recognition.

Bela Lugosi Meets a Brooklyn Gorilla (1952)

by David H. Smith

CREDITS: Director: William Beaudine; Assistant Director: Glenn Cook; Assistant to Producer: Tony Roberts; Art Director: James Sullivan; Set Decorator: Edward Boyle; Dialogue Director: "Ukie" Sherin; Men's Wardrobe: Wesley B. Jeffries; Women's Wardrobe: Esther Krebs; Hairdresser: Ann Locker; Make-up: Glen Alden; Script Supervisor: Helen McCaffrey; Director of Choreography: Lee Scott; Sound: Dean Thomas; Director of Photography: Charles Van Enger, A.S.C.; Editorial Supervisor: Philip Cahn, A.C.E.; Music: Richard P. Hazard; Songs '*Deed I Do* by Walter Hirsch and Fred Rose, *Too Soon* by Nick Therry; Screen Play: Tim Ryan; Additional Dialogue: "Ukie" Sherin and Edward G Seward; Associate Producer: Herman Cohen; Producer: Maurice Duke; Jack Broder Productions; a Realart release, 74 minutes

CAST: Bela Lugosi, introducing Duke Mitchell and Sammy Petrillo with Charlita, Muriel Landers, Al Kikume, Mickey Simpson, Milton Newberger, Martin Garralaga, and Ramona, the chimp

"This could have happened once, and we missed it, lost it forever "

The above lines, from *Youth and Art* by Robert Browning, are an apt summation of Bela Lugosi's 1950s' films, a sorry mishmash of bizarre exploitation and dated melodrama that left a sour coda on the actor's *oeuvre* of work. The years weighing down on him, infirm, disheartened by the collapse of his fourth and longest marriage, "typecast into a professional crypt," as avowed by David J. Skal's *The Monster Show*, and shunted aside by the Hollywood establishment, Lugosi died just before his earlier, classic work was released to television and a wholly new, more fervent generation of fans would have been at his beck and call.

It would seem, until the very end, he never quit hoping. On his return from England in 1952, Bela Lugosi was captured for the ages by Jack Magadan and his *Ship's Reporter* cameras for a brief but telling interview, not only promoting the just completed *Vampire Over London,* but also on the actor's aspirations:

Magadan: "... You've made many other pictures of this kind—vampire pictures and mystery pictures and things of that sort, but at the same time I know you are always yearning, as all actors are, to do a different type of stage vehicle. What would you like to do? The romantic, the..."

Lugosi: "No, I would prefer to play a comedy."

Even then, in the decided twilight of his life and career, Lugosi still wanted to flex his acting muscles. His heyday as a leading man was years behind him, and even the occasional character parts thrown him by the major studios had disappeared. Instead of the career resurgence to be expected from his critically acclaimed second go-around as Count Dracula in *Abbott and Costello Meet Frankenstein* (1948), the Hungarian-born actor was again reduced to "singing for his supper," as it were—trodding the boards as the vampiric nobleman, rather than co-starring

Bela Lugosi appeared with Boris Karloff, Peter Lorre, and Kay Kyser in the musical/horror/comedy *You'll Find Out.* Lugosi played a phony swami.

in, much less headlining, new Hollywood productions.

To a degree, the sentiment he expressed to Magadan was fulfilled by *Bela Lugosi Meets A Brooklyn Gorilla.* Unfortunately, the humor was left to a pair of novices, and Lugosi, as neatly summarized in John Cocchi's *Second Feature,* "[did] his standard mad scientist in the jungle." Again, as with nearly every producer, screenwriter, and director in the previous two decades, Bela's ability to perform comedy was short-sightedly disregarded in favor of simply exploiting his popular image for the "bogeyman" effect it supposedly conjured for the audience.

Alex Gordon, longtime friend and confidant of Lugosi, saw the error of Tinseltown's ways as well. "I don't think Hollywood ever really realized his full potential," he said in 1983's *Bela Lugosi: The Forgotten King*. "I think that, given a chance, he might have surprised Hollywood producers and audiences."

The fact of the matter is Lugosi could play comedy very well, if only by capitalizing on his imperious visage, and not necessarily by relying on audiences' memory of his turns as the master vampire. Bela's comedy roles are usually given short shrift in his filmographies, but they do deserve recognition.

For example, within months of *Dracula*'s 1931 release, he was alongside wide-mouthed comedian Joe E. Brown for a humorous turn in First National's *Broadminded* (also 1931). Playing Pancho, a magisterial South American, Bela's ire at the comedian makes the otherwise lowbrow effort a treasure, particularly the scene where Brown's fountain pen ruins Lugosi's dessert at a roadside diner. "Look what you have done to my strawberry shortcake!" he bellows with that infamous enunciation, justifiably infuriated, fearsome and intimidating despite the distaff curl of his sideburns.

In *The Gorilla* Lugosi once again starred with an ape as well as Marx Brothers wannabes, The Ritz Brothers. Lugosi portrayed the role of a mysterious butler.

However, in the ensuing years, when cast in a comedy film, Bela was reined in, painfully strait-laced amidst his co-stars' banter and pratfalls. In *International House* (1933), *Ninotchka* (1939), and *You'll Find Out* (1940) his appearances, while earning him good billing in the credits (seventh, third, and fifth), were little more than cameos, already relegated to being typecast as indignant, grousing, or mystical authority figures.

By the time of second cycle of American horror movies, commencing with *Son of Frankenstein* (1939), Lugosi's work in "A" films would be only character parts and in red herring roles. Even with so little to work with, however, his appearances often stole the shows, even in the several beguiling "haunted house" comedies he would abide for the major studios in the years following.

For 20th Century-Fox's *The Gorilla* (1939), he assumed the role of Peters, the shifty-eyed butler of Walter Stevens (Lionel Atwill), though few audiences took note that it was Lugosi that saved the day armed with a pistol and climbing through a window to prevail over the villain; again as a red herring butler, in Paramount's *One Body Too Many* (1944), he afforded some smiles as Merkle, foisting suspiciously bubbling tea on the cliched heirs gathered for a reading of a will in an old mansion.

To boost the prominence of former vaudevillians Alan Carney and Wally Brown, Lugosi went to RKO to act as a foil for a couple of that comedy team's efforts: in *Zombies on Broadway* (1945), Bela's Professor Renault was coincident with any of his Monogram or PRC mad scientist roles; lastly, in *Genius At Work* (1946), he looked tired and somewhat abashed as

Stone, the manservant of Latimer Marsh (Lionel Atwill), alias "The Cobra."

In Universal's *The Black Cat* (1941), his bit as Eduardo Vedos, the disheveled groundsman, earned him fourth billing, but as per the norm by then, his only notable scenes were straightforward and taciturn: bundling up cats to get them out of a thunderstorm (to the abstruse amusement of the authors of *Universal Horrors*), exhorting his innocence of murders committed to Myrna Hartley (Gladys Cooper), and, initially, measurably approaching a gate with a *de rigueur* close-up of his eyes, vis-a-vis *Dracula* and *White Zombie* (1932), which allowed for a segue to Hubert "Gill" Smith's (Broderick Crawford) car headlights.

With the brace of Monogram East Side Kids/Bowery Boys features *Spooks Run Wild* (1941) and *Ghosts On The Loose* (1943), his comic abilities were curtailed in favor of straight turns as mysterious magician and Axis abetter respectively; in the former, however, he did wildly overplay fear of the boys, dressed in a spooky costume, so much it becomes unintentionally funny.

Abbott and Costello Meet Frankenstein (1948), as stated, should have opened studio heads' eyes to his facility for comedy, which had high priority for filmmakers given the wane of Gothic horror films after the Second World War ended. But, as author Scott Nance wrote in *Bloodsuckers: Vampires on the Screen,* Lugosi was forgotten about, reduced to "[finding] work in cheap movies better left forgotten: *Bride of the Monster* (1955), *Bela Lugosi Meets A Brooklyn Gorilla* (1952), and the transvestite film, *Glen or Glenda* (1953)."

Following the lighthearted finale to the Universal monsters' careers, Bela went without film work for several years, and was able to return before the cameras, thanks to the largess of Richard Gordon, to earn enough money to book passage back to America following a British stage tour of *Dracula.*

In Renown Pictures' *Vampire Over London* (1952), Bela was finally able to show his flair for comedy again. Capitalizing on the dapper Dracula persona, he played Von Housen, a mad scientist who fancied himself a vampire, with a penchant for sleeping in a coffin. As the "vampire" nimbly rises from a snore-filled slumber, Hitchcock (Ian Wilson), his majordomo, expresses bafflement at the formal array:

"I'm curious to know why you always sleep in your evening clothes," Hitchcock says.

Von Housen raises an eyebrow. "Really?"

"Yes, Master," the servant insists.

Von Housen smiles devilishly. "Heh-heh-heh. I was buried in them."

Later in the film, Von Housen rallies a confederate with his plans for world conquest, explaining the function of a control panel with dials to destroy squadrons of airplanes, switches to sink battleships, and the control for an army of 50,000 robots.

"Fifty thousand?" the conspirator asks, amazed.

"Yes," Von Housen boasts with pride.

"And how many have you built so far?"

Von Housen is subdued, answering, "Err... one."

Lugosi's embarrassed reply is priceless. Again, it is sad such self-deprecating performances went unnoticed by those in power or, worse yet, unseen until too late, as in this case, given its post-mortem 1964 stateside release, as *My Son The Vampire.*

But, just before his descent into Ed Wood's egregious triune of films, Bela had one last shot at the stardom that had slipped away from him and that he sought to regain. *Bela Lugosi Meets A Brooklyn Gorilla* is the closest to the mainstream Lugosi would approach in the final years of his life, his incidental and discomfiting cameo in *The Black Sleep* (1956) notwithstanding.

With Lugosi's career at this juncture thus in perspective, a more benign exegesis of *Bela Lugosi Meets A Brooklyn Gorilla* is not only possible, but, what's more, deserved.

Talent agent Maurice Duke had a new comedy team under his auspices, Mitchell and Petrillo, who were becoming quite successful in the California nightclub circuit, and for whom Duke saw greener pastures to be tilled with feature films. The pair's success, however, was not due to originality, but rather to the duo's overt resemblance to Dean Martin and Jerry Lewis, at the time the most successful movie team.

Domonick Mitchell, nicknamed "Duke" by his father's enthrallment of John Wayne's 1932 movie *Ride Him Cowboy,* was born in 1926. Blessed with a husky singing voice, he worked the clubs as a solo before being hooked up with the teenaged Sammy Petrillo to develop an act of songs and jokes. Although Mitchell alone did not particularly favor Dean Martin, alongside Petrillo's uncanny resemblance to Jerry Lewis, the exploitative possibilities were manifest.

Arriving at Jack Broder's Realart Productions, itself enjoying appreciable success by re-releasing the original Universal horror pictures to product-starved theater chains, Maurice Duke secured screen roles for his clients, playing themselves as entertainers waylaid by fate for an encounter with a mad scientist on a tropical island. Playing to Bela's vanity, with his name in the title itself, and incorporating an approximation of the hottest show business act going, what could have, and perhaps should have, been a steppingstone back to the limelight, would instead nail the coffin shut on Lugosi's legitimate movie career.

Filmed in nine days at General Services Studios in Hollywood for $50,000, *Bela Lugosi Meets A Brooklyn Gorilla* mined out every hoary cliche from the lode of golden genres it excavated: jungle adventure, romance, science fiction, and comedy. And, in almost every instance, it came up with pyrite.

Precious metaphors aside, with print ads extolling it to be "A horror film that will stiffen you with laughter!" and promulgating "Brooklyn chumps become island monkeys in jungle full of laffs!", *Bela Lugosi Meets A Brooklyn Gorilla* was released in September of 1952. The sonorous opening narration, read over a hodgepodge of animal stock footage of varying quality, sets the stage:

"This is the jungle—the vast wilderness of giant, lush foliage, of tropical birds and fierce animal life. The killer tiger... the cunning hyena... the deadly python that can crush a giant elk... the proud lion... a fierce lioness stalking a prey to feed her young... and the buzzards, the scavengers of the jungle, soaring lower, ever lower, eager to devour the dead or the dying. Kill or be killed—this is the law of the jungle." Inasmuch as "soaring" means to fly upward, and that no natural region on earth supports such diverse animal life, the movie is really no worse in comparison to, say, any of the Tarzan movies produced by Sol Lesser. Yet.

"And here," the narrator continues as the stock footage is replaced by a shot of the familiar studio lot jungle, all plastic plants with broad leaves, "what have we here? Who are these men? What can they possibly be doing in this cruel tropical wilderness?"

The camera reveals a pair of men with long hair and shaggy beards, wearing rumpled evening wear, seemingly unconscious on the ground. Some grass-skirted natives gather them up and carry them back to their village. Just as in the myriad Tarzan and other jungle films, everyone is Caucasian, the better not to run afoul of possible backlash from the racist divisions that still existed in the 1950s' theater industry. In fact, according to Bill Warren, one of the proposed titles for the film was *White Woman of the Lost Jungle.*

A gaudily-masked witch doctor (Milton Newberger), speaking a native language, urges the pair be killed, but a beautiful girl (Charlita), as coiffed and made-up as any movie jungle queen is wont to be, intercedes. She beseeches her father, Chief Rakos (Al Kikume), to spare them. He obliges, and his daughter Nona goes about shaving and cleaning them up, dressing them in tattered clothes at least more suitable to the climate.

Trying to discover their names, Nona reads a store label in their discarded clothes, deducing one must be named "Mervyn," one of several lame jokes in the screenplay that will be at odds with the characters' real knowledge of the outside world. The two awaken, and introduce themselves to the flawless English-speaking Nona as Duke Mitchell and Sammy Petrillo.

Nona tells them they are on the southern-most island of a Pacific chain; the island is called "Kola-Kola." Sammy remarks it sounds like a commercial for some bubble water. The girl tells them they were found in the jungle and carried to the village by her fellows. Sammy asks about the carrying charges. In both of these instances, and throughout the film, Sammy laughs boisterously at his own feeble jokes, to the indifference of whomever is listening.

Curious as to their situation, Duke explains to Nona how he and Sammy were en route to Guam to perform at the U.S. military base there, but fell out of the plane carrying them while hunting for a bathroom. Luckily wearing parachutes, the pair landed on the island and survived for weeks on wild berries and raw fish.

Though this hardly explains their comatose state when found, it rationalizes their shabby appearance, though it seems unlikely the two of them could have gone for any length of time without being discovered or chancing upon the natives themselves.

Nona promises to help them, and introduces them to her father, who speaks pidgin English. The chief throws a luau to commemorate their recovery. Throughout, Sammy never stops complaining, bickering with the witch doctor in native blather, grumbling about their sparse accommodations, the lack of chairs at the party in their honor, and the fact that he, unlike Duke, doesn't have a pretty girl with which to talk.

Taking a hint, Nona introduces her grossly overweight younger sister Salome (Muriel Landers), who, inevitably in love at first sight, tries to force Sammy to eat more. Sammy rudely begs off, joining the native dancers in their performance. At its conclusion, Sammy launches into his and Duke's nightclub routine.

Sammy regales the attentive natives with several totally unfunny jokes, each met with stony silence, until the good-natured Nona translates one for her father. Though he was shown to have a keen recognition of English earlier, not until his daughter fills him in does he laugh uproariously, with all the natives joining in.

Then Duke takes a cue, instructing three native tom-tom players on the rhythm he wants. A full orchestra kicks in from somewhere, and the singer performs '*Deed I Do,* which *Keep Watching The Skies!'* Bill Warren guessed was Mitchell's signature song. In actuality, the song was written in 1926 and had, by this time, already been recorded by many performers and orchestras, including Tommy Dorsey. It was first popularized by Ben Bernie and his orchestra; a cover record was made by Ruth Etting; it was a big hit for Lena Horne as recently as 1948. The composers, Walter Hirsch and Fred Rose, were quite prolific, with many more songs to their credit.

Mitchell and Petrillo are, of course, a success with the entertainment and media-starved natives. Later, Duke goes for a walk with the enamored Nona and has a conversation that sets the stage for the rest of the movie, and, at the same time, is at odds with what has already been shown. Duke compliments her on the beauty of the island and on the way the moon shines downs on it.

"Yes, we have everything here to make us happy, " Nona enthuses. "A calm, peaceful atmosphere. No moving streetcars or automobiles. No rushing around, in and out of subways. No smoky factories smudging up the air we breathe."

Duke is nonplused. "How come you know about these things? And how come you talk like a college girl?"

"Perhaps it's because I went to college."

"Come again?" Duke asks, puzzled.

"I was sent to your country to be educated," Nona answers. "Someday I will be queen of this island, and my people would like their queen to be smart."

Of course, this would infer her studies did not include the meaning of clothing labels, much less major department stores. Nona invites Duke to stay, but the steadfast and somewhat thick-headed singer frets about the servicemen needing to be entertained on Guam. With a ship due only every two months, Nona remarks that Dr. Zabor, "the only white man on the island [sic]," may be able to help.

"So how come we never see him? Where is he?" Duke inquires.

"He lives on the other side of the island," Nona explains. "He's a scientist, working on an experiment in evolution. He's very clever, and we are in the midst of a series of—"

Duke interrupts. "Did you say we?'"

"Yes," the girl answers unaffectedly. "You see, he hired me as his assistant."

With Nona's promise to escort Sammy and him to see the doctor the next day, Duke walks her home, and they exchange a good-night kiss. There follows some more tomfoolery of Sammy trying to elude Salome, whom he calls "Salami," replete with more grainy stock footage of absurdly indigenous wildlife, climaxing with the gangling comedian impersonating the top of a factitiously-placed totem pole, to no avail.

The next day, traipsing through the jungles Sammy is afraid that Salome may be stalking him, but Nona reassures him that he has nothing to worry about, echoing the sentiments of the Transylvanian folk to Dwight Frye in *Dracula* (1931).

"None of my people venture very close to the castle. It is forbidden," Nona intones.

"Castle? What castle?" Duke asks.

"The castle where Dr. Zabor lives and works," the girl explains.

"Well, how come you go there and work?" her paramour wonders.

"I don't share all the beliefs of my ancestors."

There, just as incongruous to the island as the giraffes and such, squats a massive Balkan stone castle, origins unexplained. The trio knock, and Chula (Mickey Simpson), a burly native servant, admits them. Nona instructs the minion to announce her and her guests to Dr. Zabor.

Bela Lugosi is on screen for the first time here, working with chemicals in the lab. It is a tad unsettling now to see Lugosi as he was in 1952, out of the heavy makeup and hair dye that marked his vampire roles of the previous four years. He is much thinner, his hair a great deal grayer, his nose more aquiline than ever. Yet, the fire, the intensity is extant, the hypnotically expressive fingers unfaltering, even performing as they are meaningless manipulations of test-tubes and beakers.

At first perturbed at Chula's interruption, Zabor's eyes light up at the mention of the presence of two white men. What follows then is arguably the worst scene in the movie, as the doctor is introduced to the hapless pair.

"Dr. Zabor's going to help us get off [the island], isn't he?" Duke frets.

"Yes," Nona assures him. "Dr. Zabor's a very brilliant man."

"Brilliant man, huh?" Sammy interjects with his usual indelicacy. "Anybody who would live in a creep joint like this must be a moronic idiot."

Dr. Zabor enters the room. "Good morning. I'm Dr. Zabor. Welcome to my... creep joint."

"Oh, gosh, I-I-I'm sorry, Mr. Idiot," Sammy sputters. "I didn't mean to call your creep joint a creep joint."

"Oh, think nothing of it," Zabor allows cordially.

As introductions are made, Duke thinks he recognizes Zabor from somewhere, though the doctor pleads ignorance.

Sammy calls his partner aside. "Hey, Dukey, come here. I think I know where you know this guy from."

"Where?" Duke asks.

"Ain't this the fella that goes around with the hands and the faces, biting people on the neck and wearing capes?" Sammy offers

Duke understandably admonishes his teammate, though Sammy is unconvinced. The crooner decides to settle the matter by asking the doctor to make a face.

Zabor rears back, looking askance, his haughty features etched in perturbation. This is Lugosi at his most demeaned, lampooning his image as a screen bogeyman rather than embellishing it. As Richard Bojarski wrote in *The Films of Bela Lugosi,* "The scene is so clumsy that it comes off flat, unfunny, and is embarrassing to watch."

Sammy asks Zabor why he would go around frightening little children, but Duke intervenes with an apology, which Zabor accepts with a sinister chuckle. Now, even Duke is convinced.

Nona explains the entertainers' predicament and asks Zabor for his help. The doctor offers to do what he can, even going so far as to invite them to stay on at the castle as his guests, and to help themselves to anything in his wardrobe. At least a head taller than either Duke or Sammy, Zabor's latter overture seems particularly magnanimous if misguided. "No capes," Sammy insists to Chula as the brawny servant escorts them up the staircase.

Before departing, though, Zabor stops Sammy to examine his head and to compliment, "A most interesting cranium. Strange. But interesting." Sammy scampers away, mortified.

Zabor assures Nona after the Americans' exit he will help her new friends. "I would do anything for you in my power," he gushes.

Nona is embarrassed, and excuses herself to the laboratory. There she dons a white smock over her sarong and goes to work; Zabor enters after her.

"Why do you treat me so coldly, my dear?" the scientist queries. "You know I love you. I want you. Now then what is wrong? Why do you not accept my love?" For Lugosi, this scene hearkens back to Universal's *The Raven* (1935), wherein his Dr. Richard Vollin professed his love to Jean Thatcher (Irene Ware), although in that film there was a healthy dollop of egocentricity, rather than age, to repulse the heroine.

The native girl, fervidly working a mortar and pestle, the obvious sexual connotation no doubt unintended, demurs, "Please, Doctor, must we go over that again?"

"Yes, we must," Zabor answers passionately. It was the last time on film that Lugosi would play a love scene, which Michael Weldon's *Psychotronic Encyclopedia of Film* assented the actor handled "with aplomb."

When the freshly attired Duke and Sammy enter the lab, Zabor indulges their curiosity about his research in evolution. Naturally, Sammy isn't even clear on what evolution is, although science is pretty far removed from the script, calling a chimpanzee a monkey.

Explaining the principle, Zabor says, "Scientists have proven that all living things originated in a process of evolution. They also know that there is a growth force that tends to make genetic changes, physiologically and morphologically. Chimpanzees and gorillas are the highest members of the ape family, and are the ancestors of man. Darwin, in his provisional hypothesis, assumes that every living cell contains a gemmule which is a hypothetical granular [sic]. I have found the chemical formula that stimulates the growth force. Where nature takes years, I can, in a matter of hours, make a complete embryonic metamorphosis, both physiologically and morphologically. Do you understand?"

Aside from the wildly inaccurate theorems and the fabricated scientific terminology, this uninterrupted spiel by Lugosi at least equals his heartfelt speech to Professor Strowski (George Becwar) a few years later in *Bride of the Monster* (1955), so frequently commented on and complimented. And, for the ubiquitous and unforgiving Lugosi pronunciation critics, the actor stresses the fourth syllable of "metamorphosis." It is still a grand farewell to the patented 1930s and '40s' mad scientist vain-gloriousness known and loved.

Duke is still lost, but Sammy nods his comprehension, spouting off some equally inaccurate scientific gibberish. A caged chimp, named Ramona, unlocks her own cell door with encouragement, and comes out, taken with Sammy.

Another white man, Pepe Bordeaux (Martin Garralaga), comes in and is introduced as the representative of the law (whose?) on the island. With his small wireless outfit, he promises to try to raise help from a passing ship.

For the scene's finale, Ramona leads Sammy into her cage, locks it, and tosses the key out of reach. Ho ho.

That evening, Duke expresses his displeasure at being so far from Nona now that he and Sammy have taken up in the castle, so Nona promises to ask her father to invite all of them

Bela Lugosi portraying Pancho, a South American, is driven crazy by the annoying Joe E. Brown in First National's *Broadminded*.

to another luau. Meanwhile, Ramona gets out of her cage again and goes upstairs to the sleeping Sammy. The young man wakes up and takes Ramona back to the lab, inevitably getting locked in again. Duke checks on the sleeping pair, then bids good-night himself. Zabor sits in the front room, stewing about the turn of events, with moody lighting.

The next evening, Zabor and his houseguests are seated alongside Chief Rakos and his daughters for dinner back at the village. Though the native leader's facility with English is stilted, and what with Nona's remarks earlier about the taboo of the castle, it all seems so carelessly scripted.

"Chief is honored to have big doctor visit his humble abode," Rakos toasts. "And how goes the scientific work? Good, I hope."

Zabor is concentrating on the coquettish Nona and Duke at this point. "Eh? Oh, yes. Fine, fine. Everything is progressing satisfactorily." Stories from the set at this time insinuate Lugosi, eating mangoes, became so taken with the tropical fruit that he purposely and repeatedly flubbed his lines so as to necessitate more takes and more mangoes. This hardly seems in keeping with the professionalism he was known for in scores of other movies.

Duke and Nona sneak off for another jungle rendezvous, with the singer promising a big wedding for them back in the states. Nona worries her father will insist on the ceremony taking place on the island, and gives Duke an heirloom necklace as a sign of their engagement. She begins to hum a melody, which Duke picks up on after only a measure and sings *Too Soon* with the requisite orchestral backing.

That song is quite the opposite in notoriety of *'Deed I Do*, as its credited composer, Nick Therry, is not even mentioned in the ASCAP catalog. For treasurers of B-movie minutiae, however, the musical stars of *Frankenstein's Daughter* (1959), The Page Cavanaugh Trio, did score a minor hit record of a song with the same title on the Encore label, but it is probably a different composition entirely.

Back at the village, Dr. Zabor gives thanks for the meal and dons a black cape and hat for the walk back to the castle. Joined by Chula, who has been spying on Duke and Nona, he asks for a rundown on the couple's evening. When the muscular henchman reveals the plans for marriage and of the necklace gift, Zabor goes to the lab immediately.

There, the doctor finishes mixing a potion, then bids Chula to open Ramona's cage and bring the animal out. Zabor injects her with his concoction, then has the native return the chimp to her cage in a prone position.

Thinking this is merely another step in his master's plan to accelerate evolution, Chula proposes, "She will be big like gorilla."

Zabor shakes his head. "No. I think not."

Ramona, contrary to the medico's assertions to Sammy and Duke that results take hours, immediately goes through a lap dissolve and turns into a capuchin monkey.

"Master," Chula points out, "she is back to little monkey. What is wrong?"

"Nothing is wrong, Chula," Zabor smiles. "Nothing. Now I can change a man into a gorilla." His eyes sparkle with the gleam of madness inherent in all movie mad scientists. "Man into a gorilla..."

Chula fears that he is next to be experimented on, but Zabor allays his fear with a chuckle. "No, Chula. Not you."

When Nona arrives the next morning, Zabor tells her he has a surprise for her in the lab. Much to the doctor's chagrin, however, Ramona has reverted back to a chimpanzee, leaving a befuddled Nona to wonder why the doctor bemoans something being "not strong enough to hold."

Elsewhere, to assuage Sammy's impatience, Duke promises to hunt down Pepe Bordeaux and to see if the man has had any luck hailing rescue. Nona insists to her lover he will need a guide to find the place, but, as she is caught up in her work, tells him to go to the village for help from her father.

Duke is ambushed by Chula while on his way through the jungle, leaving the precious necklace behind as convenient evidence. Zabor dismisses Nona for the day so that Chula can bring the unconscious singer into the lab. He injects his hapless patient with a serum, then has Chula strip Duke and put him in Ramona's cage.

Now free for the day, Nona is joined by Sammy to catch up with Duke, finding the necklace en route to the village, but dismissing it as due to carelessness. The two are mortified when, talking with Salome, they learn Duke never arrived; Nona and Sammy rush back to the castle.

Duke metamorphoses into a gorilla, played by Steve Calvert. The stunt man had bought the familiar 85-pound costume from former "Three Mesquiteer" and *Undersea Kingdom* hero (and future *It! The Terror From Beyond Space*) Ray "Crash" Corrigan a few years earlier, immediately finding work in Columbia's *Jungle Jim* (1949) and in Realart's *Bride of the Gorilla* (1951). Calvert played a long scene in the suit flirting with Bob Hope in *The Road To Bali* (1953), coincidentally co-starring Martin and Lewis themselves. It also turned up in Allied Artists' *The Bowery Boys Meet the Monsters* (1954), wherein Calvert did double duty as a robot as well.

Enraged and snarling, Duke claws ineffectually for Zabor through the bars, amusing the doctor. "Now," he ponders, "let's see if my lovely Nona will prefer you to me."

When Nona and Sammy arrive, they are astonished at the doctor's results, thinking the gorilla is Ramona, progressed by the experiment.

"Do you intend to advance her one more step?" Nona asks. Zabor shakes his head. "To the human level? Nooo."

"I don't blame you, Doc," Sammy says. "This is the stupidest looking gorilla I ever saw." Apparently retaining his human intelligence, "Duke" roars his outrage at that.

Feigning ignorance, Zabor wonders if Duke has any news from Pepe. Nona tells him of her boyfriend's disappearance and says they should return to the village for any developments. Fair-weather friend Sammy begs off, complaining of being tired, so Zabor escorts Nona back to her home.

Alone with Sammy, "Duke" plays a game of charades to tell his friend of his predicament. It isn't until Ramona causes a commotion in the anteroom, and "Duke" manages to croak the chorus of *'Deed I Do*, that Sammy figures it out, and unlocks the cage.

The two decide to go upstairs to deal with it all, taking time out to bop Chula unconscious as the native is surreptitiously helping himself to the doctor's brandy. Meantime, Zabor, resplendent in his jodhpurs and pith helmet, and Nona find no new developments back at the village, giving the doctor a chance to solace the frightened girl. As expected, she cringes at his touch.

Sammy and "Duke," pacing back and forth in their bedroom, are at a loss. Sammy envisions a great singing gorilla act, and is oblivious when an actual wild gorilla climbs in the window, scaring the transmogrified "Duke" out the door.

Chula regains consciousness and runs to tell Zabor, who is still trying, without success, to console Nona. Wondering about Chula's whispered tale, Nona asks if there is news of Duke.

"No, my dear," Zabor relates. "Ramona is, ah, loose. She's dangerous! If she comes here, you have my permission to shoot her!"

Realizing he's in over his head, Sammy decides to take his friend down to the native village for help. He tries to make the gorilla put on some clothes, but, after *'Deed I Do* is croaked again and the expected double takes, finally realizes a real ape has taken the place of "Duke." He barrels out the door, "Duke" in tow, the real gorilla in hot pursuit.

Sammy and "Duke" bowl over Zabor and Chula just as the latter pair are coming through the front door, though it is obvious a double for Lugosi was used to take the tumble. Given the actor's frailty it is understandable; however, it is disconcerting that it is just as obvious the real Bela is manhandled to his feet by Chula, only to be knocked over again by the pursuing "real" gorilla.

Said gorilla gives up her(?) amorous pursuit of "Duke" when Zabor and Chula are spotted with rifles. Sammy and "Duke" get to the village, desperately explaining what has transpired. Nona is distraught, and her father vows they will find Zabor and that he will suffer for his evil machinations.

"You won't have to find me," Zabor says, brandishing his gun. Eying Nona and "Duke," he smiles. "A very touching scene, my dear. Step aside, my dear."

Raising his rifle to fire, Sammy leaps in front of his friend and takes the bullet for him. Reportedly, at a screening of *Bela Lugosi Meets A Brooklyn Gorilla,* Jerry Lewis proclaimed, "Thank God!"

But, in a denouement almost as old as motion picture history, Sammy awakens in his dressing room at a dinner club in Passaic, New Jersey to find it had all been a dream. He and Duke greet "Nona" in the hall leading to the stage, as she exits from her act with "Chief Rakos" in a gorilla suit (one wonders the content of said act); Sammy bumps into "Pepe" carrying a tray of dishes, then runs afoul of the hulking "Chula," the stage manager.

"What kept you?" Duke asks, preparing to go onstage.

Sammy shakes his head. "Ah, Dukey, the most awful thing happened."

Suddenly, "Zabor" the maitre d' turns around, remonstrating, "And you had better get some laughs this time, or you'll be collecting unemployment insurance."

The dancing girls performing then end their act, one of whom, "Salome," greets a grateful Sammy with a kiss. He and Duke bound on stage, tell a joke, then launch into yet another chorus of *'Deed I Do* for a grand finale.

Bela Lugosi films were hardly critical favorites when first released, though camp appeal, nostalgia, and fans' reassessments usually find positive aspects to mention and discuss.

Bela Lugosi Meets A Brooklyn Gorilla, however, may be the most disliked movie the man ever starred in; even its original distributors were hard-pressed to find likable selling points, it would seem.

Boxoffice, the industry trade, heralded its release with, "This is a broadly played farce which burlesques jungle horror pictures to a fare-thee-well. Bela Lugosi, who plays his formula evil scientist role straight throughout, will have marquee value for the horror devotees... neighborhood and small-town audiences will get some laughs."

So unsure of its marketability, even with the presumable appeal of Lugosi's name in the title, it was later sold to television as *The Boys From Brooklyn,* and, in England, it was known as *The Monster Meets the Gorilla.*

Variety, too, saw little to recommend, calling it a "mediocre horror-comedy," but went on to concede that "... thesping is routine. Lugosi is menacing, and Charlita lends some eye appeal as the saronged femme interest. Mitchell baritones [two songs] adequately... direction is okay as are camera and editing credits [sic]." Hardly a bona fide testimonial to be had, then.

Halliwell's Film Guide tagged it a "stupid farce which never rises to the occasion." And, in the years since its first release, critics' and fans' lambasting opinions have hardly wavered. Leonard Maltin labeled it "BOMB," sarcastically describing it as "One of the all-time greats... Proceed at your own risk." *Video Hound's Golden Movie Retriever* contended *Bela Lugosi Meets A Brooklyn Gorilla* is "worse than it sounds." *TV Guide* dismissed it as mere "jungle cliches."

Steven H. Scheuer, in *The Complete Guide to Videocassette Movies,* proclaimed that it "may be the worst film of Bela Lugosi's career... almost painfully stupid, [it] sent Lugosi spiraling downward into obscurity." *The Blockbuster Guide to Movies and Videos* called it "The absolute pits—and fascinating for it." Phil Hardy entered it into his *Encyclopedia of Science Fiction Films* as an "awful piece... neither funny, nor even unintentionally funny."

For his regrettably short essay on the movie in the first volume of *Keep Watching The Skies!,* Bill Warren seemed to want to wash his hands of it as quickly as possible, presumably so as not to draw undue attention to it. "Lugosi is totally wasted," he wrote, probably not intending any double entendre for the actor's drug addiction. "The role of a mad scientist hardly taxed him, and was pretty insulting. He's a tired, sad old man in this movie, which perfectly matches the tired, sad movie it is."

Similar sentiments were expressed by James Robert Parish and Michael R. Pitts in *The Great Science Fiction Pictures II*, wherein *Bela Lugosi Meets A Brooklyn Gorilla* was denigrated as a "strained, vapid sci-fi comedy" with "no legitimate laughs to be had and it is sad to witness the aging, obviously ill Lugosi in this low-end fare which does not even have the camp entertainment value of his 1940s' Monogram thrillers... Nothing works in [the film] ... a feature already submerged in a mire of vapidity."

John Stanley's opinion of the movie varies from one edition to the next of his ineluctable *Creature Features Movie Guides.* Once sanctioning it as "so awful it's enjoyable," he also has decried *Bela Lugosi Meets A Brooklyn Gorilla* as a "feeble excuse for a comedy-horror picture," unintentionally copping the film's "soaring" *non sequitur* by saying Lugosi, with my italics, "[is] at the *peak* of his *decline* as an actor."

Even catalogs selling the film on videocassette berate it. "This one's on just about everyone's 'ten worst of all time' list," the capsule summary reads for Sinister Cinema. "Bela looks pretty haggard."

Only confirmed Lugosi fans can ride to the movie's rescue, but there is hardly a cavalry. Richard Bojarski allowed that "Lugosi gave his usual good performance, adding the proper superiority and menace." The John Cocchi book mentioned earlier liked it, acclaiming, "With a title like that, you'd think it was funny, and you'd be right." And the exhaustive first volume of

Lugosi appeared with Duke Mitchell and Sammy Petrillo, a new comedy team modeled after Martin and Lewis, in *Bela Lugosi Meets a Brooklyn Gorilla.* Unfortunately, Mitchell and Petrillo had little of Martin and Lewis' talent.

Horror and Science Fiction Films: A Checklist, by Donald C. Willis, chose instead to comment on Petrillo's mannerisms ("irritating"), without singling out Bela or his role in it.

To executive producer Jack Broder's credit, the film looks as passable, production-wise, as any other low budget movie of the era, and he had the good sense to hire director William Beaudine (1892-1970) to keep things moving at a fast clip.

Despite *The Golden Turkey Awards* and the Medveds' nomination of him as worst director of all time, Beaudine directed quality product (Mary Pickford's 1926 *Sparrows*), as well as all those interchangeable East Side Kids/Bowery Boys films, and the scores of other, still lesser pictures he is (in)famous for.

Tom Weaver, in his superb *Poverty Row Horrors!,* was categorical, saying, "Horror fans in particular hold [Beaudine] in the lowest esteem... having dragged Bela Lugosi through the muck of Monogram's *The Ape Man* and [the] even-worse *Bela Lugosi Meets A Brooklyn Gorilla.*" Beaudine had also put Bela through his paces in *Ghosts On The Loose* (1943) and *Voodoo Man* (1944). John Stanley said Beaudine knew "just how far to go with such drivel," while Parish and Pitts shook their heads, stating, "[the director] was unable to breathe life into the proceedings."

The plot, like the direction, took no chances, and was far from original. The theme of apes being scientifically, as opposed to magically, turned into men, and vice versa, arguably first arose in literature with Gaston Leroux's story *Balaoo,* and in film with Gaumont's 1908 *The Doctor's Experiment.* This is not to ignore or impugn H.G. Wells' masterpiece *The Island of Dr.*

Moreau, but to narrow the scope of animal life transformed to apes alone.

Leroux's work saw adaptation to the screen in both direct and indirect manner, homonymously for the French in 1913, and, "updated and dressed up," according to *A Pictorial History of Horror Movies*' Denis Gifford, as Fox's *The Wizard* in 1927; movie buffs may recognize the same studio's *Dr. Renault's Secret* (1942) for the uncredited adaptation it is.

The comedic aspect of the idea, again as science and not as fantasy, was first explored by another famous movie duo, Laurel and Hardy, in their 1933 short *Dirty Work,* wherein the rotund Oliver fell into a vat of dubious youth serum and emerged a chimp.

Lugosi himself, no stranger to the plot line of men and apes changing roles, spoke and understood the language of gorillas as Dr. Mirakle in Universal's *Murders In The Rue Morgue* of 1932; in 1943, his Dr. James Brewster tried a transmuting serum on himself for unexplained reasons, but with expected consequences, in Monogram's *The Ape Man,* mentioned earlier.

The exploitation of Duke Mitchell and Sammy Petrillo as a cut-rate version of Martin and Lewis backfired, resulting in a lawsuit filed by the top comedy team's management. No second feature was ever made, and Mitchell and Petrillo amicably dissolved their partnership when the genuine article split in 1957, and the nightclubs wanted something new.

Graced with a breezy charm on his own, Mitchell went on to a singing and acting career with some success, recording several singles, performing on stage (at Dean Martin's own club, even), and landing film roles in *The Blackboard Jungle* (1955), *Crime In The Streets* (1956), *Baby Face Nelson* (1957), *Paradise Alley* (1961), and others. He eventually tried his hand at writing and directing as well, casting himself as the lead in *Massacre Mafia Style* (1974), retitled *The Executioner* for videocassette and overseas release. Friendly with Petrillo to the end, he died in December of 1981.

Petrillo, after exhausting his repertoire of Jerry Lewis impressions, faded further from the spotlight. In a genre vein, he turned up unbilled as one of the photographers of scarred model Doris Powell (Adele Lamont) as a favor for his friend, director Joseph Green, in *The Brain That Wouldn't Die* (1959/62). His only other starring role came for tawdry filmmaker Doris Wishman's *Keyholes Are For Peeping* (1972), as longhaired Stanley Bebble. Recently, it has been reported he has homes in New York and in Palm Beach, Florida, still glad to relate the saga of his brush with stardom, though with no love lost for the litigious Jerry Lewis himself.

Behind the scenes of *Bela Lugosi Meets A Brooklyn Gorilla,* however, was a young associate producer for whom the movie's crux would obviously have a lasting impression. Herman Cohen had recently become Jack Broder's assistant after a few years working for Columbia Pictures' distribution organization back in his native Detroit, then for its publicity department there in California. He left the elder man's auspices soon after *Bela Lugosi Meets A Brooklyn Gorilla*, and produced *Target Earth* (1954), coincidentally with Steve Calvert in costume as the alien robot(s).

Reeling from the financial losses of a later production, *Crime of Passion* (1957), Cohen recouped quickly with the much-scrutinized *I Was A Teenage Werewolf* (also 1957), another exercise in evolutionary retrogression. The theme of accelerated evolution formed the linchpin of Cohen's *Konga* (1961), as well. Other drive-in fare of Cohen's production includes *Horrors of the Black Museum* (1959) and the imported *Crocodile* (1979).

The opening credits reveal what may be one of the big reasons for the shortcomings of *Bela Lugosi Meets A Brooklyn Gorilla.* There is an acknowledgment for "additional dialogue," never a good sign, inferring that scenes had to be padded for length, or added in whole. This may be the reason Nona's and her father's characters seeming somewhat undefined, the language barriers, knowledge of the outside world, and superstitions coming and going as the scenes require.

But Bela Lugosi comes through it all virtually unscathed, as professional for "poverty row" producers as he was for the most polished of studio products. And, in a way, *Bela Lugosi Meets A Brooklyn Gorilla* is a sad final merging of the two most notorious personae Lugosi cultivated in Hollywood, that of romantic leading man and of monomaniacal mad scientist.

And it is nice, for one of the few times in his career, that Bela played a mad scientist that has a solid motivation for his scheming. Rather than for seeking blithe revenge against colleagues that scoffed at his ideas, sponsors that bilked him out of profits, or autocrats who persecuted him for indeterminate reasons, his Dr. Zabor has a concrete, romantic objective in mind when he injects Duke with that serum. The fact that the outcome will, in fact, validate his research is never broached, not even as an afterthought.

As Dr. Zabor, as with any role he ever assayed, Lugosi played him broadly enough to make you smile, but never broadly enough to make you laugh at him. He's at once a caricature, and yet strangely believable, and whenever he's on screen, he owns that movie.

Corresponding with Bela Lugosi, Jr., the actor's son shared with me his impressions of his father and of *Bela Lugosi Meets A Brooklyn Gorilla,* saying, "[the film] is just one example where my Dad's level of professionalism was never lessened by an otherwise poor film. He always took acting seriously and thus brought dignity to himself."

And appreciation from generations of movie audiences since, and the gratitude of film fans to come.

The author wants to extend special thanks to columnist Marvin Randolph and his "Musical Memories" for help in researching this chapter, belated appreciation to Drive-In Video and to Phil's Comic Shoppe. And to my wife Lynn, without whom, et cetera, et cetera.

And to Bela Lugosi, Jr., and his father...

Mother Riley Meets the Vampire

(1952)

by John Soister

CREDITS: Director: John Gilling; Producer: John Gilling (Gilling's receiving Producer's credit may have been arranged with Renown staffer George Minter, who is listed as Producer in other sources); Original Story and Screenplay: Val Valentine; Photography: Stan Pavey; Art Direction: Bernard Robinson; Editor: Len Trumm; Sound: W. H. Lindop; Assistant Director: Denis O'Dell; Make-up: Eric Carter; Hair Stylist: Betty Lee; Casting Director: Maude Spector; Camera Operator: Dudley Lovell; Associate Producer: Stanley Couzins; Musical Score composed and conducted by Lindo Southworth; Played by the Fernwood Studio Orchestra; Recorded by Western Electric; Released in the United States as *My Son, the Vampire;* Blue Chip Productions, 1963; Regional US release title: *The Vampire and the Robot;* no other data; Initial US release title: *Vampire Over London;* unreleased as such; Renown Productions, released July, 1952; UK running time: 74 minutes, US running time: 72 minutes; Photographed at Nettlefold Studios, Walton-on-Thames

CAST: Bela Lugosi...Professor Von Housen, Arthur Lucan...Mother Riley, Dora Bryan...Tilly, Richard Wattis...PC Freddie, Judith Furse...Freda, Philip Leaver...Anton, Maria Mercedes...Julia Loretti, Roderick Lovell...Douglas, David Hurst...Mugsy, Ian Wilson...Hitchcock, Hattie Jacques...Mrs. Jenks, Graham Moffatt...The Yokel, with Dandy Nichols, Arthur Brander, George Benson, Bill Shine, David Hannaford, Charles Lloyd-Pack, Cyril Smith, Peter Bathurst, Tom MacCauley

Growing up in Brooklyn, New York, in the fifties, I was blessed in a number of ways: cheap "Silver Age" comics (although that jump from 10 cents to 12 cents was a tad traumatic); baseball cards featuring Stan Musial, Gil Hodges, Richie Ashburn, Willie Mays, Mickey Mantle, and sundry other deities; *three* baseball teams in New York (actually, one was right *in* Brooklyn); and a local movie house whose management pandered profitably to the masses. With a bill that changed twice a week (and a special children's matinee on Saturdays), the Peerless provided us neighborhood kids (and non-discriminating adults) with an endless flow of oaters, war flicks, comedies, and monster movies. The Saturday kids' show offered some 4 hours of entertainment (3 features, 6 cartoons, and—in the early fifties—a serial chapter), all for 35 cents.

One of the talents that an habitual '50's moviegoer acquired was the ability to "weigh" a title. A regular seatwarmer could usually gauge the worth of a film by sitting through the trailer once. (True expertise was acknowledged when you could zero in on a movie just by a perusal of the poster. The opinions of individuals who had ascended to these heights were fervently sought; kids who didn't mind dropping their allowance on giant bugs didn't want a hosing if the monster turned out to be soapsuds or carpet.) Problems arose when deceptive marketing of schlock movies became more the rule than the exception. Although there were probably isolated instances of "title misrepresentation" in earlier decades, '50's science fiction/horror films really made an art out it.

Some years ago, I read Sam Arkoff smugly tell how James H. Nicholson and he had salvaged Roger Corman's stinker, *The Beast with a Million Eyes,* by poking some holes in a teapot. As an adult, I regarded Arkoff's corrective maneuvering as inventive and amusing; as a child, sitting through that film, I had been royally pissed-off. That great poster, that mind-blowing title: what happened? In lieu of the fiendish machinations of that awesomely depicted horror, the other kids and I witnessed a vague, dreary adult drama about alienation and failed potential. (Arkoff's book also revealed how Nicholson would come up with the title *first,* followed by the poster, then the film; the smarmy lawyer evidently regarded screwing disappointed kids out of quarters as his divine right.)

Famous Monsters of Filmland, Castle of Frankenstein, TV's *Shock Theatre*—they all descended on our young heads like manna from heaven. Whole worlds were opened to us; we discovered that, not only were there scads of wonderful movies lined up, all waiting to scare the drawers off us, but that **we were not alone!** I don't mean that we were being visited by extraterrestrials; there were other kids—and some adults, even—who found this stuff enchanting, too.

To a seven-year-old boy, Karloff's monster was as terrifying on a 12-inch Magnavox as he had been up on the big screen some 25 years before. Watching the famous old black-and-white stars (and those new, in-color guys: Peter Cushing and Christopher Lee) for the first time—at a time when you couldn't even dream of seeing their best work whenever you wanted (via video cassette)—was an experience both privileged and cherished. Hungering for more, I hunted constantly through the (comparatively primitive) *TV Guide*, scanned the movie ads in the newspapers, and kept one ear on WNEW where, among the latest by the King or Jerry Lee Lewis, an occasional spot would promise a couple of hours in Transylvania or on Metaluna.

My favorites—almost everyone's favorites, actually—were Boris and Lon and Claude and Bela. During the late fifties, the first three were still cranking them out; Bela had died, however, before he could delight in the impact his work was then having on zillions of kids. One by one, his most famous films (along with a liberal sprinkling of his less prestigious wheezers) were introduced by ghoulish TV host, Zacherley (nee Roland, from Philadelphia).

A couple of Bela's films, though, never seemed to turn up anywhere; Zach didn't have 'em (maybe Gaspard ate them), and they weren't among the many, many (inexpensive to rent, supremely profitable to show) second-runs screened at the Peerless. It took me years, but I finally tracked them down. One—*Mark of the Vampire*—had atmosphere up the wazoo, and moments to savor, but, ultimately, was something of a disappointment.

The other suffered from title misrepresentation, had zilch in terms of atmosphere, was a *substantial* disappointment, but, ultimately, had a couple of moments to savor: *Vampire Over London.*

Bela's first British film in over a decade fell into his lap like the aforementioned manna, due to the dedication and effort of producer Richard Gordon, who concocted the project in order to rescue the unfortunate actor and his wife from professional embarrassment.

As his fans have known for years, at various times during his career, Lugosi sat by his phone, waiting desperately for calls and job leads. For whatever reason—Karloff's assertion about language difficulties and accents, the studios' narrow-minded and total identification of actor with character, his own attitude and arrogance—whenever horror films hit the skids, the Hungarian hit the pavement. He might be offered a part in an occasional play, but it would seldom be a work of consequence, and never would it have an extended run.

The only recourse Bela had at times like these was to don his opera cloak and trod the boards as Dracula. The Vampire King was, at once, Bela's savior and his nemesis. The original film role had (briefly) posited him as top horror man at Universal, but had made his name and his image synonymous with the Voivode. It had brought him fame, but had denied him a chance at versatility. It had given him a much-needed job, but had ultimately rendered him unemployable.

Following the box-office success of *Abbott and Costello Meet Frankenstein,* Bela returned to his spot by the phone. This time around, the studio's indifference to the actor was not due to his being difficult or "aloof." During production, Lugosi had been on his best behavior; director Charles Barton would later aver that Bela, Lon Chaney, and Glenn Strange had been "dolls" to work with. There were no callbacks at UI because it was said that, with the advent of the science-fiction era, Lugosi's "type" of picture (wildly improbable plotlines, broadly drawn villainy, pre-chewed scenery) had become passé.

This, of course, was your basic crock: UI signed Karloff for two "Lugosi-type" gothic thrillers in 1951/52—*The Strange Door* (with one of the greatest ham-slicers of them all, Charles Laughton), and *The Black Castle.* Doubly frustrating to the Hungarian must have been the mining of the "Abbott and Costello Meet..." vein; although Bela and company had set the trend and had proven how much money was left in the old monsters, Universal-International had an out: the comedians had already met Dracula. Yet 1953 would find Boris Karloff cashing some healthy checks from *Abbott and Costello Meet Dr. Jekyll and Mr. Hyde* (a role with which the British actor had *never* been identified). More nettlesome was the fact that he needed play only one half of the horrific pair; unbilled stuntman Eddie Parker performed the gymnastics for which Boris got the credit. All this, however, paled beside the significance of the *first* A&C "sequel" to Bela's prototype. Despite the wealth of classic monster characters from which to draw, the studio powers had determined that Bud and Lou should first meet a genuine horror *personality:* "The Killer, Boris Karloff!"

1949 and 1950 had to be the nadir of the Lugosi career. No film work, nothing on radio: there were several baffling experiences with inveterate ad-libbers like Red Skelton and Milton Berle, but these served only to demonstrate both to Lugosi and to prospective producers that live TV was not the Hungarian's forte. At wit's end, Bela agreed to tour movie theaters in the New York tri-state area, and appear on-stage as the "live" portion of a stage/screen horror show. Film historian William K. Everson witnessed Lugosi's act, and revealed the elderly actor's humiliation in Richard Bojarski's required volume, *The Films of Bela Lugosi:*

"First the theatre would run one of his movies... one of the lesser ones... and then Lugosi, on stage, would do a horror act. This sketch hardly seemed to be written at all and merely consisted of Lugosi playing around in a laboratory with a giant gorilla and a manacled girl. The quality of the film had done nothing to give Lugosi an audience build-up. And in this era before the horror film had "come back," the kids in the audience knew nothing of the serious work Lugosi had done, so reception to the act was noisy and seldom respectful. Lugosi knew it was a wretched act and hated doing it, but at the time it was his only income."

A legitimate play did materialize, with a decent part for Bela: Fritz Rotter's mystery-comedy *The Devil Also Dreams.* With a schedule of dates throughout eastern Canada, and an eye toward a spot on Broadway, the play opened at His Majesty's Theatre in Montreal, on 22 August, 1950. However, despite excellent personal notices, Bela saw *The Devil Also Dreams* close within a short time. He was out of work again.

It was at this point that Richard Gordon intervened, and started the ball rolling for what promised to be a prestigious revival of Bela's signature play in Britain. After a series of postponements, *Dracula* opened at the Theatre Royal in Brighton in June, 1951. Due to some cost-cutting measures (not the least of which seems to have been the hiring of a less than capable supporting cast) and the lack of a comprehensive advertising scheme, *Dracula* folded, and Bela and Lillian found themselves both impecunious and stranded in England.

Hoping at least to raise enough money for the couple's steamship tickets back to the United States, Gordon made contact with Renown Pictures, producers of the Old Mother Riley series (itself on its last legs). Whereas the OMR films had had a bit of success over the years, their fame (and popularity) was virtually insular; few audiences outside British provincial influence could decipher the star's broad Lancashire accent, or appreciate his antics.

Ideally, the magic of the Lugosi name might provide the shot in the arm that the Old Mother Riley series needed; hadn't it helped provide the same tonic for Abbott and Costello's ills

Despite the nonsensical American release title, Mother Riley and Count Von Housen share no blood ties; sharing blood, however, is very much on the Count's mind.

a few years previously? Moreover, Bela's participation would mean that a name American actor headed the cast list: that couldn't hurt in terms of overseas sales. Whatever the argument Gordon used, Renown bit, and by July of 1952, British filmgoers were chuckling at what would turn out to be the last of a film series which had started some fifteen years before: *Mother Riley Meets the Vampire.*

The Mother Riley series, centered around personalities as alien to the average American as the Bowery Boys would be to the House of Lords, had begun big (all things being relative) with the eponymous *Old Mother Riley,* in 1937. British Music Hall performers Arthur Lucan and Kitty McShane (real-life husband and wife) found their niche and their fortune in portraying dotty charwoman/shopkeeper/matchseller/etc., Mother Riley, and her daughter, Kitty (respectively). As the Rileys, the couple enjoyed success for a decade and a half, carrying some 14 features.

Drawing on the British (theatrical) propensity for cross-dressing (found most recently in the Australian *The Adventures of Priscilla, Queen of the Desert,* most bizarrely in the Monty

Python output, and most venerably in any of Shakespearean England's dramatic works—no women onstage, please; we're British), Lucan adopted the unappealing but unmistakable "uniform" of a working-woman of the lower classes. McShane acted as a foil for the Mother Riley character, was the occasional love interest and, until the mid-1940s, was acceptable in her role as Riley's daughter. (Conspicuous by her absence in the Lugosi epic, McShane was nearly her husband's age. Film historian Leslie Halliwell, who found her credibility lacking in all facets of the role, referred to her as the "resistible Kitty McShane.")

While many of the series film titles (*OMR, Detective; OMR in Society; OMR's Ghosts*) indicated an imitation of Hollywood comedy themes, many others (*OMR Catches a Quisling; OMR, MP* [Member of Parliament]; *OMR, Headmistress*) reflected the British national spirit that played so well in the provinces (and which likewise severely restricted their popularity elsewhere). By 1952, the series had run the gamut of established comic topics and desperately needed an infusion of new themes, new faces, new blood. This last, of course, was Bela Lugosi's specialty, and through it, Renown hoped for at least an extension on Mother Riley's box-office life, if not for outright product immortality.

Sadly, it was not to be. At this stage in their respective careers, neither the Hungarian-American vampire nor the English comedian had enough *aqua vitae* to share, and the film did little but commemorate the virtual climax of two unique, but as of late unfashionable, individuals. Still, by virtue of Lugosi's still-commanding presence, *Mother Riley Meets the Vampire* (later titles in the series fluctuated between *Old Mother Riley* and *Mother Riley*) saw the series to its place in British cinematic history on an upnote.

A word on the picture's release in the United States. Recognizing that the title *Mother Riley Meets the Vampire* would cause American audiences to stay away in droves, Richard Gordon renamed it *Vampire Over London* for this side of the pond. Film in hand, he discovered for himself what his Hungarian client had known for several years: no studio was interested in funding, producing, or even releasing a Bela Lugosi movie. In spite of Gordon's best efforts, the film remained unwanted by the major distributors, and untenable for national release for the remainder of the decade.

In the early 1960's, independent mogul Jack (*The Blob*) Harris gave a heave at passing it off as part of the then-popular British "Carry On" comedy series; threatened litigation ended *that* nonsense. (In 1966, that series' 12th feature, *Carry On Screaming,* with its mad doctors, vampire women, mummys, Frankenstein-type monsters, Mr. Hyde look-alikes, and hip humor, made the Lucan/Lugosi effort seem tame and superfluous.)

A new idea! Seizing on comedian Allan Sherman's popularity (his albums of comically Jewish versions of standard folktunes—*My Son, the Folk Singer* being the first—were one of several current crazes), Harris unloaded the film onto unwary audiences as *My Son, the Vampire* (1963). Released through Blue Chip Productions, the movie's new title was a cypher and, despite Sherman's crooning under the credits (and his "explaining" about vampires in a special prologue), did little business.

Apparently, this was Harris' last shot at making back his investment, as there seems to be little evidence of any later regional or national campaign waged to get the movie into theaters. As *My Son, the Vampire,* the film is aired on TV (I remember seeing it as an occasional late-night offering back in the '70's), but it seems that virtually no one ever saw it under the original US release title, *Vampire Over London.*

A final note: In his coverage of the hemi-demi-semi-classic *The Blob* in his extraordinary *Keep Watching the Skies,* Bill Warren discusses the horror films being shown at the movie theatre attacked by the gelatinous monster: *Daughter of Horror* and *The Vampire and the Robot.* Warren's theory that the latter title (plastered over a poster from *Forbidden Planet*) was a regional release title for *Mother Riley Meets The Vampire* is undoubtedly correct.

More than one Lugosiphile stipulates that, during the mid to late '50s, some eager independent—it may or may not have been Harris—tried to farm the film (retitled *The Vampire and the Robot*) throughout the South via the states' rights distribution system. While the supporting evidence is little more than circumstantial, the theory does offer a solution as to why a (real) title was pasted onto a poster from a different (but also real) movie; apart from scant newspaper mention, many states' rights films were advertised only at the theaters themselves, with current titles (and those of coming attractions) being printed (or hand-written) either on the *backs* of old movie paper (usually window cards), or on blank posterboard.

There was no real poster for *The Vampire and the Robot* in *The Blob,* because there was no real poster for *The Vampire and the Robot* at all.

The 16mm print screened for this assessment was entitled *My Son, the Vampire* and, despite complete pre-print title footage in the splice-free original, there is no mention of either Arthur Lucan or Bela Lugosi in the main credits. The Charles Addams-ish title artwork cuts to footage of an ocean liner, over which the cast list is super-imposed. One can only assume that Lucan's name—of virtually no marquee value at all in this country—was dropped in an effort to further confuse the nature of the film, but the lack of Bela's name is disconcerting. If the Englishman and the Hungarian had had a shared billing in the original titles, a solo credit for Lugosi could have been shot over the new artwork. That there is no mention *at all* of Lugosi's name seems to indicate that Harris felt the expense was frivolous; in 1963, the absolute last name in big screen entertainment (save for Arthur Lucan) was Bela Lugosi. Why spend money on a credit insert for a star who, during his last years, couldn't draw flies?

As the ocean liner SS Fernwood (an inside joke: Fernwood Productions was the mother company of Renown Pictures) maneuvers to a London dockside, both the chauffeur and passenger of an ominous black touring car watch an attractive young woman walk down the gangway. The young woman, Julia Loretti (Maria Mercedes), is joined briefly by one of the ship's officers, Douglas (Roderick Lovell), with whom she has apparently struck up something of a romance. As he skedaddles back onto the ship, Julia is spirited into the touring car by the goateed Anton (Philip Leaver), who orders the car to speed away. The vigilant Douglas, however, gives chase, boards the car, and, to the accompaniment of a banging sound and the tweeting of birds, is obviously rendered senseless. (In a blatant attempt to punch up the comic elements of the film, a good assortment of cartoon noises, snores, wheezes, clanks, gibberish and the like are employed. The sound effects may not provide much help, but they certainly don't hurt.)

A remarkably well-informed newshawk cries enticingly of another "Vampire victim," and we cut to New Scotland Yard, where several higherups are attempting to piece the "Vampire" puzzle together. The contents of a telegram from "the police at Bosnick" serve to bring the audience up to date:

"The scientist calling himself the "Vampire" is a man named Von Housen, born in Bosnick in 1894. He is the descendant of Baron Von Housen, whom legend immortalized as a vampire. For reasons of his own, Von Housen claims to be an earthly reproduction of his notorious ancestor, linking his continued existence to the consumption of human blood."

Poohpoohing the vampire element, the chief of detectives nevertheless strikes home when he earmarks Von Housen as "a fanatical scientist with a stupid gang of men who have allowed themselves to be mesmerized by a legend." The chief, though, is loathe to point fingers at anyone, feeling it merely coincidental that five woman have disappeared since since Von Housen's arrival in the UK six weeks earlier. If Scotland Yard is dragging its collective heels, the media is not: a radio announcer kvetches that there is *still* no clue as to the whereabouts of Julia Loretti (the daughter of a famed Italian scientist), while admitting that she has only just arrived in the country(!)

At this point, luck has run out for the audience; amid the blaring of profoundly Irish music and a dose of the gibberish mentioned above, it is introduced to Old Mother Riley, seen (and heard) fighting with her rental agent. After a lengthy spate of insult humor, OMR breaks into a song (which seems to have the refrain, "I lift up my finger and say tweet-tweet, shushshush, now-now, come-come"), and then dances about her shop, joined not only by the rental agent, but by two female neighbors, who have been functioning as a sort of provincial Greek chorus. The entire scene is difficult to follow, not only due to the accents heard, but also to the strangeness of some of the terminology (the rental agent caps his insults of OMR by calling her "a silly old faggot," which does *not* have the same meaning as in American slang).

When the musical interlude runs out of petrol, a telegram arrives, announcing that OMR's Uncle Jeremiah has shuffled off and is sending all of his worldly fortune to his heiress, you-know-who. (The English probate procedure is apparently years ahead of the American system; news of the old toff's demise arrives on the same day as the crate containing his chattel.)

As dusk falls on the other side of London, activity picks up within a large and spooky manor house. both head-servant Freda (Judith Furse) and the diminutive Hitchcock (Ian Wilson) mobilize to their respective duties. Comic-opera snores pour forth from a casket reposing in the midst of a darkened bedroom, and Hitchcock's determined knocks produce the desired effect; with achingly familiar hand motions, the lid of the coffin is pushed open, and Professor Von Housen, the "Vampire," pulls himself erect. Looking (if anything) *better* in this introductory shot than he did in *Abbott and Costello Meet Frankenstein* (there are no evident traces of pancake make-up having been laid on with a trowel), Lugosi conjures up memories of his younger, haler, nosferatu in Columbia's *Return of the Vampire.*

The scene with the coffin allows fans one final look at the classic image of Bela Lugosi's vampire portrayal; the dialogue accompanying the scene gives those same fans an idea of how well their boy could handle a joke:

(Hitchcock) "Master, I'm curious to know why you always sleep in your evening clothes."

(Von Housen) "Really?" (excellent pause) "I was buried in them."

After a bit of silliness introducing Tilly, the housemaid (Dora Bryan, top-billed after Lucan and Lugosi in the original credits), and her dunderheaded boyfriend, PC Freddie (Richard Wattis), the film allows Bela another wonderful moment, as he explains his plans to henchman, Anton.

(Von Housen) "At last I, Von Housen, am ready to fulfill my destiny. I have created an apparatus by which the armies and machines of our enemies can be destroyed. A turn of the dial—so—and a thousand airplanes can be destroyed. Another turn, and 10 battleships can be blown up at sea."

(Anton) "Unbelievable." (points) "And what is this for?"

(Von Housen) "This is the robot control. I intend to build fifty thousand robots!"

(Anton) "Fifty thousand?!"

(Von Housen) "Yesss..."

(Anton) "But, how many have you built so far?"

(Von Housen) "Ah... errr... one."

No one could have topped Lugosi in his delivery of that shtick.

Freda enters on the heels of this great exchange, and produces a telegram: Von Housen's robot is enroute from his "secret factory" and is due to arrive in Liverpool that very day. (The British shipping concerns are every bit as efficient as the legal system.) Anton tips the comedy of errors, however, when he notes that Von Housen has chosen "a queer *nom de plume*—Doctor Riley."

As the slowest viewer by now had guessed, the crates' labels are switched, due to a group of sodden, card-playing sailors stowed away on the truck. OMR gets the robot (identified by the rental agent as a "wireless crystal set") and Von Housen, Uncle Jeremiah's worldly goods. A convenient note among the hardware allows the scientist and Anton to pinpoint OMR's house, and they begin to send instructions by radio wave to the robot.

The scientist commands the robot to go in search of the woman, Riley, and to bring her to the manor house. Rising from its crate, the robot (Mark I) approaches the wailing Mother Riley, in the most atmospheric sequence in the film. Allowing the old lady to retrieve her false teeth, Mark

I bundles her in her bedclothes, and walks her out into the street.

Unfortunately for Von Housen, just as he's seizing the drama of the moment ("Nothing can stop it now! My dear Anton, this is power!"), the constable on the beat has forced his henchman, Mugsy (David Hurst), to "move along" and take his car with him. Happily, the robot and baggage secure a lift from the local inebriate, who, dressed in the *haute* fashion of Arthur Housman or Jack Norton, piles the two into his convertible and takes off. Although, back at the laboratory, the sleepwalking Tilly manages to hit a switch marked "Arc Control" (causing the Robot and the inebriate to switch seats in the car, traffic in Piccadilly Circus to flow in reverse, and the dizzy maid's own return, backwards, to her bedroom), Mark I and OMR manage to arrive, none the worse for wear, at the manor house.

The next morning, the newspapers publish the picture of the "Vampire's" latest victim—Old Mother Riley—and New Scotland Yard reconvenes; the detectives, uncertain as to how to procede correctly, pin their hopes on the constable "on the scene," the highly obtuse PC Freddie.

Von Housen opts to keep OMR out of sight until things quiet down. In a scene amusing mainly for Lugosi's and Lucan's constant synchronized movements, the professor interviews the old woman.

(Von Housen) "When I came in, I saw you looking at that painting. Do you like bats?"

(OMR) "No, I hate them; they give me cold shivers..."

(Von Housen) "A great pity. That happens to be... my brother."

Regaling Mrs. Riley with promises of "nice, juicy steaks, and liver everyday, all day," he gives her a couple of fivers, a job, and an admonition: "Don't strain yourself, my lovely little Group 3." The implications of all that red meat go right over the old woman's head, and she giddily tells the incredulous Tilly—her new roommate—that the scientist is "smitten" with her.

OMR doesn't reckon on non-stop servings of liver, though, or on the constant cackling of Hitchcock ("You're being got ready!"), Von Housen's answer to Renfield. Evicted from the kitchen himself, PC Freddie happens upon a truckload of mummy-wrapped bodies being carried into the manor house, but, before he can discover that two of the mummys are the missing Julia, and her shipboard swain, he's chased away by Mugsy.

Seeking to work off a bit of the liver, OMR dusts about the house, and comes upon Julia. The featherduster makes the unconscious woman sneeze, and a frightened Mother Riley leaps through the window; reverse footage allows her to leap back into the room, where she promises to fetch help, and then leaps out again. Von Housen and his gang arrive moments later, and arrange to move Julia to the laboratory (with Bela giving the word the British pronunciation).

OMR peddles into town and attempts to convince the police that she knows the whereabouts of the "Vampire," the missing woman, and a whole lot more. Unfortunately, as she's been doused with gin (by the local inebriate, who's come to report that his car's been "stolen by someone from behind the Iron Curtain"), the police would rather have her arrested as drunk and disorderly. Vowing to "save her meself," the old woman starts a fracas at the stationhouse, and makes good her escape.

In the laboratory, Julia begins to regain consciousness at midnight. Von Housen's pointed questioning—he wants an Uranium mine chart—is interrupted by Mother Riley, who has returned without help, but with coffee and a newspaper. Tossed physically from the room by Von Housen (and sacked for good measure), OMR descends to the kitchen where, despite the late hour, Tilly is still up and about. The two women discover Julia's identity from the newspaper, but are prevented from leaving by Freda, who locks them in.

Unsuccessful with his direct line of interrogation, Von Housen summons Anton, and they begin to prepare Julia for shock treatment. As the villains ready the straps and electrodes, OMR and Tilly pry up a kitchen floorboard, and lower themselves into a secret passageway. Coming upon Douglas, who has destroyed *his* floorboards and found the passage, OMR brains him with her flashlight.

Chemical glassware is cheap and plentiful; no good help, however, is so hard to find, and Count Von Housen is up to some serious no good in *Mother Riley Meets the Vampire.*

The two women then find a swivel-type secret door which, after some comic byplay, deposits them in the parlor. Braining Douglas once again (the naval man has likewise stumbled onto the swivel door), OMR and Tilly are unnerved by the insane giggling of Hitchcock (who pops up from behind a variety of panels and pictures). Left with no alternative, Mother Riley does what she does best, starting a free-for-all. Freda, Musgy, Anton, and Hitchcock prove no match for the feisty shopkeeper and the dizzy servant; the two women escape up onto the roof. Tilly climbs down and runs off in search of PC Freddie, while OMR eavesdrops through a skylight on Julia, who's finally spilling the beans: the chart is onboard the SS Fernwood, still locked in the purser's safe.

Von Housen, Anton, and Hitchcock leave for the ship, as OMR works her way back into the house in order to rescue Julia. Confronting her within, however, is Robot Mark I, responding to his command to kill the old woman. An unstoppable juggernaut, Mark I follows Mother Riley upstairs. Caving in the door to the eccentric scientist's bedroom, the seemingly invincible robot is taken apart with incredible ease by the frenetic OMR and her pry bar. Mother Riley then unties Julia, disarms the explosive device Von Housen has engaged, and heads for the docks, leaving the heady young woman liplocked with her bruised-but-now-standing naval hero.

OMR jumps in the local police jitney (Freddie, having properly gone through channels to obtain a search warrant, is left behind to phone the police), and drives seaward. After a good bit of Irish chase music, rear projection, and vehicular switching, the old lady guns her motorcycle up the ship's gangway. She speeds past Von Housen and Hitchcock, held at bay by the police after a fruitless search of the safe and a brief gunbattle.

Plunging into the water, Old Mother Riley surfaces and cheerfully, albeit redundantly, speaks her last screen words ever: "This is the end," a message already inscribed on the life preserver she wears.

Mother Riley Meets the Vampire/Vampire Over London/My Son, the Vampire is neither as bad as word of mouth has made it out to be, nor as unfamiliar as one might think; it's chief offense seems to be that it is vampire-less.

Either of the American release titles (or *The Vampire and the Robot*) leads one to expect the presence of a genuine supernatural figure somewhere in the morass. (Nor should the British monicker promise and fail to deliver, just because the comic's name is first; Bud and Lou met a slew of real horrors without compromising on the chills or the laughter.) In the face of this expectation, the almost immediate revelation that the "Vampire" is not for real is a letdown, but this disappointment is not a wrinkle never before encountered: Lugosi had been a bogus bloodsucker back in *Mark of the Vampire* (and Chaney, Sr. had been guilty of the same in the earlier *London After Midnight*).

The thing that's hard(er) to take is that Bela's role—for all its comic impact—is something of a step backwards. Save for the 1935 MGM effort, Lugosi's vampires (whether his two Draculas, or Columbia's Dracula-clone, Armand Tesla) were authentic, baleful members of the undead fraternity. Failing to deliver the goods after casting the Hungarian actor in conjunction with the "V" word, is as much of a cheat as draping the cape over his shoulders in either *Spooks Run Wild* or the unfathomable *Scared to Death,* and revealing, in both cases, an eccentric magician.

Insofar as *Mother Riley Meets the Vampire* is a thinly disguised adaptation of *Abbott and Costello Meet the Ghosts* (UK title for *A&C Meet Frankenstein*), the character reversal is all the more deplorable. At first glance, with Lucan standing in for the American comics, Mark I taking Glenn Strange's place, that "stupid gang of men" filling Lenore Aubert's high-heels, and the uranium mine chart a substitute for a compliant brain, Lugosi need not have played an *ersatz* vampire.

Whether it was felt that having Lugosi play the real thing (the copyrighted name "Dracula" was out of the question) would upset the balance of the film, or would require a more morbid denouement than the comedy could handle, is open to discussion. (The only truly morbid element in the movie—the fate of the other female victims—is left unresolved; Freda mentions it only in passing, when she informs the curious Mugsy that "it's better for you not to know; it might upset your delicate mental balance.") No matter the original intent, one suspects that the constraints of a tight shooting schedule, a modest budget, and the demands of extraordinary special effects (in the days before the more "realistic" Dracula portrayal of Christopher Lee, bat transformations were *de rigueur* in vampire movies) helped put the kabosh on things.

For all the confusion regarding Lugosi as serious villain, Lugosi as comic heavy must be allowed to take a bow. Although probably due more to gratitude for the assignment than admiration for the script, Bela plunges wholeheartedly into the spirit of things. Playing broadly and to the back row, he demonstrates an impeccable comic timing and the talent for farce which could have opened new avenues for him earlier, had not the studios stubbornly insisted that Lugosi equalled Dracula, and nothing more.

This was hardly the first time he had appeared in a comedy, but it's necessary to travel back to the early thirties—before the noose of typecasting had choked the life from his career—in order to find roles wherein his capacity to menace was more than offset by his dancing about the lunatic fringe. First National had cast him opposite Joe E. Brown in 1931's *Broadminded,* wherein he not only got to sputter and fume as a volatile South American romantic, but won lovely Thelma Todd at the finale! Appearing with such comedy stars as W.C. Fields, Burns and Allen, and prissy Franklyn Pangborn, Bela had glowered with Slavic tongue firmly in cheek as General Nicholas Branovsky Petronovich in the manic *International House* (1933).

Later attempts at combining the Lugosi frisson with laughter were not so successful. The comic elements of 1939's classic *Ninotchka* (Garbo laughs!) bypassed Bela's cameo as dour Commissar Razinin, but his acting as foil to the Ritz Brothers in *The Gorilla* that same year, allowed him to peddle both snickers and snarls to the Ritzes in their last feature at 20th

Century-Fox. Prince Saliano, in RKO's *You'll Find Out,* was more concerned with attempted murder than with punchlines, and Lugosi's part as Eduardo, in Universal's second *The Black Cat* (1941), proved ludicrous rather than humorous. Paramount's *One Body Too Many* (1944) allowed Bela to do his (by now) patented butler, but with a comic twist: Larchmont's studied inability to give a cup of coffee away to guests, suspects, or policemen would have made more of an impact had not the larger goings-on been so frenetic.

Apart from his grim encounters with the East Side Kids and bits of unintentional laughter in other Monogram vehicles, only his two RKO adventures with Wally Brown and Alan Carney and the wonderful *Abbott and Costello Meet Frankenstein* bridged the gap to Mother Riley. Although the earlier RKO feature, *Zombies on Broadway,* afforded Lugosi a chuckle or two as Zombie-master Renault, *Genius at Work* was, for the Hungarian, all grimaces and scowls. Bela's swan song as Dracula, though, in Universal-International's 1948 comedy hit was a masterful portrayal, which allowed the Count his dignity and his "space," while providing him with the opportunity to maneuver among the others with double-edged humor. The happy marriage of effective screenwriting, Charles Barton's skilled direction, and Lugosi's own talent recreated the classic character and polished yet another facet of the horror-comedy jewel.

The task of adapting the 1948 Abbott and Costello farce to the style of the British cross-dresser fell to screenwriter Val Valentine, who had penned Arthur Lucan's most recent adventure, *Old Mother Riley's Jungle Treasure* (1951). Working quickly, and challenged by the effort of not making the transferred plotline too transparent, Valentine succeeded in melding the macabre aspects of Von Housen and his gang to the mundane, if slightly eccentric, world of Mother Riley.

This proportional mix, favoring the provincial comic over the international villain, might be yet another reason why there is no genuine vampire in the film. Bud and Lou's screen personas changed from picture to picture; by choice, the comedians never tied themselves down to an established continuity of character or situation. As one never knew what to expect in an Abbott and Costello movie (save that the comics would basically play themselves, no matter what their names were in this particular film), a foray into the supernatural could be taken in stride.

(Old) Mother Riley, on the other hand, was firmly anchored in stereotypical tradition. A living ethnic joke, Arthur Lucan's meal ticket danced, finagled, plotted, and schemed with a falsetto brogue, all the while drinking (or, at least, talking about drinking) like, well, like an Irishman.

Mother Riley's world was one of arguments with green-grocers, spats with rental agents, squabbles with the Inland Revenue, jousts with petty bureaucrats, rows with publicans, and bones picked with fishmongers; each confrontation was instantly recognizable to the provincial audiences for whom the films were intended. The continued popularity of the series was due not only to the comical nature of the main character, but also to the ability of the viewer to identify with the humor inherent in the (otherwise frustrating) situations. To intrude into the world beyond the grave would be to fly in the face of this set and comfortable formula, and to court disaster; better to have the movie concerned with the meeting up of two loonies than to upset the apple cart at this late date.)

Director John Gilling permits Lucan and Lugosi their moments to shine while gamely making the most of a "horror-comedy" without much horror. The first scene of the robot stalking the old woman has an air of menace to it that's missing from the later encounter; it may be that the rather diminutive status of the mechanical man, coupled with the almost casual ease with which he's dismantled, retroactively undermines the second pursuit. Gilling had had his hand in the writing end of an earlier Lucan/McShane effort—*Mother Riley's New Venture* (1949; he also wore the co-producer's hat)—but his genre fame wouldn't be assured until he wrote and/or directed a number of Hammer spookers, among them *Plague of the Zombies* and *The Reptile* (both 1966), and *The Mummy's Shroud* (1967). (Earlier than these was *Mania,* a 1959 meller dealing with notorious graverobbers Burke and Hare, and starring Peter Cushing. The film, for which

Gilling provided the screenplay and the direction, ranks second only to *Mother Riley Meets the Vampire* in terms of title changes: within a scant six years of its original release, it was known, variously, as *Flesh and the Fiends, Psycho Killers,* and *The Fiendish Ghouls.*)

Director of Photography Stan Pavey keeps his camera moving and the lights low and ominous for most of Lugosi's scenes, the two robot stalkings, and most of the manor house footage in general. By contrast, Mother Riley's various escapades in and around her shop are flatly lit and tend more to shades of gray than stark blacks and whites.

Helping mightily to create atmosphere are the sundry manor house accoutrements by art director Bernard Robinson, another technician soon to graduate to Hammer. Robinson's specific genius seems to have been the dressing of existing sets (witness the multiple incarnations the manor house at Bray underwent during the later '50's and '60's), rather than the construction of new ones. Von Housen's headquarters, replete with multiple suits of armor, extensive tapestry coverage, and endless wainscoting, indicates either Robinson's talent at stretching his budget, or the production's fortuitous access to a location made in heaven.

Unusual for an entry in a low-budget comedy series nearing the end of its tether is a customized musical score, but there's every indication that that's just what Lindo Southworth came up with. Drawing heavily on stock Irish themes, generic chase music, and nondescript phrases, the score (played with competence by the Fernwood Studio Orchestra), coupled with the constant flow of lowbrow sound effects mentioned above, provides enough background noise to keep the film moving at a good clip.

In that *Mother Riley Meets the Vampire* is the only exposure I've had to Arthur Lucan and his ethnic shenanigans, it's virtually impossible to provide a comprehensive assessment. Although the old woman is a one-dimensional character, he/she is downright funny a good bit of the time, even when making cracks that were old when the world was young. Lucan uses his voice well, blathering one moment, cajoling the next, muttering under his breath like WC Fields, or screeching at the top of his lungs, like a banshee; this capacity for variation keeps Mother Riley from becoming predictable or vocally monotonous.

There are several instances where the character is incomprehensible to non-Brits, but the frequent recourse to malapropism strikes a more familiar note, especially to fans of that past-master of garbled grammar, Leo Gorcey. Lucan's style of comedy (if I may be so presumptuous as to analyze his *style,* based on one picture) encompasses both verbal humor (including, but not limited to ethnic references, insults, provincial "in-jokes," puns, exaggeration, and the aforementioned malaprops) and physical humor (read: slapstick). If the performance under scrutiny is anything like typical, Mother Riley was a dynamic character, always moving, always scheming, capable of a broad range of comic emotion that could be traced to Arthur Lucan's music hall background.

Able to dish it out as well as take it, Mother Riley's frenetic personality might have caught on in certain areas of the USA, had the film been able to find a distributor at the time of release. Had it done so, however, the only product available thereafter to the colonies would have been the backlog of earlier titles, ripe for reissue; Arthur Lucan died suddenly, his greasepaint (as well as his garters) on, in 1954.

As long as you know what you're getting yourself into, *Vampire Over London* can be a lark. Asking no serious involvement on the part of the audience (despite those disquieting remarks about the four missing women, and a couple of dramatic injuries at the climactic gunfight), *Vampire* is a non-stop farce, its characters either chasing or being chased, and stopping only to hurl invective, set up an antique chuckle, or pontificate as only comic-book villains can.

Cultural unfamiliarity apart, the film *moves;* from the constant cutting among the British stock characters, to the blatantly sophomoric camera reversals, to the soap-box prattlings of the ultimately ineffectual Von Housen, one thing *Mother Riley Meets the Vampire* cannot be accused of is being staid and static. The borrowings from *Abbott and Costello Meet Frankenstein* transfer well, given the drop in budget and less ambitious production values, and seem to prove that the seven basic literary plots can survive even the slings and arrows of outrageous comedians.

After his repeatedly frustrated efforts to cross over into other genres, the Lugosi of the early 1950s was reduced to abject self-parody in order to stay alive. As a sop for his efforts, and a vindication of his claims at comic ability, *My Son, the Vampire* at the very least offers Lugosi a few choice moments to play with type, rather than surrender to it. Despite his addictive problems, his increasing deafness, and his undoubted lack of appreciation for Lucan's professional talents (comic transvestites were *not* big in Budapest), Lugosi seems to have given it his best shot. And for his many fans who claim never to have seen him give less than his all, there's the added consolation that this "self-parody" gave their hero a momentary respite from the worst circumstances of his life.

Poster courtesy Ronald V. Borst/Hollywood Movie Posters

Bride of the Monster

(1955)

by John E. Parnum

CREDITS: Executive Producer: Donald E. McCoy; Associate Producer: Tony McCoy; Producer and Director: Edward D. Wood, Jr.; Assistant Directors: William Nolte and Bob Farfan; Screenplay: Edward D. Wood, Jr. and Alex Gordon; Photography: William C. Thompson and Ted Allan; Camera Operator: Bert Shipham; Musical Score: Frank Worth; Editor: Mike Adams; Technical Supervisor: Igo Kantor; Make-up: Louis J. Haszillo and Maurice Seiderman; Special Effects: Pat Dinga; Electrician: Louis Kriger; Key Grip: Thomas J. Connelly; Sound Recording: Dale Knight and Lyle Willey; Sound Effects: Ray Erlenborn and Mike Pollock; Property Master: George Bahr; A Rolling M Production/Banner Productions Release, filmed in black and white, 68 minutes

CAST: Bela Lugosi...Dr. Eric Vornoff, Tor Johnson...Lobo, Tony McCoy...Lt. Dick Craig, Loretta King...Janet Lawton, Harvey B. Dunn...Captain Robbins, George Becwar...Professor Strowski, Paul Marco...Kelton, the Cop, Don Nagel...Martin, Bud Osborne...Mac, John Warren...Jake, Ann Wilner...Tillie, Dolores Fuller...Margie, William Benedict...Newsboy, Ben Frommer...Drunk, Conrad Brooks...Policeman/Suspect, Eddie Parker...Double for Bela Lugosi

Like Edgar Allan Poe's tortured prisoner in *The Pit and the Pendulum,* Lugosi "was sick... sick unto death." His "pit," however, was a black hole of poverty and despair; his "pendulum," the deadly needle he plunged into his emaciated body to anesthetize himself from both the physical and mental pain that wracked the 72-year-old forgotten actor.

It was April 1955 and Bela Lugosi had recently completed a new film... *Bride of the Atom...* a starring role which he hoped would re-establish him as a famous name once more, although his frail, drug-poisoned body belied these fruitless expectations. The director, his friend Edward D. Wood, Jr., told him they expected to preview the film in July, and had even taken some footage of Bela for another project only a few days before. Yes, it was good to know people like Eddie Wood, the Gordon brothers, Tor, Paul... but, oh how he missed Lillian, his wife of some twenty years, who had left and divorced him... taking with her his beloved teenage son Bela, Jr. Loneliness crept into that pit with him and he felt it was time once more for the needle. Not even Poe himself, beset by his own personal demons, suffered as did this Hungarian actor, now fallen on hard times and who had to rely on the generosity of a handful of friends to survive.

It had not always been like this for Bela Blasko who had triumphed on the European stage as a Shakespearean actor and matinee idol in the early 20th century. Fleeing Hungary in 1921 as a political outlaw, Lugosi arrived in New York and formed a repertory company of fellow Hungarian actors, but didn't learn English until he was cast in *The Red Poppy* in 1922. As his success grew, he was given the role of a lecherous butler in a 1924 farce derived from the German play *The Werewolf.* And during that same year, in Poughkeepsie, New York, Lillian Phillips Wood, a buyer for the Kreske Company, and her postal worker husband became the proud parents of a newborn son whom they named Edward Davis Wood, Jr.

Lugosi's link with Poe was far different in the '30s when he and Boris Karloff, as the

"Titans of Terror," helped fill the coffers at Universal Studios. Bela played the mad Doctor Mirakle in the 1932 *Murders in the Rue Morgue* in which he attempts to mix the blood of a female victim with his pet ape Erik to turn her into "the bride of science" —a title similar to the Ed Wood film of the '50s that would be the actor's last speaking part. In *The Black Cat* (1934), Lugosi, as the ailurophobic Vitus Werdegast, attempts to kill Hjalmar Poelzig (Karloff) and is initially thwarted from his mission upon seeing a black cat. And in 1935, Bela portrayed Dr. Richard Vollin, a Poe obsessed surgeon who mutilates underworld figure Edmund Bateman (Karloff) to do his bidding in *The Raven.* A 1941 version of *The Black Cat* featured Lugosi as a bewhiskered caretaker and "keeper of the cats" in a small red herring role. Of course, it was the 1931 vampire film that elevated him to fame. And so it is only coincidental that little Eddie Wood that year, at age seven and oblivious to what Fate had in store for him, saw his first horror film—Bela Lugosi as the fearsome bloodsucker in *Dracula.*

Bela's second role as a vampire, albeit a bogus one, was *Mark of the Vampire* in 1935. He had been out on loan to MGM for this remake of Lon Chaney, Sr.'s *London After Midnight.* It is thought that Lugosi's addiction to morphine to relieve an excruciating sciatica began during the filming. He returned to Universal in July for *The Raven* and then moved on to Imperial-Cameo Pictures, a California independent studio, where he was cast as both good and evil twins in *Murder By Television.* It was released in October, and around that time on the east coast young Wood was delighted by a gift given him by his parents on his eleventh birthday—his first movie camera.

Not all of the films Bela made for Universal were horror movies. In 1936, he played Benez, a nightclub owner who robs the U.S. mail, in *Postal Inspector.* Horror films were restricted in England and that is why in the third chapter of Lugosi's real life drama, a young fan named Alex Gordon, saw the famed actor for the first time in this minor program thriller instead of one of his macabre roles. Gordon does admit that the ratings board slipped up when he and his brother Richard saw Lugosi with Karloff in *The Invisible Ray.* Meanwhile, back in America, Eddie Wood and his friends were taking in the *Flash Gordon* serials at Saturday matinees. Bowled over by the then new genre called science fiction, the boys would re-enact scenes from the various chapters. While his friends would vie for the coveted Buster Crabbe part of Flash, Eddie exhibited for the first time a quirk that would become more obsessive as he grew older. Ed Wood chose to dress up and play Flash's sweetheart—Dale Arden.

After Universal's *Black Friday* (1940), and with the exception of recreating his role of Ygor in *The Ghost of Frankenstein (1942)* and being less than dynamic as the Monster in *Frankenstein Meets the Wolf Man* (1943), Bela was relegated to minor parts in that studio's horror thrillers. His *name* could still draw and was a prominent display in poster art. But Bela the *actor* found it more difficult to appear in substantial roles. Certainly his career as a leading man or important heavy was over. And so in the early '40s, disappointed by Universal's lack of regard for his talents, Lugosi signed on with Monogram Studios and Producers Releasing Corporation on Poverty Row. Though he was once again a star, his films were grade "Z" clinkers, a sad realization that must have pained the aging actor. On the east coast, however, Ed Wood was starting a band called the Sunshine Mountaineers. He had a comic book collection that was the envy of the neighborhood, had fallen in love with a gal named Catherine, and was about to graduate from high school.

With World War II raging full force in 1943, Bela Lugosi, naturally too old to serve, was doing his part for the effort. While appearing in the Harry H. Oshrin revival of *Dracula* at the Locust theatre in Philadelphia, Bela was invited to attend a dinner and production rally at the Globe Hoist Company. Having himself been forced to flee Hungary in 1918 because of his political activities, the actor was moved to say a few patriotic words at the event which would launch the shop into record-breaking production of wartime equipment: "Friends, countrymen, soldiers of the working force, this war is not an ordinary war. This is a war of skill against skill. To remain free men, American skill, workmanship, and production must triumph." And in the South Pacific, having enlisted in the marines in 1942, Private First Class Edward Wood repeatedly stabbed the lifeless corpse of the Japanese soldier who had knocked his teeth out with the butt of a rifle. Wood's kinkiness blossomed during the war when he told a fellow marine that he was glad that he had not been wounded during the invasion of Tarawa since he had worn pink panties and a bra into battle. After Wood was discharged in 1945, he attended drama school, and then joined a carnival where he alternated between playing the geek and the half man, half woman. For the latter role, according to Chuck LaBerge in Rudolph Grey's *Nightmare of Ecstasy,* he would insert a needle into his nipple and blow up his breast. By 1947, he had arrived in Hollywood, and Alex Gordon had traveled to New York as a broker for Walter Reade Theaters. He was accompanied by Richard, then a young British producer responsible for the *Carry On* series.

The following years were lean ones for Bela Lugosi. In 1946, he made only one film: *Genius at Work* for RKO, which wasn't released until 1947. A brief return to greatness occurred in 1948 when he brilliantly essayed his role as Dracula in *Abbott & Costello Meet Frankenstein,* thanks to the persistence of his agent, Don Marlow, and the brilliant restorative make-up of Bud Westmore. Wood also scored that year by directing and starring in his first Hollywood movie, *Crossroads of Laredo.*

While Wood busied himself with screenwriting over the next several years and forming his own company, Angora Productions (naturally), Lugosi returned to the stage—variety shows where he would reminisce about his career and summer stock revivals of *Dracula* and *Arsenic and Old Lace.* It was during a run of the latter in Sea Cliff, New York, that Alex and Richard Gordon visited their idol backstage. That 1948 meeting produced for the brothers a friendship with Lugosi that would last for the next eight years.

From then until 1951, Bela performed in demeaning midnight spook and magic shows to rowdy audiences on the east coast. Finally, Richard Gordon arranged for him to appear in *Dracula* in England. Due to the poor planning and limited financing of the English promotors, the play flopped, leaving the Lugosis penniless and unable to return to the United States. Richard was still representing a British producer, George Minter, and talked him into casting Lugosi as "the vampire" in *Old Mother Riley Meets the Vampire.* The film did not receive distribution in America until 1964 as *My Son, the Vampire*—eight years after Lugosi's death. Bela received $5,000 for his part... enough to get him and Lillian back to Hollywood.

In the meantime, Alex Gordon moved to the west coast and looked up a cowboy producer named Johnny Carpenter who had filmed a western for a meager $17,000. Gordon, impressed by the cowboy's frugality, wanted to discuss a new picture with him and was introduced to Carpenter's assistant director, Edward Wood, Jr. The two hit it off beautifully since both had interests in Gene Autry and Bela Lugosi movies. They made plans to produce films starring all the horror greats, and Alex introduced Bela to Ed.

Ed first approached Lugosi with an offer to appear in *Glen or Glenda,* a cheap exploitation flick depicting transvestism, a theme so personal to Wood that he cast himself as the he/she main character. So spontaneous was the offer that Ed didn't even have a part in mind for Bela. At first, the horror actor refused, saying that he could not work for an independent producer and that the $500 salary was too small. Fighting to keep her family from starvation, Lillian Lugosi persuaded her husband to swallow his pride and accept the role, and Ed spent the next night creating the part of the mystical spirit who dispensed sex advice from a weird room he shared with a skeleton and bubbling chemicals. Lugosi, uncomfortable with the role, was abysmal. In all fairness, perhaps the reason for his poor performance was that after years of verbal abuse, Lillian was leaving him. Disillusioned by her failure to wean her husband from drugs, Lillian finally received her divorce in August 1953.

Ed and Alex, now roommates, tried hard to get work for Bela. Alex lined up the haggard-looking actor for a starring role in *Bela Lugosi Meets a Brooklyn Gorilla.* Ed wrote, directed, and produced *The Bela Lugosi Review* which successfully played the Silver Slipper in Las Vegas. Between the two of them, they tried to keep their idol working and his name before the public whether it was a stage revival of *Arsenic and Old Lace* in St. Louis or a bit on *The Red Skelton Show* or even pushing a Bela Lugosi radio stint and comic book. In an effort to rehabilitate Lugosi, Ed would accompany the despondent actor to A.A. sessions since, in addition to his drug addiction, he was becoming increasingly dependent upon alcohol. Ed finally gave up taking Bela when he discovered that during the meetings Lugosi would secretly sip from tiny bottles of scotch sewn into the lining of his coat.

Gordon moved out of Wood's apartment once he and Ed completed the script for *The Atomic Monster* which was to be a vehicle for Lugosi's comeback in a starring role. Alex was tired of waking in the morning to learn that Ed's girlfriend Dolores Fuller had spent the night with him. Also, it was quite disturbing for him to return to their digs never knowing whether he would find Ed Wood, the man, or the young screenwriter in drag. Lugosi was delighted with the script for *The Atomic Monster.* Gordon remembered an impressive gigantic henchman played by Tor Johnson in *Reap the Wild Wind,* and the ex-wrestler was signed on as Lobo, a name dreamed up by Alex. Gordon took the screenplay to Realart where he and his legal advisor, cigar-chomping Samuel Arkoff, tried to sell it to producer Jack Broder and his sales manager, James Nicholson. Nothing was heard about the project until Gordon learned that Realart, a company that reissued classic Universal horror films in the '50s, was going to release *The Atomic Monster.* Thinking that Broder and Nicholson had stolen their idea, Gordon and Arkoff threatened to sue Realart, but learned that the company had only "borrowed" their title for the re-release of the 1941 *Man Made Monster* starring Lon Chaney, Jr. Broder settled for $2000 which Gordon and Arkoff split. Gordon and Wood then changed the title to *Bride of the Atom,* while Arkoff and Nicholson were later wedded in a different kind of union when they formed American-International Pictures. Strange are the matches made in Hollywood.

While all this was going on, Ed Wood was busily writing more scripts: *Dr. Voodoo, The Vampire's Tomb,* and *The Phantom Ghoul,* which was to feature Lugosi and cowboy star Johnny Carpenter in the first horror western. These screenplays, along with *Bride of the Atom,* were presented to Steve Broidy, head of Monogram Studios (which would later become Allied Artists). Broidy wanted Karloff for *Bride,* with Lugosi and Lon Chaney, Jr. to star in *Dr. Voodoo.* Then, Broidy decided he would have two new scripts developed, a vampire flick for Lugosi and Chaney, and a house of horror picture for Karloff. Changing his mind for a second time, Broidy put Sam Arkoff's brother-in-law to work on a single screenplay that would involve all three horror icons. Upon seeing the finished script, he canceled the deal. By this time, Gordon was off to Europe on a Gene Autry tour and Wood was left to handle the production and financing of *Bride of the Atom.*

Ed's attempt to raise money for *Bride* was facilitated when Paul Marco, an aspiring writer/actor, contacted his agent, Marge Usher, and told her that Wood needed money for his movie. Figuring that the young director might use some of her other clients, Marge met with Ed, was charmed by him, and suggested Tony McCoy for the part of the hero, Lt. Dick Craig. Ed agreed, but perhaps in the back of his mind was the notion that Tony's father, Donald E. McCoy, was the multi-millionaire owner of a meat packing plant. Dolores Fuller, who played the female lead in Wood's previous flick *Jailbait* and in *Glen or Glenda,* was relegated to a minor role when Ed chose Loretta King as *Bride's* heroine. According to Fuller, Loretta contributed $60,000 to assure her part, but this has been vehemently denied by King.

Paul Marco became fast friends with Wood, and Ed decided to rewrite the part of the movie's desk sergeant into a comedic patrolman to accommodate Marco. Agent Marge Usher, who lived on Kelton Avenue, suggested that name for Marco, and Wood was delighted. Thus, Kelton the Cop was born and Wood carried over Marco's role to *Plan 9 from Outer Space* and *Night of the Ghouls.* Marco also became good friends with Lugosi, and even threw an elaborate party for Bela. According to Marco in *Filmfax* Number 6, when his guest of honor arrived and saw the black Christmas tree decorated with gold balls, sitting on top of a huge white snowball, he exclaimed, "Oh, Paul! Now I feel at home."

Shooting for *Bride of the Atom* began on October 29, 1954, at the Ted Allan Studios on Poverty Row. Wood shot a station house scene plus some bits with Bela and Tor before he ran out

Bela Lugosi as Dr. Eric Vornoff along with Tor Johnson as Lobo and Loretta King as Janet Lawton appeared together in what many regard to be Ed Wood's best film, *Bride of the Monster.*

of money in three days. Work was halted while Ed tried to secure more funds, and George Becwar, the actor who played foreign agent Strowski, tried to sue Wood for the shutdown, which only delayed production further. Finally, Donald McCoy, anxious to see the film finished and his son become a rising star, contributed the needed money with certain stipulations: First, the title had to be changed to *The Monster of the Marshes;* second, an atomic bomb had to explode at the climax; and third, he had to be named Executive Producer and his son, Tony, Associate Producer, with Ed relinquishing all rights to the film. By this time, most of the cast and crew were steaming at Ed for the delays—all except Lugosi who waited until shooting resumed in March before demanding $250 be added to his original salary of $750, thereby causing another delay. But Ed was a hustler. He had bitten the heads off chickens in a carnival and with his entire cast and crew would submit to baptism in the Baptist church to appease a group of religious businessmen he hoped would back his next film *Plan 9 from Outer Space*—all to achieve a means to an end. And so this compulsive movie-maker, determined to finish what he considered would be his masterpiece, turned over control to the McCoys, leaving him with only a meager $350 director's fee as his profit from the film.

So filming resumed and the long workdays and nights took their toll on poor Bela. Often he would beg Ed for a small advance of his salary in order to buy drugs from his chiropodist or other dealers. If Wood were too busy to take him to his apartment for a fix, his friend Paul Marco would drive him home. As described in Tom Weaver's *Interview with B Science Fiction and Horror Movie Makers,* Paul tells how: "We entered his apartment, turned on the lights which were very dim, and Bela said..., 'It's not nice to watch, but I *have* to have my medicine.' ... He opened the sterilizer and took out his hypodermic and his 'medicine'.... He put the needle in his arm and took it out—I sat motionless, I just couldn't move.... 'Now,' he said with a laugh, 'I think we are ready to go!' And so we went back; it was a long, damp evening up there at the park, but Bela's medicine got him through the night. It was an experience I'll never forget."

After production wrapped, with nothing to occupy him except thoughts of his lost Lillian and Bela, Jr., Lugosi's dependency accelerated. He was sick... sick unto death, and during *Bride's* post-production period he finally took desperate measures. With his veins so scarred they could no longer accept the deadly needles, Bela Lugosi committed himself to the Los Angeles General Hospital's mental health and hygiene department. After spending a horrifying night in the hospital ward, this 125-lb walking skeleton on spindly legs covered with bandaids pleaded for treatment the next day in Psychopathic Court. A sympathetic judge commended Lugosi for his courage; he was one of the first major Hollywood stars to commit himself voluntarily for drug treatment. The judge ruled that he be sent to the Metropolitan State Hospital in Norwalk for rehabilitation.

A few days later, the cast and crew visited Bela and Ed gave him a new script to read called *The Ghoul Goes West,* a project that actually never saw light. They further encouraged him by announcing the world premiere benefit of *Bride of the Atom,* with all proceeds going to a trust fund for him. As described in Arthur Lennig's *The Count,* Lugosi was deeply moved. "This is so heartwarming, such a miracle. I cannot believe it. To know that people have such faith in me is better than medicine. I will not let them down." The premiere took place on May 11, but unfortunately it previewed on a double bill with *The End of the Affair,* a sappy melodrama starring Deborah Kerr, Van Johnson, and Peter Cushing. Fortunately, Lugosi, still in rehab, was unable to attend to see the sparse audience and hear their derisive howls and catcalls at the climax of *Bride of the Atom.*

It was another year before the film was released in the United States and Britain as *Bride of the Monster,* the title by which it is known today. Those critics who even bothered to attend the general release in July 1956, hated the film almost unanimously. But when Alex Gordon took Sam Arkoff to the Lugosi benefit the year before, Sam, who harbored no love for Wood and considered him a "loser" in his book, astonished Gordon by remarking that *Bride* was surprisingly good for the money. And indeed, it might just be the best film Wood ever directed, even though that's not saying much. *Plan 9 from Outer Space* (also 1956) is certainly the more famous, or *infamous* as the case may be, but it is because it is so incompetently made that it sparks audience interest. *Bride of the Monster,* on the other hand, benefits from Lugosi's histrionics which ranged from pure ham to personal emotional sincerity. Lugosi truly felt that the film was the comeback he had ached for, and while Wood preferred *Plan 9,* general consensus ranks *Bride* as his "masterpiece."

Bride of the Monster gets off to a frenetic start. Two hunters, Mac and Jake (Bud Osborne and John Warren) are lost in a southern swamp during a raging storm. Frank Worth's booming score competes with the claps of thunder to drown out the hunters' dialog. During a flash of lightning, they see a dilapidated house... perhaps shelter for them. Wood hung a large canvas behind a residential home to give it the appearance of being isolated. They knock on the door and the sinister Dr. Eric Vornoff (Lugosi) answers. "You can't stay! You're not welcome in my house. Go away! Go! Go! Go!" Vornoff threatens them. The lumbering giant Lobo (Tor Johnson) appears and the hunters think he is the legendary monster of the swamps. They flee, and Vornoff chuckles to the mute Lobo saying "They think you are the monster." The scene was shot toward the end of filming and it was at this point that Lugosi walked off the set demanding more money.

Vornoff and Lobo (Could Lobo be derived from lobotomy?) retreat back into the shabby interior of the shack, walk through a secret passage in a fireplace, and enter one of the phoniest labs ever committed to film. The flimsy sets painted to resemble part stone dungeon, part walk-in kitchen, are truly ludicrous and must have been a source of embarrassment to Lugosi who had been accustomed to the realistic Universal dungeons during his glory days. Vornoff tests some machinery and then peers though a window that looks out *under* a lake, although the house has no cellar. There he is startled to see a gigantic octopus, although his surprise is surprising since he later makes reference to the creature as being a long-time resident of the area. Stock aquarium shots alternate with those of a rubberized mechanical octopus which had been used in the John Wayne action thriller *Wake of the Red Witch* and which Ed and some crew members acquired from Republic Studios' attic warehouse. The motor no longer worked and the misappropriators snapped off a tentacle during the heist. The only thing that could make the creature appear less than inert was to hoist around the other tentacles with invisible wiring.

Meanwhile, the hunters rush through the swamp and Mac falls into nearby Lake Marsh and onto the lifeless arms of the rubber octopus. Actor Bud Osborne wraps a tentacle around himself to simulate some realism in the scene. The four-foot lake was created when Wood dammed up a small stream in Griffith Park. Lobo grabs the other hunter and carries him off to Vornoff's laboratory.

Jake is strapped to the table, his wrists handcuffed for some reason when they could have been bound beneath the straps, and his skull encased in an ill-fitting bowl that keeps sliding down over his face. Lobo wheels the deadly ray machine, actually a photo enlarger, to the table as Vornoff examines his patient. Observing a bruise on Jake's neck, he slaps his imbecilic assistant: "Lobo, you're too rough with my patient." Introducing himself to his victim, he chuckles and promises his patient that "soon you will be big as a chi-ant... with the strength of 20 men... or else—like all the others—dead!" Alas, the experiment is another failure and Vornoff stares thoughtfully through that mysterious window at the octopus: "Isn't it strange, Lobo, how our friend always returns home after his long, tiring swim?"

Headlines flash upon the screen: "Monster Strikes Again and Monster Takes Two"—how any newspaper except the *Weekly World News* could assume such illogic simply from the discovery of a lost shotgun and a torn jacket could only by dreamt up in an Ed Wood movie. The film then grinds to a tedious halt as the scene shifts to the local police station. Kelton the Cop (Paul Marco) is introduced as a bungling idiot, interrogating a drunk (Ben Frommer) picked up near the scene of the murders—although, remember that no bodies have been found. Frommer, a vaudevillian, begged Wood to let him use Lawrence Tierney's famous speech from *Dillinger:* "No tank town jail can hold me; I'll be outta this here rat trap in 24 hours!" and Ed, always appreciative of film tributes, agreed. Kelton then takes the newspapers with the exploitative headlines into Captain Robbins (Harvey B. Dunn) for some more lame comedy bits. Dunn, a professional party clown whose shtick was a trick bird, used a live parakeet that sits on his shoulder during the police station scenes, making the official appear as asinine as the dialog he recites from Wood's script.

Lt. Dick Craig (Tony McCoy) is called in and is soon joined by his girlfriend reporter Janet Lawton (Loretta King). Both exhibit the very nadir of acting, and King, who refrained from drinking liquids on the set because she was afraid of putting on weight, became severely dehydrated. Lugosi would tell her that she was going to shrivel up and look like a mummy. Ed claimed that Loretta had hinted that she had a million dollars, and so in addition to awarding her the starring female lead over his current girlfriend Dolores Fuller, he almost married her.

After bickering with Captain Robbins over the twelve swamp murders, Janet quarrels with Dick, a wimp of a cop, and then storms off in her 1938 Chevy sedan to begin her own investigation. First she consults with Tillie (Ann Wilner) in the advertising department of her paper. Tillie, who can't seem to locate the pencil tucked into her hair (Ed never did retakes when someone screwed up), lets Janet go through her real estate files to learn who bought the property out by Lake Marsh. Assigning Tillie to make a myriad of phone calls for her, Janet then asks another employee, Margie (Dolores Fuller in an abbreviated role), to make excuses for her. The brief scene between Loretta and Wood's girlfriend literally drips with venom not in the script.

Professor Strowski (George Becwar) arrives at the police station to talk about the murders. Considered an authority on the Loch Ness monster (Ed was always ready to include a timely news item in his films), the professor points out that the events are similar to sightings in Scotland. Robbins assigns Dick to Strowski and they plan to visit the lake in the morning.

Janet drives to the swamp wearing Wood's trademark piece of Angora clothing—this time a cap. Another storm breaks as she careens through the jungle. Wood, according to sources, strapped himself to the roof of the car, and, with watering can in hand, sprinkled "rain" on the windshield as cameras rolled. Naturally, Janet totals her Chevy, tumbles out into the underbrush, and screams at the sight of one of the rubberiest snakes this side of a novelty store (intercut, of course, with stock snake shots). Lobo arrives, beats up the rubber serpent, and then picks up Janet's Angora cap, fondling and smelling it before carrying off the reporter to Vornoff.

In the laboratory, the mad scientist tells Janet that she is tired and must rest. He waves his hand hypnotically, a bit that Wood claimed he recreated from Lugosi's scarf scene in *White Zombie,* and Janet falls into a trance to his mesmeretic voice: "Sleep... sleep for a lovely young lady."

Lt. Craig and his partner Marty (Don Nagel) arrive at the swamp looking for Strowski who had not kept the promised appointment. As they stare at the stock jungle footage, Marty complains how the swamp is "alive with crawling things... crawling death." Another storm arrives which the detectives blame on a timely fashionable occurrence—atomic testing. They drive around some more and come upon Janet's abandoned car. Dick phones Robbins from a convenient coffee shop in the swamp—an interesting scene since a set was created instead of using an actual establishment. But there are no customers or employees... just a phone on a wall with canned background conversation. Craig is told by his boss to forget Janet and to look for Strowski.

When Janet awakens, she is startled by the sight of Lobo. Vornoff tells her that he came upon Lobo wandering around the wilderness of Tibet —one more attempt by Wood to include a then-current theme—the abominable snowman, sans hair. He tells Janet, "Don't be afraid of Lobo... he's chen-tle as a kitten." Now for some reason, everyone assumes that Lugosi is making the first of two dialog mistakes—that he is saying "chen-tle as a *kitchen."* Perhaps it is because of the *ch* he pronounces in gentle that people think he is repeating it in kitten. John McCarty in *The Sleaze Merchants* also debunks this popular myth, and you will also if you listen closely.

Lugosi does, however, make a slip in the next scene when Professor Strowski arrives to take Vornoff back to the homeland (presumably Russia). Vornoff has just placed Janet in another trance. The close-up of Lugosi's eyes—taken to resemble his hypnotic orbs in *Dracula* and *White Zombie*—are a pathetic reminder that the actor had not aged well. Lobo has taken Janet to Vornoff's quarters as Strowski slips into the house. This is the first of several shots when someone enters the front door and passes through an entirely different style of door once on the inside. The front room is in shambles and one would think that Vornoff would have Lobo do some light housecleaning in his spare time—at least straighten the pictures.

Vornoff greets the professor and reflects on how he had been banned from creating superbeings, separated from his wife and child, branded a madman and a charlatan, and condemned by the profession that had once honored him—dialog which reflected Lugosi's personal insecurities and current lifestyle. Vornoff continues: "Now, here in this jungle Hell I have proven I am *all* right." As reported in Lennig's *The Count,* "Bela is so intense here that he makes a Freudian slip; instead of 'I have proven I was right after all,' he delivers 'I have proven I am all right.' And indeed he was—the dignity, charisma, and charm of the man would never diminish; only the producers were simply unwilling to make use of his aging but by no means vanishing gifts."

Lugosi's next speech is perhaps his most emotional in the film. It appears to come from deep within his heart: "Home," he sobs. "I have no home. Hunted. Despised. Living like an animal. The jungle is my home. But I will show the world that I can be its master. I will perfect my own race of people... a race of atomic supermen which will conquer the world." The speech, as written by Wood, is—charitably speaking—trite; but as delivered by Lugosi, one of his most memorable... maybe even to rank up there with "I never drink... wine."

But Bela was terrified about making this speech. He complained to Wood that he was an old man, that he couldn't memorize lengthy dialog anymore. Wood promised him cue cards which only incensed the actor whose pride would not let him stoop to such unprofessional measures. Paul Marco volunteered to rehearse with Bela. As Marco reported in *Filmfax* Number

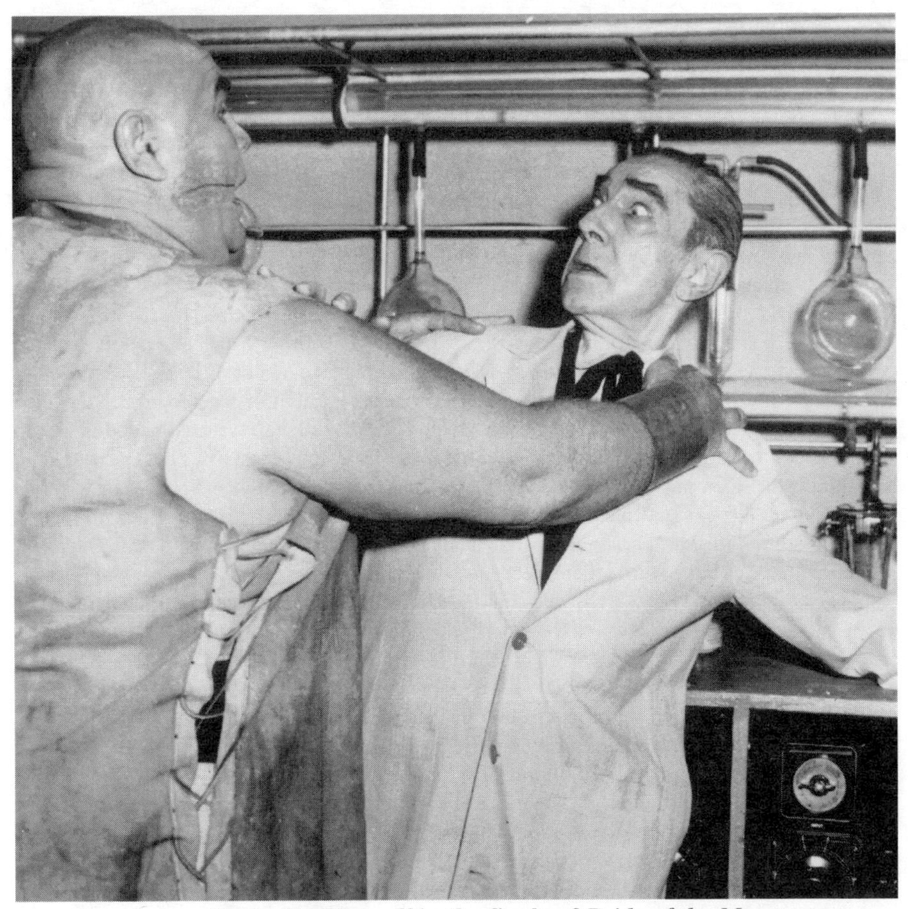

Lobo attacks Dr. Vornoff in the finale of *Bride of the Monster.*

6, when it came time for the take "he was looking right at me.... He used me as his focal point, center... as he gave that long speech to George Becwar. And when Bela finished—he did it all in one take... I was stunned. Everyone, the crew, was still as could be. You could have heard a pin drop—and when he was finished, everyone just applauded, everybody had tears in their eyes for the wonderful performance he gave, knowing that he was in pain." He grabbed Paul and hugged him and asked him how he had done. And Paul said that he had just heard how he had done from the applauding cast and crew... and that he was Number One in Paul's book. And Bela replied, "As long as I am Number One with you, Paul, I'm happy."

When Vornoff tells Strowski that he will not return home, the agent pulls a gun on him. Lobo intervenes and Strowski is thrown to the rubber octopus. "You will disappear, Strowski, just as all the others have disappeared," Vornoff chuckles.

Craig and Marty, driving through the swamp, find Strowski's rental car. Craig, trampling through the weeds, falls into a pit and is attacked by alligators... courtesy of stock footage again. He pumps bullets into the slithering reptiles and scampers out of the hole. Robbins, meanwhile, without the bird on his shoulder, questions Tillie at the newspaper and learns that Janet has gone to Vornoff's. What he doesn't realize is that at the very moment the doctor is using his fancy hand movements to summon Janet from another room. Janet enters in a trance... dressed in a white bridal gown! When Lobo sees her, he is smitten by her lovely appearance.

Craig arrives at Vornoff's, enters the door of many styles, and finds Strowski's cap in the front room. He also discovers the professor's glasses and briefcase which contains a nice 8 x 10 still of Lugosi in *Scared to Death*—Bela's only color film. In the laboratory, Vornoff commands Lobo to strap Janet to the table. The brute is hesitant at first, but acquiesces when Vornoff beats him with his whip.

The detective finds the secret passage in the fireplace just as Vornoff places the photo enlarger over Janet, promising her that "it will hurt for just a moment, and then you will emerge a woman of super strength and beautiful... the bride of the atom!" Dick enters the lab and Lobo karate chops him on the shoulders, knocking him unconscious.

Captain Robbins and Kelton arrive at the swamp and hook up with Marty. In the laboratory, Dick has been secured to the wall in a convenient pair of shackles. He vows to Vornoff, "I'll live to see you hang." Vornoff checks the straps and the ill-fitting bowl on Janet, then stares at Lobo and scratches his chin in bewilderment—either trying to remember his lines, or some other action that perhaps only Ed Wood understood. He strides to the control panel to turn on the juice as Lobo pulls the Angora cap from his pocket and looks sadly at Janet. With a thundering growl, Lobo charges toward Vornoff. The mad scientist fires the detective's gun at the giant who then hurls him to the floor, unconscious. Lobo releases Janet, pats her gently, and returns to Vornoff. Janet picks up the gun and places it in Dick's holster before releasing him. Lobo straps the struggling Vornoff to the table and proceeds to activate the monster-making equipment. Dick, gun in hand, commands him to turn off the mechanism. The detective fires at the giant and finally runs out of ammunition as Lobo shreds his shirt and chops him again. As Janet administers to her boyfriend, Lobo manipulates the dials, ignoring the pleas of his master—sweet revenge for all those beatings.

Robbins, Marty, Kelton, and other cops break into the shack as the now super-charged Vornoff climbs off the table and attacks Lobo. The dumb giant has succeeded where his brilliant master had failed so many times! During the strenuous fight, stuntman Eddie Parker doubled for Bela, just as he had done during the filming of *Frankenstein Meets the Wolf Man*. Parker tries to shield his identity by keeping his hands before his face in the same manner that Wood's chiropractor Thomas Mason filled in for Bela in *Plan 9 from Outer Space*. It is very obvious, however, that it is Parker performing the rough stuff, even though shots of Lugosi in bloody make-up by the noted artist Maurice Seiderman are inserted.

Vornoff hurls Lobo against the lab equipment; it explodes and kills his servant. He then scoops up Janet as Dick regains consciousness and scampers about the burning room. Finding the secret passage, he enters the living room where Robbins and Marty have just smelled the smoke and have decided to clear out. Outside, Kelton points to the fleeing Vornoff carrying Janet up the side of a mountain (in a swamp?). The monstrous doctor then puts Janet down, presumably so Lugosi could step in for the doubling Parker, and watches as lightning (yes, another storm has arrived) strikes his house and blows it up. The police can now fire off a volley of shots at Vornoff, who has unexplainably developed an odd spasm in his shoulder. Dick rips off the remains of his shirt (to show off his scrawny physique?) and charges up the hill, covered from the waist up only by a pair of suspenders... a truly odd sight. Kelton charges down the hill, but trips and sprains his ankle. Robbins looks disgusted—but whether it is at Kelton or at Wood's inept direction is unclear.

As Vornoff advances on Dick and Kelton, the detective rolls a gigantic Styrofoam boulder down the hill, knocking Vornoff into the lake and into the limp arms of that octopus. Lugosi wraps the tentacles around himself and screams wildly. Another bolt of lightning strikes, this time hitting Vornoff and the octopus, and they explode in an atomic blast. As Dick and Janet watch producer McCoy's required mushroom cloud rise majestically over the swamp, Captain Robbins gazes sadly in astonishment and intones the often-cliched remark, "He tampered in God's domain."

With filming of the lake scene completed, the local fire department informed Wood that he would have to demolish the barricade that dammed up the stream. Wood obliged, but when the dam was broken apart the four-foot deep body of water that had built up deluged a golf course across the road and it couldn't be used for days. This and other strange stories about the filming of *Bride* are legendary. Incredible incidents fill Rudolph Grey's book on Ed Wood, *Nightmare of Ecstasy,* such as how Ed learned that his director of photography Bill Thompson was color blind. Bill gave Ed a ride in his car and asked Ed to tell him when the stoplight turned green. Or David Worth reporting in *Sleaze Creatures* that one of the props used for a chemical reagent was a bottle of Pepto Bismol. And, of course, there is the recent 1994 Tim Burton film *Ed Wood*, a somewhat exaggerated if not partially inaccurate biography, introducing the director to a general public not already fans of his cult films. But what is truly incredible is that Martin Landau's moving performance as Bela Lugosi garnered him an Academy Award for supporting actor in Burton's film about the career of a man some critics consider the worst director of all time. There are those of us who would disagree with these critics. Having endured the 1964 *Creeping Terror,* I personally nominate director Art Nelson (who supposedly lost the soundtrack for that film in Lake Tahoe) for that dubious honor. Nelson's flick is a bloody bore. Ed Wood's enthusiasm for the genre always shines through in his films no matter how ineptly they were made. They are never boring!

After Lugosi was released from the hospital on August 5, 1955, he went on to make two more films, ones in which he had no speaking parts: *The Black Sleep* for United Artists and Wood's *Plan 9 from Outer Space* which used only a few clips of Bela that Ed had filmed the previous year. He married for a fifth time, a thirty-nine year old Hope Lininger who had sent him daily notes of encouragement during his hospital stay. But Bela's days were numbered... the years of abuse had taken their toll that no therapy could correct. On August 16, 1956, Hope returned to their apartment to find her husband had passed away quietly while reading a new Ed Wood script, *The Final Curtain.*

Wood himself followed in Lugosi's footsteps to a living Hell... dwelling in poverty, with alcohol as his drug of choice. Reduced to directing cheap nudie flicks and writing pornographic smut books in order to survive, Ed's ravaged heart finally gave out on December 10, 1978, at the age of 54.

But before Death claimed these two now cult giants, Ed took Bela to see the film which Lugosi hoped would bring him fame and fortune once more. It was July of 1956, only one month before Lugosi's demise, and Wood's film was now in general release as *Bride of the Monster.* Wood claimed that Lugosi liked it. It is not known what Bela secretly thought of the grade "D" trash he had just sat through. But that's not important for either us or Lugosi. What is important is the incident that occurred after the two left the UA theater in Los Angeles. As related by Robert Cremer in *Lugosi: The Man Behind the Cape* and by Ed himself in *Nightmare of Ecstasy,* an elderly fan stopped Bela who was smoking a cheap stinking cigar and asked the aging actor for his autograph. The fan told Bela that he was 62 and that he felt very old. Lugosi puffed out his chest and proudly boasted, "I'm 71, but the brain, the brain, it never feels that you're old. Only the body looks old, but never the brain. The brain is young, then the body is still young, like a young man."

Bride of the Monster, certainly not Bela Lugosi's best work and probably one of his worst, may on the other hand have been the most important film that he ever made. This grade "D" horror claptrap, directed by a booze-sodden hack director who liked to dress up in women's clothes, actually did more for Lugosi's personal self-esteem than his vampire role in *Dracula.* While *Dracula* established Bela as a horror icon, it also typecast him forever, dragging him slowly and painfully down into the world of cheap horror flicks and eventually into drug-induced degradation and self-pity. *Bride of the Monster,* while in itself no different from the ilk that had nearly destroyed him, actually lifted the despondent actor form the pit of despair. This movie took Bela at his lowest ebb and instilled in him a sense of self-worth. Bela Lugosi's name was once again up in lights and he could face his last remaining days... with Hope.

Many thanks to Victor Torres who provided the tape, Laura Parnum who committed this chapter to computer, and to Edie Parnum who graciously edited it.

The Black Sleep

(1956)

by Tom Weaver

CREDITS: Released in June; A Bel-Air Production; Executive Producer: Aubrey Schenck; Produced by Howard W. Koch; Directed by Reginald LeBorg; Screenplay: John C. Higgins; Story: Gerald Drayson Adams; Photography: Gordon Avil; Editor: John F. Schreyer; Music: Les Baxter; Assistant Director: Paul Wurtzel; Characters Designed by Volpe; Makeup Created by George Bau; Set Designer: Bob Kinoshita; Wardrobe: Wesley V. Jefferies & Angela Alexander; Property Master: Arden Cripe; Lighting Technician: Joe Edesa; Key Grip: George Fenaja; Operative Cameraman: Ben Colman; Makeup Man: Ted Coodley; Hair Styles: Cherie Banks; Sound Mixer: Joe Edmondson; Sound Editor: Mike Pozen; Music Editor: Sam Waxman; Rerecording: Charles Cooper; Photographic Effects: Jack Rabin & Louis DeWitt; 81 minutes

CAST: Basil Rathbone...Sir Joel Cadman, Akim Tamiroff...Odo, Lon Chaney, Jr....Mungo, John Carradine...Bohemond, Bela Lugosi...Casimir, Herbert Rudley...Dr. Gordon Angus Ramsay, Patricia Blake...Laurie, Phyllis Stanley...Daphne, Tor Johnson...Curry, Sally Yarnell...Nancy [Female Monster], George Sawaya...K6, Claire Carleton...Carmona Daly, Louanna Gardner...Angelina Cadman, Peter Gordon...Investigative-Sgt. Steel

Bela Lugosi fans may grumble about this book's inclusion of *The Black Sleep;* it's an impressive "B"-budgeted horror movie with an all-star "once-in-a-lifetime" cast, but it's also a standout title on lists of embarrassing Lugosi credits. And yet it's an "important" Lugosi credit for various reasons; for one, it's our only opportunity to see him acting after his drug rehabilitation. (Actually *acting*—not just wandering around, making faces, or twirling a cape in the home movie-ish footage that would later turn up in *Plan 9 from Outer Space*.) It's also, of course, his last movie.

Sadly, *The Black Sleep* finds the 73-year-old actor on his last legs. He plays a mute part (as do others in the cast), and it's awfully tough for a professional actor to screw up a non-speaking part, particularly when it's a minuscule one and he's kept in background and out-of-focus most of the time. But Poor Bela comes dangerously close. The film's producers wonder if Lugosi even knew he was there. It's a heartless-sounding comment, but probably quite accurate, and Lugosi's performance seems to bear it out.

Aubrey Schenck and Howard W. Koch formed their own production company in the early 1950s and began supplying economically-made exploitation pictures for United Artists release. Their first was *War Paint,* an actionful Pathecolor Western shot in 19 days in March, 1953; the enterprising pair followed up with dozens of Westerns, action dramas, and crime movies for UA release. Schenck (now living in retirement in Northern California) was the "idea man" for the company, dreaming up potential plotlines and then turning them over to screenwriters. "I *had* to be [a prolific idea man]," says Schenck, "because with the money Howard and I had to spend on the movies we made, I *couldn't* go out and buy stories or plays or anything like that."

"Aubrey Schenck was the story man—a brilliant story man, and a wild, enthusiastic kind of a guy," adds the still-active Koch, still headquartered at Paramount many years after his reign as production boss there in the 1960s. "[Aubrey] gave me every opportunity I had in my life—whatever break I got was from him. I owe him everything. I was the down-to-earth guy that made the pictures—either I directed them or I produced them. I was a 'factory picture' maker—I knew what it took to make a film. A lot of producers in those days only knew about finding a script, casting, hiring a director. They didn't know one thing about how the below-the-line was done. Having been an assistant [director], I knew that pretty well."

Standard procedure for Bel-Air Productions (Schenck/Koch's production company) was to come up with a title and submit it to UA for approval and receive moneys to use toward production. "Then we'd write a script for it, check one member of the cast with UA, and shoot the picture," Koch reveals. "That was the time of exploitation films—second features were still hot then. All of our pictures, except maybe three of them, were second features. We'd come up with a title and then write the story; that's precisely how *The Black Sleep* came about."

Schenck doesn't recall whether the idea for an old-fashioned horror movie came from him or if it was presented to them by an outside party; "All I can remember is that I said, 'We'll get every goon in the business for this that we can lay our hands on!'" The "goons" of the movie business were a glut on the market in the mid-1950s, horror pictures having become a nearly-extinct genre after the mid-'40s. The primary role of Sir Joel Cadman, an obsessed brain surgeon and medical researcher, went to Basil Rathbone, an actor seldom-seen on movie screens since he rejected the chance to continue his Universal Sherlock Holmes series in 1946. "For an actor to forsake so lucrative and comfortable a niche in Hollywood was almost unheard-of," wrote Greg Mank (*The Hollywood Hissables*). "In fact, the movie colony never quite got over Rathbone's defection, and one might imagine—considering the actor's later screen roles—that it never forgave him for it." (Actually, most of the actors who specialized in costumers were out of vogue by the 1950s unless, like Vincent Price and others, they worked to change their image.) Rathbone returned to the stage, worked on radio and TV, and also toured with a one-man show of memories and dramatic readings, *An Evening with Basil Rathbone.* He came back to the screen after years of absence for *Casanova's Big Night* (1954), a Bob Hope costumer/comedy, and followed it with *We're No Angels* (1955) and *The Court Jester* (1956).

"Rathbone was great fun, not at all the kind of person you'd expect after seeing him playing all those historical roles that he did with such grandeur," remembers Gloria Talbott, co-star of *We're No Angels.* "There was a bunch of Russian teenagers or young adults who were going to be visiting the set—it was one of those weird 'foreign exchange'-type things, and about 20 kids who wanted to do films were coming. And so Basil, who was always doing strange and funny things anyway, bought a nice, *beautiful* piece of wet *shit* from a novelty store. I don't know which shop he got it at, but it was the best one I'd ever seen—it was not hard, it was sort of like Silly Putty, and it was horrible and wet-looking! And as you opened the stage door, you'd step in *one* and then take the *second* step and you'd step right into the shit. (He had it fixed so that it wouldn't slide.) Those of us who had gotten there early had watched Basil set it up, we were all in on it.

"Well, the first person he caught was Bogie! And, of course, the expletives flew—'Mother-f! Son of a b!' Bogie kicked his leg and the shit dropped off. He looked down...and he looked around...and of course everybody was watching. Basil said to Bogie, 'Good morning, old boy!' [*laughs*]—and Bogie just looked up at him with that *look* of his, his head down and his eyes up. Then he turned, and went *straight* into his dressing room! After that, everybody came in, including the Russians, and we caught at *least* the first seven people. But by that time everybody was screaming and yelling, and word got back to the rest of the Russian kids what was happening. I sat there and watched with glee—I wet my pants, it was so funny! Basil and his teenage daughter and Aldo Ray and I—we stood around and waited for 'em all to come in! We were *children*!"

Goon #2: Akim Tamiroff as Odo, a glib Gypsy who procures human subjects for Rathbone's fiendishly unorthodox experiments. The Russian-born actor trained at the Moscow Art Theater drama school and acted in America from the 1920s on, first on stage and then on film; 20 years before sharing the screen in *The Black Sleep,* Tamiroff and Rathbone were in competition for the Best Supporting Actor Oscar of 1936 (Rathbone for MGM's *Romeo and Juliet,* Tamiroff for Paramount's *The General Died at Dawn*). *Black Sleep* was the first Hollywood film in two-and-a-half years for Tamiroff, who had been acting in Europe.

Goon #3: Lon Chaney, Jr., whose battle with the bottle had caused professional and physical deterioration since the War years when he ruled the roost as Universal's number one horror star. Unlike Rathbone, Tamiroff, Lugosi and John Carradine, Chaney worked regularly in mainstream Hollywood movies in the early '50s, but usually in brutish, blustery parts that were a long way from his Larry Talbot and the sophisticates he played (badly) in the *Inner Sanctum* movies. Low-budget moviemakers, who had no money to waste on blown takes, often cast him in mute roles (*The Black Castle, The Big Chase, Indestructible Man*), as did Schenck and Koch on *The Black Sleep.*

Goon #4: John Carradine, Chaney's elder by just five days, was *another* once-busy screen performer who retreated to stage, TV, and radio in the early 1950s. *Casanova's Big Night* was Carradine's "comeback" picture as well as Rathbone's; the two were also featured in *The Court Jester.* By the '50s, moviegoers were reading more about Carradine on the gossip pages of tabloid newspapers than in movie magazines; he was arrested in August, 1953, for non-payment of back alimony, and as soon as that was squared away, the I.R.S. got after him for back taxes, marital battles with new wife Sonia Sorel hit the papers, and he was even named as a "john" at a prostitute's well-publicized trial(!). Carradine was one to always land on his feet, however, and he managed to work in prestige pictures like *The Egyptian, Around the World in 80 Days* and *The Ten Commandments* during these otherwise dark days.

And Goon #5, Bela Lugosi. Enough, perhaps too much, has already been written about the tragic hand that Fate dealt Lugosi during the last decade of his life: Drug use, heavy drinking, a divorce from his wife of 20 years, an ever-worsening list of movie credits, frequent unemployment, money troubles, and finally his headline-making self-commitment to Los Angeles General Hospital's mental health and hygiene department in April, 1955.

"The court wants to commend you for this very courageous act of yours," said the judge who committed him to Metropolitan State Hospital in Norwalk, California. "It is commendable that you have come forward voluntarily wanting to cure your addiction to the use of drugs. After all you are only 72 years of age. And it will be wonderful to get well and live the rest of your life as you should."

The cast and crew of Lugosi's recently-completed *Bride of the Monster* flocked to his charity ward bedside and announced that the proceeds from the film's premiere would go to Bela. But very little money was raised, and production of Lugosi's next-announced picture, Ed Wood's *The Ghoul Goes West,* was cancelled. As he was being discharged from the hospital, Lugosi told a pushy interviewer that he had given up drinking, but he was soused at his August 25, 1955 wedding to longtime fan Hope Lininger. Lugosi was supported by his young bride; legit movie offers had long ago ceased to roll in.

"The highest-paid [horror star in *The Black Sleep*] got 10 or 15,000, that was Basil Rathbone," Aubrey Schenck reminisces. "Chaney would get about five bills a week, Carradine the same, maybe 750. Bela—well *[laughs],* what was the minimum then? Three hundred fifty or four hundred a week....Oh, my God, we had to carry him from place to place, he didn't even know he was gettin' paid. He was so drugged, he didn't know where he was.... [Lugosi] was numb! That's the best word to describe *him*!"

The film's initial announcements stated that Allen Miner would direct and that Peter Lorre would be part of the cast. (Lorre asked for too much money, and the role earmarked for him went to Akim Tamiroff.) "Allen Miner had directed a picture called *Ghost Town* [1956] for us and he did very well—five days, $100,000," says Koch. "We had a nice relationship with him and announced him for *The Black Sleep,* but then when we got deeper into the picture we figured it would take a guy who had done that kind of stuff, knew that genre better. So we switched over to Reginald LeBorg." LeBorg, a veteran of the Universal horror factory (*The Mummy's Ghost, Calling Dr. Death, Weird Woman, Dead Man's Eyes, Jungle Woman)* took the reins on *Black Sleep,* which rolled at the Ziv Studios on February 9, 1956.

THE STORY: The film opens in 1872 London, where Dr. Gordon Ramsay (Herbert Rudley), convicted on circumstantial evidence for the murder of moneylender Curry, is awaiting execution at Newgate Prison. Amidst the sound of hammering (the building of his gallows, outside and off-camera), he is visited by his surgical mentor Sir Joel Cadman (Basil Rathbone). As Cadman leaves, he deposits a small quantity of powder in Ramsay's metal cup and tells him that it is a sedative he should take just before he walks the last mile.

The powder is actually an East Indian drug, nind andhera, and it gives Ramsay the appearance of death; the prison surgeon examines the body and surmises that Ramsay died of heart failure. (The nonspeaking role of the prison surgeon's assistant is played by executive producer Schenck.) Ramsay's body is claimed by Odo (Akim Tamiroff), a Gypsy tattoo artist who brings the coffin to the back room of his Limehouse studio. There Cadman administers an antidote, bringing Ramsay out of his state of suspended animation. "...I don't believe that any government has the right to take human life," Cadman explains. "Only should life be taken when unavoidably necessary—for example, in the furtherance of medical science." Cadman offers Ramsay a chance to assist him in the research work he is doing in the area of brain surgery, and the grateful Ramsay immediately agrees.

Cadman and Ramsay travel secretly to the old abbey on England's East Coast where Cadman has set up shop. They are being admitted to the abbey by the mute watchman Casimir (Bela Lugosi) when a blood-curdling woman's scream is heard. A lurching, subhuman figure, Mungo (Lon Chaney, Jr.), chases servant girl Laurie (Patricia Blake) through the foyer, brushes aside Cadman and Ramsay, and begins to choke the girl. Daphne (Phyllis Stanley), Cadman's surgical nurse, appears, chiding the now-submissive brute.

Unbeknownst to Ramsay, Cadman's young wife Angelina (Louanna Gardner) is in a coma, a victim of a deep-seated brain tumor and in desperate need of a delicate operation; in preparation for this revolutionary surgery, Cadman has operated on live human subjects, damaging their brains in order to further his store of knowledge. Casimir and Mungo are two of Cadman's "lobotomized" victims; Laurie is actually the daughter of Mungo, formerly Professor Monroe, a one-time colleague of Cadman's. Since Laurie's mother died in childbirth, Mungo in his brain-damaged condition reacts violently to the sight of the girl. Laurie sobs to Ramsay, "Each time he operates [on Mungo], he'll destroy a little more, each time, a little more, to satisfy his own curiosity! Dr. Cadman is the monster of this place!"

Searching for Cadman's medical records, Ramsay and Laurie find a secret passageway that leads to a cave-like dungeon where other victims of Cadman's scalpel are kept in chains: Bohemond (John Carradine), a madman in rags and long white beard who believes himself to be a medieval Crusader; a madwoman (Sally Yarnell) with a bald head, her body covered with small tufts of hair; a homicidal sailor (George Sawaya) with an infected face; and moneylender Curry (Tor Johnson), now a mindless, blank-eyed brute. (Ramsay was framed by Cadman for Curry's "murder.")

Ramsay and Laurie are discovered by Cadman, Daphne, Mungo, and Casimir and made prisoners. Cadman plans a double-operation: To sacrifice Laurie as an experimental surgical subject just prior to performing the needed operation on Angelina. But the dungeon mutants free themselves and rove the castle; led by Bohemond (chanting "Kill! Kill!"), they hold Daphne down on blazing fireplace logs and choke Mungo to death. Cadman, carrying the comatose Angelina, flees from the rampaging monsters and topples from a high staircase. Police arrive, the remaining mutants are (presumably) rounded up (off-camera), and Ramsay and Laurie are free to enjoy the future.

"Seldom, if ever, has the X certificate been so richly earned," wrote a reviewer for England's *Kinematograph Weekly,* reacting to the amount of on-screen gruesomeness in *The*

"Herr Director, give me more to do—I do not speak!" Lugosi asked. "Well, your tongue is cut out, I can't give you more, you can't speak," the director replied. Lugosi was unhappy with his mute valet role in *The Black Sleep.*

Black Sleep. The film ought to be required viewing for Hammerheads who like to boast that that company's *The Curse of Frankenstein* (1957) was the first film to break a number of "taboos" that were actually already broken by *Black Sleep.* The sounds of stabbing and sawing are heard as Basil Rathbone cuts open the sailor's (George Sawaya) scalp; closeup shots of his exposed fluid-seeping brain are seen; there's also some strong on-camera violence, including a closeup of Phyllis Stanley's screaming face as she's held down in the blazing fireplace. (By the way, none of this is meant to imply that scenes like these make for a good horror film.) Truth be told, one has to wonder if some Hammer exec may not have seen *The Black Sleep* (it was double-billed with a Hammer film, *The Creeping Unknown*) and taken a shine to its Gothic setting, its story of a ruthless medical experimenter and his unwilling assistant, and its ahead-of-their-time horror effects; all are to be found in the company's subsequent *Curse of Frankenstein.* (Both movies open with virtually the same scene—one of the two monster makers awaiting execution in a prison cell.) Of course, *The Black Sleep*'s not in color, and Basil Rathbone doesn't have the stupid habit of wiping off his bloody hands on his good clothes, and nobody carries around phony "joke shop" body parts; and not many Hammerheads are in the habit of cluttering up their writings with facts anyway. So, in *that* circle, *Curse of Frankenstein*'s rep as a groundbreaker will probably stand.

But *The Black Sleep* also shares with the later Hammer horrors the unwanted tendency to feature too many talking-heads scenes. Rathbone and Herbert Rudley seem to discuss everything twice; dead-end scenes of police investigation clutter the plot; and Akim Tamiroff plays an unbearably unctuous and garrulous character. The midsection of the movie is ruined by a long (almost ten minutes) scene involving Tamiroff, a female street beggar (Claire Carleton), and some Scotland Yard men—ten minutes of actors we don't want to see, playing in a scene that doesn't advance the plot. (In fairness to Tamiroff, Peter Lorre would probably have been just as off-putting in the part, which is marked by an endless stream of nonsense dialogue, bowing-and-scraping, and unfunny schtick; even the other characters in the movie tend to look annoyed when Odo is around.)

Among the "horror stars," all acting honors go to Rathbone, who gives a fine performance as Cadman. Peter Cushing has the reputation of inaugurating the character of the titled, elegant, silver-tongued but singleminded monster maker, but Rathbone did it first and did it much better; Rathbone in his impassioned scenes gives a real thoroughbred, sit-up-and-take-notice performance ("I will reach out after [Angelina] down the corridors of eternity and I'll bring her back, I'll bring her back!") quite different from Cushing's businesslike posturings as Dr. Frankenstein. Rathbone, notorious for bad-mouthing his horror roles, had no reason to look down his nose at this movie, *Tower of London* (which he may not have even considered a horror film) or his later *Tales of Terror*. (*Son of Frankenstein*... well, he might have a point there!) But, unlike the jovial, joke-playing Rathbone of *We're No Angels*, Rathbone socialized with perhaps no one on the set of *Black Sleep.* "Rathbone had sunk low, and I think he found it uncomfortable to accept the lesser members of the hierarchy as being social equals," says his co-star Herbert Rudley. "Now, I'm accusing him of a kind of snobbery and I can't be sure that that's an accurate evaluation of his position, but at least that was my feeling at the time. He would leave the studio as quickly as possible."

Playing a role far beneath his capabilities, John Carradine does all the talking as the mutants' self-appointed spokesman and leader, the crutch-toting lunatic Bohemond. (He looks like a bedraggled version of Aaron, the Biblical character he played in DeMille's *The Ten Commandments.*) The character is a big favorite of fans of the actor's outrageously overdone horror roles, and (of all the stars featured in *Black Sleep*) Carradine's the only one who could have played it. (Carradine could also have played Cadman, and in a way he did—a year later, Carradine filled the mad-doctor slot in the *very* very similar *The Unearthly.*)

Like Carradine, Lon Chaney's the only one who could have played *his* role, Mungo. (Oddly, Rathbone gives the monster man—formerly Prof. Monroe—that nickname, but later chides Herbert Rudley for using it!) Chaney, who turned 50 on *Black Sleep*'s second day of production, still looks as though he could whip his weight in wildcats; in the film's best scene, he limps down a castle corridor, left leg dragging *a la* Kharis, chasing after the leading lady. It's the best-directed scene in the picture, with the camera "becoming" Chaney, strangling hands extended into view, as he closes in on Rathbone, Rudley, and Patricia Blake. Of course it's just another Lennie-like characterization from an actor who went that route too many times, but the uncontrolability and mindlessness of Mungo make him a more formidable brute than similar Chaney characters (Gargon in *The Black Castle,* "Butcher" Benton in *Indestructible Man*, Mannon in *The Alligator People*) who could conceivably be reached through reason.

Then there's Bela Lugosi, whose part (unlike Carradine's and Chaney's) could have been played by anybody. (Or by a nobody.) The role is so small, it should be almost impossible to judge his acting, but Lugosi seems so completely "at sea," so befuddled, that (unfortunately) he stands out. About all he gets to do is react, and every reaction seems inappropriate to the situation: In his first scene, he opens a small viewing window in the abbey's front door and puts on a hammy expression of surprise at the sight of the guy (Rathbone) who lives there. Later, as he lugs a couple of bed warmers down a castle corridor, thunder rumbles and lightning flashes; Lugosi arches his back and directs a belligerent, "You-lookin' at-me?"-type glare at nothing in particular. When the thunder fades away, he puts his woebegone face back on, shakes his head, and shuffles away. What Lugosi's part really boils down to is a series of unintentionally semi-comical walk-throughs.

Lugosi may not have made his presence felt in the movie the way he wanted to, but he certainly made his presence on the set felt:

- According to Aubrey Schenck, Bela had Tor Johnson carrying him on and off the stage.

- According to Lugosi's teenage pal Dick Sheffield, he was drinking on the set.
- According to set visitor Olive Mosby of the *Inquirer,* he complained about his role: "There is Basil Rathbone playing my part. I used to be the big cheese. Now I'm playing just a dumb part." (Reginald LeBorg: "That was typical silliness for Lugosi, to be petulant like that.")
- According to Greg Mank's *Karloff and Lugosi,* Rathbone presumably detected Lugosi's resentment, and felt compelled to send him a note meant to smooth things over. (Rathbone and Lon Chaney, Jr. had already presented Lugosi with a bound copy of the script, autographed by the cast; in fact, Lugosi seems to have been treated with a great deal of deference by all concerned.)
- According to Reginald LeBorg, Lugosi pestered him for dialogue. "Lugosi came to me all the time asking, 'Herr Director, give me more to do—I do not speak!' I laughed, 'Well, your tongue is cut out, I can't give you more, you can't speak.' He said, 'Give me more lines! I've got to do more!' I said, 'You *can't* do more—you're Basil Rathbone's valet, and all you can do is stand next to him and nod.' Finally I compromised. I told him I'd put him into some shots where Rathbone was speaking. So when Rathbone had a discussion with Akim Tamiroff, I put Lugosi in there with them. And he started to *grimace,* while Rathbone spoke—that spoiled the shot! But to placate Lugosi, I took a couple of close-ups of him, knowing they would end up on the cutting room floor. But that satisfied him, and he thanked me." [Richard Bojarski's *The Films of Bela Lugosi* and set visitor David Carradine both state that Lugosi did deliver dialogue in at least one scene, a scene which was, obviously, not used.]
- According to LeBorg, Lugosi also picked a fight with Lon Chaney, Jr. "There was—I won't say hate—but a rivalry going on between Chaney and Lugosi from the Universal days when they both played Dracula. You see, Lugosi was the great Dracula, but then something happened at Universal and they gave the part to Chaney [*Son of Dracula*]. There was a terrible rivalry between them before I even arrived at Universal. It came out on *The Black Sleep*: Chaney was sore at something Lugosi brought up and it nearly came to a fight. Chaney picked him up a little bit, but put him down—we stopped him. We kept them apart quite a bit."

Lugosi's on-set antics provide great grist for us scandal-mongers, but it's also very sad; it doesn't take much of a stretch of the imagination to picture Lugosi just ten-years-younger, playing a Cadman-like role in a *Black Sleep*-type movie of the 1940s (it would have to be a Monogram—or better yet a PRC!), and doing it in grand style, giving one of his full-steam-ahead, wonderfully entertaining performances. But by 1956, the spark was gone, and things had deteriorated to the point he was *lucky* to get the non-speaking bit part in *The Black Sleep.*

"Even though surrounded by friends [on the set of *The Black Sleep*], you've got to go it alone," Lugosi told interviewer Harold Heffernan in a non-pain-in-the-ass moment. "I keep telling myself I must believe I will make the grade again. If I stop believing for even a minute I find myself sinking into despair. It's fighting this feeling—a thing that comes to all former drug addicts—that saps up my energy.... God has been good and given me this second chance, and I'll do my best not to fail."

Forgive the continuing Hammer references, but the horror films of Reginald LeBorg and Terence Fisher had some similar qualities: Both directors' dialogue scenes tended to be frequent, repetitious, and often insufferably boring, and both tried to spruce things up with their horror scenes, which were characterized by their luridness and "pushing-the-envelope" brutality. (The horror scenes may have seemed a bit more grisly than they really were, engulfed by the slow, "polite" and stately—i.e., dull—nature of the other scenes in the movies.) LeBorg had a leg-up on Fisher, however, working as he did with the blue-chip, "real-deal" horror stars (Karloff, Lugosi, Chaney, Price, Carradine, Rathbone, etc.) and handling horror scenes with a bit more imagination. (LeBorg was big on effective subjective shots—they're found in *The Black Sleep, The Mummy's Ghost, Calling Dr. Death,* and probably others.)

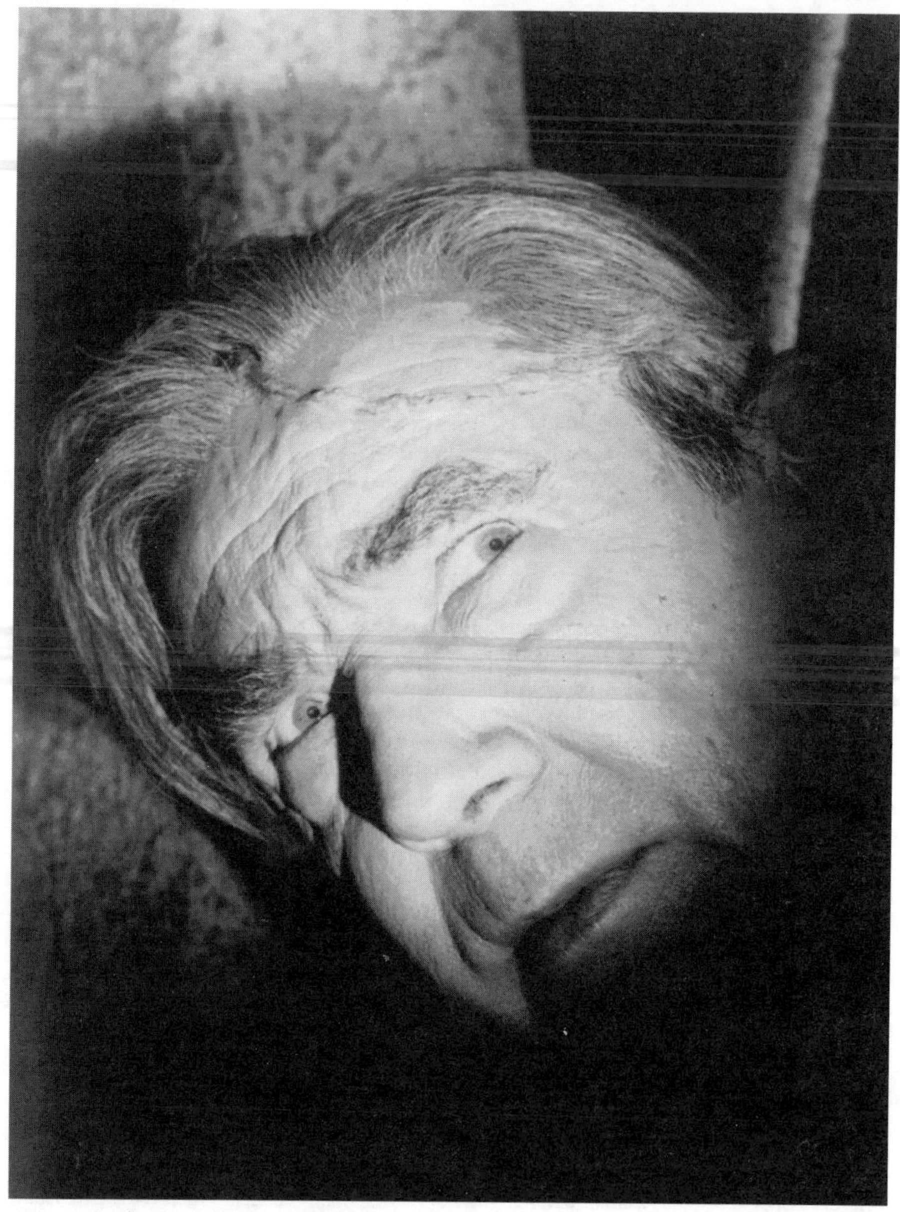

Bela Lugosi in one of his last publicity stills during production of *The Black Sleep*.

While the pacing in *Black Sleep* occasionally falters, overall it's well-acted and entertaining, and in 1956 this gloomy Gothic stood out nicely from the welter of flying saucer and big-bug movies that were then the rage. (The "English" atmosphere had more than its share of dubious moments, Rathbone being the sole Englishman in the cast.) Les Baxter's score is a good one and Bob Kinoshita's castle sets are large and quite impressive, which is fortunate, since practically the whole movie takes place indoors. The highlight of the film is the Herbert Rudley-Patricia Blake "walking tour" through Rathbone's catacomb of horrors, spotlighting one by one all of the maimed "guinea pigs" (Carradine, George Sawaya, Sally Yarnell, Tor Johnson). Volpe, a California-based artist, "designed" the characters, George Bau created the makeups, and Ted Coodley applied them—although Sawaya says he doesn't remember Coodley, and says emphatically that his makeup was applied by Lou LaCava. [Sawaya was a stuntman/heavy frequently employed by Koch/Schenck, in addition to doing stunts and playing gangsters for countless other producers. ("I played gangsters 100,000 times—I had that 'Mafia look'!") Sawaya wore a skull cap to play the bald sailor ("They knew they didn't have enough money to ask me to shave my head"), and he remembers *Black Sleep* as a "very, very quick movie. In those days, they used to do ["B" movies] in five days. Some of 'em, the *big* ones, went 11 days!"]

As for the other actors, Herbert Rudley is so unlike the usual horror/sci-fi leading man that he seems wrong for the part, but actually he's just right: Rudley, who was in his mid-40s, is old enough to play a qualified surgeon but young enough to fight monsters and clinch with the leading lady. He was also a good enough actor (his stage career went back to the 1920s) that Rathbone isn't able to "steal" their shared scenes—not 100 percent, anyway. Patricia Blake (The Girl) isn't very good, but neither are some of the lines she's asked to deliver; Blake was pretty, but her career went nowhere. Easy to miss (or to take for granted) in the supporting cast is Phyllis Stanley as Daphne, an interesting but poorly motivated character. "I would do *anything* to help you," she tells Cadman, waiting for his reply with a starved-for-approval, why-doesn't-he-notice-me? look; when Cadman doesn't respond, she turns away with a pained expression. Daphne obviously loves Cadman but at the same time she seems unaccountably eager to help him restore the comatose Angelina (whose hair Daphne tenderly combs). Sometimes Daphne seems to be "in" on Cadman's evil plans, other times she's not. She's warmly devoted to poor Mungo, but at the end she turns "heavy," helping to drag Laurie into the operating tower where Cadman plans to butcher her. Screenwriter John C. Higgins probably assumed that very little attention would be paid to the character (he was right), and he just had her do whatever was needed to keep the story rolling along.

"[One] afternoon, Tor [Johnson] reflected on his friendship and years of travelling with Bela Lugosi," Johnny Legend wrote in *Fangoria #22*. "His most vivid memory centered around one night he and Lugosi were on a barn-storming tour of small towns to promote *The Black Sleep*. Bunking together in the upper floors of a cheap hotel room, Tor recalls that Bela was at his lowest spiritual ebb, deeply depressed and suicidal, continuously muttering that he 'just wanted to die.' Growing weary of Bela's constant whining, Tor snatched him roughly by the collar and held him dangling from their hotel room several stories above street-level. 'Is this what you want, you miserable Hunkie?' Tor demanded. Lugosi finally came to his senses and admitted he wanted to live, at which time Tor hauled him back in to safety."

"When we opened *The Black Sleep* in San Francisco," says Howard Koch, "we sent Lugosi and a press agent, Chuck Moses, up there for the opening of the picture. Chuck walked into the hotel room one night, and Lugosi was standing on the sill overlooking San Francisco, with the window wide open, saying, 'I'm gonna fly!' Chuck cried out, 'Wait a second! You *can't* fly!' Lugosi was so drunk, he was going to jump out the window of the hotel! Chuck nearly fainted—he didn't know whether to run and grab him, or to stand there and not disrupt Lugosi's thinking. Anyway, Chuck got him in, called me and said, 'What should I do?' I said, 'Put a handcuff on him, take him to the theater, put him on a plane with you, and *come home*!'"

Lugosi fans like to belittle studio execs who no longer gave him work in the 1950s. My question to *them* is, "Would *you* have hired this man?"

Kinematograph Weekly: "The cast, which includes many specialists in Grand Guignol, really gets to work on the grisly malarky and, except for an unintentional near slapstick climax, invests it with plausibility."

Harrison's Reports: "Those with weak stomachs, particularly women, may become nauseated by some of the scenes... The picture has been produced well—so well, in fact, that it is sure to cause chills to go up and down the spines of all who see it."

Variety: "Handling of the script... plays the horror tale fairly straight so what's happening is not too illogical until the finale wrapup, when all restraint comes off and the melodramatics run amok."

Motion Picture Exhibitor: "Rathbone has a grand time as the mad scientist, assisted nobly by some of the best names in the horror field. Audiences should be frightened plenty, and past experience proves that this can mean good grosses... Sure, a lot of it is corny, but it is all good fun in a grisly, frightening manner."

United Artists promoted *The Black Sleep* very heavily, commissioning George Bau to create life-sized figures of Rathbone, Tamiroff, Lugosi, Chaney, Carradine and Louanna Gardner(!) to be used in country-wide exploitation. (The figures, made at a reported cost of $20,000, were shipped to New York in individual coffins on May 9, 1956.) There was also a West Coast personal appearance tour for Lugosi, Chaney, Carradine, Tor Johnson, and TV horror hostess Vampira; the Howard Koch and Johnny Legend anecdotes above should provide a rough idea of what *that* was like, Lugosi-wise. (Readers who thirst for yet more *Black Sleep* horror stories can consult Greg Mank's *Karloff and Lugosi.*) *The Black Sleep* grossed nearly a million dollars in less than a year. In 1963, the film made even more money for UA when they re-released it as *Dr. Cadman's Secret.*

Lugosi's *Dracula* and the actor's final film *The Black Sleep* are interesting "bookends" to his horror movie career: *Dracula* led off the very first parade of screen monsters while *The Black Sleep* was the vanguard of the first horror movie "revolution," combining surgical gore and violence (but *not* at the expense of plot or atmosphere). The Lugosi *name* is more important to *The Black Sleep* than his role or his performance, but (little as he does in it) the picture would be a lot less fun and interesting and "all-star" without him. It's too bad that *Plan 9 from Outer Space* is generally cited as Lugosi's last movie; *The Black Sleep* has a more legitimate claim to that distinction, and (obviously) it's an infinitely better movie.

It's sad to see how far Lugosi slipped as an actor, sadder to hear from the filmmakers that he was sometimes less than a professional on the set, and saddest of all to learn about the self-destructive streak that tormented him in his final days. But one interesting "souvenir" from *The Black Sleep* is that familiar posed photograph of Rathbone, Tamiroff, Chaney, and Carradine gathered around the throne-like chair where Lugosi is seated; *if* any implication was intended, the only possible one is that Lugosi was the King of Horror Films. I'd like to think that Lugosi, the greatest of all horror personalities, *did* feel at that moment that he was receiving the recognition and respect of his acting peers.

Ed Wood and the Lugosi Mystique (1994)

by Bob Maidson

CREDITS: Director: Tim Burton; Producers: Denise Di Novi, Tim Burton; Co-Producer: Michael Flynn; Executive Producer: Michael Lehmann; Screenplay: Scott Alexander and Larry Karaszewski; Musical Score: Howard Shore; Film Editor: Chris Lebenzon; Production Designer: Tom Fuffield; Director of Photography: Stefan Czapsky; Editor: Chris Lebenzon; Costume Designer: Colleen Atwood; Key Makeup Artist: Ve Neill; Makeup: Carry Angland; Bela Lugosi Makeup Designed and Created by Rick Baker

CAST: Johnny Depp...Ed Wood, Martin Landau...Bela Lugosi, Sarah Jessica Parker...Dolores Fuller, Patricia Arquette...Kathy O'Hara, Jeffrey Jones...Criswell, G.D. Spradlin...Reverend Lemon, Vincent D'Onofrio...Orson Welles, Bill Murray...Bunny Breckinridge, Mike Starr...Georgie Weiss, Max Casella...Paul Marco, Brent Hinkley...Conrad Brooks, Lisa Marie...Vampira, George "The Animal" Steele...Tor Johnson, Conrad Brooks...Bartender

Bela Lugosi was little appreciated in his lifetime. After his triumphant turn as Dracula on the New York stage, and on tour, he immortalized his classic portrayal in Universal's 1931 film version. After that one, myth-making performance, his career started its decline, ending only with his frustrated, pained final days.

With the start of the "Monster Boom" in the late 1950s, Bela Lugosi was rediscovered by a legion of new, devoted admirers. Too bad the man himself died just before this incredible groundswell of popularity. Throughout the 1960s, Lugosi appeared on countless "monster" magazine covers, almost nightly on television, became the horror star most fun to imitate, and was the basis of a cult less visible now than the "Monster Boom" heyday, but no less fanatical.

To the Lugosi fan, critics were little better than a nuisance, and not to be taken seriously. For a long time, talking about his remarkable presence or theatrical delivery to the uninitiated would result in nothing more than blank looks. Worse, the stupid would mention their only point of Lugosi reference with exploitive cracks about his tragic drug dependence.

Fans would argue that Karloff was the better actor, that after 1939 Lugosi made few (if any) films of interest, that Lugosi always played himself. But such criticism is meaningless to those who fall under Lugosi's peculiar charm. It is the personality, the man himself, that is magnetic. There are few performers who could be as compelling, as watchable, as Lugosi even in his worst films.

Lugosi was the cinema's first professional bogeyman. Lon Chaney, Sr. was a peerless character actor who employed remarkable and oft times grotesque makeup. But his classic forays into melodrama, like *The Hunchback of Notre Dame* and *The Phantom of the Opera,* are horror films only in retrospect. They are grandfathers of the fantastic film genre, but by no means actual begetters of this specialized corner of movie history. The concept of a "horror" film would not start until Lugosi and *Dracula.*

Nor was Chaney, Sr. a "horror movie star." During the course of the 1920s, he played a wide variety of character types, the sheer scope of which were denied those equally fine actors who worked under the "horror" label. Chaney displayed his range in such non-horror fare as *While the City Sleeps, Outside the Law,* and *Mr. Wu;* an opportunity to flex his thespic muscles that was generally denied such horror-branded talents as Lugosi, Karloff, and Price.

So it is not Universal-International's 1957 *Man of a Thousand Faces* that is the first biographical film treatment of a horror star—but Touchstone's *Ed Wood.* As such, it is worthy of the serious genre buff's examination.

It is with the story of legendary "bad" film director Ed Wood and the frail-but-proud Bela Lugosi that director Tim Burton has fashioned his warmest, most human film to date. Wood emerges from the telling of his life a guileless naïf, history's greatest optimist doing his best in an industry riddled with compromise and hardship. In the film, Wood seems an innocent in every respect: innocent of talent, innocent of insight or judgment, and innocent in his child-like relations with people.

Johnny Depp plays Wood with all the freshness and enthusiasm of an overgrown boy. It's a rich, full performance that has an unsuspected subtlety to it. His optimism is never for the sole benefit of his friends or potential employers, but for himself as well. Throughout the film, we see Depp as Wood convincing himself that he has the talent and know-how to make his dreams come true.

Depp's work is full of little touches, just visible under the bluster. His voice cracks when especially excited, and there is a slight whistle to his speech, the aftermath of upper dentures. It is the kind of thoughtful playing that makes Depp one of the most intriguing young actors on the cinema scene today, and a staple of Burton's repertory of players.

Is this counter with the portraits of the historical Wood, handed down throughout the years among the Hollywood fringe? No matter, because that is not the game Burton is playing. Screenwriters Scott Alexander and Larry Karaszewski take the Wood that history hands us —an alcoholic, exploitive hack—and transform him into an almost Chaplinesque figure. As written, Alexander and Karaszewski have produced the ultimate anti-biopic: their Ed Wood has all the tenacity and drive of a Great Man, but none of the genius. He is a clown despite himself.

Under Burton's directorial baton, Lugosi comes off better. Bela Lugosi is the film's most human character: flawed, yes, but commanding, proud, courageous. The Lugosi of *Ed Wood* is no paragon, he is drawn with very broad and not always accurate strokes, but it is a fine memorial to him, the first of all the great cinematic monsters.

Lugosi is the butt of most of the film's jokes. Hollywoodites and Ed's friends are all amazed to learn the he's still alive, and Lugosi's Dracula obsession is sadly comical. Amazingly, his dignity remains unscathed, and our respect for him grows as he struggles to overcome these casual rebuffs.

And through it all, Lugosi is *fun*. No matter how harrowing his addiction or painful his circumstances, the film is truly alive when dealing with Lugosi. It's impossible not to leave *Ed Wood* doing some of Lugosi's dialogue, or imitating his trademark hand gestures.

The tone throughout the film is unfailingly sweet. Wood, and his crew of friends and followers, lived on the very fringe of the Hollywood experience. But rather than poke fun at the untalented director, Burton treats them with sincere affection. This is no mean-spirited bashing of an unfortunate artist—something along the lines of the Medved brothers' witless *Golden Turkey Awards.* On one level, *Ed Wood* is a buddy-film, the story of Bela and Eddie. But on another, deeper level, the film is actually about building an alternate family.

As the film tells it, Wood, a transvestite who fought courageously during World War II, manages to bring together a group of amiable misfits. His entourage included people like the "psychic" Criswell, such untried and untalented actors as Conrad Brooks and Paul Marco, Swedish wrestler Tor Johnson, and transsexual Bunny Breckinridge. Together, they build a small community for themselves with Ed at the helm. In an age when contentious debate on the meaning of families and their values fill the nation's rhetoric, along comes *Ed Wood* to explain what families are really all about. The world of *Ed Wood,* at least within his small coterie of companions, is one of acceptance and unconditional love. Perhaps the underlying ethos of the film is best relayed in a snatch of dialogue among Ed, his wife Kathy, and former horror film hostess Vampira, going through the script of what would become *Plan 9 From Outer Space.*

"The Ghoul's wife?! God, I can't believe I'm doing this..." Vampira grimaces.

"You should feel lucky," Kathy says. "Ed's the only guy in town who doesn't pass judgment on people."

"Hell, if I did, I wouldn't have any friends," he says.

It is obvious that Burton has great affection for Wood, and a deep understanding of his need to get close to his idol, Bela Lugosi. Like Wood, Burton grew up a movie-monster loving kid in suburban America. And where Wood later befriended his boyhood hero Lugosi, Burton managed to work with his idol, Vincent Price. Price narrated Burton's masterful (and surely autobiographical) short film *Vincent,* and later played the Inventor in *Edward Sissorhands,* also starring Johnny Depp.

Ed Wood can be seen as a dark, mirror-vision of Burton's relationship with Price. The tragic Lugosi ended his career in isolation and obscurity, while the luckier, more successful Price left this life a figure beloved by many generations of Americans, an artist working in projects worthy of his talents until the end. Wood struggled to put together work for Lugosi, while Burton had real Hollywood money and viable projects for Price. And, in both cases, both directors were obsessed more with the image their idols projected on the screen than the actual men: Wood with Lugosi's immortal Dracula, and Burton with the Poe-inspired, doomed aesthetes of Price.

Ironically, it is Vincent Price who was heir to the mantel of Bela Lugosi. Many genre buffs consider Price to be the second generation Boris Karloff, but that is only true in so far that both were famous and successful throughout their long careers, both lives ending on high notes. But it is with Lugosi—a fine actor revered more for his mesmerizing personality than his very real talents—that Price has his deepest affinity. Price became a personality, a brand name as reliable at drawing scare-hungry crowds as Lugosi. Where Bela traded on his eyes, his magnificent gestures, and his legendary voice, Price used his right eyebrow, his super-theatrical delivery, and his own "sinister" intonation.

Price made many sleazy exploitation films at AIP in the late '60s and early '70s, films that worked solely on the strength of his charisma alone. Lugosi made nine films for Monogram in the 1940s, and while not as flashy as the AIP product, they too traded exclusively on star power. Many film buffs still make the distinction between "horror films" and "Bela Lugosi/Vincent Price movies." They are genres in-and-of themselves.

Most historians believe that the Wood-Lugosi relationship was more important to Wood than Lugosi. (The same was probably true of the Burton-Price relationship. Price was never recorded describing Burton as more than "an amusing little fellow.") Screenwriters Alexander and Karaszewski have deepened their friendship, giving the film a richer emotional core. As to whether Wood was an actual "friend to" Lugosi is open to debate. Bela Lugosi, Jr. is quoted as saying, "The jury is still out on that." But to make theirs an almost father-son bond, several facts of Lugosi's life had to be edited out. These include Lugosi's fourth wife Lillian, his final wife Hope, and his own son, Bela, Jr. These omissions are painful to the film buff who demands nothing but accuracy, but they make artistic sense for the film.

Heroically, Burton shot the film in black-and-white. (Columbia Pictures, which originally had the option for the film, backed out after Burton insisted on this artistic decision.) Howard Shore wrote the wonderfully evocative score, replacing the usual Burton standby, Danny Elfman. Shore's music is rich with fruity "science fiction" excesses, as well as the driving bongo drum sounds of Hollywood's "beat" era.

Because it is interesting to see where the film departs from actual events in Lugosi's life, let's look at Lugosi's scenes and references in *Ed Wood* closely. We will also look at elements dropped from the original screenplay.

The film opens with Wood's (largely fictional) adventures in getting *Glen or Glenda* off the ground. After grabbing a quick drink (the actual Conrad Brooks does a cameo as the bartender), Wood walks the streets. And, passing a mortuary, he sees in the window...

Wood removes his sunglasses, unable to believe his eyes.

We first see Martin Landau's Bela Lugosi lying in a coffin. The mortician stands over him, expectantly. After a beat, the "corpse" snaps to life. "Too constrictive," he thunders. "This is the most uncomfortable coffin I have ever been in."

"Gee, Mr. Lugosi, I've never had any complaints before," the mortician chimes in.

"The selection is quite shoddy. You are wasting my time!" Grabbing his cane and broad-brimmed black hat, Lugosi storms out.

Suddenly *Ed Wood,* already amusing and entertaining, gets infused with some of the Lugosi magic.

We not only feel it, but Wood does himself. He stands there, awe-struck by this real-life glimpse of his idol. After approaching Lugosi, the two engage in some of the film's most priceless dialogue.

"Why are you buying a coffin?'' Wood asks.

"Because I'm planning on dying soon," Lugosi says, chomping on one of his infamous cigars.

"Really?"

"Yes, I'm embarking on another bus-and-truck tour of *Dracula."* Landau gives the famous name all the classic Lugosi cadence. "Twelve cities in ten days, if that's conceivable."

"You know, I saw you perform *Dracula*. In Poughkeepsie, in 1938."

"Eh, that was a terrible production. Renfield was a drunk! "

"I thought it was great. You were much scarier in real life than you were in the movie."

Lugosi pauses, happy. "Thank you."

"I waited to get your autograph, but you never came outside."

"I apologize. When I play Dracula, I put myself into a trace. It takes me much time to re-emerge. Oh, here's my bus. Shit, where's my transfer?! "

"Don't you have a car?"

"I refuse to drive in this country. Too many madmen."

In Wood's car, the exchange deepens. "But you're a big star!" Wood protests.

"No more. I haven't worked in four years. This town, it chews you up, then spits you out. I'm just an ex-bogeyman."

Outside Lugosi's home, the horror master assesses changing tastes, and the decline of his fortunes. This was the era of the science fiction/ horror film, as exemplified by movies like *Them.* Lugosi says: "They don't want the classic horror films anymore. Today, it's all giant bugs, giant spiders, giant grasshoppers—who would believe such nonsense!"

Wood agrees. "The old ones were much spookier. They had castles, full moons..."

Lugosi puts his finger on their secret easily. "They were *mythic.* They had a *poetry* to them. And you know what else? The women prefer the traditional monsters."

"The women?"

"The pure horror, it both repels and attracts them," Lugosi emphasizes with his cigar. "Because in their collective unconsciousness, they have the agony of childbirth. The blood. The blood is the horror... Take my word for it. If you want to score with a young lady, take her to see *Dracula."*

This snippet of dialogue about women and horror is pure Lugosi. It is culled almost verbatim from various interviews he gave throughout his career. It became part of his standard interview repertoire.

Lugosi opens the door of his simple tract home. Visible inside is a huge portrait of him young, in full Dracula costume. Dogs yap in the distance.

"Ugh, what a mess. My wife of twenty years left me last month. I'm not much of a housekeeper. [To the dogs.] Shh! I'm coming, my darlings. I will feed you. [To Wood.] The children of the night are calling me." And, laughing the famous, sinister Lugosi chuckle, he vanishes behind the door.

The initial meeting between Wood and Lugosi remains one of the highlights of the film. Landau has such a handle on the man, that the transformation is almost complete. Little nuances, like the way Lugosi's eyes would narrow while delivering dialogue, the expressive and theatrical hand gestures, and, most of all, the mock-diabolical laugh, he has down pat. If Lugosi has been dead for 39 years prior to *Ed Wood,* surely Landau had magically brought part of him back to life.

Part of the effect is Rick Baker's magnificent makeup job. A longtime fan of the classic movie monsters, Baker lovingly transformed Landau's distinctive features into Lugosi's. Appliances covered Landau's prominent upper lip, and Baker blackened the actor's teeth, removing his natural piano-smile. Add to that a dimpled chin, enlarged ears, and craggy brows and wig and the transformation is complete. But Landau never simply plays the makeup. The Lugosi visage is so familiar that a lesser actor would walk through the part, playing the face and voice. But Landau puts the life and fire back into a man who has descended (unhappily) in the public mind to little better than a cartoon. He plays a now bent old man, but it is Lugosi. It is a vivid performance.

Ironically, when Baker received a well deserved Academy Award for Best Makeup, he thanked his inspiration, Lugosi's old nemesis, Universal makeup ace Jack Pierce.

Stepping away from the film, how factual is this sequence? It says much, but distorts a great deal as well. Lugosi was performing *Dracula* in sad stock companies throughout his latter career. Actor David Manners has testified that Lugosi put himself into a trance-state while playing the Vampire King. He was a life-long cigar smoker, and he never learned to drive. (Driving was the duty of each of his three American wives.) He was deeply resentful in the shift of interest from classic horror, and his views on women and horror are well known. So what could be wrong?

Several things. Lugosi and Wood did not meet in a mortuary, but rather through Alex Gordon, one of Wood's early business partners. At the time, he was married to his fourth wife Lillian, and Wood was trying to interest him in *Glen or Glenda,* which already existed as a project. Nor did Lugosi have a home at this point, but rather an apartment. Lugosi was a life-long dog owner, but he favored huge hounds and not small, yappy dogs. The celebrated portrait of Lugosi from the early 1920s, dashing in winged collar, with bowler and overcoat draped elegantly over his arm, hung prominently in his living room, not a painting of the young Lugosi as Dracula.

Buried deep in the wallets of both Alexander and Karaszewski are their poetic licenses.

Home, Wood tells Dolores (Sarah Jessica Parker) that he met a great horror star, the first of many Lugosi jokes.

"Boris Karloff?" she asks.

"Close! The other one!" He imitates Lugosi's celebrated hypnotic hand gestures.

"You met Basil Rathbone! "

"Oh, the hell with you. I met Bela Lugosi! "

"I thought he was dead."

"No! He's very alive. Well... sort of. He's old and frail—but he's still Bela Lugosi! And he's really nice."

Ed Wood's Halloween sequence is perhaps the film's ultimate comment on Lugosi as a character. While children trick-or-treat outside, Wood sits on the couch with his hero, both of them beneath the huge portrait of Lugosi as Dracula. The old and sickly Lugosi sits in his Dracula evening clothes, watching his younger self on television and holding his dogs for comfort.

White Zombie plays on television, and both men are illuminated by the flickering light of the screen. Stefan Czapsky's stunning photography and Baker's makeup create an almost perfect illusion, again it brings Lugosi to the life.

Vampira (Lisa Marie), the first great horror host, breaks into the action. Wood is annoyed at her lack of respect for the film.

"I think she's a honey," Lugosi says. "Look at those jugs."

In a breathtaking evocation of the man, Landau as Lugosi briefly imitates Lugosi's locked hands from *White Zombie* before employing his famous Dracula hypnotic hand gestures. His eyes blaze, and his sinister smile is touched with the salacious.

"Vampira! You will come under my spell! You will be my slave of love! "

Wood, fascinated, mirrors Lugosi's actions. It's a beautiful image. (And, honestly, how many people reading this book have not tried it themselves during some forgotten childhood late show? We simply weren't lucky enough to do it with Lugosi himself.) "Hey Bela, how do you do that?"

"You must be double-jointed and you must be Hungarian."

Fatigued, Lugosi leaves Wood to the television as he takes his medicine. The action is seen taking place in shadows behind a curtain to Wood's side. Seconds later Lugosi, energy restored, emerges. "I feel better now."

The doorbell rings. "Children! " Lugosi cries. "I love children!" He hustles into his cape, dons fangs, and throws open the door.

The terrified children scurry away, except for one child, dressed as a cowboy. He is unimpressed, despite Lugosi's best efforts to frighten him.

Wood jumps through the door and pulls the upper teeth from the front of his mouth. The cowboy runs in panic.

Lugosi's impressed. "How'd you do that?"

"Dentures," Wood replies. "I lost my pearlies in the war."

Again, how are we to take this as an actual representation of Lugosi's life? Lugosi's medically induced drug addiction is now too well documented to detail here (and the film *Ed Wood* makes full use of it). And film historian William K. Everson records that during Lugosi's live "horror show" that played in smaller theaters along with one of his lesser films, atomic age children howled at him. By 1950, horror had a radioactive face, and Dracula, the only face Lugosi had, was passé.

More importantly, this scene serves as the perfect, heartbreaking metaphor for Lugosi's final years. It is the film's most unforgettable image, the perfect summation of all that could be said of Lugosi at this time of his life. There he sat in obscurity, under a portrait of earlier and past glories, shrouded in the costume of his greatest triumph—the costume that would become, literally, his shroud. Lugosi never forgot his earlier success, and never completely came to grips with his later poverty and failed career. Everywhere, from the momentos in his home to daily television, came the constant reminder of who and what he once was.

In more ways than one he sat under Dracula's shadow.

Cut from the completed film, Wood and Lugosi, both drunk, break into a local cemetery, something Lugosi does "every Halloween." Lugosi, still in Dracula's formal attire, cavorts around the graveyard. Finally, he playfully flaps his cape and says: "I am Dracula! I will live forever!!!"

Wood meets again with George Weiss (Mike Starr), producer of *Glen*. His new pitch is that he can deliver something that a picture needs to be a success... a star! He holds up a beautiful, early 1930s' photo of Lugosi.

"Lugosi?" Weiss asks.

"Yeah! Lugosi!"

"Isn't he dead?"

Wood seals the deal, promising a script in three days.

Home, Wood furiously hammers out the script that would become *Glen or Glenda*. On the phone with Bunny, he cajoles his friend into rounding up transvestites and transsexuals. There is a knock at his door and Lugosi, excited at working again, enters.

"I need transvestites!" Wood tells Breckinridge, and hangs up.

"Eddie," Lugosi guardedly asks, "what kind of movie is this?"

Wood explains it's about people with two personalities.

Ed Wood and his troupe of actors wave a warm good-bye to another bunch of potential investors, in *Ed Wood.*

"Oh, like Jekyll and Hyde!" Lugosi is thrilled. "I've always wanted to play Jekyll and Hyde! I'm looking forward to this production." In this sequence, Landau looks and sounds more like himself and less like Lugosi than any other portion of the film.

Wood explains that, instead of the character with dual personalities, he is more like the puppetmaster that looks down on the characters, overseeing everything.

"Ah," Lugosi says. "So I pull the strings."

Wood, inspired, dashes to his typewriter.

(In actuality, Wood first met Lugosi with hopes of casting him in *Glen or Glenda.* Lugosi initially wanted nothing to do with the picture, but when his salary was doubled to $1000, he relented. Wood had to re-write the script to accommodate him.)

Switch to a dingy studio labeled LARCHMONT STUDIOS. With great ceremony, it's announced that Mr. Lugosi has arrived. Speaking through a megaphone to his staff that is standing right beside him, Wood admonishes the crew not to be too excited and to treat the man with respect.

The door opens and Lugosi enters.

Ed runs up to him like an excited kid.

Landau's Lugosi wears a dark suit, a black, caped-coat, and carries a broad-brimmed hat. He carries a cane, but his bearing is regal, proud.

"Eddie," he whispers, "do you have my money?"

Wood peels some bills from a large wad, and the two set to work.

Sitting in the *Glen or Glenda* armchair, the makeup man applies powder to Lugosi's hands. Snaking up his arm are dozens of black needle marks. Lugosi looks at the man, resigned, pained, still proud.

What follows is the film's most hilarious—and infamous—vignette. As Lugosi prepares to shoot, Conrad Brooks approaches, asking Lugosi to autograph his script.

Lugosi beams, all gracious n*oblese oblige.* Brooks gushes, Lugosi smiles indulgently.

"You know which movie of yours I love, Mr. Lugosi? *The Invisible Ray.* You were great as Karloff's sidekick."

Lugosi freezes. He looks up at Brooks, a picture of barely controlled rage. "Sidekick??... Karloff!!" He pulls the autograph from the book and tears it to shreds. "Fuck you!! Karloff doesn't deserve to smell my shit! That limey cocksucker can rot in hell, for all I care!!!"

Wood dashes over, looking daggers at Brooks.

"How dare that asshole bring up Karloff?!! You think it takes talent to play Frankenstein?! No! It's just makeup and grunting!" Here Landau magically mimes Lugosi doing the monster, grunting, his face contorted with disdain. It is an hysterically funny bit.

Wood placates him. "Now Dracula, that's a part that takes acting."

"Of course!" All of Lugosi's stagecraft comes to the fore, instantly becoming Dracula. "It's all in the voice, and the eyes, and the hand..."

Wood suggests he takes a little rest before shooting.

"Bullshit!" he cries, folding his arms, bottom lip jutting forward. "I am ready now! Roll the camera! "

Wood sheepishly dashes back to the crew. They all stand back, cowed by the great man's fury. "Action," Wood whispers.

And suddenly, Lugosi is on and the magic happens. He utters Wood's atrocious dialogue with all of the old fire and style expected from the First Man of Horror. The mesmerized Wood mumbles the dialogue behind the camera, slowly raising his megaphone to cut.

Lugosi stops him with a masterful gesture. "Pull the strings!" He commands, with all the fury of some great, dark god. A god, perhaps, more formidable than ever. "Pull the strings!"

Wood cuts, he and the crew flabbergasted by Lugosi's tremendous power and presence.

Again, how is the Lugosi buff to digest this? It is wonderful movie-making, but is it true?

Again, yes-and-no. Lugosi and Karloff were not friends in any real sense, and Lugosi certainly harbored a strong resentment for his English rival. But there are few instances of Lugosi flying into such an intense, foul-mouthed rage. Usually, it was a sigh of resignation and blank look of puzzlement.

Many genre magazines, particularly one still aimed at children, have taken *Ed Wood* to task for Lugosi's use of profanity. Actually, it serves a dual purpose. To hear the famous Lugosi voice spew obscenities is undeniably funny. Also, it somehow makes him more human. Lugosi—as a man and icon—has often seemed so imperious, so in control, as to be something slightly more than human. Something larger. Humanizing him makes Lugosi more accessible, and, hence, much more likable. It's unlikely Lugosi swore the constant blue-streak portrayed here (the reader would do well to remember stories of Lugosi insisting his cronies keep their language clean around ladies), but he was human, after all. It is interesting to note that other character's obscenities were cut from the screenplay to emphasize Lugosi's.

Much scripted material follows that did not make it into the final film. Wood and Lugosi screen *Glen or Glenda,* only to learn that Weiss has inserted stag-party style footage. Afterwards, Wood and Lugosi plan additional films to ride the wave of the expected *Glenda* success. Lugosi denounces Universal (which is probably the reason why this, and all other negative references to Universal by name, were cut) which controls the rights to *Dracula.* Wood concocts a new character, Dr. Acula.

That night, Lugosi calls in desperate need of help. Wood pulls up in front of the house, finding no answer to his knocks at the door. Inside Lugosi lies sprawled on the floor. Beside him are a rubber tube, a needle, and his whimpering dogs. Heartbreakingly, Shore's score breaks into a mournful snatch of *Swan Lake,* the only music in the original *Dracula.* To underscore the poignancy, Wood helps him to the couch where he lies under the portrait of young Lugosi as the immortal Count. A ruined man under his monument of former glory.

"Is there anything I can get you? Water? A blanket?"

"Goulash," Lugosi weakly replies. He's so broke, he doesn't know what to do.

Wood promises to find something.

Dolores convinces Wood to work as an independent outside of the studio system. In a series of montages, Wood makes his sales calls. "Yes," he tells one hopeful, *"The* Bela Lugosi. Yes, he's still alive."

Wood books Lugosi on a live, television comedy show. Backstage, he and Lugosi, in full Dracula regalia, go over the script. Lugosi struggles with the language. (Actually, it was Alex Gordon who wrangled Lugosi onto *The Red Skelton Show*, and coached him with his dialogue. The sequence is inspired by Lugosi's fatal foray into live television comedy. Skelton would not give Lugosi his cues, and the weakened actor left the show almost in total collapse.)

On the monitor, Wood sees Criswell (Jeffrey Jones, who is a delight), predicting colonies on Mars by 1970. He is enraptured.

The skit starts and the comic, Slick Slomopavitz (a name inspired by Skelton's Clem Cadiddlehopper, but the actor here uses the voice, mannerisms, and delivery of Huntz Hall), disturbs the sleep of the vampire. Slomopavitz ad libs, confusing the flustered Lugosi. The curtain goes down, killing the scene before it really starts.

Backstage, Slomopavitz says: "I told you we should've gotten Karloff."

Still backstage, our heroes meet the majestic Criswell. Jones imbues the role with all of its showy, razzle dazzle. He predicts that Lugosi's next project will be an outstanding success.

Later, at the Mocambo Room, Criswell and his cronies entertain Wood and Lugosi. Criswell confesses to Wood that all of his predictions are made-up. "If you dress nice and talk well, people will swallow anything." He offers Lugosi a glass of wine.

"I never drink... wine," Lugosi says.

Wood and Criswell roar.

We see the adventures of filming *Bride of the Atom.* Wood guides Lugosi, and later Tor Johnson, through a corridor door, giving both the same direction. "At Universal, they shot two scenes a day," Lugosi tells Johnson. "Eddie can knock off twenty or thirty. He's incredible."

Cut from the finished film is a sequence where Wood awakens the sleeping Lugosi to shoot his next scene. The finished film cuts to Wood, Lugosi, Johnson, and Loretta King in a huddle, blocking out the next scene. Wood motions Lugosi to the Tesla coils. Lugosi balks, saying one of them burned him on *The Return of Chandu.* (Not quite. There are no Tesla coils in *The Return of Chandu.* Instead, Lugosi wouldn't go near the laboratory set of *Glen or Glenda,* afraid the test tubes would explode and burn him.)

After filming shuts down due to lack of funds, the screenplay details a Lugosi-Wood visit to an Eastern-type, pseudo religious temple. Both sit through a lecture as Lugosi gives him some fatherly advice: "In life, the decisions that haunt you are the ones where you just don't know... where right or wrong will never be answered." (In fact, Lugosi was deeply interested in mysticism, and was friends for over twenty years with Dr. Manly P. Hall, a Hollywood "mystic." Hall hypnotized Lugosi during *Black Friday*—an event debated to this day—and officiated at Lugosi's fifth marriage. It's a shame this sequence was cut, if it was ever filmed at all.)

In Griffith Park at night, *Bride of the Atom* readies its terrifying climax. Wood and his cronies dam the stream as young Tony McCoy practices his lines. Up at the car, an ailing Lugosi asks for a chance to rest. Once Wood leaves his friend, Lugosi pulls a rubber tube from his pocket and wraps it around his arm.

The stream has now deepened, and Wood wants the motor that works the octopus. But Marco didn't think of stealing that along with the mechanical beast. Meanwhile, a revived Lugosi comes down the hill to shoot his scene.

Lugosi's courage is detailed in the following scene. Never is Landau more poignant.

"Let's shoot this fucker! Where do I go?"

"You'll be fighting with the octopus."

Lugosi looks at the black water. "Out there?! What happened to the stream?"

Poor old Lugosi wades into the freezing water. A crew member throws him a bottle of whiskey. "Okay. How do you turn this thing on?"

Wood explains they have no motor, and that Lugosi will have to make it look like it's killing him.

"Do you know I turned down *Frankenstein*?" Lugosi asks. "After I did *Dracula,* the studio offered me *Frankenstein.* But I turned it down. The part wasn't sexy enough. It was too degrading for a big star like me."

Landau is chilling. He uses Lugosi's voice with a wistful cadence, full of lost chances and missed opportunities. It is almost possible to hear Lugosi's thinking: if I had made different choices, I wouldn't be in a cold stream at 4.00 A.M. with a broken octopus, making crap for Ed Wood.

A trooper, Lugosi throws the bottle back and falls onto the octopus, screaming and thrashing like a dying man, which, in fact, he is. It's an incredibly moving bit, and Wood and the crew watch, stunned.

It's morning, and the exhausted crew return to Larchmont Studios. Wood thanks Lugosi. The old star smiles warmly, telling him there aren't many people he'd do it for. Wood then gives him a new speech. Lugosi reads it, impressed. (In actuality, Lugosi balked at the new dialogue.)

Interestingly, Lugosi's role, Vornoff, had great resonances for the actor. The speech, which Landau delivers with all of Lugosi's magic, could almost be about the sad actor's life. "Twenty years ago I was banned from my homeland. I was classed as a madman—a charlatan outlawed in the world of science which previously honored me as a genius. Now here in this forsaken jungle hell, I have proven that I am all right." Lugosi, in a telling Freudian slip, read the line "all right" rather than "right." *Ed Wood* makes this look intentional. Better yet is Landau's reading of the almost weeping Lugosi: "Home. I have no home. Hunted... despised... living like an animal—the jungle is my home! But I will show the world that I can be its master. I shall perfect my own race of people—a race of atomic supermen that will conquer the world!"

Did Lugosi read these lines fully conscious that he was speaking metaphorically about himself? I can only answer: how could he not? Watch the actual footage from *Bride,* and you'll see Lugosi putting all of himself into a part that required so little. Visible there is Lugosi's hurt, and his pride; his early success, crushing downfall, and dreams of future glories. It's heartbreaking in life, and moving in *Ed Wood.*

What is the legacy of *Bride of the Atom* (later *Bride of the Monster*)? It is another darling of that inane "worst film" crowd, boobs who find greater amusement in trash than quality. But while *Bride* is undoubtedly poor, it is by no means the worst film ever made, and is Ed Wood's best film by far. *Bride* is nothing less than one of Katzman's Monogram pictures, made 10 years later for less money.

More importantly, it is Lugosi's last speaking part on film. And though visibly debilitated, his magic and intensity remained. Watching the film may take heroic effort, but it is nothing compared to the heroism of the man who made it.

Wood gets another desperate call from Lugosi. At the actor's home, the young director is held at gun point by the depleted bogeyman. Drunk, despairing, the actor talks of suicide. His unemployment has run out, and now without money to pay for his home, he has nothing to live for. He considers taking Wood with him.

Wood, desperate, talks Lugosi out of it. As the actor realizes the enormity of what he was about to do, he collapses in sobs on the director's shoulder. Landau, again, is superb. Never in the film does he look so old, so frail, or so helpless as in this sequence.

At the desk of South Metropolitan State Hospital, a frightened nurse looks up. "My goodness," she says. "You gave me the willies. You look just like that Dracula guy. "

Lugosi, proud, terrified, says: "My name is Bela Lugosi. I wish to commit myself. I have been a drug addict for twenty years. I need help..." And the aged, stooped actor is led away.

Again the Lugosi historian checks truth at the door. The story of Wood, the gun, and Lugosi's suicide is one that first appeared in Cremer's Lugosi biography. We have no assurance of its truth other than Wood's word. According to Wood, Lugosi was upset when kids wrote a local

Bela Lugosi (Martin Landau) shows Ed Wood (Johnny Depp) his classic hand gestures.

station after an airing of *Dracula,* asking if Bela Lugosi was still alive. (Discovering if *Dracula* was aired before the *Shock Theater* package might help confirm or reject this tale.) Is it something Lugosi, even in the depth of despair, would have contemplated? From my readings on the man, I am inclined to reject the story. Lugosi's fear of death is too well documented to make this suicide attempt probable, nor was Wood the first person Lugosi would turn to in despair.

More importantly, Lugosi committed himself on April 21, 1955— Lillian Lugosi's birthday. It was both a cry for help, and a tremendously spiteful attack on his former wife. Wood was in no way involved.

Later, Wood is outraged at reporters exploiting the recovering Lugosi. Wood throws the newsboys out, calling them parasites. Lugosi demurs, "There is no such thing as bad press... [I'm] the first celebrity ever to check into rehab." (A line which relies a little too much on historical hindsight.) Lugosi plans a return once his strength is back.

In actuality, Lugosi received much press attention during his hospital stay, but Wood never sent anyone away.

Wood and Kathy meet in the hospital waiting room. Later, she has has knitted some booties for Lugosi. "They're black. To match his cape."

Wood is informed that Lugosi must leave the hospital, as his insurance will no longer cover him. And so, the concerned director leads the aged star from the hospital. Lugosi looks more than half dead as Wood lifts him from his bed. Ill, frail, Lugosi is eager to work on another picture.

Again, no. In life, Lugosi left the hospital under his own steam on August 5, 1955, a cured man. He would live for another year, marrying for the fifth time.

As scripted, Wood borrows a camera and some film to shoot some footage of Bela to raise his broken spirits.

In the finished film, Wood and Lugosi stand outside of the actor's home, shooting footage that will end up in *Plan 9 From Outer Space.* (Lugosi was really living in a small apartment at 5620 Harold Way at the time. The home in *Plan 9* belonged to Tor Johnson.) In caped-coat, with his broad-brimmed hat, Landau looks more like Lugosi than ever. Wood is working just to get something in the can to make Bela happy, and they improvise some business on the spot. "What if I'm not in too big a hurry?" Lugosi asks. "What if I take a moment to slow down and savor the beauty of life? To smell a flower?''

The two shoot, and, as played, it is a beautiful and moving scene, a sad look at what both had been reduced. Lugosi, fighting the demons of age, illness, and death, humbled but unbowed, working as best he can, and, Wood, a minor-leaguer who refuses to quit. It's impossible not to feel for them.

Real life was just as interesting. Wood had gotten $800 front money to start shooting *Plan 9.* The first thing he did was get as much Lugosi footage as he could. Days later, Hope Lugosi found her husband lying in bed, dead of natural causes. In his hand was a script for a film titled *The Final Curtain.*

Wood, Lugosi, Vampira, Johnson, Kathy, and Criswell show up for the premiere of *Bride of the Monster.* As scripted, our gang ride a hearse, unable to find the theater for some time. At the movie house, the manager tries to quiet a waiting and unruly crowd (mostly youngsters).

In the finished film, Wood and crew arrive at the theater. The crowd of kids and teens are worked up to a near riot. Criswell leads Tor Johnson down the aisle (he is in his white contact lenses and can hardly see), while Vampira escorts the ailing Lugosi. Kids pelt them with trash and popcorn, hoop and holler, and one even grabs Vampira's breasts. A roughneck steals Criswell's wallet.

Wood races after them in a rescue attempt. The film starts as our heroes make for their hearse.

In front of the theater, thugs are stripping the car.

Behind them, the doors explode with rioting movie-goers. Kathy runs to the street and literally jumps on a cab. They pile in, speeding away from the angry crowd.

"Now *that* was a premiere," Lugosi says.

Great scene, funny story. Didn't happen. A benefit premiere for *Bride* occurred while Lugosi was still in the hospital. Lugosi only saw the film at a local bijou with Wood after his recovery. But if this premiere didn't happen, well, it should've.

Lugosi and Wood stroll down the streets of Hollywood. Lugosi is still talking about the night before (he envied the kid who grabbed Vampira), and tells Wood he admires Kathy's heroism with the cab. "I know none of my wives would've [done that]."

A reflective Lugosi says: "Eddie, I want to thank you. These last few days have been a *good* time."

"I only wish you coulda seen the movie. "

"No problem. I know it by heart..."

The camera lowers, the building behind Lugosi surrounding him like a proscenium arch. The magic is on again, and he delivers the soliloquy from *Bride.* Again, Lugosi is in his glory, plying his craft with all the old passion. The camera pulls back, and we see applauding tourists. They ask for his autograph.

Delighted, he signs. When a tourist asks him about his age, Lugosi replies: "I'm seventy-four, but I don't know it. If the brain is young, then the spirit is still vigorous... like a young man." He puts his arm around Wood.

It's a touching scene, and our last glimpse of him alive.

It's comforting to realize how much of this is true. After Wood and Lugosi attended *Bride,* Lugosi was met by an older fan in the lobby. The film quotes him almost word-for-word. And while walking down a Hollywood street, Lugosi broke into the *Bride* monologue, amazing and delighting passers-by.

But was this really a *good* time for him? Unfortunately, the real life Lugosi was far more tragic than the reel life one. Lugosi was bitterly unhappy about his health, felt the loss of youth acutely, and still desperately wanted a comeback film. He greatly feared death, and was not entirely content in his fifth marriage. Unhappily, Lugosi died in a cloud of despair and desperation. The acceptance and calm he displays in *Ed Wood* are largely fictional.

At home, Wood receives the call that Lugosi has died. At the funeral home and graveside, our heroes mourn the loss of their beloved friend. Landau lies in state, wearing Lugosi's Dracula attire, looking like the tacky photos we've seen of the actual man in his coffin. In the film, it appears that this cast of characters were the only people in attendance, with Wood as chief mourner. Again, Lillian, Hope, Bela Jr., and scores of friends and well-wishers are missing.

After the funeral, a broken-hearted Wood screens and re-screens his *Plan 9* footage. Again the strains of *Swan Lake* are heard, a bitter reminder of the Lugosi tragedy.

Cut from the film, too, is Kathy helping Wood recover from his loss. "I'd seen him in a coffin so many times," he laments, "I expected him to jump out..."

"Ed," she says, "You've got to snap out of this. Bela's dead—you're not!"

"I might as well be. I made shitty movies that nobody wanted to see. I blew it. All he wanted was a comeback... that last glory... I was a fuckin' hack! I let people re-cut the movies, cast their relatives... I let Bela down."

With Lugosi dead, the film rapidly recounts how Wood came to make *Plan 9 From Outer Space.* As his opus takes shape, he exhorts: "This will be the ultimate Ed Wood film! No compromises! " We now track the production of his "masterpiece," a film the historical Wood called "my little gem."

Plan 9 is now in production. Marco arrives with three potential Lugosi doubles, two old men and an Asian. "This guy doesn't work at all," Wood says of the last one.

"Well, I was thinkin', like, when Bela played Fu Manchu."

"That was Karloff."

At coffee house meeting with Vampira, Wood meets bald, 35 year-old Tom Mason, Kathy's chiropractor. Wood holds a napkin under his nose, and Lugosi's double is found!

At the Hollywood premiere of *Plan 9* at the prestigious Pantages Theater (didn't happen), Wood thanks his fans, and adds "This film is for Bela." As the movie plays, our heroes watch from the balcony, immortality assured. Wood speaks the film's narration to himself, caught up in his own genius. He says: "This is the one. This is the one I'll be remembered for."

Fortunately, the film ends with quick summaries of the cast's later lives. Wood's end note reads: "Edward D. Wood, Jr. kept struggling in Hollywood, but mainstream success eluded him. After a slow descent into alcoholism and monster nudie films, he died in 1978 at the age of fifty-four. Two years later, Ed was voted 'Worst Director of All Time,' bringing him worldwide acclaim and a new generation of fans."

Lugosi's runs: "Bela Lugosi never rose from the grave, but after appearing in 103 films, he is more famous than ever. Today, his movie memorabilia outsells Boris Karloff's by a substantial margin."

What is one to make of *Ed Wood?* The screenplay portrays a harder edged man, one who was often drunk and, while sweet, had flashes of temper. Burton removes Wood's seedier edges, fashioning the real man into a heroic (if misguided) artist: a child-like creator who never stopped believing in himself. In Depp's good natured playing, what could have been an exploitive huckster becomes an incompetent, misunderstood artist, struggling to preserve his vision against greater odds than a more generous God would have allowed.

Rather than an exposé of the Hollywood fringe element in the '50s, Burton has created an incredibly warm and life-affirming comedy. The laughs are bittersweet (Lugosi drinking formaldehyde, or his harrowing descent into addiction), but to Burton the laughs are there. We chuckle at the hero's expense, but we never loose our affection for him. In Burton's typical Baroque way, he has made a dear little movie about an extended family of odd-balls and the

Ed Wood gives direction to some of his cast members on the set of *Bride of the Monster* in the film *Ed Wood.*

persistence of their dreams. Burton furthers his exploration of the outcast artist-hero (the Joker in *Batman,* Edward Sissorhands, Jack in *Nightmare Before Christmas)* and his place in society, with continuing penetration. Thematically, it matters little to Burton what mode these character's aestheticism takes (homicidal mania, topiary, macabre stylization) but how they remake the world around them. Wood's films may be dreadful, Burton argues, but he was an artist unto himself, and as such, made his mark.

And what does the film do to Bela Lugosi and his reputation? More importantly, what is "the Lugosi mystique," and why has it continued to hold sway over successive generations of filmgoers and fans?

Lugosi's reputation will survive. Such legends as Harlow, Fields, and Barrymore have weathered warts-and-all bio-pics. Their legends have, in fact, grown more profound and have survived longer than the films inspired by them. That *Ed Wood* may simply be the best Hollywood bio-pic ever made is of little consequence: Lugosi's legend exists independent of *Ed Wood,* and not because of it. If anything, the film simply adds more gist for the mill—a chance to further explore the Lugosian enigma.

But, the devotee must return again and again to the simple, inescapable question: what is it about Bela Lugosi? What is the hypnotic hold of the man that not only warrants a major biographical film, but this book of essays, today, some 39 years after his death?

Such a question may be impossible to answer definitively. But I suspect that the truth lies in the man's remarkable *presence.* When Lugosi was truly "on," his presence was something mysteriously akin to magic. It is impossible to isolate the components that made the man work so well: it was more than his inimitable delivery, greater than the balletic gestures, more intangible than his fierce and regal bearing. But the total combination of these disparate parts create a sum

Ed Wood and Bela Lugosi film the infamous *Plan 9 From Outer Space* footage in front of Lugosi's home in *Ed Wood*.

much greater than the whole... and transcend into an indefinable magic.

In *Ed Wood,* Lugosi continually amazes Wood and his production crew with his ability to produce this mysterious magic when the camera rolls. Awe was the only possible response to Lugosi's other-worldly, undeniable, *presence.*

Listen to Lugosi on one of his many radio appearances. The voice, so unmistakable, is there with all its power. The delivery, pure Lugosi. But the total effect falls short of perfection—Lugosi was a complete package, and had to be taken with all his component parts for that magical *frisson* between performer and viewer to take place.

Look at Lugosi in *Mark of the Vampire.* He is mute for most of the film, and so, is not "classic" Lugosi at all. With full vampire costume it looks like this should be a winning role, but one of the vital elements is missing. When not a complete package, Lugosi's power is diluted. Bela Lugosi cannot be distilled.

Martin Landau's Bela Lugosi is a classic, and perhaps destined to be as legendary as the original itself. But for all of his bravura playing, he is not Lugosi. (Of course, no one ever could be!) There is too *much* Lugosi for any one actor to incorporate. Landau has most of the particulars, and many of the subtleties, but not all of them. His voice is fine, but Lugosi's matchless use of phrasing and pauses is missing. The hypnotic hand gestures of Landau are fine, but Lugosi's arm had a curious tension, arching almost impossibly at its middle like a cat's back. The live-wire quality is missing as Landau moves with easy fluidity.

Lugosi was an original in the truest sense of the word. Of course, he emerged during Hollywood's Golden Age, when originals were a much more common commodity. So, what, aside from his *presence,* has Lugosi to offer worthy of continual study?

The sad incidents of Lugosi's life: his short-lived success, his creation of a definitive portrayal (Dracula) that became a curse while ensuring immortality, the abuse at the hands of myopic studio heads, his drug addiction and cure, and his sorry exploitation by grade-Z filmmakers all conspire to make Lugosi the classic Hollywood tragedy. That Lugosi did not sink into obscurity with a whimper, that he heroically continued to live as much as he possibly could, committing himself for a drug cure, working and waiting for a comeback film when lesser men would've quit, marrying and building a new life when most men are grandfathers—create a noble figure who rose above the setbacks of fate and his own misguided talents. Hollywood creates stars and then discards them; Lugosi would not quit. While struggling to survive, he created a legend. Lugosi was a large spirit in a town with a small soul.

Tied also to the Lugosi mythos is Dracula. Lugosi succumbed to the kiss of the vampire, securing immortality at the cost of his own life. Bela Lugosi may have breathed life eternal into the King Vampire, but he also became the fiend's most celebrated victim. He gave his face, his voice, *his presence* to the character... qualities Lugosi could not remove like so much Jack Pierce makeup. The tragedy of Lugosi's career was not that he was a personality and not an actor, or a limited actor, but that he could not escape the shadow of his own towering creation. Lugosi was not ultimately crushed by the poverty-row films that engulfed him, but by the majesty of his own greatest achievement.

Landau's textured performance manages to capture these disparate strains. His Lugosi is strong, proud, stalwart, and human. Even if the film distorts the facts, isn't this a fine way to memorialize the man? And for those unfamiliar with the man and his work, isn't this a fabulous introduction? Lugosi is the most fully realized character in the film, and in Landau's playing we feel Lugosi's urgency, his battle against illness, hardship, and his own mortality. Never before has the man's desperation been rendered so real to his legion of admirers.

Landau comes to his empathy for the character naturally. A fine actor who showed early promise, his career later hit extreme lows. He has worked with Hitchcock, and played the villain in *The Harlem Globetrotters on Gilligan's Island.* He starred in more than his share of sleazy, exploitation shockers, and it was not until *Tucker* in 1988 that his career was revitalized. It was a second chance Lugosi was never granted.

The happiest result in the wake of *Ed Wood's* release was Bela Lugosi winning the Oscar.

Kind of.

When Landau won the Best Supporting Actor Academy Award for *Ed Wood*, thousands of Lugosi fans shared in his vindication. On that night, "Monster Boomers" around the globe sat back in satisfaction. We had known Lugosi's worth as a performer when as children we sat in our basements and watched *Shock Theater.* He has moved from cult figure to the heights of Hollywood history. While it was Landau's performance that won, it was a performance soundly grounded in Lugosi, the man and his work. Landau was the author, but Lugosi the creator.

Lugosi was never accorded the honor of an Academy nomination during his troubled lifetime, but now, albeit by proxy, he has an Oscar to his credit.

It would do the old spook proud.

Ed Wood is a meditation on Hollywood's ability to create legends and then cast them aside. Lugosi's vindication came, and with it, he has won undying fame, much as Dracula won immortality, once life had left him for good.

Instead of ending the Lugosi story on an elegiac note, *Ed Wood* strikes a chord of triumph. Lugosi passed through hardships and obscurity and entered into American folklore. His myth continues to be celebrated, helping to sponge away the pain, loneliness, and anguish of the man's final years.

Bibliography

Compiled by John E. Parnum

Ackerman, Forrest J (Editor): "Bride of the Monster" (Filmbook), *Monster World* (Number 5), October 1965, pp 34-43.

Bojarski, Richard: *The Films of Bela Lugosi,* The Citadel Press, Secaucus, New Jersey, 1980.

Brunas, Michael; Brunas, John; and Weaver, Tom: *Universal Horrors,* McFarland & Company, Inc., Jefferson, North Carolina, and London, 1990.

Clarens, Carlos: *An Illustrated History of the Horror Film,* G. P. Putnam's Sons, New York, 1967.

Cremer, Robert: *Lugosi: The Man Behind the Cape,* Henry Regnery Company, Chicago, 1976.

Crocker, Keith J., and Reis, George R. (Editors): "The Richard Gordon Interview," *The Exploitation Journal,* Volume 2: Number 2-3, 1995, pp 6-12.

Gordon, Alex: "My Favorite Vampire," *Fantastic Monsters,* Volume 1: Number 5, 1963, pp 46-49.

Gordon, Alex: "I Remember Eddie Wood:" The Pit and the Pen of Alex Gordon, *Fangoria,* Number 25, February 1983, pp 26-29.

Grey, Rudolph: *Nightmare of Ecstasy: The Life and Art of Edward D. Wood, Jr.,* Feral House Press, Los Angeles, 1992.

Henderson, Jan Alan: "Paul Marco Remembers Ed Wood," *Filmfax,* Number 6, March/April 1986, pp 37-51.

Lennig, Arthur: *The Count: The Life and Films of Bela "Dracula" Lugosi,* G. P. Putnam's Sons, New York, 1974.

Mank, Gregory William: *Hollywood Cauldron: Thirteen Horror Films from the Genre's Golden Age,* McFarland & Company, Inc., Jefferson, North Carolina, and London, 1994.

Mank, Gregory William: *It's Alive: The Classic Cinema Saga of Frankenstein,* A. S. Barnes & Company, Inc., San Diego, New York, 1981.

Mank, Gregory William: *Karloff and Lugosi: The Story of a Haunting Collaboration,* McFarland & Company, Inc., Jefferson, North Carolina, and London, 1990.

McCarty, John: *The Sleaze Merchants,* St. Martin's Griffin, New York, 1995, pp 19-13.

Prawer, S. S.: *Caligari's Children: The Film as Tale of Terror,* Oxford University Press, Oxford, New York, Toronto, Melbourne, 1980.

Riley, Philip J.: *Dracula (The Original 1931 Shooting Script): Universal Filmscripts Series Classic Horror Films—Volume 13,* Magic Image Filmbooks, Atlantic City, Hollywood, 1990.

Skal, David J.: *Hollywood Gothic: The Tangled Web of* Dracula *from Novel to Stage to Screen,* W. W. Norton & Company, New York, London, 1990.

Skal, David J.: *The Monster Show: A Cultural History of Horror, W. W.* Norton & Company, New York, London, 1993.

Stritto, Frank J. Dello: "The Road to Las Vegas: Bela Lugosi in American Theatre," *Cult Movies,* Number 11, 1994, pp 56-65.

Twitchell, James B.: *Dreadful Pleasures: An Anatomy of Modern Horror,* Oxford University Press, New York, Oxford, 1985.

Weaver, Tom: *Interviews with B Science Fiction and Horror Movie Makers,* McFarland & Company, Inc., Jefferson, North Carolina, 1988, pp 249-259.

Weaver, Tom: *Poverty Row Horrors,* McFarland & Company, Inc., Jefferson, North Carolina, and London, 1993.

Worth, David Earl: *Sleaze Creatures,* Fantasma Books, Key West, Florida, 1995, pp 18-23.

The Feature Films of Bela Lugosi[1]

compiled by Gary Don Rhodes

Hungary:

1. *A Leopárd (The Leopard)*
[Lugosi appeared under the pseudonym Arisztid Olt]
Star Company, 1917.

2. *Álarcosbál (The Masked Ball)*
[Lugosi appeared under the pseudonym Arisztid Olt]
Star Company, 1917.

3. *Leoni Leo*
[Lugosi appeared under the pseudonym Arisztid Olt]
Star Company, 1917.

4. *Tavaszi Vihar (Spring Tempest)*
[Lugosi appeared under the pseudonym Arisztid Olt]
Star Company, 1917.

5. *Az Ezredes (The Colonel)*
[Lugosi portrayed the Colonel]
Phoenix Company, 1917

6. *A Nászdal (The Wedding Song)*
[Lugosi appeared under the pseudonym Arisztid Olt]
Star Company, 1917.

7. *Küzdelem A Létért (Struggle For Life)*
[Lugosi appeared under the pseudonym Arisztid Olt]
Star Company, 1918.

8. *Casanova*[2]
[Lugosi most likely appeared under the pseudonym Arisztid Olt]
Star Company, 1918.

9. *Kilencvekilenc (Ninety-Nine)*
[Lugosi appeared under the name Bela Lugosi]
Phoenix Company, 1918.

10. *Lili*[3]
[Lugosi appeared under the name Bela Lugosi]
Phoenix Company, 1918.

11. *Az Élet Királya (The Royal Life)*
[Lugosi appeared under the pseudonym Arisztid Olt and portrayed character Lord Harry Vatton]
Star Company, 1918.

Germany:

12. *Slaven Fremdes Willens (Slave of a Foreign Will)*
[Lugosi portrayed a hypnotist]
Eichberg Film, 1919.

13. *Nat Pinkerton*
Dua Film, 1920.

14. *Der Fluch der Menscheit (The Curse of Man)*
[Lugosi portrayed Maelzer, a saboteur]
Eichberg Film, 1920.

15. *Der Januskopf (The Head of Janus)*
[Lugosi portrayed Dr. Warren's loyal butler]
Lipow Film, 1920.

16. *Die Frau im Delphin (The Woman in the Dolphin)*
Gaci Film, 1920.

17. *Die Todeskarawane (The Caravan of Death)*
Ustad Film, 1920.

18. *Lederstrumpf (Leatherstocking)*
[Lugosi portrayed Chingachgook]

19. *Die Teufelsanbeter (The Devil Worshippers)*
Ustad Film, 1920.

20. *Johann Hopkins III (John Hopkins the Third)*
Dua Film, 1920.

21. *Der Tanx auf dem Vulkan (The Dance on the Volcano)*
[Lugosi portrayed a Parisian aristocrat]
Eichberg Films, 1921.

America:

22. *The Silent Command*
[Lugosi portrayed Benedict Hisston]
A Fox Picture, 1923.

23. *The Rejected Woman*
[Lugosi portrayed Jean Gagnon]
Distinctive Pictures, 1924.

24. *Daughters Who Pay*
[Lugosi portrayed Serge Oumanski]
Banner Productions, 1925.

25. *The Midnight Girl*
[Lugosi portrayed Nicholas Harmon]
Chadwick Pictures, 1925.

26. *How To Handle Women*
[Lugosi portrayed a bodyguard]
Universal Studios, 1928.

27. *The Veiled Woman*
[Lugosi portrayed a suitor to Nanon]
Fox, 1929.

28. *Prisoners* [4]
[Lugosi portrayed Brottos]
First National, 1929.

29. *The Thirteenth Chair*
[Lugosi portrayed Inspector Delzante]
Metro-Goldwyn-Mayer, 1929.

30. *The Last Performance*
[Lugosi dubbed Conrad Veidt's voice for a Hungarian-version release which was also perhaps screened in Hungarian communities within the United States.]
Universal Studios, 1929.

31. *Such Men Are Dangerous*
[Lugosi portrayed Dr. Goodman]
Fox, 1930.

32. *Wild Company*
[Lugosi portrayed Felix Brown]
Fox, 1930.

33. *Renegades*
[Lugosi portrayed Sheik Muhammed, the Marabout]
Fox, 1930.

34. *Oh, For A Man*
[Lugosi portrayed Frescatti]
Fox, 1930.

35. *Viennese Nights*
[Lugosi portrayed an Ambassador]
Warner Brothers, 1930.

36. *The King of Jazz*
[Lugosi acted as an onscreen host for the Hungarian release only]
Universal Studios, 1930.

37. *Dracula*
[Lugosi portrayed Count Dracula]
Universal Studios, 1931.

38. *Fifty Million Frenchmen*
[Lugosi portrayed a magician]
Warner Brothers, 1931.

39. *Women of All Nations*
[Lugosi portrayed Prince Hassan]
Fox, 1931.

40. *The Black Camel*
[Lugosi portayed Tarneverro]
Fox, 1931.

41. *Broadminded*
[Lugosi portrayed Pancho]
First National/Warner Brothers, 1931.

42. *Murders in the Rue Morgue*
[Lugosi portrayed Doctor Mirakle]
Universal Studios, 1932.

43. *White Zombie*
[Lugosi portrayed Murder Legendre]
United Artists, 1932.

44. *Chandu The Magician*
[Lugosi portrayed Roxor]
Fox, 1932.

45. *Island of Lost Souls*
[Lugosi portrayed the Sayer of the Law]
Paramount Pictures, 1932.

46. *The Death Kiss*
[Lugosi portrayed Joseph Steiner]
World Wide Pictures, 1933.

47. *International House*
[Lugosi portrayed General Petronovich]
Paramount Pictures, 1933.

48. *Night of Terror*
[Lugosi portrayed Degar]
Columbia Pictures, 1933.

49. *The Devil's In Love*
[Lugosi portrayed the Prosecutor for the Military]
Fox, 1933.

50. *The Black Cat*
[Lugosi portrayed Dr. Vitus Werdegast]
Universal Studios, 1934.

51. *Gift of Gab*
[Lugosi portrayed an Apache]
Universal Studios, 1934.

52. *Best Man Wins*
[Lugosi portrayed Dr. Boehm]
Columbia Pictures, 1935.

53. *Mysterious Mr. Wong*
[Lugosi portrayed Mr. Wong, Mandarin]
Monogram, 1935.

54. *Mark of the Vampire*
[Lugosi portrayed Count Mora]
Metro-Goldwyn-Mayer, 1935.

55. *The Raven*
[Lugosi portrayed Dr. Richard Vollin]
Universal Studios, 1935.

56. *Murder By Television*
[Lugosi portrayed Arthur Perry and Houghland's Assistant]
Imperial-Cameo Pictures, 1935.

57. *Mystery of the Mary Celeste*[5]
[Lugosi portrayed Anton Lorenzen]
Hammer Studios, 1936. Made in England.

58. *The Invisible Ray*
[Lugosi portrayed Dr. Benet]
Universal Studios, 1936.

59. *Postal Inspector*
[Lugosi portrayed Benez]
Universal Studios, 1936.

60. *Son of Frankenstein*
[Lugosi portrayed Ygor]
Universal Studios, 1939.

61. *The Gorilla*
[Lugosi portrayed Peters]
Twentieth-Century Fox Films, 1939.

62. *Ninotchka*
[Lugosi portrayed Commissar Razinin]
Metro-Goldwyn-Mayer, 1939.

63. *The Dark Eyes of London*[6]
[Lugosi portrayed (Dr. Orloff/Dr. Dearborn]
An Argyle Production, 1939. Made in England.

64. *The Saint's Double Trouble*
[Lugosi portrayed the partner]
RKO Radio Pictures, 1940.

65. *Black Friday*
[Lugosi portrayed Eric Marnay]
Universal Studios, 1940.

66. *You'll Find Out*
[Lugosi portrayed Prince Saliano]
RKO Radio Pictures, 1940.

67. *The Devil Bat*
[Lugosi portrayed Dr. Paul Carruthers]
Producers Releasing Corporation, 1940.

68. *The Black Cat*
[Lugosi portrayed Eduardo]
Universal Studios, 1941.

69. *The Invisible Ghost*
[Lugosi portrayed Dr. Charles Kessler]
Monogram Studios, 1941.

70. *Spooks Run Wild*
[Lugosi portrayed Nardo]
Monogram Studios, 1941.

71. *The Wolf Man*
[Lugosi portrayed Bela, a gypsy]
Universal Studios, 1941.

72. *The Ghost of Frankenstein*
[Lugosi portrayed Ygor]
Universal Studios, 1942.

73. *Black Dragons*
[Lugosi portrayed Dr. Melcher/Colomb]
Monogram Studios, 1942.

74. *The Corpse Vanishes*
[Lugosi portrayed Dr. Lorenz]
Monogram, 1942.

75. *Bowery At Midnight*
[Lugosi portrayed Professor Brenner/Karl Wagner]
Monogram Studios, 1942.

76. *Night Monster*
[Lugosi portrayed Rolf the Butler]
Universal Studios, 1942.

77. *Frankenstein Meets the Wolf Man*
[Lugosi portrayed Frankenstein's Monster]
Universal Studios, 1943.

78. *The Ape Man*
[Lugosi portrayed Dr. Brewster]
Monogram Studios, 1943.

79. *Ghosts on the Loose*
[Lugosi portrayed Emil]
Monogram Studios, 1943.

80. *Return of the Vampire*
[Lugosi portrayed Armand Tesla]
Columbia Pictures, 1943.

81. *Voodoo Man*
[Lugosi portrayed Dr. Richard Marlowe]
Monogram Studios, 1944.

82. *Return of the Ape Man*
[Lugosi portrayed Professor Dexter]
Monogram Studios, 1944.

83. *One Body Too Many*
[Lugosi portrayed Larchmont]
Paramount Pictures, 1944.

84. *The Body Snatcher*
{Lugosi portrayed Joseph]
RKO Radio Pictures, 1945.

85. *Zombies on Broadway*
[Lugosi portrayed Professor Richard Renault]
RKO Radio Pictures, 1945.

86. *Genius At Work*
[Lugosi portrayed Stone]
RKO Radio Pictures, 1946.

87. *Scared to Death*
[Lugosi portrayed Leonide]
Screen Guild Productions, 1947.

88. *Abbott and Costello Meet Frankenstein*
[Lugosi portrayed Count Dracula/Dr. Lejos]
Universal-International, 1948.

89. *Mother Riley Meets the Vampire*[7]
[Lugosi portrayed Von Housen]
Renown Pictures, 1952.

90. *Bela Lugosi Meets A Brooklyn Gorilla*[8]
[Lugosi portrayed Dr. Zabor]
Realart Pictures, 1952.

91. *Glen or Glenda*[9]
[Lugosi portrayed a Spirit]
Screen Classics, 1953.

92. *Bride of the Monster*
[Lugosi portrayed Dr. Eric Vornoff]
Banner Productions, 1955.

93. *The Black Sleep*
[Lugosi portrayed Casimir]
United Artists, 1956.

94. *Plan 9 From Outer Space*
[Lugosi portrayed the Ghoul Man]
A D.C.A. Release, 1959.

95. *Lock Up Your Daughters*[10]
[An on-screen Lugosi narrates clips from a handful of his films]
New Realm, 1959. Released in England only.

[1] Only feature-length films have been included in this listing. Short Subjects, newsreels, serials, and other celluloid appearances have not been covered. Moreover, while an attempt has been made to point out commonly-used alternate titles, it should be clear that many of the listed films appeared at theaters across the world under multiple titles.
[2] Questions persist as to whether Lugosi actually appeared in *Casanova*, and—if he

did—whether he would have used the name "Arisztid Olt" or "Bela Lugosi."
[3] Many sources list this film as *Lulu*, although original ads prove the Hungarian release title was *Lili*.
[4] Though *Prisoners* itself was only 10% sound, the film marked Lugosi's entry into talkies. He never again made a full-length silent film.
[5] *Mystery of the Mary Celeste* surfaces regularly as *Phantom Ship*, its American release title.
[6] *The Dark Eyes of London* generally appears on audio/visual formats and television as *The Human Monster*, its American release title.
[7] Prints of this film generally circulate under the American-release titles *Vampire Over London* and *My Son, the Vampire*.
[8] *Bela Lugosi Meets a Brooklyn Gorilla* often appears under the alternate title *Boys From Brooklyn*.
[9] Though best-known as *Glen or Glenda*, the film most often appears on audio/visual formats under one of its many other appellations, *I Led Two Lives*.
[10] While various period sources indicate "new" footage of Lugosi appeared in this film, definitive proof as of 1995 escapes film historians.

INDEX

Poster courtesy of Ronald V. Borst/Hollywood Movie Posters

AUTHORS

Dennis Fischer is the author of *Horror Film Directors: 1931-1990*, a much acclaimed reference work detailing the careers of almost a hundred directors of horror films. He has been a regular contributor to numerous genre film publications including *Midnight Marquee*. He lives in the L.A. area with his loving wife and charming two-year-old son, who will never have to ask, "Bela *who*?" When he is not working as a high school English teacher, he is preparing chapters for upcoming Midnight Marquee Press books and is preparing a follow-up volume of *Science Fiction Directors*.

Richard Gordon, movie producer and movie fan, was born in London in 1925. Gordon graduated from the University of London in 1943, served in the British Royal Navy 1944-1946, and soon emigrated to the United States (writing for numerous fan publications), eventually forming Gordon Films, Inc. in 1949. Gordon, over the years, has produced films such as *The Haunted Strangler* (with Boris Karloff), *Fiend without a Face, First Man into Space, Corridors of Blood* (with Karloff and Christopher Lee), *Devil Doll, Curse of the Voodoo, The Projected Man, Island of Terror, Horror Hospital*, and *Inseminoid*... among many more.

David J. Hogan has been a film enthusiast since 1960, when his mother was featured in *Famous Monsters of Filmland* #7. Since 1973 he has contributed to a variety of magazines, including *Cinefantastique, Moviegoer, Photon, Filmfax*, and *Outré*. His essays have appeared in editions of *Magill's Cinema Annual* and he has written three books: *Who's Who of the Horrors and Other Fantasy Films*, *Dark Romance: Sexuality in the Horror Film*, and *Your Movie Guide to Drama Video Tapes and Discs*. He is associate publisher, automotive division, with Chicago-based Publications International, Ltd. Hogan lives with his wife, Kim, and three children in a rambling house filled with books, music, and and movies.

Don Leifert is one of the earliest contributors to *Midnight Marquee* and has written for many film publications including *Video Times, Filmfax*, and *Movie Club* (where he was Co-Editor). When not teaching Drama and secondary English, Leifert haunts antique shops and auctions unearthing incredibly rare memorabilia, looking for the ultimate finds. Instead of sleeping-in on weekends, Leifert usually sets up shop at flea markets/ swap meets across the area.

Bob Madison has written for *Wonder, Cult Movies, Scary Monsters*, and *Scarlet Street* magazines. He lives in New York and is finishing a novel. A portrait of Bela Lugosi hangs in a place of honor in his living room and still Bob has managed to stay a married man.

Gregory William Mank is the author of the books *It's Alive! The Classic Cinema Saga of Frankenstein; The Hollywood Hissables; Karloff and Lugosi*; and *Hollywood Cauldron.* Greg currently is completing a book on Actresses in Melodramas, and starting a book (with Jim Coughlin) on Dwight Frye, with the cooperation of Frye's son, Dwight David Frye. Active in regional theater, Greg is currently enacting the juicy role of Captain Hook from *Peter Pan.* By day he teaches high school English.

Mark A. Miller contributes articles and interviews to *Midnight Marquee* and *Filmfax* magazines. His first book, *Christopher Lee and Peter Cushing and Horror Cinema* (McFarland), was published to critical acclaim in 1994. He lives in Columbus, Ohio, with his wife, Teresa, and teaches English in nearby Gahanna.

John E. Parnum is an author, editor, archivist, and magician extraordinaire who worked for 31 years in the advertising department of Merck Pharmaceuticals before retiring to devote full time to writing, collecting horror memorabilia, and prestidigitation. He was Editor-in-Chief of *Cinemacabre* and has written articles and stories for such publications as *Midnight Marquee, Photon, The Monster Times, Gateways,* and others. Inspired by his pet python Monty, he is currently working on a book on snakes in horror and science fiction films called *The Slithering Cinema.* He lives in Wayne, PA with his wife Edie and daughter Laura.

Gary Don Rhodes is the author of *Lugosi: A Portrait of His Life and Career*, the 1996 McFarland reference book. He is also the former editor of the *World of Bela Lugosi* newsletter. Along with founding a "Bela Lugosi Society" as a teen, he has continued to write for film journals ranging from *Classic Images* to *Cult Movies.* Rhodes currently teaches at the University of Oklahoma, instructing courses such as English Composition and his own creation, The History of the Horror Film. His numerous documentary films cover such topics as jazz and cultural history, being offered on videocassette through companies such as V.I.E.W. after their initial PBS broadcasts.

Bryan Senn, a psychometrist at a Seattle-area hospital, is co-author of *Fantastic Cinema Subject Guide: A Topical Index to 2500 Horror, Science Fiction, and Fantasy Films* (McFarland, 1992). Besides contributing to magazines such as *Midnight Marquee, Filmfax, Monsterscene, Movie Club*, and *Cult Movies*, he has recently completed a book entitled *Golden Horrors: A Critical Filmography of 46 Works of Terror Cinema, 1931-1939* which will be published by McFarland in 1996.

David H. Smith lives in Florida with his wife Lynn and son Colin, and a morbidly obese cat named Lobo, along with a vast comic book, magazine, CD, and video collection. David tends to enjoy remakes as much as the originals, and sequels even more so. He likes that Gary J. Svehla has referred to him in print as "elusive," and is a firm believer that Moody Blues albums cannot be played too often, that Paul Naschy will never get enough recognition, and that people shouldn't take Jerry Warren movies as personal affronts. David has had articles published in *Amazing Heroes* and *Midnight Marquee*, as well as letters of errata in *Scarlet Street, European Trash Cinema, Monsterland, Bits & Pieces*, and *The New York Times*.

Don G. Smith is an associate professor of educational history and philosophy at Eastern Illinois University. Besides owning a major collection of movie memorabilia related to Bela Lugosi, Lon Chaney, Jr., and Hammer horror, he has published in *Midnight Marquee, Fangoria, Scarlet Street, Filmfax, Movie Collector's World*, etc. He is also the author of *Lon Chaney, Jr.* and *The Cinema of Edgar A. Poe*, both forthcoming from McFarland & Company, Inc.

John Soister, an avid Brooklyn Dodger fan until the Bums left town when he was seven, has never let his otherwise impeccable taste get in the way of his love for horror movies. A sixties' fanzine editor (one-shot *House of Horrors*), co-editor (*Photon*, briefly), and all-around LoC curmudgeon, John picked up his quill pen for the first time in three decades in an effort to spill a little ink about some of his favorite Lugosis. (Astounded that the rest of his one-time colleagues were in the computer age, John has vowed that his children: Jake, Katelyn, and Jeremy—named respectively for Bela Lugosi, Boris Karloff, and Claude Rains—would have an easier-to-edit life than he.)

Living (and partly living) in Orwigsburg, PA, John teaches modern and classical languages (and whatever the hell English is considered to be) to uninterested high school students.

John's lovely wife, Nancy, shares his bewilderment.

John Stell, new to film criticism, has contributed to *Movie Club, Midnight Marquee, Monsters from the Vault*, etc. John, an avid collector of horror/fantasy/science fiction films on video tape, is now working on his first solo authored book for Midnight Marquee Press (a book documenting horror movies produced during the decade of the 1980s). Stell is a CPA by day and thus dreads tax season (January through April) whereby he puts in 70-hour weeks (thus, the reason for taping so many movies—who has time to watch them!)

Gary J. Svehla, who as an eccentric 13-year-old monster movie fan created the first issue of *Gore Creatures* in 1963, today some 32 years later, finds himself to be editor/publisher of the world's longest running horror film magazine (*Gore Creatures* became *Midnight Marquee* in 1976). After producing the magazine as a labor of love for over 30 years, Gary and his wife Susan decided to get serious, expand, and inaugurate Midnight Marquee Press, Inc. in 1995. *Bela Lugosi* is the debuting paperback and we hope it is only the first of many, many more to follow.

Until becoming a publishing magnate, "Citizen Gary" will continue teaching secondary English and officiating as President of the Horror and Fantasy Film Society, the Baltimore-based organization that sponsors the tremendously popular FANEX movie conventions every Summer in Baltimore. He has contributed to *Monsterland, Amazing Cinema, Movie Club, Monsters from the Vault, Bites & Pieces*, and *Monster Times*.

Susan Svehla, now married to Gary for 11 years, convinced the complacent Gary to inaugurate Midnight Marquee Press, Inc. so the happy couple could carry out their dreams, turn a hobby into a profitable business, and, hopefully, be successful enough that MidMar Press can lead to an *earlier* retirement from their day jobs. Susan has contributed to *Midnight Marquee* (of course), *Scarlet Street, Bites & Pieces*, and *Movie Club* and is currently working on a Hollywood Musical book for Midnight Marquee Press. She has chaired or co-chaired all the FANEX film conventions for nine years and is gearing up for the 10th Anniversary film expo in July of 1996.

Tom Weaver, a North Tarrytown, New York-based movie fan, has written for *Midnight Marquee, Fangoria, Starlog, Starlog Explorer, Cult Movies, Comics Scene, Videoscope, Filmfax, Movie Club, Fantastic Films, Scarlet Street, Monsters From the Vault*, and many other genre-related magazines. One hundred of his interviews with sci-fi and horror moviemakers have been compiled into four McFarland books; he also wrote McFarland's *Poverty Row Horrors* and co-wrote (with the Brunas Brothers) *Universal Horrors*. Contrary to his public image, he sometimes wears pants and actually does admire Bela Lugosi's acting.

Bret Wood is a freelance writer whose documentary on Lon Chaney is distributed by Kino on Video (800-562-3330). His biography of Tod Browning is being published in France by Editions Macula.